4/20/23

W9-CQW-101

OPENING OUR
SPIRITUAL EYES

OPENING OUR
SPIRITUAL EYES

Karmic Clearing for Humanity and the Earth

SRI'AMA QALA PHOENIX

North Atlantic Books
Berkeley, California

Copyright © 2011 by Sri'ama Qala Phoenix. All rights reserved. No portion of this book, except for brief review, may be reproduced, stored in a retrieval system, or transmitted in any form or by any means—electronic, mechanical, photocopying, recording, or otherwise—without the written permission of the publisher. For information contact North Atlantic Books.

Published by
North Atlantic Books
P.O. Box 12327
Berkeley, California 94712

Cover art by Demetri Condos
Cover and book design by Suzanne Albertson
"The Miracle Story of Ease" © by Sue Short is reprinted courtesy of *Living Now* magazine. www.livingnow.com.au.
Printed in the United States of America

Opening Our Spiritual Eyes: Karmic Clearing for Humanity and the Earth is sponsored by the Society for the Study of Native Arts and Sciences, a nonprofit educational corporation whose goals are to develop an educational and cross-cultural perspective linking various scientific, social, and artistic fields; to nurture a holistic view of arts, sciences, humanities, and healing; and to publish and distribute literature on the relationship of mind, body, and nature.

North Atlantic Books' publications are available through most bookstores. For further information, visit our website at www.northatlanticbooks.com or call 800-733-3000.

Library of Congress Cataloging-in-Publication Data

Phoenix, Sri'ama Qala.
    Opening our spiritual eyes : karmic clearing for humanity and the earth /Sri'ama Qala Phoenix.
       p. cm.
    Summary: "Opening Our Spiritual Eyes is a book of channeled spontaneous wisdom the reveals 'the true nature of the divine plan' through an enlightened master's eyes. According to the author, humanity can and will quickly shift into a higher state of consciousness with ease and grace as a soul's personal and collective karma is transformed through the power of prayer and forgiveness"—Provided by publisher.
    ISBN 978-1-55643-963-6
1. Karma. 2. Spirituality. I. Title.
    BL2015.K3P46 2011
    202'.2—dc22   2010049598

          1 2 3 4 5 6 7 8 9 UNITED 16 15 14 13 12 11

DEDICATION

The hearts of all humanity and the minds that dare open their spiritual eyes are my inspiration and to them I dedicate this book. To question, inquire, and explore beyond that which is known and seen, through endearing windows of new awareness and consciousness . . .

. . . to all skywalkers who dare explore all possibilities

. . . to all pathfinders, those that brave creation from the heart

. . . to all who tempt the sacred glimpse through alternate eyes

. . . to Little Owl, Dreaming Heart, Golden Phoenix, and Jehraan

. . . to my daughter, Razmia, and my grandson, Indiana

. . . to my mother and father, my grandparents, and my ancestors

. . . to my sisters Amaya, Illumina, and Lelama

. . . to all who have quested the path with me

. . . to the mystery within all Seven Worlds of the Earth

. . . to my dearest friends, the Enlightened Masters

. . . to Mother Gaia and all beings

. . . to our Holy Spirit

. . . to Love

CONTENTS

CHAPTER FOUR
Our Potential: The New Human Being—
Our Evolutionary Path 137

CHAPTER FIVE
Humanity's Call to Transformation and Illumination 193

CHAPTER SIX
Your Contribution to Your Family,
Your Community, and Our World 233

CHAPTER SEVEN
Assisting the Clearing of Collective Karma
or Humanity's Burdens 291

CHAPTER EIGHT
Our World's New Cities of Light:
The Celestial Project 2009–2013 353

PREFACE

Each night as I go to sleep I ask to see through the eyes of grace, love, and divinity. This new view I offer you now. I simply ask that you consider this as an alternate angle on your world, neither denying your truth and reality nor presuming that my perspective offers a higher view. Each of our views marry and may live in the realms of oneness as we open our spiritual eyes to see new and very different aspects of life on Earth.

All that I share comes from my personal experience of living in the companionship of many Enlightened Masters who graced me many years ago with a gift that I can in no way return, except through my service to the world and the illumination of others who wish for this.

Life has struck a deep passionate kiss upon my soul—ever long and everlasting communion through body, mind, soul, and spirit, which has left a taste of possibilities throughout my being. I have a yearning to give myself once again in surrender to the deliverance that God holds for me, and I understand that there is no greater source than that which lies in my own heart, awaiting to greet and welcome me.

Through a journey of homelessness, loss, aimlessness, and self-abuse, I rise like the phoenix from the flames of my own self-creation of karma, to meet myself in my many forms, re-piecing gently my mind, body, and soul to become the chalice for my Holy Spirit. A death like no other, my old self is gone. I am held within the temples of the Holy Mother as I am bathed in special frequencies and granted journeys into other worlds to rediscover the Earth as my jewel, my greatest gift: a land of creation, play, and pleasure.

Awakening, I emerge from within my holy flame. I write this book so you may see the light within you and know deeply that there is always a way to create a different reality, re-piece yourself, keep the truest source of you, and allow your consciousness to activate, illuminating the Divine You.

Illumination as a path is built upon the heart: upon the strength of the mother's love, the father's wisdom, and the child's innocence. This book is a journey through the realms of the Enlightened Masters, exploring our evolution—as individuals and as a collective—on the shift into the fifth dimension via the clearing of our collective, planetary, familial, and personal karma. Our ancestors have gifted us our DNA and brain chemistry. As we illuminate, a new view of our feelings ignites, and we understand where our emotions source from, where our spirit dwells, and who we are throughout the physical and nonphysical worlds.

We share a journey into the world with these divine beings who shine their wisdom, love, and faith in each one of us. They are here to remind us that we are precious, sacred, and loved deeply by many who wait in the wings of spirit, by many in angelic form who have known us before, and by many whom we are still to meet and be graced by their unique form. My book presents simply one angle that mirrors back to you all that you hold within you on your own journey of life. As you travel with me, your soul will find a path of healing, grace, and illumination. Your spirit will receive a new level of recognition.

Let that which you dream be held as you read this book and trust that your soul's return into the light that lives within you is only expanding your view and inviting you to see through another's eyes spiritually. Your spiritual eyes, in opening to the new, will activate a new level of awareness and consciousness within you.

In divine trust and the holy sacrament of peace the unveiling of your soul—your inner reality and your eternal self—is an aspect of the journey. To trust in your own heart is all that is asked.

In the timelessness of light you will find one jewel in this storybook—a soul who came into oneness through what appeared to be a breakdown in conscious understanding but was actually an awakening of what lay underneath all of her being. Internally, nowhere is more important than here; as karma rises up there is nowhere to go but here, if you hold responsibility for your own soul's creations and call out from within for enlightenment.

On the journey, finding Presence became the hidden goal of life's ploys, plays, and pleasures. Through accepting responsibility, the fires of life began to burn, soothe, and then sensationally deliver bliss to the body; ecstasy and energy welled up from a deep pool of hurt and learning; loss and grief transfigured into innocence and passion for creation. Only love can be responsible for this. Light held a great hand and guided the way. On the way, I discovered the purpose of life: "To marry thyself through thy heart, spirit in all forms of thyself, all ways, embracing all that has been and all that can be and uniting it within thee."

Simple gifts lie within this story, and, as you read, divine codes will transfer into your body. Frequencies are encoded into different journeys. You will receive ripples of light, sensations in your body reminding you of your spirit and how vast you truly are as your Presence sinks deeply with you into the evolutionary path of your soul.

Take your time with each passage and let it open your eyes to another way of looking, listening, hearing, receiving, and transferring your consciousness and energy. New and quite incredible events will be described to you, and each one of them is true. This has been my journey as a soul. This book holds a thread of me within it and the teachings I have received through over four thousand visitations from the Enlightened Masters. Take that which appeals to you, resonates in you, and delivers you a gift. You may be revealed to yourself more deeply through this.

Blessings of love,
Sri'ama Qala
April 2010
Montana, USA

ACKNOWLEDGMENTS

With all my blessings I wish to deeply thank and honor the many people that have helped me and continue to be by my side, offering assistance and their smiles, open hearts, and gifts of time, service, and skills to the Divine University Project and the Academy of Energy Science and Consciousness, and to the Celestial Project.

I wish to thank Amaya for her incredible heart, gifts, and ongoing tireless service to humanity and Mother Earth. You are an inspiration to us all!

Blessings and my gratitude to Katherine, Gordon, and the guardians and spirit of their sacred land for the amazing welcome, comfort, and love I received while in hermitage during the creation of this book, and thank you Zeph for the deep healing.

I wish to thank De and Nat for their loving assistance. I wish to thank Vonnell for her love, charity, and companionship in her deliverance of me to the Grand Canyon and North America for the birthing of the Celestial Project.

All my blessings and gratitude to Raphia, my personal assistant, who is a treasure of divine grace. My love and gratitude to Ra, Saajz, and Zjael for their loving service to the Celestial Project.

Blessings and deep gratitude to Stella, Katherine Elaine, Katherine, and Shala for assisting me in creating the Karmic Clearing Program. I wish to thank Veronica for all the yummy, nurturing food.

Blessings and gratitude to Leilani, Ishtar, Bill, Colleen, Lelama, and Kishalah for allowing me to share their stories within this book.

My blessings and gratitude to Richard at North Atlantic Books for the offer and the support to make this book real, with an extra big thank you to Jessica for the great work she offered as my editor.

CHAPTER ONE

The New Paradigm Shift into the Fifth Dimension

Opening Our Spiritual Eyes is a journey of faith, beauty, and unconditional love, and a testament to our trust in the development of the holy sacrament we hold as a collective—our caretakership of the Earth. The journey can no longer be avoided by those in slumber, for it is the time of awakening. Every second, someone is seeding the light on Earth. This is awakening our collective to become aware that life is sacred here and needs to be respected through all our actions, words, and intentions. Mother Earth can no longer wait. It is her time to be fully blessed and protected.

The children of our Earth are calling out to us as adults to remember the truth of who we are so we may take the necessary steps to no longer simply allow that which is not serving our growth to take place in our lives. Simultaneously, we are reminded every day—through simply experiencing our world and the parallel realities occurring in the lives of our friends, neighbors, and families—that we are one, and that together we are either creating karma or transforming that which is not serving our lives and our world to be at peace.

Pockets of brilliant, radiant, and glowing human beings are forming around the Earth, each having made the decision to love and transform all and to no longer place their energy into the creation of karma. They have each promised to seed the light into all they are doing, thinking, feeling, and creating, working consciously with the universal laws of love, grace, oneness, divinity, karma, forgiveness, and liberty in service to all beings. They are each taking responsibility for their karma. Becoming aware that we are all ready is the first key, and choosing to hold this truth within our consciousness for all other beings—those we hear about, meet, or see to be in need of assistance—is truly an amazing gift. This is called faith in our fellow humanity.

Mother Earth is inviting each one of us to understand and recognize the faith she holds in every single member of our society. The continual abundance she produces through the food on our tables, the beauty of her nature, the kindness of her warmth, and the coolness of her breath is a testament to her unconditional love for each one of us.

Life is very simple through the spiritual eyes of Mother Earth.

Those in need are to be given to. Those with abundance are to share. Those with fear are to be held closer to our hearts. Those in power are to be wise and humble in all they choose for the greater good of all. Those in love are to spread their wings and ignite this love in all who carry sadness in our world. Those in pain are to surrender so they may receive and be assisted to heal their deepest fear and come into a state of peace. Those in good fortune are to be thankful and to support others of lesser fortune.

Those in a state of grace are to let the blessings flow abundantly through them, to fill others with grace. Those in peace are to anchor the light and truth for all others on Earth. Those in happiness are to help others believe and have faith in themselves. Those in oneness and bliss are to heal the sick. Those who have strength are to carry on their backs all others that cannot yet stand on their own two feet. Those with intelligence are to use it wisely to build a new society based on peace. Those with compassion are to hold the hands of all the new children as they walk into the new world. Those with worries or doubts are to pray for the blessings for all beings in our world.

This simple parable of love serves as a divine blueprint for developing unconditional love, which can guide us through every moment in our lives. These are the principles of love and wisdom that spiritual aspirants or initiates follow on the practical path of enlightenment. Our souls are being called to recognize that these principles hold the fabric of integrity within our society. When acted upon, the unconditional love flows within our communities, our families, and our own personal lives. Whenever unconditional love is given, a greater experience of unity takes place for all receivers and givers, and we create a better world based on peace.

Mother Earth offers us this blueprint for the development of our fifth dimensional society of peace, love, and equality so we may unite our world and ourselves through the fabric of our truth and integrity. This vision of peace is our birthright as human beings, and it is the reason we are awakening and preparing for our collective journey or shift in consciousness.

As we close our physical eyes, the light held within and around our physical world can be sensed more deeply. Our spiritual eyes open as this light becomes more apparent to us in our everyday lives. This light awakens our memory of the true nature of our humanity and guides us to hold faith in our society to create peace through a journey of reclaiming our truth and integrity. Behind the surface of what we witness through our physical eyes is the light. It is here, in the sacred space that is often not visible through the physical eye, that the karma or cause of all that takes place can be seen. With our spiritual eyes open, true forgiveness can occur instantly, effortlessly, and with such grace to change our shared reality.

When the true cause of all is seen there is no blame, shame, guilt, resentment, or anger to project at oneself or another, for the flame of compassion grows so strong in one's heart that it emanates equally for all beings, including oneself. No matter who, what, why, or how situations are enacted, when the true cause is seen through spiritual eyes, all souls are seen as innocent. Through one's spiritual eyes, one is able to see and love each soul equally as a divine being on their eternal path of learning and cocreation.

Learning to see behind the physical reality can only occur if the heart has forgiven the collective of humanity for the creation of the world as it is and can see war, suffering, disease, poverty, greed, fear, abuse, and control as merely aspects of humanity's creations from old karma. It is this forgiveness of humanity and our ancestors that seeds our spiritual eyes to open. From this point on we are able to see with eyes of compassion, grace, and love and to be of benefit as peacemakers in our world.

May this book bless you with understandings and new ways of perception to support you on your unique and amazing journey of opening your spiritual eyes. In gratitude and peace, may you take from this book that which resonates and leave the rest for God. Blessed be on your journey. Be at peace.

> Let you not forget who you are and why you are here
> to be Love ... to live the truth ...
> to create the highest heart manifestation of all lifetimes and to heal all
>   that does not serve you any more.
> Let us gather as one family of Love to experience the Divine ...
> We know the truth ... no more, no less ...
> and we offer this to you, only from the Grace of God that we serve with
>   our hearts ...
> May it be that you receive all that you are willing to give to yourself
>   through your own open heart

one thousandfold again, as we hold you in our hearts and all that is not
love lifts from you . . .
You are freed to feel your soul love to the brim of your being and over-
flow the Golden Chalice that you are.
—*Maitreya*

Entering the Fifth Dimension—Your Journey with the Collective of Humanity as a Light Seed

Humanity has chosen to awaken via a specific plan, which is based on one
person in each family seeding the light and opening the hearts of other
family members. These ones are known as the light seeds of humanity. It
is these light seeds of humanity that chose to be the peacemakers on Earth,
to activate their gifts and service to create fifth dimensional energy bodies,
organizations, families, and projects, and to awaken others through the
power of their hearts. They seed the light into their relationships and
endeavors, guided by unconditional love as their principal motivation in
life.

It is such a blessing, though not always seen by veiled eyes, that our
collective has chosen to fully awaken from the illusion that our physical
world exists as our only reality. It is with the grace and love of the pure
deeds of our ancestors and of our own loving deeds in life that we are now
able to create together a new reality based more deeply on unconditional
love and peace and less on personal desire.

Many other species live with their base frequency resonating to the
fifth or higher dimensions, where unconditional love flows easily as a first
level response to all situations in life. These ones—Pleiadians, Sirians, Arcturians, Andromedans, Venusians, and many other collectives of light
beings—paved the way long ago for their sister species, humanity, to also
open their hearts and heal the past that has held them trapped in the illusion that nothing exists but the physical in their world.

Many councils of light beings that hold their hearts wide open to
humanity have been gathering in support of humanity taking this step

together as a collective. Long ago, councils of light from many of the stars beyond our sun and celestial councils from the suns and moons in other galaxies and universes made a sacred contact with individuals of our collective to prepare them to be representatives and receive the highest healings, energy assistance, and understandings so they could make this shift into the fifth dimension, hold this as their new base frequency, and lead the way for humanity's collective. Long before they came to Earth, each light seed was prepared within the spiritual planes of love, and each one was given gifts and all that they would need to create the transition on Earth.

Long before humanity's star-seeding or creation, many presences of love made a contract to be the loving guardians of the Earth and to assist the Earth and its beings in their evolutionary process. These ones are known as the Enlightened Masters. These ones have since guided the process for the preparation of all light seeds on their journey into incarnation.

As the light seeds were prepared, they were each gifted the faith, trust, and love to be able to incarnate on Earth and fulfill their holy service. They were each told the story of the Earth and shown their path ahead. They were shown the veils around the Earth, but also the different world they would enter—one of beauty, where they would learn to embrace and to smile rather than to react with duality to their experiences. The nature of this learning was shown in great depth, and within every light seed there is the memory of the truth of how they are to move through their journey. They were told they would experience feeling alone, although they would never be alone in truth, and Spirit would always be there. They were told they might experience emotions of great strength and were asked not to fear these, but to remember that they were always held by love in every moment.

They were told they would experience humanity at its worst and best, be asked to enter forgiveness as a representative of humanity, and experience times when they felt abandoned by their own Divine Presence—yet their Presence would always be with them. They would experience angst or worry, but they would always be shown the truth and a lighter path to walk upon, and there would be an angel that would meet them when they truly needed to leave the angst and worry behind.

Each light seed met the other souls who would share their journey, and learned why these other souls had chosen to incarnate with them. But they also were shown that they might forget to completely trust these other souls. The light seeds saw the family they would be a part of again and learned why this family was so important to them. They were asked to recognize that the journey would create them to heal deeply with love something that they felt they were unable to love during an alternate journey with Mother Earth and that this was their lesson and doorway to unconditional love. Lastly, they were shown their heart, how large it was, and what they had already created from the base of their heart and how, from this base, all of their journey on Earth could feel easy and be experienced as a deep blessing.

Every light seed still receives this preparation, and many more are coming to the Earth via the waves or soul pods of the new children that began to incarnate in the latter part of the 1980s. These ones carry less karma than the souls who were generally incarnating prior to 1987. Many of them do not carry personal or soul karma but come to the Earth to assist the transformation of their family or the collective karma. Inside they carry a higher consciousness that is initiated when one is given unconditional love. The frequency they carry is the medicine for all members of their family and, as they grow older, for the communities they live within.

Every light seed on the Earth was given three responsibilities before they incarnated. These are presently being reactivated through the awakening of our collective shift in consciousness. These responsibilities are the responsibilities of the collective, but the light seeds were asked to hold them as a member of the collective, as many on Earth have forgotten them. Each light seed made the sacred promise that, as they awakened their gifts and balanced the karma of their soul, family, and community, they would allow themselves to be reminded to care for themselves energetically, for the Earth in the highest way, and for all of the new children who would bring the higher frequency and consciousness to the Earth.

Each one was shown the collective of humanity they were joining upon incarnation. They were shown the power, creativity, and strength of humanity and all that was possible for them to create. They were also shown the veils of karma that humanity had become attached to, partially created by their ancestors and partially by living in ignorance and continuing to create pain and suffering. Each was given a road map that was laid inside them and to this day is held by every light seed on the Earth. It is held by their heart as a form of higher consciousness and activated as inner knowing when they are acting, speaking, or intending from a place of unconditional love.

Through the grace of God, the journey of the light seeds—though many of them work in the background and their light work is not seen— is to light the world with their higher frequency. As light seeds, we must ask ourselves whether we are willing to live in equality and use all of the gifts we presently hold to create peace in our world. Your gift may be your consciousness to see something for the collective that others cannot see. You may have the awareness of what is needed by someone so they are able to flower or free themselves emotionally. You may have the awareness of a truth that another has discarded and you may, with love, be able to bring that truth to their heart, but this can only take place through the acts, words, and intentions based on unconditional love.

The gift of a light seed as they awaken on the Earth is to share their consciousness with others who do not have the awareness to "see the light" in certain life situations. Because of their awareness of the sensitivities of others, light seeds have the responsibility to share their consciousness, offering a loving, new perspective in a very gentle process—never in haste or in an unclear, emotional state. This gift, when offered without judgment or fear, always opens the hearts of others to hear, listen, and receive, beloved. A natural resonance of the truth is already held within every soul, and when truth is spoken with love it always ignites the heart.

The souls on Earth whose consciousness is sleeping or still awakening are more delicate and vulnerable, for they carry less of their light as their natural protection and feel the karma of humanity weighing down upon them. They may feel less of their light, strength, and magnificent heart. They may access less of their divine consciousness, and therefore may need to be more protective of what they allow into their heart.

A light seed that is careful with the delivery of new consciousness, ensuring that it is shared with unconditional love so another can receive it, is seeding the light in their communications with others and grounding their light on Earth. The preciousness of your words, love, light, and all you are seeding with your beautiful intentions for humanity can become dispersed, scattered, ungrounded, or rejected by others when communications are shared without the unconditional love that unites each being within any collective experience.

Light seeds have the innate gift to sense when things are not in balance. This is also always a sign that karma is present, wishing to be acknowledged, forgiven, and loved, free within the environment. When a light seed recognizes that karma is present and lovingly acknowledges that it is not created by one being alone—that karma is a universal experience shared by all beings—they hold the light and therefore cannot be affected negatively by the karma. When they remember there is oneness even in the karma and no man, woman, or child is a single island unto themselves they feel empowered within to take the next step by taking responsibility for the karma they have acknowledged.

To enter the fifth dimension as light seeds we are asked to let go of any expectation of the collective or of any individual to heal, balance, or transform that which we are shown with our spiritual eyes. In other words, when we recognize karma is present it is our responsibility to begin the process of balancing and transforming it. We are asked to understand that unless a soul has their spiritual eyes open karma can be a burden for them until another assists them.

Taking responsibility for the karma simply means that you are willing to create something toward its shift or transformation. This may begin with a simple prayer calling on God's grace for another being that you witness struggling in life. With your spiritual eyes, you will be shown only

what is important for you to embrace with your heart and bring unconditional love to. It may be a man you pass begging in the street, and you
may be guided to give him a donation instead of rushing past him with
closed spiritual eyes in avoidance of this experience. At another time,
guided by your heart, you may walk past and say a prayer as you witness
him. Each time, your unconditional loving actions are touching the heart
of another with human kindness, assisting them with their karma of
homelessness and poverty.

Through this simple act you are seeding the light on Earth so members
of the collective can shift their consciousness and experience peace on
Earth. Know that the seeding of the light is your puzzle piece in the Divine
Plan for the balancing of the karma of the Earth. Seeding the light with
small acts of love also opens the sacred journey of your return to the heart
of your Divine Presence and your release from the karmic wheel onto the
wheel of grace. As you give love to the balancing of all beings' karma on
Earth, your own karma also begins to transform naturally and easily
through these regular, openhearted gestures.

> No more divine than you, yet truly divine I am . . .
> This is my truth and the truth I hold for you . . .
> Come into the arms of the Divine Mother and Father
> Love and Wisdom
> and be nurtured and raised until
> you feel you could be no more filled . . .
> Source awaits you!

Divine Intervention—My Story

About fourteen years ago my life began to change deeply, and a new direction for my life journey became apparent to me. It was as if the hand of
God picked me up and moved me. Very quickly my consciousness altered
completely, and my personal shift into the fifth dimension took place. I
was assisted by the Enlightened Masters, whom I consciously met for the

first time in this life through a process of divine intervention. All I share as my knowledge in this book is sourced from over four thousand visitations or direct contact experiences I have personally had with the Enlightened Masters since this divine intervention took place in my life. May this story take you on a journey, activate your path of karmic clearing, and initiate a shift for you. Know your emotions may arise and you may experience a connection to your karma as your consciousness journeys with this book. Also know that your heart is magnificent and, through holy forgiveness and the support of the Enlightened Masters, you may release your karma and shift into a higher state of consciousness.

I was studying for a bachelor's degree in naturopathy at university in 1997. That special day when my spiritual eyes were fully opened I was sitting in a large auditorium listening to a lecture on the physiology of the brain. My lecturer was speaking about the pineal gland at the time, and it became obvious to me that very little was known about the true nature of our brains. Following this thought, many questions on the missing puzzle pieces of the brain began releasing from my consciousness. I had always had a fascination with the brain and now, finally, I was in a situation to receive the highest teachings, but so much was missing. I was slightly disappointed that university did not have the answers to my questions.

Just after this moment of contemplation, time seemed to slow down, and as I took another breath the whole auditorium filled with white light. I suddenly became aware of large, light beings about seven feet tall in the auditorium. Angels of such beauty were present with many of the other students. I had never seen angels before. I looked a little closer, as I was amazed at what I saw. Their wings were gently directing rays of light to the students, as if they were nurturing the students with their light. They seemed unaware that I could see them. They seemed to be in total service, and, as I connected to them, a great love began to fill me. Suddenly, my eyes cast over to my lecturer on the stage, and I was amazed to see three or four beings of light glowing and standing around her. Some were far behind her but one was by her side, and, as she spoke, golden light came out of her mouth and floated in spirals around the room—almost like the release of dancing, musical notes—spiraling streams of sound particles releasing consciousness into the room.

Through this experience I lost connection to my lecturer and what she was saying. I began to feel wonderful inside and transfixed by these amazing light beings. They held such immense love and peace. Out of the corners of my eyes I became aware of another three tall, large light beings. One was standing on my left, another on my right, and one directly behind me. As I became aware of them it was as if a switch had been turned on inside my head and I had been attuned to the signals of a special radio station. Within my mind I could hear them communicating; they were discussing the brain and responding to every one of my initial questions regarding the human brain. They were discussing this topic with immense intelligence and wisdom that obviously was not of the Earth, as if they had the knowledge of the whole universe at their fingertips. There were no doubts or limitations in their words. The love that I felt as they spoke was profound—a love I had never experienced on Earth. It washed over my whole body and soul and calmed the fear I felt as my initial response to seeing and hearing them.

My mind was hoping that this wacky experience would be over when I removed myself from the environment I was in. I planned to leave the auditorium once I felt I could walk. When the lecture ended, I waited until all the students had left and braced myself to enter the greater world. The angels had all moved on. They seemed to dissolve into clouds of white light as the students left the building. The three were still with me. They seemed to have a stronger presence than the angels, and I also noticed they had no wings. They seemed to be in robes of light that were very long. The one on my left had a long white beard—a male presence like a wise old man. The one on the right was a taller male presence, but younger looking with a beautiful, loving, peaceful face. I could not see the face on the being of light behind me, but she was also in white golden robes and I sensed she held an immense grace. They were made of pure light and not at all human. From the very center of their chests a stronger light, like a star, emanated and radiated in every direction. This light was so strong it almost blinded me.

The three beings completed their conversation about the brain, and then each of them focused upon me and together they said, "Welcome to the world of light. Please do not worry!"

My mind raced at a million miles an hour. How could I not be worried by the sudden presence of such huge beings of light in my life? This must be a figment of my imagination or a hallucination. Had someone spiked my water?

The three heard my thoughts, and shared that I was experiencing a divine intervention through the hand of God. I could not even ask them who they were or what they wanted with me, and I certainly could not embrace that I was experiencing a divine intervention.

Immediately, I started to leave the building, possibly in an unconscious move to get away from them. As I went outside the colors of our world were very different. There were streams of colors flowing around the plants and trees in every direction. The clouds and the sky were filled with a soft, loving light, and I could see a fine grid of light that seemed to link everything in a realm of oneness and love. Every person I passed was communicating in multicolored energy, with richer colors if they were more focused and brighter colors if they were active. No longer could I sense harsh energies. Everything was softened. Every smile I saw on people's faces seemed to fill me with color and love. Angels were with some of the people I saw, comforting or loving them as I walked past. I sensed these souls were sad.

I watched two people kissing passionately and embracing, their colors of energy expanding out across the oval on my right as I passed by. I was heading toward where I had left my car, thinking it was time to go home. I needed a place of safety. As I walked, the three presences walked with me, slightly behind me. If I had a thought or question or fear they would immediately respond, explaining, calming my mind so I would not worry.

I jumped into my car, and suddenly they were with me. It was the strangest experience, having a continual vision of my physical reality overlaid with another reality, as if there were two realities or planes of experience. I was in shock, but somehow I had been prepared for this experience. Previous visions and encounters with Spirit passed through my mind, confirming that I had been opened to the spiritual planes for a higher reason that would unfold over time. I had been chosen for this, and I also had chosen for this to take place at this time.

I drove home through landscapes of beautiful colors, a surreal world. I went straight to bed so I could hide under the covers. The three presences filled me with love as I lay on my side, blocking out my thoughts, trying to numb my mind, which was still racing at a million miles an hour. Each time they responded, my mind calmed and my soul felt a deep peace—but then my mind would have a thought and again begin to race with fear. This went on for many hours until I had released some of the fear. The colors slowly dulled as I fell asleep.

The next day I awoke, and all seemed normal for a few moments—and then they came. This time, six Enlightened Masters arrived. They seemed to appear out of thin air—I was just suddenly aware of them being there. Our telepathic communication seemed to have strengthened overnight. They shared with me that they were the Enlightened Masters Kuthumi, Sananda, Metatron, Mahatma, Sanat Kumara, and Archangel Michael. They shared that they had come to teach me as I had a mission and would be a teacher for humanity. They shared that a great shift was coming and I was a part of this shift, and I would now train with them in the Divine University on the spiritual planes. Part of my mind was really spinning, not sure if they were real or if this was my imagination. Was I going mad? Every time my thoughts went in this direction they calmed me down with their soothing love and wisdom, as if they were deeply linked to every emotion and thought I was having.

I was unable to be with other people at this time. The presence of their guides, angels, and loved ones confused me and caused me anxiety. The plants and trees were all I could deal with. They were communicating with me and showing me many things, but at least they did not expect anything of me. I could not disappoint them, and they did not judge me.

If a friend visited I would be aware of three conversations occurring simultaneously. Both my friend and their guide would be speaking to me, and, if I got anxious, an Enlightened Master would also speak with me. I was often so dumbfounded that I could not speak, or, when I did, I was not understood by those around me.

I could no longer return to university or even get into a car to drive somewhere. My whole reality seemed out of control, yet I could still see the world as it was before, just with an extra layer of these radiant beings and radiant energies pouring forth from everything. The natural world was absolutely incredible—plants, crystals, and animals all took on a whole new light as I walked through the paddock of long grass and the trees spoke to me, emanating rays of color into my body, sharing I would be alright. Fairy spirits that lived in the paddock came and brushed my hair, placed golden ki's (geometries of light) into my chakras, and said I would need to release my fear. Golden unicorns appeared, and Pan and the nature spirits came to me out of the trees and shared they would help me. All of this was beautiful, yet overwhelming. My heart felt like it had been stretched across universes, and I was being cracked open. I could feel a sea of despair, yet I sensed I could do nothing about it.

It had been three or four days now and these beings were always there, speaking to me, comforting and loving me, and bringing me wisdom. New forms of beings were arriving to inform me of their existence. The feelings I experienced moved from terror to complete bliss and joy, but then my mind would begin to doubt and I would feel immense fear. This world I was seeing did not fit into my belief system. Why had I been chosen? Surely there were others who would do better with this?

A part of me was angry. The Masters explained my life would be very different now, as a higher plan that I had chosen was being activated. Yet why did I feel this was occurring against my will? I had promised myself that, no matter what, even if university was boring, I would complete it so I would have a degree and be able to build a life for my family. I was angry that my plan to return to university and study natural medicine was being interfered with, even though when I chose this, I knew inside I would never be a practicing naturopath. I had never been able to envision myself actually working as a naturopath, but my spirit was passionate about pursuing this career.

I felt so out of control of my own reality. How could I become normal again? How could I return to my classes and study? All of this raced through my mind and, of course, the Enlightened Masters appeared again. They took me by the hand and shared they had something to show me.

Whenever they came close to me I felt peace and love flood through me instantly. My mind would calm, and my energy field would open again. I could see my energy field, which was golden. They explained that my brain chemistry was changing, and this was my evolution. They explained it was not intended for humanity to stay the same, and this experience was only created through fear that was locked in the mind or body of a soul. As they took my hand I became light like them. Streams of enlightened energy flooded through me to expand wings of light out from my body. I was pure light as I traveled with them through a portal of immense blue light. On the other side we were in the stars, traveling toward another great light.

They said, "The light you see is Sirius A."

As we got closer I saw cities of light on the surface. A huge temple structure made of pyramids, in golden light, was the first thing that attracted me.

"You are going home, our child. This is the last place you traveled to before you incarnated into your human form."

We entered the pyramid temple, and it was so beautiful, so peaceful. They shared I was within a civilization of light, and all beings here were in group-consciousness, communicating through the field and via telepathic group mind communication. My group mind connection had been activated as part of their divine intervention, and the crystal known as the pineal gland had been fully activated in my brain. From now on, they explained, I would always see and hear Spirit, as I would need this for my work.

As I traveled with them I experienced no fear or reaction. We traveled through the light pathways to other worlds where I saw beautiful things I could never have imagined existed. I simply listened to the Masters as they educated me. I felt only a great peace and love as we explored and they showed me many planes of existence within the realms. From the light cities on Sirius they took me to the libraries of light, and Sanat Kumara took me into a small room that had technology within it. He offered me something that appeared similar to headphones, but made of light, and asked me to place these on my head. As I did this I could hear a council of beings conversing in languages I could not understand, but I sensed that whatever they were discussing was important.

Sanat Kumara explained that there are many beings from many worlds that speak in ancient languages with very different sounds. The technology I had on my head allowed me to understand and translate all I heard. As I listened he told me to simply intend to receive their transmissions. He explained that my vibrational lightbody was at a high enough level that all could take place through my intention. I did as he requested, and suddenly I could hear the voices within my inner voice speaking in English. A group of three presences was discussing the karmic band within the Earth Mother and how it would dissolve through the Divine Plan. I was fascinated but caught only a fragment of the conversation. It made an impression on my mind as I had never consciously thought about a Divine Plan, nor had I considered that a band of karmic energy could cause the Earth and humanity to be limited.

Sanat Kumara had taken me under his wing, so to speak, making sure I was understanding all and not struggling with all that I was experiencing. He developed a more personal relationship with me than the others. Over the coming months, he held me as I fought inside and my spirit and mind battled with my new path. I was not able to return to university as, over time, the fear caused my body to become immobilized so it would lose all of its energy and collapse to the ground. Sometimes this would happen a few times a day, when I was walking outside, in the field or forest or on the way to my yurt sanctuary.

When my body lay immobilized, my awareness of the colors of the world would grow stronger and my psychic abilities would increase. I could hear the butterflies communicating to the flowers as they fluttered their wings. They seemed to be knitting together blueprints of light for each flower to come into its full beauty—so much exchange taking place within this field of light that linked everything together. As I lay on the ground, sometimes for many hours, the larger trees around me would send me their energy via the grids of light in the field until my body had enough energy to stand and walk again. Spirits would come out of the forest, form a circle around me, and begin to heal my energy body. The Masters shared that I was in a process of transformation and I needed to surrender. My mind was impatient and angry that I was trapped in this situation. I was a mother, and I needed to care for my daughter. Sometimes I could barely make her dinner. My partner at the time, Dreaming Heart, held me, letting me know it would be okay. Wonderful things were happening, although it did not always feel great. He was the ground rock in my life, my soothing presence that reminded me I was not mad. All was in divine order. My visions were amazing to him, and he would have liked to experience them with me.

Sometimes I would lie on the ground for three or four hours, as my body could not move until the trees finished their work. I could then stand up, but I would walk only twenty feet and collapse again. The Enlightened Masters visited me every day. In between their visitations, nature seemed to be caring for me. It took more than a year for the fear to fully release that was trapped in my energy field that had compressed through the diamond plates linking each chakra within my lightbody. Sometimes this process was blissful, and my heart was so expanded I felt I had met God within me. At other times I was taken to the edge as all of my paradigms were shattered. Somehow I was always held on this journey, no matter how much my mind resisted.

Eventually one day I felt myself fully surrender. My body was on the ground again. I was in the long grass, and I felt my will align and my spirit come into my body. I began to sound, for hours, in an ancient language.

Each sound seemed to activate a part of my brain to open to the light. Then as the sounds grew in strength, each cell began to respond in turn. One of the abilities I had received in my training during the thousands of hours of journeys I made with the Enlightened Masters into the other worlds was the ability to see into the physical body. I could literally see the filaments of light attached to each cell in my body expand and grow longer as I sounded. I could see the fear locking my body's cells and beginning to release as clouds of dark energy. As it dispersed it transmuted to light. I could see the diamond plates that connected the different chakras of my energy body being aligned and reactivated.

I could see a large presence with me, helping me. It seemed like it was me, but in a huge body of light that could not fit into my physical body. I recognized it as the presence that had stood behind me in the auditorium. I could see hundreds of thousands of filaments of light running from my cells, through my body, forming the meridians and then running through the organs and glands into the chakras, and from my chakras into this vast body of light, my Holy Spirit. As I sounded, these filaments lit up and my field seemed to expand at least one hundred feet in each direction.

My Presence spoke to me and said, "You are opening your field to me. You have chosen the new path to be one with me. You have chosen to place your will into your positive path ahead. All of the fear will release now. Your sound is your power of creation. We create together through our sound."

My body arched as I heard these words through my inner voice, and it felt like the fear, in the form of an old body, released from my spine, brain, bones, muscles, and cells. My body began to sob deeply from relief. A whole new body of light seemed to weave through my body. Giant butterfly beings who shared they were Andromedan emissaries, began to weave a pure cocoon of light around me. I was lifted in the cocoon to Andromeda. I saw the most beautiful feminine being made of blue light. She seemed like a Goddess. I looked into her eyes, and oceans swam within them. I looked more deeply, and I could see dolphins and whales inside them.

She smiled and shared I was a part of her. She was my Andromedan Presence. I would be meeting many parts of myself so I could open my abilities, evolve, and assist humanity to ground the new fifth dimensional teachings on Earth. She explained I had to forgive myself now for all of my past so the karma would lift. I would need to open my heart to every small challenge and learn to live in the world without escaping all I was confronted by. She shared she would support me, and others would come to help and we would build new streams of education that would shift humanity into its new world.

Then I was returned, aware I was lying on the Earth in the long grass. The sun had long set, and I had energy running through my body and could walk effortlessly. The ancient sound had healed my fear of the great transformation that my mind did not understand.

This led me to fully surrender to my training with the Enlightened Masters within the Divine University. Every day I would sit in the spiritual practices the Enlightened Masters had taught me in preparation for their visitations. Then they would come and take me, sometimes for six hours, into the worlds of light, to heal the karma I carried. The love was so profound my mind eventually stopped thinking about my future, and the Masters began to show it to me. I would travel the world with them, supporting others to open. They showed me my mission of grounding the Divine University on Earth. For two years all I did was travel into this infinite temple system on the spiritual planes, known as the Divine University, to meet with councils and other species and to learn about the energy sciences of the universe, the lightbody and field structure of humanity, and the call for the shift to bring about peace. During this time, I began to access the wisdom needed for all I met in life.

The Enlightened Masters became a large group of over one hundred Masters, as I met many more over this time, and they began to teach me. They each took me under their wing for a period of weeks or months and accelerated me or activated me to remember what I held within. They shared I was a powerful teacher. This was hard to believe as I had never taught anything in my life and found it difficult to complete anything.

They shared this was my karma, for in my last life, I had been a great teacher and I was unable to complete what I had come to Earth to do. They shared I would step into teaching again and meet many that I had known or assisted in some way in my last life, and they would remember me and what I had done for them. They would help me achieve what I was unable to complete—the anchoring of the Divine University on Earth.

The Enlightened Masters showed me a vision that has never left me. I saw a very large temple and education center in Australia where many people from around the world would gather to do service and experience a new consciousness birthing within them, a small prototype school for children that would birth near this center, and a community based on God Presence that was also nearby. People who came would receive the enlightened teachings and frequency and learn to live in accordance with the principles of love, wisdom, divinity, faith, service, communion, and charity so they could embody their Divine Presence. Many would come, create charitable service, and assist in the creation of new education that would be sent all over the world. Each individual would accelerate in their consciousness, and their Presence would ground into their hearts, minds, and eventually their bodies. The Enlightened Masters shared that I would have a hand in this collective transformation.

This seemed quite improbable considering my background and considering I had not achieved anything in my life up until this point apart from the creation of my beautiful child. In fact, I had periods of being quite destructive and very lost. How could this be and why me? This question ran through me and lived within every cell of my body until I fully accepted my Divine Presence into my life. This was a journey of many years, for even after I became a spiritual teacher with many activated, extraordinary gifts, it was not until I truly accepted my Divine Presence that I stopped wondering why this was occurring to me. The answer was that it was simply my choice and that I had been living under the false belief that what I saw and experienced physically was all that existed in my life. I had chosen to open my spiritual eyes and meet my vaster consciousness. This two-year period, when the veils were pierced and my eyes opened to the world of spirit to see how it feeds the physical world, was truly the greatest blessing in my life.

The universe is far more creative than the seeds of time, the winds of change, and what your single hand can construct in one life.

Your life, though, is your instrument for witnessing what your love can move, create, and giveth to this immense creation, your universe. Stand in the light and know that the power you truly hold is humble in its love, strong in its wisdom, and wise in its actions.

—*Babaji*

A Message from Buddha—
The Power of Your Incarnation

The power of your incarnation carries so much for you that you may not be fully aware of yet. In your awakened state, you may be very aware that your birth or journey into human form was not the beginning of your life, but was simply the beginning of one leg of a larger journey to create your soul's growth, development, and discovery of love and oneness.

I speak to you now from the realms of enlightenment as a sage who has lived on the Earth for over three hundred incarnations. Many have known me as Gautama, others as Buddha. The journey of your soul is not dissimilar to mine, yet you may not yet be aware of the power you hold within to awaken and illuminate your divine nature beloved, or you may wonder how your soul's purpose could be as simple as this. I share with you now that the journey of returning to the truth of your light is all it simply is.

On the path of incarnation, there are many distractions and beautiful jewels, but the biggest distraction that will take you away from your holistic manifestation and experience of love is your karma. Many lose themselves temporarily due to karma or the fear associated with karma. Written within your Akashic records is all you have mastered, all you have chosen to meet in this life to forgive and ignite with love, and all you chose for this incarnation. You have prearranged the journey to be a powerful instrument for your learning and awakening.

It is sometimes hard to believe, says the mind, that this could be true, that you have chosen the primary events of your life, even the difficult ones that possibly left an emotional wound. And you have the power to change your experience and liberate the karma of your soul. Yet the very nature of truly accepting responsibility for your experiences to liberate the karma of your soul and change your experience is often swept away, pushed aside, doubted, or denied by the mind due to the fear of what this responsibility would mean for you.

I address you with great respect and love for your soul and the immense journey you have led in life, and not only this leg of your journey. I look into your Akasha now and see the journey of your soul and share that between you and the truth of who you are, the great gifts you hold, and the unconditional love and wisdom your carry there is a small package of karma that needs to be acknowledged and embraced so you may interconnect with the power you hold as a soul, which when ignited leads you to the experience of divine love. It is now the time to recognize that your life may hold fragments of your soul's memories that carry the learning needed for you to enter a new doorway where all is lighter, more loving, and fulfilling, where you may experience a New You.

This New You I speak of is in fact yourself in a higher state of consciousness, where your heart is expanded so powerfully that your mind, soul, and body are able to feel the oneness and grace of divine love. The doorway we offer you through this book is a journey for your soul to open your consciousness to the interconnection you carry with All That Is, God/Goddess, the universe in its infinite expression of love and grace within the oneness.

This journey will take you into the exploration of your connection to your family, your community, and the Earth as your planetary mother, so that you may reach the highest potential that you seek as a soul. Remember that all primary events in your life have been chosen by you. You may ask, Why have I chosen to experience these events if they have involved suffering? Why would I do this to myself? I would not choose this, you may think.

You may have known that this was the best way for you to understand what others may have experienced before you, we say. But why would I wish to experience what others may have experienced if it was an experience of suffering? you may ask. This leads me to share with you that if you were ever responsible in any way as a witness, creator, or facilitator of another's suffering, then you carry karma with this experience. To balance this karma, you may have chosen this experience so you could understand and forgive it and thus reclaim the power you lost on that previous leg of your journey as a soul. You may not now be aware of what you experienced or witnessed, yet it is held in your Akashic records until you are ready to transform it. A great disappointment can be felt when karma is misunderstood as a punishment rather than an opportunity for the reactivation of gifts you have lost or closed.

This incarnation has brought you to the very people you need to open your heart. It has brought you to the very place, area, or community you need to heal your heart connection to Mother Earth. It has brought you to your current age, your physical body, and your unique personality. It will continue to bring all you need to you, offering you the opportunity to evolve beyond any personal karma you hold.

To be beyond karma may subtly imply to some that they can avoid what needs to be forgiven and brought into unity consciousness. There is no soul who is beyond karma until all beings are free from the karmic wheel and there is peace on Earth, as all souls live as a collective on Earth. All souls have aspects of themselves that at times would like to deny, push aside or avoid what is obviously needing to be forgiven. These aspects sometimes get triggered when karma is present in their environment. Yet when karma is acknowledged and a small, loving action is created to take responsibility, these aspects enter peace, bliss, and oneness, knowing all is held by love. The more loving actions you take in this way, the more the parts of self that fear the karmic energies experience a knowledge that all is being held by the love.

This growth of the heart is the central focus of a soul, and when the heart is not growing, the soul feels old and disempowered. The concept arises that there is a force outside oneself creating one's reality, an illusion many minds attach to so they may avoid responsibility for the Earth's karma or their collective, family, or personal karma. As a soul, you have been given free will, and no other being can in any way create your reality unless you choose to give your power away.

The gift of all karma is that it brings back to you a great love and power. It is often seen as a primary challenge in life which when avoided or judged creates suffering through the body, mind, soul, or spirit, or a combination of these. Consider your own life journey and what your greatest learning has been. You may attune to this easily by looking at any experience you have been avoiding or repressing inside, even though it arises in your life each day. Your karma is a primary challenge in your life, that which will teach you to love unconditionally something you originally closed your heart to. Your karma is a part of the grace God has bestowed upon you, yet when you deny or disown your karma, it disempowers you. Yet, if it be your will, I share that you always have the opportunity to embrace, heal, and balance this karma and receive karmic absolution from the Enlightened Masters. Call my name, Buddha, and ask for karmic absolution once you choose to enter a process of love and forgiveness.

What is it you need to forgive to allow yourself to evolve into the New You? This is a question you must answer from your own inner knowing. Then trust this, for the New You is free of the old ways of thinking that create disempowerment. For is it not true that your experience is created by the feelings and thoughts within you? To own your karma is to liberate your soul from the plane of duality. Illuminated and activated you will be as you choose to embrace all aspects of karma that may arise in your life.

I bless you on your path of karmic illumination, resolution, absolution, evolution, and activation. I encourage you to know that the love of the universe is behind you, empowering your soul with every act you take to align yourself to the truth of your learning. Choose to see that your karma is simply showing you where the power you have given away is stored so you may reclaim it through forgiveness, love, acceptance, and oneness.

Blessed be. Blessed be. Blessed be. Blessed be all beings!

CHAPTER TWO

Karmic Healing: The Journey of Reclaiming Ourselves

Your karma is naught but the energy and consciousness you gave as power to others, returning back to you. The key is to receive it as a blessing of energy that you may transform into any form that you wish. The power you hold is the power to embrace the form that your karma returns in. It shall be resurrected to the form you wish it to be upon the moment you choose not to judge it.

—KUTHUMI

When you make a deep heart connection within yourself, you access the Divine Presence of your soul, a powerful and conscious inner force of love and grace. This is your greatest support in life and is also known as your Holy Spirit. It is your unconditional love, wisdom, divinity, and faith, and it has the power to shift any karma you hold.

Each of the cells of your physical body also holds the key to your liberation from the karmic wheel. Your DNA is a carrier of your consciousness, and when it is freed of your karma, it activates and grounds new consciousness, or what is known as more of your Presence, into your physical body. This is a frequency shift that raises the vibration of your body and your energy field.

The wheel of karma influences all souls who incarnate on Earth. Individuality is influenced either by the consciousness of the astral plane, where the cause of suffering is held, or by the realms of light, where one's Presence is held. An individual's energy body resonates either to the frequency of the light realms or to the fear-based vibrations of the astral plane. The realm of light and the astral plane are simply doorways for a soul's experience. Neither one is greater than the other; yet, the realm of light offers a soul the experience of pure light. The wheel of karma is a doorway that souls must enter to travel from one plane to the other, from the astral into the planes of light or vice versa. The astral plane also must be traveled through upon death, when one is leaving one's light form or incarnation permanently, even if only briefly. If a soul's heart is open or ignited through forgiveness, they travel into the light planes and merge back with their spirit and Divine Presence, leaving behind any unresolved fears within the karmic wheel, or karmic plane of the Earth.

Unfortunately, souls that close their hearts in deep fear can become temporarily stuck between these planes, either on the wheel of karma or within the astral plane. Souls without an ignited heart are also unable to easily enter the realms of light, so they often interconnect with the astral plane or the wheel of karma until they feel ready to embody their truth more deeply and forgive their karmic experiences. All souls with the support of their spiritual guides reach the light realms during sleep, either traveling first through the astral plane or entering the realms of light directly. As long as the journey through the astral plane is not long, souls have beautiful and very important experiences in their dreaming bodies. However, if an astral connection is made for too long, a soul can embody the collective karma or suffering held in the lower aspects of the astral plane and temporarily lose connection with their essence. They therefore will need the assistance of the angels who spend a great deal of time in the astral plane assisting souls.

Those that have been harshly judged as dark or not of the light, so to speak, are simply souls or aspects of souls who have strong connections to the astral plane and to the collective karma. These ones are unable to be in touch with their true essence, as their heart has become embodied with the astral memories or traumas of the collective, and their soul is locked out of their body by the astral energy. This can cause them to be unconscious vessels for the astral energies. Their personalities and bodies continue to act out these traumas, usually leaving a path of destruction behind them. This is what is known as a lost soul—someone who loses their essence and is overpowered by astral memories. It is important that we begin to see these ones with spiritual eyes, as they are the souls that need the most love, forgiveness, and assistance on Earth. To embrace these souls with compassion even after the darkest deeds have taken place will free them from the astral plane. When this powerful act occurs, the veils of our ancestors' karma lift from our collective more deeply than through any other act of love.

The deepest aspects of the collective's karma carry elements of destruction and heartlessness and are stored in the astral plane for safekeeping for this very reason. All so-called dark beings are actually souls who suffer from our collective's memories of trauma and pain. Some may consider the lower astral plane as a mirror of the religious belief in the existence of "hell," and the doorway from the karmic wheel to the astral plane as "purgatory."

Just as the memories of deepest suffering are held within the lower astral plane of Earth, the Akasha and truth of all that has occurred is held within the light realms of Earth. The connection that souls on Earth hold to the living libraries or Akashic records brings all souls together in a field of collective consciousness. This collective refers not just to humanity, but to the living matrix of all souls who have incarnated on Earth in any living form, any time, any dimension, and any reality.

Your body is made of pure light, fabricated from the essence of Mother Earth, and is therefore a living library in its own right. Your body's cellular structure deeply resonates to the frequencies of light that source from the light realms. In other words, your body is an instrument for your soul to draw in the resonance and vibrational rays of light each day, connecting to the greater field of the Earth and universe known as the unified field. Yet, when a soul holds karma on a personal level or with family, community, or the planet, the flow of light rays into the body is blocked, creating pain, disease, ill thoughts and feelings, or disempowerment, until the karma is embraced and forgiven.

In your own life, you may perceive that all that occurs is created either through your influence, the influence of your circumstances, or the choices of others that are beyond your control. The truth is, the karma held within your body and energy field is the only influence, apart from your free will, that dictates how your life is manifested. The belief that you are a victim to circumstances beyond your control disempowers you and keeps you from truly balancing your karma. The joyful manifestation of your heart calls you to sincerely look within to understand what learning experience your karma may hold for you. Your power lies in your choice to forgive that which may seem to be beyond your control.

Discovering the Part of Your Consciousness That Carries Your Karma

Take a moment with me now to pause and sink into your own breath and awareness of yourself as you rest and allow your energy to embrace what I have shared with you in the deepest way. When you are ready to feel inside yourself deeply, you will find that you can access a sensitive part of yourself that lives hidden within you, on the inner of your being. This vulnerable part of your being is more sensitive to the world and to feelings. This is the part of you that is most affected by your personal, family, collective, or planetary karma. As you meet this part of you and give it love, you will come to understand that this is not a wounded part of you. This is a part of you that is very powerful, and it will release this power to you when it is liberated by you with unconditional love.

Take another breath and simply accept with me that inside you and within all beings there is a vulnerable aspect of self that holds the next level of power in its birthing process. This part of you also holds the memory of karma from beyond this life, from the eternal journey your soul has experienced in all incarnations.

This memory is also held in the library of the Earth, for the Akasha of all souls is held by Mother Earth, deep inside her body within the crystalline matrix. This Akashic record is also held within the chakras of your energy body, stored for you until you embrace the part of your consciousness that may have closed down long ago. The Akasha held in your chakras awakens via the cells within your physical body in divine timing for your soul growth, to bring you to the awareness of what needs to be forgiven.

The processing of your DNA within each cell carries consciousness and translates your consciousness between dimensions of yourself. In other words, your body can be likened to a battery of divine energy that has formed physically for your soul to temporarily experience your consciousness in a denser or more concentrated body. The battery of your body was created by the Earth Mother and carries her light.

The chemistry of your body as a vessel of light sustains your consciousness only when your soul continues to evolve. When your consciousness focuses on manifesting, creating, being, thinking, or feeling that which is not of your true light or vibration, your body acts as an attractor for the unresolved collective karma that is stored within the libraries of the Earth and the astral plane. Sometimes, if great focus is placed on negativity, astral connections can be made that affect a soul deeply, causing difficulty. You have returned to the Earth not only to experience love and what you have chosen as important for you to learn, but to gather and reclaim parts of your consciousness that you may have left behind in other times, dimensions, or worlds within the Earth. These parts of self can be seen as your karma or as parts of your own consciousness and power, ready to return to your heart for your soul growth. Many on Earth struggle because of a denial that they have chosen their life experience. This denial can create a soul to give their power to an astral fear that is held in the collective consciousness.

What can occur is that the body, your biological vessel, can become charged with cellular memory or consciousness that feels trapped inside, unable to express itself as love due to the attachment to fears that arise when the Akashic records or memories are activated by the light. Then the soul can become caught in a karmic loop, and even reexperience some form of suffering from other times or dimensions on the Earth. This often terrifying and debilitating re-embodiment only occurs when a soul has attached to the astral fears of the collective through the denial of their original choice to meet their karma and empower themselves as a soul.

The body is so powerful, as powerful as the Earth Mother, and therefore able to transform all that comes into it via the cells, including all streams of consciousness. To understand the true nature of the body, one must embrace the truth that the body has many dimensions to it, and the physical aspect of the body is only one dimension.

Consider with me now your body and its response to your consciousness. How you think and feel determines what occurs within your body. Consider your body to be a vessel and every cell a translator of your consciousness, which is so large that it cannot possibly fit into your physical body or within one dimension of experience. In fact, it can only move through your body as streams of energy, temporarily offering you new experiences and opening you to new dimensions of yourself. This movement of consciousness is also known as the flow of light through your body. As you contemplate this, I ask you to recognize how it feels when you open yourself to the truth that there may be much more of you.

A larger light or form of your consciousness is held within the spiritual planes as higher dimensions of yourself. The spirit of your soul extends through all dimensions, often unseen and unknown by you, and is in truth returning to you via each of your incarnations. This larger you comes in a spiritual form of light, which carries qualities of love, compassion, and divine expression. Each stream of consciousness that grounds into the cells of your body activates a new opportunity for your evolution in consciousness and greater experiences of oneness or God consciousness.

The journey you have chosen in life is not at all based on what you see as occurring in your life. It is not based on your job, the one you are closely in relationship with, or what you may believe about your self-identity. These are not the aspects of your life you chose before you came into incarnation.

In other words, you did not choose *how* you would learn your life lessons. What you did choose was the nature of these life lessons so you could reclaim any aspects of your power that your soul may have closed down to in other dimensions or lives on Earth. You foresaw the nature of what the Earth held for you in her libraries, in the Akasha. Before you incarnated, the councils of Light and your spiritual guides revealed to you your Akashic records so you could consciously make this choice.

Thus, although you did not choose every single aspect of your incarnation, you did choose the essence of your path of learning. Much may have occurred in your life that has not always made you happy, but I ask you to consider balancing any karma so the most vulnerable part of you may transform and open the true power of love within you. Each time you say within yourself, "I am able to meet this with the support of my Divine Presence, and I am able to forgive what I need to forgive to let go of the old consciousness that no longer serves me to experience my divinity," you set your path with the empowerment of your light and you align yourself to your spirit and to the realms of light.

The spirit of humanity is so powerful when it is aligned to the light of its true nature. The spirit of humanity is equally destructive when it is misaligned through loss of consciousness. Humanity as a collective has been experiencing the journey of learning together, discovering what the spirit can create for the benefit of all beings and what it can create that is not for the benefit for all beings. This learning has led the collective to choose to work together to create a shift into the fifth dimension. The journey into the fifth dimension is a journey of consciousness, and every being that enters this dimensional connection where unconditional love can be accessed with one's free will awakens their true power and choice to act in accordance with that which benefits others as well as self.

The Purpose of Your Karma

Earth's history has shown, over the last two thousand years, a light growing stronger, year by year, as a darkness or ignorance has been gently lifting over many generations to allow more on the Earth to access their true consciousness. In most countries of the world, some pockets of the collective are still acting out the karma from previous civilizations. This karma is most deeply manifested in areas where war, slavery, disease, and poverty are prevalent. Yet, our role is to embrace the whole world and love it, even the pockets that are acting out the karma for our collective.

In your unique individual journey, you have your own perceptions of what is occurring in the world and why you relate or do not relate to what you hear, see, know, or feel. This individual perspective makes up the fabric of your belief system, forming your perceptions not only of your reality, but of everyone else's reality. Yet, what if it is only your karma that influences you to see the world this way? What if the karma lifted, and you no longer believed what is truest to you now? Would you be willing to open your mind and heart and body for a journey with the Enlightened Masters to learn whether there is, in fact, a truer reality of your soul that lies behind your karma?

According to the universal laws of creation, karma, and love, every soul holds the power to resurrect from the planes of suffering to the planes of light. This ascension is a choice, and many souls on Earth have chosen to be representatives of the collective and agreed to their ascension in this life. It is the ascension of these souls that takes the collective on the journey into the fifth dimension and beyond, into higher states of consciousness.

Within the astral plane of the Earth, a thin band of deeply unresolved memory and consciousness holds the collective thought forms of unresolved traumatic experiences of our Earth's ancestors. These beings are simply large, astral thought forms. They have been claimed by many to be an invasive force or a psychic force of interference, and some healers who work with clearing the energy field see them as astral entities. In truth, these entities have no will of their own and simply live within the astral band. Any soul that gives power to their deepest fear can attract a connection to this astral plane.

The manifestation of collective beliefs that is created when souls attach to astral energies no longer needs to be experienced by humanity. Many light seeds have incarnated on the Earth for the journey into the fifth dimension, whereby humanity will no longer be affected by the astral plane, which is held by the Earth's oldest etheric body within the fourth dimension.

In your own personal journey, your consciousness either does or does not have karma with the astral plane. If you have learning with the astral plane, it is because you have given your power to it on another leg of your soul journey. You now have the opportunity to balance this karma by accepting that you no longer need to give your power to a collective fear, as it is not personal or true in regard to you.

In the true nature of your reality, these collective thought forms hold an effect upon you only when you fear your path, your future, your responsibility, or your karma. As fear is simply polarized energy or light, it can easily be transformed. The pain and suffering of karmic experience is only manifested when you close your heart to your experience. When you begin to see that all is able to flow in accordance with where you focus your consciousness deeply, you begin to draw closer to the true nature of your dharma, or your path of service in life. Extraordinary events occur to all beings that embrace their karma, not because they are lucky, but because of the release of the old Akasha, the old consciousness that was blocking their true self. Through the law of attraction, as you balance your karma, you attract the true reflection of love into that area of your life.

Ninety percent of the path of transformation can be made manifest by your Divine Presence, simply through prayer, intention, and the sacred alignment of your will to the embrace of any karma with love and acceptance. Ten percent of the transformation comes about through a heart opening process that can only take place through the will of your soul as you make the choice to bring love to yourself rather than enter into and embody the suffering and pain of an old memory, triggered by a challenging experience.

This takes great strength at first, as it is sometimes unavoidable to reignite the Akashic record, the memory of an original experience when the soul closed their heart in a previous time or dimension on Earth. The sense of the pain that had been locked away can create a soul to begin to close their heart again and to believe it is impossible or too difficult to embrace this lesson with love.

Contemplate your own heartbreaks in your life and consider for a moment the experiences where you have been most disappointed, or the experiences where you have been hurt most deeply. There lies your power, hidden inside you as a form of karma. Why is it karmic? you may ask me. How is it my karma that creates this, when another hurt or disappointed me or broke my heart deeply?

In the nature of love, there is always an equal exchange of energy. In the nature of karma, which is simply energy left in an unbalanced state, the exchange has not been equal. If you have karma with certain experiences or people, then you left a situation unresolved, and when you enter a connection with these people again, you always feel the imbalance in the energy between you. If you are unaware that this is your karma and instead you project the responsibility onto someone or something outside yourself, you will re-embody the original feelings that formed the imbalance. Simply understand that if you experience it, it is your karma.

For example, if long ago you exchanged deeply with a group and you shared an immense amount of anger with these ones, and the exchange was not equal, then you have karma with anger. This karma could arise when you are in the presence of these souls again, or when you enter a situation that reminds you in some way of this original experience. You may find yourself reexperiencing the anger you long ago projected at others, as others are now attracted into your life who project anger at you. Until you embrace the anger you are receiving and forgive yourself for sharing such deep anger unconsciously, you will continue to experience the karma of others projecting anger at you. You chose this lesson, for in another life or dimension on Earth, you were unable to learn it, beloved. Resolving karma is about completing your lessons in life.

The universal truth that the Enlightened Masters hold for your soul is that you are a divine being and deeply deserve to free yourself from the wheel of karma, and that all of the assistance that is possibly able to be shared with you will be brought forth as soon as you begin to embrace your Earth karma as your doorway to empowerment via the highest alignment of your free will in oneness with your spirit. Archangels and angels have been sent to assist you and others like you who are on the journey as light seeds, for your role is to seed humanity's collective consciousness into the light planes of the Earth and release the old etheric body of Mother Earth. This action will dissolve the astral plane of fear from the collective consciousness of humanity and the Earth.

Consider this astral plane as a small part of a great spirit or divine consciousness known as Mother Gaia. The astral plane of the Earth is transcending slowly and surely from the fourth dimension into the fifth dimension as Mother Gaia rises in vibration, octave by octave, receiving the higher frequencies of her ascension. See it with me now: the Earth's consciousness healing, transcending, and liberating. All souls who have collective karma will have this karma absolved, freeing them from the wheel of karma.

This collective release from the wheel of karma does not take place all at once, in one moment on a specific date. It has already occurred for some on the Earth. These souls are known as the souls of the first wave of ascension, and their response to all in life is based on love. They have their spirit firmly grounded in their bodies and speak with a loving energy. Their eyes do not flicker to the left or right when they speak. They carry a centered energy that feels supportive and embracing. They speak with compassion and sensitivity toward others, and they live in a state of peace.

You may be one of the light seeds who have ascended, and therefore you experience life from the core response of your heart, with unconditional love. If this is true, you carry a greater responsibility now than you have had before. You have been given a divine opportunity to ground more of who you are, use your gifts more wisely and contribute in a deep way to the transformation of society. Although your personal and family karma may be balanced you may still be affected by your collective and planetary karma, which relates to your relationship with humanity. Your personal karma creates the pain and suffering experienced in your life, whereas your collective karma with humanity creates your disassociation, isolation, or fear of being in your true power as a divine being in the presence of others.

How do you feel about yourself and your life when you take away all that you do and all that you own or have created here, and simply look at yourself as a soul? Do you feel loved and accepted here, not for what you own, what you do, or what you have created, but for yourself as a being? When you have balanced your collective karma, you truly begin to feel the love of humanity rather than believing only in the misfortune, duality, lack of empowerment, or apparent lack of love. How you perceive your own soul family of humanity is directly related to the beliefs stored in your Akashic records. To experience feeling loved by humanity, you must clear and balance your collective karma and transform the beliefs that share that humanity is not made from love.

The divine timing of events in your life sets the pace for an acceleration through the activation or reactivation of your sacred path as a light seed for the evolutionary path of humanity. Your DNA carries the codes in specific sequences, and specific streams of your consciousness are now wishing to return to you via the balancing of your karma and the opening of your heart in the holy act of forgiveness. You alone, as you walk with so many in spirit by your side, have the last say through your free will as to whether you will abide any longer in ignorance and simply stand by, witnessing your karma, pushing it aside into the "too hard basket" that lies by your side.

As you choose to no longer ignore or avoid what your spirit is calling you to embrace as your karma, you will receive empowerment from your Divine Presence, and little miracles, changes, and openings will occur for you. As you continue to take responsibility for your situation in life, no longer blaming others, becoming the victim, or holding shame, a great door will open and your spirit will begin to truly merge, flowing through you to benefit new, amazing, joyful experiences to take place within you.

The journey of embracing one's karma is a step-by-step journey. The first step on the journey is to see what is directly in front of you that would seem to stop you on your path—your challenge with your physical body, your mind, another person, or an aspect of your life—and recognize this as your karma. If it seems that another is stopping you or you have ill feeling when you are with them, you have karma with them. In a dimension or previous time, you have exchanged energy in an unequal way with their soul or another dimension of them.

To work with your karma offers you the greatest opening of your heart, for when the most hidden, vulnerable parts that normally lie inside, curled up and protected from the world, awaken, aspects of your heart grow and new gifts begin to open. The journey is not an overnight experience, but embracing karma and living in forgiveness always improves one's circumstances almost immediately. Eventually, once the energy is balanced, you will be fully liberated from the unresolved situation. This creates a new reality. You will be free of the old pain, free of any pattern of fear. The limitations and suffering that were symptoms of karma will never manifest in your life again.

A New View through Spiritual Eyes

In 1998, the Enlightened Masters told me that a great experience was about to take place that would be very unusual for me. I thought, How could anything be more unusual than the phenomena I have already experienced? They shared with me that I was being offered an unusual form of grace. I would be taken out of my physical body to travel to Sirius, where I would be given the Divine Plan. I had been traveling to Sirius and other realms with the Masters every day for over eighteen months, and I wondered how this would be different. Suddenly, I was shown a vision of my body slumped to the ground. They shared it would not be an experience where I meditated and my consciousness expanded and traveled with them. Instead, all of my consciousness would leave my body. During this time my body would be cared for by them as an empty vessel.

I was very unsure of how all this would occur but sensed it was important, so I agreed to follow their recommendations. Down by the ocean on a beautiful headland called the Furry Mammoth's Back was a portal that was directly connected to the enlightened realms. The Enlightened Masters recommended that I go there and be held by this portal to have my new experience. They promised me that my body would be fine and I would return into it with no difficulty. I spoke with my partner, and he was so beautiful and shared that he felt it would be fine. So off I went down to the portal the next day. I remember walking down the small, windy track that meanders to the tip of the headland and feeling the fear rising inside me, a little more with each step I took. As I got closer, my legs were shaking, and I realized that a part of me was in terror. I calmed myself and told myself it would be okay. As I came out to the clearing on the tip of the headland, I felt myself relax, and I thought that the fear had left me.

I did as instructed and meditated in the portal for an hour or two. I had a lovely journey to Sirius, but it was just like all other times, very powerful, but not the journey they had shared about with me. I came home and was in the arms of my partner, sharing my story, feeling it had not occurred. I simply let go of it and felt it was just a strange occurrence, unexplainable at the time.

I forgot about it until a few days later. I was in the middle of a healing session with the Enlightened Masters and was offering an energy recalibration to a woman from my local area. A great bolt of light began to flow through me, so strong and powerful I could barely stand. I had become accustomed to the large waves and currents of the Enlightened Masters' energy, but this felt as if they had turned the volume up one hundredfold. I could hardly breathe. Eventually, I placed my hands to the ground and bent over, trying to ground myself while the light only increased, stronger and stronger. Then I was gone. I imagine my body slumped to the ground at this time, just as they had shown me in the vision.

I was not sure how long I was gone, but it felt like a four- to five-year period to me, based on all that occurred while I was away—the beings I met, the councils I sat within, and the teachings I received and gave. I remember meeting every being in the world of light that I would meet in my physical life on Earth. I learned that everything takes place first in the world of light, and then it can physicalize. I was given many dispensations, teachings, and forms of new education to bring back with me. It felt like a lifetime of work and enough to also offer a lifetime of creation work to many others if they resonated with it. These teachings and dispensations were placed in hundreds of time capsules, and I knew that these would open at specific times on my journey in the presence of another who had a puzzle piece with me, or a contract to also support the creation of this new education to take place. This new education was from the Divine University.

As my final experience in the world of light, I stood on a precipice in space on a large crystal platform, almost like a crystal river, and all of the Divine Presences of humanity that were coming to the Earth were gathered to bless me on my journey. I was to be a bridge between the worlds and assist souls to meet and embrace their Presence, surrender their wills so they could have their highest potential shift and become genuine love and light frequency transmitters for the creation of a new world. As the Company of Heaven was blessing me, hundreds upon hundreds of thousands of Presences before me and millions behind them, my consciousness began to spiral inwardly. This experience of being blessed by all of humanity's presences before I returned to Earth became etched so deeply into my consciousness that even now I can see them all with me; we are a united force, working together so there will be peace.

All of a sudden, I was aware of journeying through a huge tunnel of light that looked like it was one hundred miles wide, and thick with pulsing, liquid energy. It was organic, and it breathed with me. The fabric in the universe was a sentient being, breathing with me. With this united sense of breath, I suddenly became aware of transmission upon transmission of higher consciousness traveling with me and through me, becoming me. I heard my voice speaking the wisdom of the Divine Plan. It was like a discourse from the Enlightened Masters, sped up, and the volume of information of hundreds of thousands of discourses concentrated into the one stream.

This speaking and the downloading of the Divine Plan was amazing. My awareness was fascinated by what I heard and simultaneously transmitted. Over a period of time, maybe ten minutes or longer, I had a sudden flash of awareness, as if a lightbulb had been turned on in my mind. I was on Earth! I was astounded. The transmissions continued at high speed, and I continued to speak of the Divine Plan. I could hear the words floating far away and yet simultaneously very close to me. I felt myself enter the Earth more deeply, pushing through the veils.

A great door opened in my being. Another sudden flash of self-realization came. Oh my God, I was Qala Serenia Phoenix! My light, spirit, and soul traveled back into my body through my crown chakra, and all of a sudden I was aware of my body. It sat upright, and discourse came through my physical voice, transmissions from the Divine Plan that I had been given during my journey. The experience of self-realizations drew closer together; I was slowly becoming more aware of time. Oh my God, I was in my yurt. I spoke this out loud.

Transmissions continued to flood through me. I was alternating between speaking from the Divine Plan to speaking of my sudden flashes of self-awareness—shifting from a place of God consciousness, where there was no individual awareness of self as separate from others, to my sudden flashes and moments of awareness of who I was as an individual, through my incarnation. This was a strange experience as my soul and spirit were squeezing themselves to their best of their ability back into my little frame, and the hemispheres of my brain were integrating this new form of communication with each other. Another sudden flash ignited. Oh my God, I was in the process of healing when the Enlightened Masters lifted me out of my body!

I suddenly became fully aware of being in my yurt, with the healing table to my left and my client by my feet looking worried but quite amazed. Even with this awareness, I could not stop the transmissions that were speaking through my voice or even try to rationally control myself so I could somehow comfort my client. Finally the transmissions completed and grounded with me. I was very shaky as I spoke to my client. She did not fully understand what had occurred, and I was not in any position to continue our healing. I was deeply grateful she was there to help me ground from such an immense experience. Later, the Enlightened Masters came and shared that it needed to be done this way due to my deep fear of the experience. I would carry the Divine Plan now in my being and always would know all that was needed to occur in accordance with it. From this day forth, I was led to make many new choices through the knowing that this was what was in the highest for myself, and all beings. The Enlightened Masters shared with me that evening that a lot of their work would come from the Divine Plan through me, and it would assist to prepare humanity for their journey and what they called the "great shift."

My journey off world seemed endless and timeless. In the moments where time stood still, I was aware that every Divine Presence of humanity was coming to Earth, the veils of the collective would be lifted, and the Holy Spirit would be recognized and accepted. I met friends and family

I knew deeply, but all in different forms. I spent a great deal of time on ships made of light, which are large *merkabahs* made from the group-consciousness or mergence of the energy of very advanced sentient beings, archangels of light. The merkabah is a form of light technology that activates one's consciousness and allows a soul or group to travel multidimensionally. The Galactic Federation of these archangels and emissaries of light took me on journeys into the field of the Earth so I could study the lightbody and the maps of the portal systems. They taught me how the plates of the Earth would shift and how humanity was only a small aspect of the greater shift, which would take place with or without humanity's alignment to it. At the same time, they showed me how important every single being is, how each carries an important puzzle piece in the plan. Even those who seem asleep or unconscious hold a piece of the puzzle that is Gaia.

The emissaries of light explained that humanity's perceptions would change quite rapidly during the first level of their shift in consciousness. For those in the process of transition, time would appear to speed up. But once a soul truly entered a higher state of consciousness, time would seem to slow down, and much more would seem to be created or accomplished in a shorter period of time. They explained that a soul's love, conscious awareness, and power of creation would each grow as their shift in consciousness and new energy bodies stabilized. They described the shift as an inner experience; the lightbody of the Earth was the vessel to create this for every living being on Earth, and humanity's perceptions would change quite rapidly due to this. The second level shift would then be guided by qualities of love, compassion, and fifth dimensional consciousness. They explained that was what was truly occurring was a deepening of our closeness with God, our direct contact with God, and that a release of the fear vibration was taking place that has held our collective prisoner, creating old beliefs that humanity's reality is purely physical.

As we traveled through the portals, I met so many teams of light beings who worked in oneness to create from the Divine Plan, in service to all beings. Each of these spirits of great consciousness, made of pure light, shared that they also were incarnated on the Earth as a human being. Every single one of them was deeply connected to one human being. They shared they were the higher selves or presences of these ones. As spirit, they were extensions or parts of the vaster consciousness of souls that had incarnated on the Earth. They shared with me the agreement that was held between the spirit and the soul of a being, and that as the chakras of an incarnated soul opened and the soul chose to live in closeness with their own heart, the spirit would be able to share the higher consciousness and light with them. One part of our vast consciousness would stay in the light realms (our spirit) and become the guide, while the other part incarnated (our soul) for the learning and experience in the physical world. They shared that as the soul was supported through their spirit's guidance and conscience, their spirit would merge with them to create the soul to ascend into a higher dimension while still incarnated. This would be experienced as a slow transformation of the brain and body as the higher vibrations of light grounded into the cells. They shared that the alignment of a soul's heart to the vibration of Mother Gaia's heart is what creates a soul's ascension, and that this was occurring on a larger scale than ever before. They showed me the energy science of the Earth core and spoke of the Inner Earth as a giant heart, pulsing, holding together and feeding not only the physical world but also the other worlds within Earth.

My experience of divine intervention has continued, and most days there are visitations where higher communication is delivered from the enlightened planes for the benefit of humanity. As we left each other and the presences blessed me and I traveled down the tunnel of light back to my body, they shared it takes only 51 percent of the collective's karma to be lifted from Earth for the chain reaction of humanity's inner transformation to create peace on Earth. It is to these words that I have given my light and life since that time. To make a small difference is all we are asked to do.

Aspects of My Personal Journey with Karma

My highest truth in life has always been based on giving love, for I have always believed that it is only through love that we truly live and experience life as a gift. I have experienced many powerful, life initiations through a journey of meeting what lies between our love and our pain, that which I call karma. My own karma has been very deep for me.

As a child I was a seeker of what lies beneath all that is seen. I always wanted to understand life, and this led me to seek a closer connection to Spirit from a very early age. At first, the search seemed pointless, as my karma took me to experience the loss of myself. I had created a reasonable amount of karma in my early youth with my body, my family, and my community. I was driven from a place that related primarily to what I believed was right and wrong in our society and blamed others deeply for all that took place, believing I and others like me were innocent. As a sixties child, I grew up with the awareness of the bomb, and the concept that humanity had the power to nuke hundreds of thousands of people with the simple push of a button. I was deeply shocked to discover the events of Hiroshima and Nagasaki that we had created as humanity, and I found these atrocities almost unforgivable.

It took only one cruel event to switch me into a state of fear in which I chose not to be present any more and firmly took the stance that our society was not a place I wanted to coexist in. I was sexually abused as a young girl. I felt deeply ashamed, and the only person I had the courage to share this with did not believe me. This was my closest friend from school, who many years later ended up marrying the person who had abused me. While I was sharing my experience with her as we walked to the local pool together, I had my very first experience of déjà vu. I remember it like it was yesterday as it was the strangest sensation. To have this experience of a memory so strong, of experiencing the exact same scenario with the same person before, created it to be deeply ingrained within me as a memory.

This was the first appearance of karma in my life. It took me many years to forgive this experience of being abused as a young girl entering puberty in this life. I felt a lot was taken away from me through this act. The innocence of being able to love and connect through the heart to a boy was lost for many years. The unconscious fear that men would just be using my body as a vessel or instrument for their pleasure lay seeded in my body as a memory until I was twenty-eight, when much began to change on every level of my being, and the path of true healing began.

The act of this abuse was the single cruelest and most unloving event that turned the switch of my consciousness to a level of fear. As I felt unsafe to share it with others, I bottled it up inside and it haunted me for many years as I grew to a young woman. I turned to drugs to soothe the fear, knowing no other way. I had started university at eighteen but soon left, unable to commit to creating any future for myself. By then I had begun deeply tapping into the collective karma of humanity and the deeper problems on Earth—apartheid, poverty, animal cruelty, war, disease, homelessness, and the destruction of our rainforests. I continued to feel despair and disappointment at humanity's plight. I felt I could not be a participant in our society. From the ages of sixteen to nineteen, I deeply believed that humanity had got it all wrong and unless there was a major change to the present structure, our society would stay corrupted and broken. I felt deeply for all the people without—the victims of war, those persecuted, those in poverty and homeless, and all the people I judged to be wronged by our society. I wanted to be their protector.

I was angry at humanity. I was unable to see all of the angels and people offering goodness in the world, and had no awareness that I needed to clear my own karma and do my piece in the balancing process. I wanted to express my difference and protest against the status quo, so I dressed differently and spoke out against the hierarchical system. The church, religion, government, banks, and corporations were all in my bad books. I could not identify with society as I knew it. Although I seemed gifted and bright, my deeply unresolved emotions directed my path at this time, rather than my intelligence. During my drug-based years, I had many close calls and lived on the edge of life and death until I fell deeply in love and met the person whom I thought would be my life partner. I call him Little Owl for he was so connected to these birds. We shared the same philosophy, and all felt beautiful when I was with him. We were young and in love, yet righteously believed that we needed a new society, one not based on hierarchy. We felt we had the right to do everything outside the laws of society since it was damaged and corrupt. We conceived a child, which changed my priorities, for I was finally given a reason to care in a more loving way about life and myself.

My karma really began to show itself fully once our child came into the world. Her light was so strong and pure, such a strong soul to choose to be with two young parents who were unable to be fully present in our society. Her innocence and love began to change me quickly as I began to sort myself out to make room for her and learned to mother and nurture her. Little Owl was deeply depressed about the world and our society. He was shyer than me and held things in more deeply. During pregnancy, I had begun to close down my intimacy and sexuality with him without meaning to. I began unconsciously rejecting him. I felt fear run through me physically that created my body to contract every time he touched me. The rape energies went into an overprotective state and built walls around my body, protecting my child from any potential enemy. I seemed to have no control over this, but it hurt my partner deeply. He gave me the space and grace to sleep alone while I was pregnant, but this sent him into a deeper depression. I loved him deeply, but my body was rejecting him out of fear, and I did not know how to deal with it.

Once our child was born, all my energy was focused on her, and my partner asked me many times if I was ready to be with him again. I felt pressured. I wanted to be, but his touch still affected me to close down and cringe inside. So much was changing inside me, in my body, mind, and soul due to this amazing light, my child, and all so quickly. When I finally held her in my arms, I felt peace for the very first time.

I had no recognition that I held fear or that karma was arising inside me and had no idea what was about to occur that would set the new direction for my life. I lived in regret for many years and thought, If only I had known, been wiser, been more aware, more present and considerate. Several times, Little Owl tried to commit suicide and I intervened and stopped him. He was deeply depressed about our world and what our child was going to meet. He also felt he was losing me, as I was changing deeply. With the pressure of being a new mother and receiving little assistance, I became overwhelmed and began checking out of my reality of being a partner to him.

We separated bedrooms to give each other space and to see if things would improve. He spent time with a close friend of mine who fell in love with him, and I met another guy, whose voice and energy somehow created me to feel safe. Each time we met, I began to feel closer to him. I felt my sexual feelings and openness return for the first time and developed feelings for this man. In a state of ignorance, I hurt Little Owl deeply. This led to our eventual separation and then to both men fighting as they came together one evening. A few days later, Little Owl took his own life at twenty-one years of age.

This was the hardest karma for me to meet, feeling the grief of losing him, feeling my own guilt that his love for me was unfulfilled and that our relationship was the major reason he gave up on himself. I grieved, as nothing could now be undone, as he was gone and I loved him. I cried myself to sleep for many years. It was as if a mask was taken off at the end of each day, and I would feel the karma as a heavy weight upon my chest. After spending the day using all of my strength to not let the grief overtake me, I had to have this release when no one could hear me. I had no understanding that the loss I felt was connected to my karma or that if I forgave this, the pain would lift from my heart, chakras, and body.

Of course, time does heal aspects of a wound when such traumatic experiences are met, but unfortunately time does not lift the karma of the experience or balance it. Even after seven years, the pain inside was as red and raw as it had been on the day he died. It was just buried underneath the strength I willed myself to access each day to be able to move on with my life and be a mother to my child. When I entered another deep relationship seven years later with the same level of intimacy and connection that I had created with Little Owl, the karma began to arise. It came as a fear that my new partner, whom I call Dreaming Heart in this book, would leave me and I would not fulfill him. It manifested as neediness toward him. This again was unconscious, as most karma is, but it did not feel like the "true me" and I was determined to learn from my past and apply the wisdom of the journey. I was living with Dreaming Heart at the time of my experience of divine intervention and the presence of the Enlightened Masters in my life.

I began to study universal law deeply, as the Enlightened Masters continued to assist me and visit me each day. I chose to apply all I had learned from the Masters to all that arose in my life experience, to align myself to the laws of the universe. They shared this would clear my karma and my consciousness and activate my higher consciousness. As I became closer and closer to Dreaming Heart and gave my trust and love to him and he gave his trust and love to me, I experienced my largest shift in consciousness, which led me to become a spiritual teacher. During this time, my karma arose as five large experiences, and only through studying universal law was I able to see my karma in each situation and take responsibility and heal it.

The first experience arose after Dreaming Heart and I had formed a deep relationship and were living together as partners. It arose through our sharing of truth, which was important to us. He shared with me that he was having attractions to other women. He would be adoring and present with his love when we were alone or at home, but when we went out, he seemed to experience a disconnection from me. I was aware that it was not what he truly wanted, but one part of his consciousness was definitely not committed to me. He had experienced this before in a committed relationship.

When he shared this with me, I was guided by the Enlightened Masters that everything was a reflection and this was my initiation of my heart and of unconditional love. They shared I had commitment issues to myself that I needed to shift, which were a part of my karma. They asked me to keep my heart open and work with the law of reflection that stated that each time my heart closed and I reacted to another, how I perceived them was a direct reflection of a part of me that I needed to embrace. With this, and the karma of neediness arising from my previous relationship, I had my hands full with taking responsibility for what was being experienced as the undertow within our beautiful relationship.

Well, the triggering soon began, for my partner learned he could say almost anything to me, and because I was training with the Enlightened Masters, I would stay in my heart with him, and if his truth affected me to react with deep feelings, I would look at my reflection to heal the part of me that reacted. The number of buttons my partner pushed over the first year of our relationship seemed to go on and on forever. Just as I would come to a place of peace and feel the immense love again, there would be another deep, inner journey. Yet, within a very short period of time, all of the neediness cleared, simply through my working with universal law whenever a triggering occurred.

With each experience, the love between us would grow stronger, and our connection would empower us. The karma arose and cleared layer by layer through my nonjudgment of Dreaming Heart and his nonjudgment of me. He eventually entered a deep commitment with me as I cleared my reflection. It was a profound, beautiful journey to meet myself this way. I became confident and clear in my being. Over a year or more, I gave love to my partner instead of withdrawing, blaming, criticizing, or separating from him, and a deep level of my personal karma cleared around my true commitment to myself.

The second experience arose with one of my friends. He was a great influence on my being, yet his influence was not always positive. I had to make a choice to not spend time with him so the karma could clear. I spent many months guiding myself through deep processes of forgiveness, clearing my field of the unresolved aspects of my consciousness. I call this process "aspect clearing." I had been unaware of a great deal of karma held in my mind, existing as negative thoughts, judgments, and insensitive attitudes toward myself and others. This reflected my friend deeply, as he had always been critical of others. Upon my completion of this process, I was able to hold unconditional love toward him and myself.

The third experience arose as a fear that a dark force would interfere with me. I was taken on a journey where I met a deep fear that appeared to me in vision as an astral lord. I had many enlightened beings and advanced sentient consciousnesses with me, yet this was the first time I had met the astral in a conscious way. This one appeared to me in dark robes, something like Darth Vader from a *Star Wars* movie, speaking to me of negative events that may take place, obviously trying to scare me. I realized that I had attracted this to me through the law of attraction and resonance, and somewhere inside lay a part of my consciousness, locked in an astral form. This opened up a whole new world to me of meeting the astral plane. As I met other astral energies, I noticed these beings had no souls, no essence, and in truth, they had no personal power. I looked more deeply into them and noticed they were simply projections made from the deeply unresolved thought forms of the collective; there was no presence of light in their hearts. Instead, they lived off a soul's light as a soul gave their power to focusing on negative thoughts. I realized that if I gave only positive thoughts and love, the astral energies would have no power to attach to me. The Enlightened Masters shared that these astral beings were made from the unresolved energies of the most traumatic experiences. Through this, I also learned to meet, embrace, and not judge parts of myself from the layers of my unconscious, or more hidden or darker aspects of myself. I held my heart open to them as I met them inside and gave no power to them, accepted them but guided them to receive the love and compassion. I learned to see these energies as no different from any others and to bring my love to them as my first response when I became aware of them. Eventually I had no fear of the astral or of any part of me as either light or dark. This created me to open my heart to all beings and to no longer judge souls for their choices, intentions, and actions. This was another level of karma that was cleared—my karma with the collective and also my spirit.

The fourth experience of karma arose with anger and my power of creation. Deep down, I realized that things were not going my way in life even though in my eyes I had been so positive and loving. During this period I felt blocked and angry inside. I was angry about little things, then larger things, then little things, and anything that seemed to not be flowing how I wished it to be. I met the karma of my own anger. I found that this was karma I had created through simply bottling up my anger for many years. I was angry with myself. A deep healing took place as I acknowledged my anger and understood that this energy was my creative fire and passion that I had turned in on myself. As the karma shifted, my creations flowed, deeply filled with my love and power. Another level of karma had cleared, known as my karma with creation. Creative flow has taken place in my life every day since clearing this karma.

The fifth experience arose with my karma with my heart as my Divine Presence guided me to surrender something I was deeply attached to. I was asked if I would surrender my life with Dreaming Heart and my beautiful lifestyle of living in isolation on the land with him, my daughter, and my soul family. It was shared with me that if I could open my heart and give my lifestyle to God, this would open my planetary service work, and I would travel and teach many more on Earth. This was a period in my life where God's grace supported me although a part of my heart deeply feared the experience. I had had twelve years of beauty, peace, and oneness with nature, living on very large acreage, my heart connected to the spirit of the land. Yet my planetary karma would only change if I were willing to release my attachment to living in this isolation and working with just a small group of people. This form of karma was very silent, hidden in the comfort of what I enjoyed and loved. How could this be karma? I asked the Enlightened Masters. They shared that this was my planetary karma due to entering deep isolation in my last life, which was in Ancient Egypt. I had closed down my connection to the wisdom teachings of my

Presence and pushed many away so I could be alone and live without responsibility, and I had created karma with humanity and the planet, based on this isolation and non-sharing of my wisdom.

I reluctantly let go at this time and was relocated in a magical way, through another divine intervention, to the local town, where I began to gather with more people and work more deeply to assist others. This led to international travel with the Enlightened Masters' work the following year, and this work has only expanded since that time. This was a clearing of my planetary karma, which is the most hidden and invisible form of karma a soul holds on Earth. My planetary work birthed as I chose to let go of my lifestyle and I began to travel the world to many countries, with the Enlightened Masters' work.

Surrender into the Light

It can sometimes be a shock to our souls when unexpected experiences occur that change our circumstances or our life direction quite suddenly. It can feel as if a force outside us has come along and created this against our will, and we had no part in its creation. Often, our life direction, our relationships, and our ideas about how things should be become set in our minds, and when something occurs that does not fit into our personal plan it can be quite confronting. Sometimes these surprises are beautiful, and we can give thanks for all we receive. But when the events that arise ask us to let go of something we are attached to, fear is often the first response. These experiences of deep surrender are the key to the transformation of our DNA and to the release of fear that has been stored within us from the karma we carry as souls. If we surrender and the fear is released and our karma balanced, then we are taken through a doorway by Spirit into a new world where grace lives. This was my journey of entering that door and embracing what Spirit wanted for my partner and me. It was what truly set us free from each other and allowed our love to move from a place of personal attachment into the expression of God's love.

About five years ago, my partner and I were having difficulties. This was many years after Dreaming Heart and I had completed our intimate journey with each other, and I was in partnership with my twin flame, Golden Phoenix. I was away overseas with my work quite a bit that year. Our relationship and karma had hit a new level in life and there were so many areas that seemed not to flow beautifully. We had come together in a powerful, magical way, but over the years, three karmic experiences had taken place that we had not yet been able to balance. Although we did feel a huge amount of grace and support and held an immense love for each other, there was also an underlying struggle within our relationship. We were vibrating to different frequencies, and our consciousness was anchored in different dimensions.

My communication with the angels, archangels, and Enlightened Masters, and the continual visitations I experienced, the volume of new educational materials I received, and my ability to quickly shift from one project to another as needed, triggered within Golden Phoenix a fear of the power of his own light and Presence. He was unable to meet me spiritually, due to deep, unresolved projections he held about himself. As a couple, our energy bodies were unable to resonate with each other. It was almost like placing chalk and cheese together, yet we loved each other beyond our difficulty to actually synergize as beings. Our karma started to arise gradually, one experience leading to the next, until we found ourselves embodying physical karma with each other. This was our karma of the physical body.

Our first karmic experience occurred one evening while we were making love. I experienced a vision of being raped by many men, of which one appeared to be Golden Phoenix. My sexuality closed down during the experience, and although we loved each other deeply and knew in our conscious minds that this vision was not our reality, my body deeply rejected being touched or held by him after this. If we connected sexually, my whole body would feel like it was crawling with black snakes because of the level of fear or karma trapped in my body. This was a reoccurrence of my previous experience in my early youth, and it was this same trapped karma that partially led to Little Owl's suicide. This time, the unconscious energies had become even more deeply incorporated in my body. I realized it must have been a very large, old memory trapped in my consciousness, as it was powerful enough to instantly close my body down in the presence of any sense of intimacy with Golden Phoenix. This led me to work with the Enlightened Masters to discover how to heal the karma of loss of one's sexuality, which led me to developing healing programs based on the source of this karma from Ancient Egypt. I was determined to heal this. The Masters shared that this would take time, but if I did this, I would not only heal my sexuality but also activate my tantric energy and create a lot of bliss within my body.

Not long after the loss of my sexuality, the second karmic experience occurred. Golden Phoenix began to experience sciatica and then a loss of power in his legs; eventually there were times when he was not able to walk at all and suffered great dizziness. No one at that time could find a diagnosis for his ailment, but he was suffering from the beginning stages of Parkinson's disease. At times he would pick up, and his amazing, healthy glow would return. But then he would plummet and his body would close down, and he would experience a complete loss of physical power. There was also fear that accompanied his attacks.

The third experience was that Golden Phoenix would occasionally be overtaken by his alter ego. During these times he would say very hurtful things that the next day he would never remember saying. He just seemed to experience a lapse in consciousness and then be affected by the astral energies of the collective. His physical pain always grew stronger whenever he was unconsciously overtaken. It was a catch-22, for as his physical body weakened from illness, his brain chemistry switched to the frequency of fear and he would temporarily lose consciousness and be overtaken. It was painful to witness and also to receive the hurtful words of his deep, repressed anger as it rose to finally be expressed. So much healing took place, but the karma was very deep and it would need to be balanced.

When he was overtaken, we knew it was his spiritual and physical pain speaking, which had been locked in his soul and body for a very long time. Golden Phoenix felt a lot of guilt over his lapses of love and clarity. When this pain blocked his heart, he lost himself, and only when he forgave would he find his way back to his truth and feel his heart again. It was like witnessing a soul heal the inner darkness they had repressed. I forgave each time he hurt me with his words, and knew that in accordance with the universal law of reflection, a part of my unconscious was very angry, blaming, and venomous. I also realized that I had attracted this experience to me, and that I must have projected a massive amount of anger at Golden Phoenix in a previous life.

This was my karma. I wanted to run away many times or push him out of my heart, but I knew if I did I would simply attract it to me in another form. I had something very big to forgive—verbal abuse. I could not remember when or how I had sowed the seeds of verbal abuse, but I recognized this was my karma and now I needed to balance this with love and forgiveness. I worked with the universal laws of reflection with myself—the laws of oneness, grace, karma, forgiveness, and love—and he mirrored my own inner change. He became more balanced and no longer was overtaken by rage and anger. This took some time, as it was very deep karma. Our love strengthened through this and is still very deep to this day.

I was told that these forms of karma were much deeper than what I had met before. My role was to bring unconditional love to the situation every time, no matter what occurred. The Enlightened Masters shared it was my heart initiation, and my heart would open to a much more expanded state as I did this regularly. During this time, my own personal experiences of bliss, inner ecstasy, and divine love grew within my meditations and spiritual teaching sessions, and I was taken into deep states of oneness with all of life and God Presence.

As I had these experiences, my heart reached out to Golden Phoenix, whose fear did not allow him to meet Spirit as easily or receive the light without pain. He also knew his karma with the body was very deep, and he would need to balance the spiritual pain that created his physical pain. He wanted to have the same experiences as me or just be free of pain, but he was only just learning to surrender to his own heart and he could not rush this. The karma between us was not a simple reflection, as this karma was held in many dimensions of my field and not just on a soul level within me. In other words, this was not my personal karma but was connected to our collective and planetary karma as twin flames, which was held through many dimensions of our being.

Because of our profound love, we were committed to supporting each other as well as healing and forgiving miscommunications if they arose between us. Yet we had not only come together to be in union with each other, but also to be in service to humanity, by working with the Enlightened Masters on the development of new education and forms of new consciousness grounding. We were aware as we were grounding new programs from the enlightened realms and being carefully guided by the Divine Plan and the Enlightened Masters that aspects of our own consciousness, as well as aspects of the collective and of the Earth, were also in a process of gentle transformation.

It was our busiest time of year. As I was overseas and he was at home, our communication lessened. When we were able to talk, work-related issues became the focus of our conversations, and we simply lost touch with each other for a period. I was teaching retreats, and my schedule took me to Egypt. Returning to Egypt was the key for me, after many months of forgiveness, for balancing the karma that created the loss of my sexuality. When I was there I felt renewed and healed on all levels of my being as the karma was cleared and my sexuality was returned to me.

After working many months overseas, I came home to find my Golden Phoenix with very deep feelings for another woman. This of course was not part of my personal plan in life, and at first I experienced all of the feelings that normally arise from a situation like this—the initial shock of the discovery, questions about our future, and very deep feelings of being hurt, although I knew that in no way did he mean to hurt me. The hardest thing was that he still loved me and I still loved him, yet he was so torn inside and also needed his independence from me. We cried together and in the best way we could, tried to give it over to God, but a part of me could just not fully let go. What did this mean? Were we to complete our relationship? Could I be happy without him and could I be happy with him?

The difficulty for me was that I deeply loved the friend he had developed strong feelings for, and we also worked professionally with each other in my office, which was on the ground floor of my home. This placed me in a confronting situation. Would I lose a friend? Fears arose about what I might lose and what this meant for me as a woman. Who was I? All of a sudden, I felt myself being flung into a small passageway inside myself where I felt my consciousness shrink, as if it were being squashed through a sieve. I started doubting, questioning, and arguing with myself. Was I not enough? Had I not given enough? Who was this other woman? Why me, and what would happen to me? The need to control my reality took my mind in every possible direction. Some part of my consciousness was determined that only the worst scenario would take place, while all parts of me felt like the rug had been pulled from under my being. It was all so unexpected, just when my sexuality had returned.

All of the anger, pain, grief, and feelings of betrayal began to arise, while at the same time, the love for my partner and my friend and compassion for the situation arose as another part of me tried to see the light within the situation. The nature of my truth as a spiritual teacher overtook me and guided my way through the path of unconditional love, but underneath there was a deep part of me that I knew was about to surrender to the hurt and rage. Strangely enough, it almost felt like these two parts of my personality were arising from two different hemispheres from my brain. I was simply forced to witness. Wondering which part of me would win, I quickly took myself away from others so they would not be affected.

Some part of me knew not to make a decision until I could feel my heart again. My heart felt like it was being thrown from wall to wall around my house, and that the walls were crashing down. It felt like it was dying inside, closing, frizzling, and turning to a small rock. Such deep pain I felt inside. I was aware that I needed time to heal, yet my commitments were still asking me to be strong and move forward on my path. How would I find the way, I wondered, when I was so devastated?

Golden Phoenix had not made a decision about what he was doing, but I knew he would need to make his own choice. He seemed to be the one in control of my reality, and not me. I felt deeply hurt inside, yet I still loved him deeply; I wanted to close my heart but I could not, as my love for him was larger than the pain. I knew the pain would only cease if I closed my heart like a rock and cut him out of my life so I could not feel it. So many people had done this on the planet already, and the ones they had loved were no longer an important part of their lives.

A small part of me asked, is there not another way? So many parts of me tried to close down but the searing pain would burn through my cells and my soul as another stronger part of myself was determined to keep myself open. My heart moved in a cycle, closing itself down and then opening, over and over again. I lay numb on my bed, blankets over my head. Let the world go . . . let the world go. . . . This part of me echoed in my mind, the part of me that felt dead. This part of me felt so exposed . . . could I not just hide inside, place the blankets over my head, send the world away and not arise? It felt like a true death.

This was true, for a part of me was dying. This feeling of deep pain that can at times bombard our hearts is truly a doorway for our transformation and change. In ancient times, we had rituals for these passageways. Womanhood was acknowledged by life initiations around the menstrual cycle, the connection to the moon, coming into partnership, the birth of children, entering eldership and wisdom—but the life passage was also recognized as a journey of initiations of the heart.

What was my initiation? I had many choices, but a part of me felt like I had no choice. Was this true? As I lay numb inside, swaying and rocking on my bed, trying to manage the grief and pain that riveted through every bone, every cell of my body, a small voice spoke . . .

The love will return, but you must trust that this path is leading you to heal a wound that you buried long ago, deep inside. Take the time my child to listen to me now. You are wise beyond your years, yet the part of you that feels the pain is bound inside you, alone, feeling shattered, bitter, and deeply fearful that she will be abandoned here. Hold her in your heart. Do not just listen to her screams. Guide her to a place to receive healing, my child. She is but a part of you that is feeling the pain of a loss long ago, and this creates her to fear the path ahead, believing that there can only be more loss and pain on the path ahead.

As you lie down, let me bring the love into your heart. Open it to me. Golden light will bless you now. The angels will come, but you must let them in and allow them to do the healing with you. She is a part of you that is strong, has held so many hands in this life, helped so many, yet she has not learned to receive the grace, fully. She still believes she is to give and give and this will only lead her to abandoning that which she loves most deeply. Your partner is simply asking you to enter unconditional love, and this hurts you because this part of you has conditions on this love. Will you help her heal so she may open to unconditional love?

God has a path for you, and although you may not know what this is and fear may arise, it will take you home into your heart as long as you do not give your power to these fears. Watch them, but do not place your faith in them. See them as pain and anger from the past, needing a witness of compassion and love. See this part of you, so unforgiving and hurt, as an abandoned child that only you can love. Comfort her and guide her to know she is loved. Let her know she is not alone and that you and I are there with her.

I became held in that moment with a beautiful energy, and my energy field began to support me. The swaying stopped, but the rock was still inside my heart. A beautiful presence, Nada, an Enlightened Master, was in the room with me, comforting, guiding, and supporting me. When my heart opened for short periods I would feel the love Nada was offering me as she spoke to me through my inner voice. She was asking me to make a choice to own and support the part of myself that was in pain, to not just be a victim to this crisis but also become a loving participant. There was no rush, she said, but the longer I left it, the more destitute I would feel. Had I asked for help? she said. I realized in all of my anger and grief, I had forgotten to simply ask directly for the grace I needed from God. I had forgotten to love myself.

What was my lesson? Could I love myself through this journey no matter what direction it took? This was my initiation of the heart. The part of me in pain wanted to close the heart, push my partner away, cry out his name in anger, call my dear friend the betrayer. Yet, another possibility did exist. It was my choice! A part of me could see their new love and feel that their connection could be strong and healing in their love for each other. I knew my partner needed this, but no matter how much I had tried, regardless of the truth that my consciousness was so different, regardless of all the love I had given, I still felt I had failed him as a partner. A part of me could see this was the path Golden Phoenix needed for his soul growth and healing. I knew if it would help him heal his pain, I would have to let him go.

The journey surely would take time if I chose this path. Could I embrace my karma? Could I forgive? Or would she, my wounded self, hold this forever? In isolation, I was the only possible support to this part of me that felt like she was drowning in memories. She felt like a zombie, stiff and dead inside as I went to the kitchen for a glass of water. My body felt heavier and heavier as I walked, my feet somehow dragged themselves step by step, spiritless, and my hands shook as I reached for a glass to quench my thirst.

Nada appeared again, and a small loving voice inside said . . .

You are dry inside, my child, the waters of life have ceased to flow, the cellular memory of this pain that you buried so long ago has arisen and filled your body. It is trying to release. Every cell is reliving it presently, instead of releasing it from your DNA. It has been stored there until you are ready to open your heart beyond it, and forgive the karma, beloved. This is the most vulnerable and sensitive part of your being at this stage, needing the love from the mother. Connect inside to this part screaming inside and hold her with me. Bring compassion to her rage.

I looked in the mirror. My eyes swelled like oceans, and my skin was like a lizard's, so dry. I felt like the oceans were spinning inside me, with torrential rain and wind howling through dark skies. I knew this would be a deep journey, and sighed deeply inside, as I was so tired of it already. The small voice continued . . .

There is nowhere to go but to your heart. She will quieten and be brought to peace if you enter your heart. Surrender and you will begin the journey back to your heart. The rage will cease.

I took a breath, and step by step my feet dragged me back to the bed, where I collapsed in a heap and started to cry. The tears felt like an endless river, and shame flowed from the waters of my body. My cells seemed to be shedding an ancient shame I did not understand, not from this life's experience, but sourced from something I had buried long ago.

What did I have to be ashamed of? I had not been the betrayer, my mind said. Yet my body spoke a different story. As my body sobbed, shards of my old memories of loss left my cells. I saw a river of light beginning to form inside me as the shame released from my DNA. Finally there were no more tears. The river inside my soul had unlocked.

Nada spoke again . . .

You are a mother of love, yet she has forgotten to love. The shame is her burden or belief she does not love enough. She has carried this for so long, from so long ago when she mothered many and gave great love but could not love enough to create her partner and herself to be happy. She blamed herself then, and has held the shame since then. She is letting go. She is a part of your heart opening, but she must first let go of the shame that has held her in suffering.

A resonance so strong was felt by me, a knowing that somewhere on one leg of my eternal journey I had lost my partner and family and blamed myself. I now owned this creation. I felt her let go. The rock inside softened, allowing me to breathe again. Curled in fetal position, my body murmured for the love that was always held back. Every organ in my body began to open. I felt as if someone had removed an old crust from my body, and a beautiful new skin formed, a little raw and sensitive but flowing with light. I was placed in a cocoon of light.

It was then that I saw the twelve angels around me, their hearts wide open, transmitting rays of many-colored frequencies. I entered an altered state, my frequency began to rise, and my spirit expanded in my body. I saw myself lying on the bed, and pearls of silver-white light were being placed in my body and chakras. A beautiful, tall angel was by my side, gently filling me with elixirs of love from a golden chalice of light. Within ten minutes, I felt the pain leave me, and I no longer felt the pressure of my situation with my partner. I no longer searched for answers or felt the devastation, although I felt deeply raw inside. I could feel my cells altering as I was being gifted with love and being healed.

The small voice spoke again, and I realized Nada and the angels were blessing me and I felt safe, so safe inside. Maitreya and Serapis Bey also stepped by my side.

You will come to a place of peace now, and you will know what is right for you on your path. There are no mistakes, only synchronicities, and no longer will this pain be felt by you in this or any other life. You have opened your receptivity and more grace will now come to you. No matter who may choose to be with you or not, beloved, this grace is yours as your forgiveness is yours.

From this day forth, you will no longer fear being abandoned here. This is a great time for you. What you must ask now since the healing has taken place is what and whom do you need to forgive to complete this so the karma is fully released. This karma is ancient, and long ago you gave and gave, yet you forgot one thing, which was to let God give you all you needed, not only to make you happy but also to free you of all your fears that may otherwise not leave you. Through this, beloved, you abandoned yourself, and your partner felt this. You abandoned yourself and from this you felt the shame of abandoning others. You are learning, our dear one, that fear is a mysterious energy, unconscious and therefore unseen. It can have a powerful effect on a soul if they do not honor it and instead choose to give their power to it. You have now met the part of you that had given her power to the fear and pain. Thank this part of you now for the journey and simply ask this part to travel into the light so it may live in the experience of love again.

As this occurred I saw beautiful bridge of light anchored from the heavens. I was suddenly aware that I was in another dimension in a beautiful temple, and the presences and angels that were with me were illuminating the part of me that had held the pain. I saw this part of me in another dimensional form. She looked like an Egyptian being of great stature. She carried in her arms a golden ankh, but it felt like a great burden to her. Nada stepped forth and brought golden books to her, my Akashic records. As she looked through them and remembered why she had felt such shame and guilt, she cried.

She looked me in the eyes, and a great power of love was released that she had bound inside because of the guilt and shame of feeling she had failed her flame. She had chosen forgiveness, after thousands of years. She was a feminine part of my consciousness, my receptivity from my last life where I had chosen to close down and isolate myself. She offered her shame of closing down in this way, and chose in that moment to forgive and enter the light. She stepped into the bridge of light, and I witnessed her transform to pure golden light. In this moment, I became aware of my sacral chakra opening, my heart chakra expanding, and a golden bridge of light forming between my sacral and my heart. It was glowing powerfully and my lower chakras were growing larger. I was evolving, not only healing.

Over the next hours, the pain released from my body, soul, and chakras. I had a few sensitive months after that, but we were all able to love each other through the experience as long as we gave each other sacred space. Golden Phoenix and I still deeply love each other and are very close friends. My dear friend and I held our friendship through the process and still do to this day, even though she entered an intimate relationship with Golden Phoenix after he and I spent three final months together, completing our partnership with unconditional love.

I can now give only gratitude to Golden Phoenix for taking me on this journey and for holding me through it, as I see deep surrenders like this as a very deep service to the Earth Mother and our own personal transformation. I honor all who embrace their true power to surrender even when unbearable circumstances arise, as the power of forgiveness only brings people closer.

May this story assist you in some way to prepare for your own journeys of surrender when you are called to clear karma. As brave souls, we do have the power of love to surrender and forgive all. In every instance, know that this same grace that touched me and supported me will also be there for you. All you need to do is to be willing to receive it by surrendering your fear. The angels, archangels, and Enlightened Masters promise to be there for you in any circumstance where you need assistance to transform your karma, and only ask that you be willing to open your energy to receive from them by calling on their assistance, love, and powerful healing dispensations for the benefit of your soul, your spirit, and all beings on Earth.

CHAPTER THREE
The Divine Plan, as Held by the Enlightened Masters

The vastness of spirit is unfathomable to the mind and can only be experienced. The infinite nature of all possibilities of expression of ourselves lies within our true nature as one with our Divine Presence. This vastness is the power to take the breath away and then give the breath back to ignite life again. The force of our life and incarnation and all energy we hold is the gift our Divine Presence giveth us for our temporary experience in physical form.

—SRI'AMA

Every soul on Earth has their direct connection with God or the creation energy of life, as their Divine Presence. Even those who have no faith in their own light and love, who have no faith in a universal spirit or larger force, and who cannot feel their hearts have this Divine Presence watching over their lives. The Divine Plan for humanity is based on the awakening of each soul to a higher state of consciousness through the guidance and overlighting blessings of the Divine Presence. This awakening is taking place in stages and in accordance with the karma and the free will of each member of humanity.

When one soul in each family is guided to open their heart and they choose to awaken, the journey begins. The soul begins a process known as the purification of the mind, which prepares them to heal on a much deeper level with their family and thus begin to clear the genetic line. This is the first work that most souls are guided to during their awakening process, to spend time patching up old miscommunications and heart connections with their family members. Once a soul has completed this work to a certain degree, they begin to open their heart connection to others in their local community. This activates a deeper level of connection to the plan for humanity's evolution and shift in consciousness.

The plan for humanity is then activated through three unique stages that alter the energy body of a soul so they can begin the recalibration to the frequency of their soul's divine blueprint or personal Divine Plan. This divine blueprint lies inactive in the etheric body of a soul until the soul has awakened spiritually.

The first stage of the Divine Plan for humanity's evolution is based on the "unlocking of our genetic code." This takes place as souls are guided by their Divine Presences to three specific forms of activity that allow the DNA to receive the codes of light and higher intelligence sequences of divine energy from the unified field. As the DNA filaments of consciousness expand, the super-consciousness is activated, and new streams of consciousness ground through the body. The consciousness of many people is trapped in their physical bodies, and until the genetic code is unlocked, they perceive the world as simply a physical experience.

The first activity takes place as souls are guided to create healing in the family. This begins the process of a karmic clearing of the wounds or old fears held in the genetic line that often are sourced from one's ancestors. This is not based on changing people but based on changing your own consciousness to fully accept and embrace every member of your family through love and forgiveness. The heart clearing created as one member of the family connects deeply to every other member stabilizes and naturally brings the family karma into its first level of balance. Often, once one person in the family is awakened and has made the heart connection to all others, another in the family begins to awaken, and then another. When three have awakened, it is a sign the genetic clearing is deeply taking place, for every ancestor as well as every family member and all future children birthed within the lineage will be free of this karma.

The second activity takes place as souls are guided to sacred places on the Earth to receive the codes of light or special energy and frequency they need for their evolution. People are guided to these places by their spirit or led by their hearts, sometimes on holidays or for their work, but there is always a higher reason that their circumstances have been arranged for this specific place to be visited. The higher purpose is the activation of their energy with the special energy that travels through the ley lines or portals of this land. This frequency offers a slow recalibration in preparation for their shift in consciousness. Some are also called to help the ancestors of humanity heal and forgive the past by clearing the sacred sites on the Earth where traumas have occurred. This reopens the portals between the worlds and assists other beings that live on the Earth to also release from the karmic wheel. It also opens and strengthens the connection between the soul's consciousness and their Divine Presence.

The third activity takes place as many of these souls are guided to fully take the mantle of the light into their hearts by recognizing they are light beings. They promise to hold to their divine relationship or source connection to the oneness, the force of creation within all of life that many name as God/Goddess, by no longer giving their power away to a false belief in a force outside of themselves creating their reality and by holding sovereignty over their own experience. The reclamation of personal power through the clearing of personal karma is the essence of this activity.

The second stage of the Divine Plan for humanity takes place as souls are deeply guided by their Divine Presences to reclaim more of their consciousness by creating deeper and more expanded connections with their own heart. Within the Divine Plan, there are six specific activities that souls are guided to for the expansion and deepening of the heart connection.

The first activity that supports a soul's heart connection is charitable service to others in need. This service balances a soul's unseen karma that is held within the veils of illusion or between the worlds. This karma is known as the collective and planetary karma of a soul.

The second activity that creates the heart expansion is the forgiveness of self. The journey of meeting limitations that seem immovable calls us to forgive ourselves, as forgiveness is the only way to shift the stuck, rigid consciousness within us and create transformation on the path of our evolution.

The third activity for deeper heart connection is releasing all false attachments based on fear. Our false attachments hold us in illusion as we give our power and light to beliefs that we created when we closed down our hearts during experiences of suffering. These attachments feel real and important to us, as we have placed so much of our power into protecting ourselves from meeting these experiences again. As we acknowledge what we are attached to and resolve the memories these are sourced from, we will surrender to our Divine Presence so our hearts may expand more deeply and we may reclaim the power we have lost.

The fourth activity that ignites the heart connection to grow is choosing one's happiness as a priority in life. As we release our attachments, we are shown by our heart what our path of happiness is. Through our journey of making new choices in life as our heart guides us, we begin to reprioritize and realign our life energy, consciousness, and direction toward happiness.

The fifth activity that expands the heart connection occurs through transforming the focus of our life when our heart is not fulfilled. Our heart expansion at this level is about learning to receive assistance, and one of our hardest lessons is learning to realize that our spirit is supporting us in life and that the universe is a positive force that is helpful and benevolent when we are in need of assistance. The rearrangement of our life's direction can feel like one of the hardest forms of change unless we invoke our Divine Presence to arrange the change to be filled with grace and ease.

The sixth activity that expands the heart connection is the embodiment of love, as we focus on sharing love through open-hearted experiences as a priority. This comes to us as we cultivate the first five activities. As our heart opens, it attracts large amounts of love from the vastness of our Divine Presence, and sharing this love with others, not for the purpose of receiving, but for the pure experience of feeling love, allows for deeper levels of love to flow through our being and to fill us.

The third stage of the Divine Plan for humanity is the empowerment of each soul through the next level of their heart opening. This empowerment takes place through three specific activities.

The first activity for a soul to empower their heart is to place their action and power into creating a new path for themselves and others around them. Once a soul feels the love deeply supporting them and feels secure in their own connection, they have the power to create a larger experience known as their heart dreaming, which benefits not only themselves but all others around them. As they follow their heart to this deeper level, they access the strength of their heart and empowerment to change their life circumstances and path in resonance with their core being.

The second activity that empowers a soul's heart is forgiving the collective of humanity. It is not until a soul embodies love deeply that they are able to see where they may hold a lack of forgiveness for their fellow humanity and see their own subtle judgments. As forgiveness is made, they release their collective karma, and the relationships in their life are then filled with love and divine experiences.

The third activity that empowers a soul's heart is the release of all personal karma. As a soul completes this clearing, a great shift occurs for every other soul that has experienced a connection with this soul, and it also creates the balancing of the karma of the Earth. This stage of the Divine Plan completes with the balancing of the Earth's karma, as when this occurs, peace shall manifest on Earth.

The Divine Plan and Humanity's Shift in Consciousness

A universal trust was built long ago between the heart of a soul and their spirit, and this trust is known as the Divine Plan. The spirit of a soul carries this trust until a soul is ready to place their free will into their path of evolution and take responsibility for their creation and experience.

Just as each soul has its own spirit, a collective spirit is held for all of humanity, known as the spirit of humanity. The spirit of humanity carries the Divine Plan for the collective of humanity. This plan involves the evolution of a higher level of consciousness within the collective through the heart opening, connection, and empowerment processes described above as stages of the Divine Plan.

When you give your trust to your Holy Spirit, also known as your Divine Presence, you begin to ignite the Divine Plan for your soul and awaken the knowing of your higher purpose in life. When you develop this trust in your spirit or spiritual path, you also ignite the Divine Plan for other members of humanity's collective, so they may embody the true spirit of humanity with you. Those closest to you also begin to gently change as powerful changes occur to you.

The true spirit of humanity is kind, generous, charitable, loving, peaceful, intelligent, wise, and very creative. The development of these qualities and the evolution of all souls within humanity's collective can only truly occur when all brothers and sisters choose to accept each other as equals and share these qualities as they work together. This is taking place right now all over the world, and the humanitarian aims and principles are grounding consciously and becoming a force of enlightenment for the whole collective. This Divine Plan for humanity begins with activating your trust in your fellow humanity.

To truly align your will, thoughts, feelings, and actions with the Divine Plan of your soul, you must be willing to look at any distrust you hold in your fellow humanity and forgive anything that may lie between your heart and soul and your trust in the capacity of humanity to evolve. Your planetary karma or collective karma can influence your soul to distrust others, and this causes separation between you and the collective of humanity and thus separation from your own soul family. The plan for humanity is peace and unconditional love.

There are three elements that deeply influence the manifestation of this reality. The first of these elements is related to the history of humanity on Earth and all that lies in the ancestral lineage that has not been resolved, forgiven, or healed. The second element is based on the karma that is held in humanity's group structures and relates to the sharing of power, finance, and resource. This aspect of our collective karma is balanced as humanity opens its charitable heart. The third element is based on humanity's relationship with Mother Earth and relates to the care of our environment. As humanity practices forgiveness and honors all kingdoms and species on Earth, this aspect of the karma is balanced.

Humanity carries the collective karma of all human acts that have taken place that are unresolved, and this karma is held within the karmic plane of the Earth. An aspect of this is connected to you through the unconscious body of your soul as it connects you in oneness with your mother, your father, and all who share your genetic line through the past seven generations. In other words, your ancestors live within you, unconsciously, if they have unresolved energy here on the Earth.

You may ask, How does this affect me in a positive way? The journey of your ancestors through their own incarnation here brought the light in to seed you to be able to incarnate and also journey to the Earth. Consider that as a light seed you had been waiting for the right moment to come, and your ancestors laid the path for you. They are still with you in spirit, as many are angels and others are ancestral spirits. They see your world, and through you, they are also able to forgive some of the experiences they had when they were in human form. As they witness you and the other members of your family, gifts that they have held activate within you. If there are any threads of old consciousness or ways of being that no longer serve your family lineage, it is your ancestors who are guiding you to heal what may be held in your ancestral family tree and genetic line.

Within the Divine Plan for your life, your ancestors are always with you so they may assist the healing of the past and bring the wisdom and gifts they held, so you may live in a wiser and more gifted way through all that they experienced. Through your genetic line, the consciousness of your ancestors is able to merge with your soul and your body, and at times, you may need to ask them to forgive the karma that affected them if you sense you have unhappy ancestors with you. If there is unhappiness within you when you consider your past, your ancestors need healing. Your genetic line is not yet clear of the experiences your ancestors may have left unresolved on Earth, as these memories still lie in your unconscious body, via the link through your DNA, waiting for love and forgiveness.

The journey of opening your heart is the very purpose of the Divine Plan, and it is this heart opening that supports the divine nature to arise from within and light up a soul's life. In each moment that you are giving your energy to your ancestors, your past, and your family via your clear heart, you are creating a recalibration of your genetic structure within your physical body, opening new parts of your consciousness that may have been closed, and activating the higher centers within your body and brain that are interconnected with your light. This light is the larger form of yourself, your Divine Presence, and it is able to support you when you accept that the Divine Plan is serving you.

What Is the Divine Plan?

The Divine Plan is the plan that your Divine Presence or divine consciousness flows and creates through, in your life. It is a blueprint for the creation of the highest form of your reality, the highest expression of yourself in oneness. There is a Divine Plan for your soul, which is also known as your soul blueprint. It is a plan for your soul's growth, specifically for your present incarnation. It is a flexible plan that is not fixed, yet you seeded it prior to this incarnation and it seeded your etheric body with your life purpose. It is constantly being ignited in new ways through the alignment of your will and your choices.

Even when the Divine Plan is recalibrated through your life choices or the realignment of your will, it will recalibrate your highest potential path as an energetic blueprint inside your etheric body. Your etheric body is the level of your energy that is closest to your physical body, and thus the Divine Plan seeds your divine consciousness into your physical reality. When your soul acts against the Divine Plan, your divine consciousness is unable to seed into your physical reality.

There are three forms of plans in life. The first is the Divine Plan, which is an aspect of the plan of creation. This is stored within the field of oneness that many also call the "unified field," and also stored in your etheric body in a personalized form. It is the plan that your spirit follows and your light adheres to, the plan that your soul assisted to create through choices you made prior to your incarnation. When you are feeling the flow of light through your being and growing to your full potential, you are aligned to the Divine Plan for your life, and this also serves all beings to grow to their full potential with you.

A second form of life plan is the plan we create within our mind's structure, based on what we know as our experience of the past and what we do not wish to create in our future. This form of plan is known as one's personal plan. The Divine Plan and your personal plan are not always synonymous, as the Divine Plan is a blueprint that was laid prior to your incarnation and created by your soul and spirit with the purpose of achieving the lessons you set out to master in this life. Your personal plan may be based on personal desire and takes none of your lessons into account. In other words, your personal plan may not always attune to the higher picture for your evolution. When souls on a spiritual path attempt to follow a personal plan, it does not often work out as their spirit and true power of light are on another life plan.

The third form of plan is the old Divine Plan that may karmically ignite from a previous soul incarnation. These ancient memories may awaken in one's etheric body when karma activates. If one has cleared one's genetic line and balanced personal and family karma, one is not affected by an old plan, for when the personal and family karma is cleared, all attachment to previous lives is also cleared, and the karmic memories will no longer affect a being to fear that their personal plan or the Divine Plan will not serve them to develop their life as they wish to.

As a soul experiences new levels of guidance, they always meet influences from each of these three unique plans until they have balanced all of their karma. Once a soul's karma is cleared, only their inner guidance and the Divine Plan can influence them. A soul's personal life plan, created by their mind, simply falls away and becomes unimportant. If they were carrying an old Divine Plan in their consciousness from another incarnation, this will be dissolved by the absolution of the karma.

The Three Soul Pods of Humanity's Collective Consciousness

From a broader perspective, humanity in its present process of evolution is in three stages of development, or, more accurately, it is resonating to three soul groups. In other words, the greater collective of humanity is presently holding three levels of consciousness as a species. One level or soul group is fully awakened. The souls of this group carry their consciousness as light and have an activated lightbody and live from a heart resonance.

This is presently the second-largest soul group, approximately 30 percent of humanity. These are the souls who have experienced their heart awakening and are working directly with the collective to support all other souls to awaken. Some of them do this very quietly in unseen ways, and others in a more public way as guided by their Divine Presence. They are scattered in all areas of the world, with varying lifestyles and with many different beliefs, yet they all are guided by their heart energy.

The second level of consciousness or soul group carries the "consciousness of the self." This group forms the larger proportion of humanity, presently approximately 50 percent. This form of consciousness is needed before souls are able to awaken to their greater potential. These souls are preparing to have the heart awakening experience and they have been given all they need to do this and are now simply waiting for the time when they feel ready. Their lives are centered on themselves.

The third soul group needs assistance, as they are influenced by the astral plane and the fear held as the collective karma of all beings who have incarnated on the Earth. These ones are not clearly conscious of themselves or the repercussions of their actions, thoughts, or words. This soul group is affected in the deepest way by the collective karma and by their own personal karma, and they cannot awaken until some of the oldest karma has lifted from the Earth. They live in unconsciousness, or what is known as ignorance. This is presently the smallest soul group, a little less than 20 percent of the world's population.

To understand the plan for humanity, it is important to understand humanity itself and what creates a soul to be either awakened, conscious of self, or unconscious, beloved. The first understanding needed is that although a soul's level of awareness is created by their free will, it is not always the level they would choose if they could be more conscious of the astral connections or unconscious aspects they hold, which deeply influence all of their actions. In other words, the reason people do what they do is not always sourced from a conscious choice. It is for this reason that it is so important to always hold compassion for those who seem to act from a place of ignorance, rather than judge these ones for their actions.

To understand that humanity operates instinctually from their unconscious when their chakras are closed, via the fear-driven fight-or-flight response of the brain, will support you to hold more compassion for these souls, beloved. Their feeling centers within their brain and centers of logic and compassion are not yet fully activated. They have underdeveloped neurology within their brain chemistry and have fewer neurons firing than other souls on the Earth and therefore do not have the ability to access more of their consciousness until their brain chemistry alters.

The brain is a vessel for the discharge of consciousness and is a primary director of one's intelligence as well as one's creativity, and as centers of the brain activate, higher levels of consciousness can be accessed. There has been interest in the connection between the development of the brain of a child and the experience of love and nurturance. Neuroscientists have linked the underdevelopment of the brain to a lack of loving nurturance, and it is suspected that those who do not receive the love frequency as small children when their brains are first developing do not activate the higher centers of their brain function.

It is equally important to recognize that those within the soul pod who presently hold "consciousness of self" act in life through conscious choice but usually operate from a personal level only. Therefore, their thoughts are focused on themselves, their immediate surroundings, what affects them personally, what their personal needs are, and how to be sure they will be fulfilled as an individual. These souls may seem self-centered, and when you are in their presence, they may have little awareness of your reality, as their consciousness lives in a bubble, and they will only have the access to more of their consciousness when their brain chemistry alters and they have a deep heart-opening and awakening experience.

When a soul has a heart awakening, their bubble of self-consciousness is burst, and as they receive the unconditional love, their brain chemistry begins to change. They begin to be freed from the bubble that has kept them separate, and the more they free themselves in this way, the more their minds begin to be more fluid and relaxed as both hemispheres of the brain come into balance. Eventually the centers of logic and intuition activate and harmonize and the brain begins to operate in unity consciousness.

When a soul is awakened to new levels of consciousness, the brain centers of logic and intuition are linked and the soul can begin to receive deeper levels of support from higher functions within their brain. These brain centers support compassion, love, and higher levels of knowing to open. Souls who are moving to a full awakening begin to tap into levels of their super-consciousness, which activates various levels of higher self-connection to take place through their chakras opening and developing. These souls perceive life through awareness of the collective, and their intentions express deeper levels of love than those belonging to the other soul pods or levels of consciousness. These awakened souls have the ability, through the expression of love, to fully activate their brain chemistry, balance it, and then access vaster levels of consciousness to benefit their service to the collective and their enlightenment process.

Understanding humanity in its stages of evolution in this way supports us to let go of any expectations, judgments, or distrust we may have in our fellow humanity in regard to their evolution and specifically their commitment to planetary peace. Through this recognition, we are also able to see that personal choice or free will plays only one part in a soul's creation and that karma is an equal influence within the creation of reality. Through the natural process of the unfoldment of the Divine Plan, more and more souls from the soul pod that holds only consciousness of self will awaken to increase the percentage of awakened souls to over 50 percent, which will generate a shift within the wheel of karma. Our collective will then be able to receive dispensations to be able to clear some of the oldest karma of the Earth for the freedom of those souls who are still unconscious. The Divine Plan for humanity is not a complex plan, although it is diverse and multidimensional in its nature. The basis of the plan is the return to the truth of one's soul and the expression of one's true spirit as a human being.

Embracing the Four Forms of Earth Karma through the Divine Plan

The purpose of the Divine Plan is to ignite communities to be established worldwide, based on love, unity, and peace. Within the Divine Plan, it is the gatherings of the light seeds and the sacred work of each light seed working in cooperation with others that will accelerate this plan over the next four to five years in this great time of alchemical change. As each light seed continues to travel wherever their spirit sends them to do their work, others will then activate and awaken as they meet them on their path and exchange the codes of light with them.

The consciousness shift that takes place when a soul awakens from the level of consciousness of self, the second soul group, to a greater union with their spirit, is so powerful it generates a high frequency that expands its signal six miles in every direction. The psychic field of an awakening soul is so powerful it can affect electricity and other forms of energy. The experience of awakening also raises the vibration of the physical body and alters the brain chemistry, and it takes time for the endocrine and nervous systems to realign and operate via the signals and chemistry of the new firing of light codons within the brain.

The awareness that one is connected intimately on every level of one's being to a greater field or larger self, or to Spirit, All That Is, via the unified field, ignites this shift in consciousness to continue to take a soul into vaster and higher levels of awareness. With each shift in consciousness there is the opportunity for a whole new level of karma to be balanced and also raise the physical body's vibration.

The four levels of karma are your personal karma (your soul's karma), your family karma, your collective or community karma, and your planetary karma. Your personal karma is the unresolved energy and consciousness from this lifetime and your last three incarnations on Earth. This is created purely from your own actions, words, and use of will, and your energy and consciousness during these lives.

Your family karma is the unresolved energy of your relationships with all of your family members from this lifetime and your last three lifetimes on Earth. The unresolved karma of the last seven generations of your ancestors is also a part of your family karma if it is creating a lock within your consciousness and your DNA or genetic code that does not allow your consciousness to expand beyond their unresolved beliefs and feelings.

Your collective karma, also known as your karma with community or groups, is the unresolved energy and consciousness left within your collective consciousness (your soul and your spirit within all worlds and realms) from your soul or spiritual relationships with groups, communities, soul family, and collectives from your last three powerful lifetimes on

Earth. These are the lifetimes where you held a very developed consciousness. Often this karma traces back to Ancient Egypt, Atlantis, and Lemuria. This karma is usually balanced and cleared through service.

Your planetary karma is the unresolved consciousness and energy you hold with Mother Earth herself, from all lifetimes on the Earth. This is related to your energy exchange with the Earth and her resources, and the use of your gifts to contribute and be of equal benefit to the Earth and all beings that she supports.

Each of these levels of karma is connected to a soul's development and potential and is activated by their Divine Plan. A soul who may be slumbering in unconsciousness may deeply shift in consciousness as their personal and family karma is cleared and balanced. The beauty of the Divine Plan is that this shift could take place even without the soul consciously creating it, if the collective karma keeping the soul unconscious is cleared or balanced by others.

Similarly, a soul who is conscious of themselves yet unaware of the effect they have on others, may shift to awakening if they balance their personal and family karma and partially shift their community karma. This could also take place during a deep heart exchange with an awakened soul who carries the codes of light within their energy system. During such an interaction the codes of light release from the awakened one to the partially conscious soul, altering their brain chemistry and activating a heart awakening.

Similarly, an awakened soul who may be acting as a representative of the collective of humanity may shift into oneness with their Presence and activate their ascension and the next step of their journey of enlightenment if they balance and clear their personal karma, family karma, community karma, and planetary karma. This can also take place at any time if they are awakened by others who carry the necessary codes for their next shift to a new level of consciousness.

As a soul shifts in consciousness from one soul group to another, a great change occurs on all levels of a being and they begin to receive a new energy body that will support them to continue to evolve as a being. The nature of the Divine Plan is dynamic, in that every time a soul shifts a level of consciousness, they take another three souls with them.

As the soul shifts in consciousness and moves from one soul group to another, their heart is awakened so powerfully that the first three souls they connect to through the heart chakra receive all of the divine energy that has been generated in this transformation. This divine energy comes in the form of codes of light, exchanged simply through the heart or eyes, and activates these three souls' consciousnesses to also make the shift, without their awareness of why or how. This may be a smaller shift, but it is nevertheless the same consciousness shift occurring within a different level of their being.

Through the Divine Plan, it is the heart connection that carries the frequency from one soul to another, and this natural process is guided by the spirit of a soul. You may be directed to see a friend and the opening of your heart to them may be the very key that activates their shift, if they are ready. The gentle love released through this interaction creates the shift and then grows and is shared with others. As each individual attracts others they need to meet to activate their consciousness; in this way the collective is supported to shift into the fifth dimension.

As you travel in your life, journeying from place to place, you are also receiving codes from the Earth Mother and from the different sites you visit. For within the Divine Plan, Earth herself is generating a new consciousness and holding this for humanity until they know they are able to fully shift as a collective. The choice to shift in consciousness was made long ago by the collective of humanity, and this will continue to accelerate as Mother Earth raises her vibration to create her own vibrational shift.

In addition, as the genetic line is cleansed and many balance their family karma, the collective consciousness will enter its largest shift in consciousness as humanity's ancestors release their karma. This offers a cleansing of the astral plane and the release of the oldest collective thought forms that lead souls of the third soul group to stay unconscious of their words, actions, intentions, and thoughts. Within the Divine Plan for humanity, the focus upon family karma is a priority, for as the balancing takes place collectively, the most unconscious members of humanity will be freed to be conscious of themselves as beings once again.

An immense amount of divine assistance has been sent to the Earth via angels and archangels, returning for higher levels of service. These ones simply witness humanity and respond to all who call for assistance. Their love and light encourages us to recognize we have no reason to feel fear about the direction humanity is taking, and they ask all to understand that grace is available if we are willing to take the time to be deeply connected to our heart and to receive assistance with balancing karma.

Origins of Karma on Earth

Long ago on the Earth, aspects of humanity's empowerment were displaced during a gradual collapse of ancient civilizations where many souls, now incarnate on Earth, held a much higher level of consciousness. These civilizations are known as Lemuria, Atlantis, and Ancient Egypt, and some of the oldest karma held within humanity's consciousness is deeply sourced through the collective experience of the collapse of these civilizations.

Whenever a member of humanity feels pain and suffering, the cause of this is held within their consciousness as a soul or genetic memory. This memory is usually locked in their body by their DNA, which is a broadcaster or transmitter and anchor for one's consciousness to flow through the cells of the body. Our DNA is linked via filaments of light that extend from our cells and travel through the nervous system into each neuron. These filaments of light grow long and strong in the presence of higher frequencies and the love vibration flowing through the body; they grow short and fat in the presence of lower frequency waves and fear, creating energy blockages and illness within our body.

If the billions of filaments of light linking our DNA, cells, and nervous system are strong and long, they extend into the endocrine system or glands of our body via the meridians. It is our consciousness that determines whether our cells, nervous systems, glands, and meridians are flowing with light and energy and raising the vibration of our body. Our consciousness is not able to anchor clearly in our body without the unlocking of our genetic code within our DNA. It is the unlocking of the genetic code via the clearing of our family karma that allows our DNA filaments to grow, ground, and expand our consciousness and also free our body of unresolved fears and our soul or genetic memories.

In ancient civilizations, many of our collective carried powerful abilities and extraordinary technologies that were all energized and activated by a being's energy body and chakras, carrying and grounding immense amounts of light frequency on Earth. Their DNA filaments of consciousness were all very long and strong, and their energy systems were able to produce large amounts of excess energy that they were able to direct for the creation of what would now seem like extraordinary feats. Some of these were spiritual and mental feats and others were accomplished through telepathy, soul travel, seership, and higher forms of communication via group-consciousness. Others were combined spiritual, emotional, and physical feats such as levitation and bilocation.

These presences held powerful energy bodies and consciousness that were fully connected to the unified field and carried higher frequency light technologies, which could be ignited by their consciousness for specific purposes. Drawing their unlimited source energy through their chakras and utilizing their energy field's connection to the unified field, these beings would merge their energy bodies and link in group mind and group heart to create extraordinary feats.

In these worlds where there were many awakened, fully activated beings of unified consciousness, our collective accessed great power. Within each civilization, there came a time of completion. Each time this took place, there was an imbalance between the free will and divine will of the collective, which led to a partial displacement in consciousness for some of the souls who chose to use their free will before igniting their divine will.

During this time of completion within each of these civilizations, those that aligned the use of their power and intentions with their divine will completed their incarnations with grace and traveled into the next world in brilliant bodies of light. They evolved to later become archangels and Enlightened Masters. But those that chose to deny their divine will and aligned their intentions through the use of their free will experienced a displacement of their consciousness. They moved from being fully activated light beings into a state of self-consciousness, and some even entered unconsciousness. Some of their feminine or masculine consciousness was caught in a vortex, and parts of their consciousness became trapped within the lower dimensions of the Earth. These beings were forced to seal their energy fields so more of their consciousness would not become trapped in the lower dimensional states.

Some of these beings were then able to complete their incarnations and leave in the same way as the others, for they surrendered and eventually also aligned to their divine will. As they did this, though, they were forced to leave behind the parts of their feminine and masculine consciousness that had become trapped in the lower dimensions of the Earth. They left the Earth with less consciousness than they had incarnated with, and were known as the fallen ones. These beings knew they would have to return to the Earth to retrieve these parts of their consciousness; they became angels and made a promise to serve over the Earth. Whenever possible they would incarnate and reclaim the parts of their consciousness that were left on Earth so they could then ascend and evolve in their higher bodies of light.

In some ways, not a great deal has changed since the completion of these civilizations, but in other ways everything has changed and we have evolved on all levels of our being. What has not changed? The Earth is still our mother, made of a liquid quartz crystal, and she still holds the power to guide and align us to our divine will, which is our inner power that holds the clear direction for our actions that are for the highest good of ourselves and all beings. We will continue to be caretakers of the Earth until our work is complete and we have created a civilization based on peace. Our bodies still hold the key to our enlightenment, Mother Earth's wisdom is still the activator of our bodies, and our DNA filaments still facilitate our reality, as directed by our consciousness.

What has changed? The Earth herself has evolved. She has changed the movement of her seasons, and new life forms have evolved; her oceans have altered, as has the direction of some rivers. Within humans, our whole biochemistry has evolved. Our bodies have crystallized, and we are still developing in this way.

In fact, what may seem to our minds to be a devolution in consciousness has actually created us to evolve in a whole new way. Since Lemuria, we have been learning to become more aware of ourselves, for we were such collective beings of love, living in oneness, that we had not yet learned self-awareness. Those that experienced the fall of Lemuria as fallen ones learned self-awareness in a painful way. Since Atlantis, we have been learning to become humble, for we were so young, bright, and powerful, we sometimes forgot to give space for things to take place with no effort and simply come into an alignment with nature. Those that experienced the fall of Atlantis as fallen ones learned humility in a painful way. Since Ancient Egypt, we have been learning to empower ourselves, for we were so deeply reverent of Spirit that we forgot this holy fire was also our own power of creation. Those that experienced the fall of Ancient Egypt as fallen ones learned about their power of creation in a painful way.

This karma or unresolved learning left in our collective on the Earth from each civilization has had immense benefit to us in the development of many qualities within our collective. Deeper levels of compassion are birthing from within us, and a deeper understanding of how to use our wisdom for the benefit of many.

The outcome of closing down our consciousness was a disconnection from others sharing our world; our hearts were unable to expand, and we became individualized consciousnesses. Before this, all experienced life in group-consciousness, and the central focus was not held upon the individual self. When these fallen ones reincarnated, their consciousness continued to close, and they entered what is known as unconsciousness.

Presently, our whole collective is in the process of healing the cellular memory of losing a state of oneness with others and entering a state of self-consciousness or unconsciousness. The most amazing aspect of this journey is that we are able to create from all of our collective learning, and even if we have not experienced any of this personally, the wisdom from the shared journey is held in the libraries of light on Earth and is accessible when we open our hearts deeply to the Holy Spirit of the Earth, known as Gaia. We will truly learn all of our lessons as a race when we choose to listen to the wisdom of Mother Gaia.

A Journey to Sirius

While I was in deep training with the Enlightened Masters, Lord Sirius and Lord Arcturus arrived one day with a group of Sirian archangels who were blue crystalline, winged light beings of about seven feet tall. As they looked at me and I looked into their beautiful eyes, I received many codes and it activated a deep remembrance inside me. Their frequency was so pure and as my connection and experience of friendship grew with them over many years, I realized how much they held for humanity as a sixth race or archetype that helps to seed our new consciousness. As Sirians live in much higher dimensional crystalline forms, based on the sixth dimensional frequency, they always live in group mind, allowing their minds and intelligence to be held and grounded in their open hearts. They are an exquisite race of star beings.

On that day, the Sirians opened their hearts and minds and invited me to link my chakras with theirs so they could open my connection to travel with them on the inner planes to Sirius A. I saw my chakra pillar open and their higher frequency pillars merge with mine; in that moment, a flooding of pure love came into my being, and my frequency and energy grew inside until I felt myself only as light.

My vision always opened powerfully whenever I received frequency transmissions from the Family of Light. As they opened a group merkabah for us to travel in, they shared with me that they were utilizing higher dimensional technologies made of high frequency to open the portals and remove the veils to allow my consciousness to experience what they experienced.

We became a beam of light, and the next thing I could see and feel was myself standing on a crystal platform in the stars above the Earth. There were large light portals in the heavens, and they showed me one that was blue and shared that it would lead us to Sirius A, where members of my spiritual family and lineage would meet me.

As we traveled into the blue light, it felt like I was stepping through a crystal mist. As we grounded on Sirius, I saw many large, domed white temples to the left, and on the right were beautiful lakes of colored waters. They took me to the waters and asked me to bathe in them, sharing it would change my frequency. As I did this, small dolphin-like beings came toward me, playing and joyfully greeting me.

The taller Sirians said, "These are our children. The younger Sirians live in dolphin bodies."

I smiled to think that dolphins were on Sirius. They shared that their ancestors helped star-seed the dolphins on Earth. Very gently, the dolphin children of Sirius snuggled around me, and I felt them gifting me something. I could see my heart chakra glowing with a soft, pink energy. I thanked them for it.

Once they had completed, they swam away, and the Sirian beings said, "They took your sadness away so you could be happier as a soul."

I came out of the water, and they took me to one of the domed temples. I could see it was connected to a huge complex of temples and halls that were all made of crystalline light. I asked them where I was, and they shared we were in the central city of light, where the libraries of light and university of peace were held.

It astounded me that they had libraries and that their world was so vast. An amazing light shone from everything I could see. They shared that I would go with them to meet the librarians of light and that for the next four months I would be traveling to Sirius with them each day, to train and open my access to the libraries and Akasha.

They took me into a large temple, which had many sections within it, and many beings connecting together. I witnessed a very large group gathering together, and I could see all of their hearts connected with streams of light. A current of golden and emerald light was emanating from their bodies, and I saw them build a large geometric field with this golden and emerald light. As divine energy poured out of their beings, a beautiful crystal formed. They shared they were creating a new light technology, and the Sirian archangels with me explained that this was how technologies were formed.

We entered a very tall hall that led to many chambers. I was led toward one and taken inside, where there were sacred scriptures or tablets of fire letters upon each of the walls. As we entered, the Sirians placed their hands on a wall, and I witnessed as fire letters or codes flew out from the wall, up into their hands, up their arms, and then lodged within their hearts.

They shared that they received frequency and consciousness through this process. I asked, "What type of consciousness?" They shared that they had received the consciousness from the libraries and from my Akasha, in relation to the highest experience they could facilitate for me to learn from.

Around me in the room were many golden tablets emanating energy. The Sirians shared that these were aspects of the Akashic records related to my spiritual journey. They explained that my spirit had the ability to travel far from my physical body, for it could not be contained by time, space, or dimension, but I was always one with my spirit even if it was not merged with me in the physical body. They shared that as my spirit built its light frequency, my soul's heart would grow, and I would feel my wholeness as a divine being. There were parts of my spirit in different dimensions, and these would come together and merge with me when important experiences were to take place. Then I would be held by the field of life to allow my spirit to incarnate through me.

At the time, it felt like a very big concept for my head to comprehend, and the archangels could hear me struggling with this and continued to share.

"The journey of your soul is not independent of your consciousness but is simply a reflection of the lessons, love, gifts, and choices you are embracing while you access your consciousness."

I wondered about what they really meant by this.

"Your consciousness is what links you to all in your universe. How you direct it and what you do with it creates your reality for you. If you do nothing with it, it simply goes to sleep."

They showed me a vision of a soul that was not using their consciousness and simply closing down. It looked as if they were switching off the light in all areas of their field, in all directions, and slowly their field was becoming smaller and smaller.

They said to me, "This was you."

I was shocked. They asked me to connect with the first tablet by my side.

"This is your Akasha, our child."

As I touched the tablet, I was taken to Ancient Egypt. It was a little over ten thousand years ago. I was a tall man, and I saw hundreds of people gathered. We were all receiving streams of frequency, dispensations, and love, and all of life was of great beauty. I was opening a huge field and knew what I was doing. Many people were receiving love and communing. Many people sang, and their lightbodies activated as they experienced communion with the Holy Spirit. We did not call it the Holy Spirit then. I saw myself as a young boy, growing to be this man, training as a representative for the people in a highly disciplined way. I then saw myself as a man again, with my wife and my children. I saw myself in happiness and ecstasy. Then I saw darkness, and I was alone, feeling guilty inside and hiding away. I saw many coming to help me. I saw myself refusing to allow others to help me and saw my heart broken inside, feeling the need to send my family away to protect them. I saw myself in immense pain, and one by one, the beautiful lights in my field went out as I chose to close myself down, giving up on myself and losing all faith in myself. I saw myself take my own life, because I could not bear the pain.

I wept as I remembered this journey I had left unresolved, where so many parts of me had closed down.

They continued, "This is why you are here, to restore all you closed down, and to return to a life of holding this love and immense grace without fear. Your spirit was scattered to all parts of the Earth, and when your soul left the body, your spirit had no doorway to travel back to Source. A large part of your spirit was trapped on Earth as your field had closed the gateway of light. All of the lights of your spirit are waiting for you to return, and you will reclaim them as you may now build your field again, our beloved heart. They will be returning to you over the years ahead. You will know when you meet them, as you will feel life is a challenge and you may want to close down your field again. Your lesson in this life is to choose to not close down, no matter what you experience. As you choose not to close your heart down, all that you feel you lost will be returned to you and you will experience bliss in your physical life."

I was a little overwhelmed but felt their truth resonate to my core. They continued to share and asked me to receive my second Akashic tablet. I looked at the floor, and there were two more. I sensed it was the one on top. I touched it and saw the codes and fire letters travel up my hand and my arm into my heart chakra and then flood through my whole body.

I suddenly saw myself trapped in a body, my body, as a beautiful Egyptian woman. I appeared to be paralyzed from my waist down. I saw a beautiful river. People were coming to help me, leaving me flowers and presents, but I rejected them. I had lost my partner, my legs, and my womanhood, and I was not sure what else could be lost. I was in grief and unable to forgive myself. I could see my partner lying ill by my side, and I could not help him. I felt helpless and guilty. No matter what I did, he did not heal. So many people were loving me, but I was not free to help my partner. Darkness occurred again. I was an angel and no longer was held in my physical form; I was freed, and I could fly, but everywhere I went I was haunted by my partner's pain and the memories that I had left him alone and he was suffering. I could not fly high enough into the light. I could not escape this pain.

I sat on a mountaintop, my wings hidden and frayed. I looked over the world and decided to stay and watch over all that were suffering. I flew to Egypt and to my partner and promised I would not leave him.

He looked at me and said, "Sing to me."

I sang to him, but it did not lift his suffering. I wanted to fly away, but I held my promise until he passed away. He was very sad and angry about his life and refused to become an angel or go into the light. I watched him as he shut himself away in a dark cave and swore he would never forgive God. I stayed as he avenged his pain and tormented himself over and over again. I whispered to him to forgive and go to the light, but he promised he would never again enter the light. I broke my promise to him and told him I had to go into the light and we would meet again when he was ready to forgive. I would always love him and would hold his hand when he chose to return into the light.

This Akasha did not mean much to me at the time and did not touch my heart like the other, but it meant a great deal five years later when I found myself in a similar situation with my partner Golden Phoenix.

The Sirian archangels shared there was another tablet for me to receive. They shared this one was very important to me.

I connected to the third tablet, and as the energy streamed through me, I became a rainbow snake sweeping through the lands. Valleys formed as I moved my body. I was timeless, and the world seemed to be forming itself over millions of years as my body moved through pathways deep inside the Earth. Darkness came. I was asleep, coiled up in a cave; I was grumpy and did not want to be bothered by anyone. Many came to visit me, and one of my eyes would open and then close. A fire rumbled in my belly. Small snakes birthed from me; they traveled while I slept and returned to feed from my source. I gave them all my light. In my dreams I was in a beautiful world where everyone loved each other, and when I opened my eye, I remembered the world where all had lost their love. I was sad and so large as mother, and my creation fire was needed. I shared it with the others, as a source for them to receive the creation energy. Then darkness came again, and I made a promise to not wake up until I could love all beings even if they had lost their love. My serpent self closed her eyes and went to sleep until it was time.

I was taken aback by this last Akashic tablet and did not understand it until about six years ago, when I met myself as this rainbow serpent through a powerful experience in the First World. As I met myself and saw how my personal initiations were related to my choice to love all beings even if they had lost their love, the serpent healed and chose to awaken. A current of energy rose up from the Inner Earth, healing my lost sexuality and creation power, filling my body with tantric energy and activating my tantric heart.

The journey back from the libraries that day was quick. We left the temple and traveled like a beam of light through the blue portal and the stars, back to Earth and then into my room. Many records were revealed to me over the months, some of which had more relevance at the time, as they directly related to my experience with my partner Dreaming Heart. Each time I received from the Akasha, the Sirian archangels supported me to have self-realizations so I could forgive my karma and reclaim my true gifts.

If you wish to work with your own Akasha, simply call on the Sirian archangels of light and ask to be taken to the libraries of light. If it is not a conscious experience, know it will occur in your dream states, and honor your dreams as a part of the journey of connecting to your Akasha.

Your Invitation to Consciously Shift with Gaia

The great mother carries us into her womb, holds us, and feeds our body with grace so we may know ourselves as physical beings in our world. Our cells are doorways to our union with her; our mind is our doorway to expand her wisdom with ours in the creation of magical manifestations in the physical realm; and our body is her breath, aligning with each step we take. May we take the steps that will always feed back to her, the light she endows upon us in every way. Let us guide our lives, from our heart connection to hers.

—SRI'AMA

Gaia lovingly invites us to know that our collective holds the power to reactivate our hearts. Although we presently hold our base level of awareness in one of the three soul groups, we need to remember this could shift at any time through the gentle awakening of our awareness. Even though our base consciousness may rest on one level, each of us holds aspects of all three different states. For example, even the awakened souls have aspects of their consciousness in a state of self-consciousness and aspects in a state of unconsciousness. But the base level of awareness is awakened if at least 51 percent of their consciousness is awakened. For a soul in unconsciousness, aspects of their consciousness may be awakened or self-conscious, but 51 percent or more of their consciousness is unconscious.

What is beautiful about the Divine Plan is that every soul does not need to connect to their karma to clear it. Some are simply guided to do charitable service, and this creates them to balance their karma. Also, the Divine Plan offers to support all of humanity to shift, rather than only supporting those that have gifts or awareness. Each individual only needs to make the shift partially, and the collective lifts them the rest of the way. It does not matter how you forgive the karma that causes you the greatest suffering. You could be assisting older people and caring for them, and unbeknownst to your mind, your soul is balancing your karma with death or old age. However, it is necessary for all light seeds to accept their puzzle piece in the Divine Plan and step fully into the light with the awareness of what is influencing them to not be a beacon of light.

The most painful aspect of a soul's personal and collective karma usually occurred in one of their previous incarnations on Earth. Lemuria's was a loss of universal love, family, and soul family. The original heart connection to love was severed deeply. This is the collective karma humanity carries from Lemuria. Atlantis's was a loss of the mind's empowerment and clarity, group-consciousness and open-mindedness. The mind's original connection to the light was severed deeply. This is the collective karma humanity carries from Atlantis. In Ancient Egypt, it was a loss of divine union, communion, love of self, and empowerment of the body and spirit to unite as one. The power of creation and the body's original connection to the Earth were severed deeply. This is the collective karma humanity carries from Ancient Egypt.

It is not important to know the source of one's karma or to return to past lives, but forgiveness is essential. For within the plan, humanity is held by their sacred spirit until they have learned to forgive themselves and each other. This forgiveness, once learned, creates the heart chakra to open and stay open, allowing the shift into the fifth dimension.

The Three Primary Elements of Our Karmic Clearing

As mentioned earlier, there are three elements that most deeply influence the collective of humanity. The first element is our history as a collective, the past experiences of humanity that have not been resolved. Through our forgiveness of ourselves and our collective we will be able to accept humanity's history without judgment and release the past acts that caused suffering. Our history has been the most powerful influence within our collective karma, and as the genetic code is unlocked within the family lineage, our ancestors will be freed to forgive with us, allowing the unresolved karma to be released from the Earth plane.

The second most powerful element is humanity's present methodology of living and working together as a group, for the energy humanity carries in its organizational structures or group-consciousness is affected by the collective karma. These structures within society also carry karma within them if they are built on a system or hierarchy that is not humanitarian or heart based in its principles.

Within the Divine Plan, the transformation of these structures is blueprinted and is already being seeded by the light seeds on Earth, who presently represent 30 percent of the population. They are letting go of the belief they need to care only for themselves, and trusting that their connection to the universe will support them deeply in their lives. As they awaken, they are establishing fifth dimensional structures for others to connect to when they are ready to shift. Those yet to awaken are also being prepared to activate their puzzle pieces and transform the old structures, liberating humanity from the karma of hierarchy that created slavery, war, greed, abuse, fear, disease, and poverty. A great shift is occurring that will continue to dismantle this hierarchy completely.

The true sovereignty of a soul is their open-heart connection to all beings in a state of fearlessness, in an awakened, activated light energy. This is known as one's empowerment. The Divine Plan for humanity holds the blueprints for the sovereignty of each soul to their being, and it is this that forms the basis for the new structures of light that are being designed, implemented, and seeded into society by the light seeds who are fully awakened. As these new organizations for living and working in group-consciousness are based on equality, they are liberating the collective karma of humanity.

This karma is sourced back to Atlantis, where light structures were implemented with great power and beauty, yet through a fall in consciousness and loss of empowerment of the mind, a false hierarchy was developed as a safeguard. This hierarchy led itself to become a control matrix, which has operated through the etheric body of the Earth and has been empowered by the fear or polarized light of humanity's collective, held in the astral plane of light. As more and more members of humanity dissolve their karmic link to the astral plane and fully awaken in their spiritual empowerment and sovereignty, the control matrix that was seeded into the Earth's old etheric body after the fall of Atlantis dissolves rapidly.

As the old control matrix is dismantled and humanity begins to enter the fifth dimensional connection, it will become apparent and acceptable that we share the Earth with many other life forms. Contact with the Family of Light and races of light beings from other worlds and from the inner worlds of the Earth is already occurring, and as a soul awakens fully, this contact is made deeply on a heart level so the light seeds can be guided clearly in their sacred work in the Divine Plan for humanity and the Earth.

The third element that holds karmic energy for the collective and also affects the manifestation of peace on Earth is based on the original journey or first incarnation of a soul on Earth, when their relationship to Mother Earth was determined. This karma carries a memory of disconnection from the spirit of the Earth and the original role of caretakership that was handed to each soul as they first incarnated.

The imbalance between humanity's giving to the Earth Mother and receiving back from her is the karma of the collective, sourced from this original incomplete experience where not all of the energy and consciousness of a soul remained intact, beloved. This has created a learning or potential for the whole race as a collective. The imbalance is obvious in all aspects of environmental care, and humanity, in accordance with the Divine Plan, will experience a great awakening to their true relationship as caretakers of the Earth. This will initiate each soul as they accept a greater responsibility as Earth caretaker to balance the Earth karma of taking from the Earth more than is given or needed by humanity.

A gentle journey of transformation seeds the way for the collective to shift its past. While our history, our group structures, and our relationship with Mother Earth hold deep karmic energy for humanity, these are hurdles we can overcome, and we have the powerful assistance of our forefathers and foremothers, as well as all of the Presences who evolved into archangels and Enlightened Masters.

Anchoring the Divine Plan through Developing Your Trust

The generous, kind, loving, charitable, peaceful, intelligent, wise, creative spirit of humanity will rise as these three primary elements of karmic clearing are balanced and peace on Earth is made manifest between all races within the collective. As this true spirit of humanity rises through the planes of karma, the old etheric body of the Earth will release, and a new etheric body grid system will support the fifth dimensional connection to be ignited. The old astral plane and the collective thought forms which have influenced so many over the last thirteen thousand years of Earth's history will then dissolve into the void, allowing the collective consciousness to increase in vibration and liberate each soul's mind.

It only needs your trust for this to take place—your trust in your fellow humanity to be generous, kind, charitable, loving, peaceful, intelligent, wise, and creative in the true nature of their spirit. Beloved, as you place your trust in humanity, humanity will serve you in accordance with the Divine Plan. If you distrust humanity, you will attract the karma of the collective as an experience to learn from so you may be supported to see what you need to forgive to balance your collective or planetary karma as another part of your puzzle piece. But if you are awakened on the path of your spiritual journey, you no longer have a choice to distrust your fellow humanity for you are powerful as a soul and spirit. The larger you is infinite in its ability to stream consciousness into all you focus on, no matter whether it is enjoyable for you or whether it is activating karmic experiences or deep challenge for you. Your Presence has no preference and will simply enlighten and energize all that you focus your consciousness upon.

Your greatest learning is to trust yourself and others in your world by using your will to focus on what you wish to create rather than what you would like to be separate from. As you do this, the true nature of your reality will be shown to you via the naturally occurring journey of inner alchemy that is presently taking place for all. This awakening cannot be avoided by any being, as it was consciously chosen by every soul who presently lives on the Earth, and in support of this choice, a sacred promise was made to every soul before they embarked on their journey to the Earth that their spirit would follow them, guide them, and lead them to their awakening of oneness with all beings. This promise by each soul's spirit will be initiated over the next five years in the most powerful way, for in accordance with the Divine Plan, many souls have agreed to the embodiment of their spirit via their higher self or Presence. This oneness with Presence will open the way for those who hold a puzzle piece within the Divine Plan to birth and implement new ideas within society.

As the Presence of a soul guides and creates transformation of the DNA structure, divine energy and bliss merge through the molecules of the body, igniting a soul to enter the fifth dimension. Through the Divine Plan for humanity, a new chakra system is being given to all souls who are ready to receive this recalibration of their energy fields, and this process is initiated by many hours of visitations from archangels and angels and Enlightened Masters. It takes place through free will once a soul is ready to fully awaken and enter self-realization as a God conscious creator being, and it releases the soul from the astral field of the collective consciousness of humanity. The soul's energy field then links into group-consciousness with the fifth dimensional energy field, the sixth dimensional mind, and the seventh dimensional heart connection to the spiritual planes. Once a certain number of souls have received the DNA ignition into the fifth dimension, a rapid acceleration occurs as the new DNA braiding activates a new energy field for the whole collective to shift into.

These light seeds, contracted to become embodied by their Holy Spirit or Divine Presence, have chosen to give over their free will completely to fully serve the Divine Plan. They are presently working in every field of society on Earth, and their primary role is to balance the collective karma of humanity, wherever they are in the world. Their larger self is flowing through them most hours of the day and guiding their way. They have a solid fifth dimensional or even higher dimensional connection activated, and they are unaffected by other people's energy fields. They are usually unaffected by the collective karma of humanity unless they have a contract to clear it as they integrate a new part of their higher consciousness. These souls live in a different state of consciousness known as group-consciousness, and their thoughts are focused on service to all beings.

The beauty of the Divine Plan is that no matter what a soul may decide within their mind regarding their life on Earth, their eternal journey will not be interrupted or their evolution blocked by any small choice or fear that may become locked within their consciousness. In other words, as each soul needs only to make a partial shift to be taken all the way once the collective shifts, no soul will be forgotten or lost in the astral or unconscious realms. This is the true beauty of being a collective and sharing life within the Earth's energy field. All that occurs to one, occurs to all. The timing of this, though, is activated through the code exchange between our dimensional selves and the journey of opening the heart. Our heart opening allows us to receive all that others have collectively created, including all of the light and codes of transformation and evolution they have released by unlocking their genetic code.

Every soul will either shift into a state of consciousness of self or become fully awakened. How each being makes their shift in consciousness will be their choice, and no other individual, Presence, or Enlightened Master can take this power of choice from a soul. What we need to trust is our fellow humanity's choices even if we do not resonate with them. As humanity shifts into the fifth dimension, the unconscious and astral veils, which create the karma of slavery, war, greed, abuse, fear, disease, and poverty, will be released. It may not seem as if much is presently shifting in society, but we are asked to understand that changes first must take place within each being, and the outer reflection of the shift will only occur when 51 percent of the collective has made a transformation.

This collective shift will activate all souls to enter either one of the two soul groups left on Earth. Alternatively, some souls who deeply fear the process will leave the Earth plane for a more suitable destination, as the oldest and third soul group transforms, and the oldest karma of the Earth dissolves back into the void. This is the Divine Plan for humanity's path of evolution in accordance with the collective's wish and in accordance with Mother Earth's natural path of evolution. It is essentially the healing of the veils of ignorance and darkness that cloud humanity's collective from entering their hearts and empowerment as divine beings. And as it is God's will, so it will be. The Divine Plan activates now through all the trust you give to your fellow humanity.

Encountering the Divine Plan for the First Time

The Divine Plan is a fluid, ever changing, alternating matrix of love that only serves to guide souls and groups of souls to live in oneness and harmony with the universe and all that they create or encounter on their path of incarnation. It is carried out through the overlighting guidance of the Divine Presence of each soul as the soul incarnates or leaves the source of their spiritual home to serve in alternate realities such as Earth.

Since my own original awakening approximately twenty-three years ago when I birthed my beautiful daughter Razmia, and my partner, Little Owl, completed his incarnation through the tragedy of suicide, I have met the four levels of my karma as a soul and learned to embrace these to balance them easily with God's grace. This has been my soul's freedom and my personal gateway to a very powerful, extraordinary life journey.

The deep grief I experienced after the shock of my partner's suicide led me on a journey to understand the mysteries of life and death and eventually onto my spiritual path, where I met the Earth spirit who began to heal me of this grief and gently lift it from me. It took many years before I was ready to forgive myself and my partner for the separation and for the loss of a father for my daughter. This was my personal karma, and as it lifted and I forgave, learning to trust a man again to support me and not abandon me, learning to trust myself as a woman not to hurt a man or herself through ignorance, I shifted in consciousness and became more awakened. Gifts activated from within me that I was unaware I held, that had been deeply repressed. I began to help others in small, loving ways to support them to be clearer and to guide their lives using these gifts.

This journey was all about trust and finding the original beliefs that I had given my power to. As I was shown my karma of having abandoned my partner and the guilt I carried inside from walking away from him in another life, I began to see how we had the possibility of completing our journey together, even though he was on the other side. To have the opportunity to heal something with a soul I loved so deeply and to know that when we meet again there will be no blame between our souls gave me peace of mind. I then had the strength to say yes, I could accept that I was responsible for my own reality of feeling abandoned. No one else had created this for me; it was my own karma of abandoning myself and others that led me to the experience of feeling abandoned so deeply. This had all occurred so I could heal a hidden part of me, an unseen part of my consciousness that was keeping me protected against men, just in case I would be held guilty for hurting them, or in case they would not love me because I could not give them all they wanted. Simply acknowledging this vulnerable part of myself was the first step that freed me from feeling guilty, grieving the loss of partnership, and longing for him to return, or for another to come and fulfill me. This acknowledgement was the first step that then opened a free space within me so the healing could take place.

In my early thirties I began to create the ancient sounds of my higher self to come through, activating my merkabah, recalibrating my energy field and my brain's DNA chemistry through the science of sacred sound to activate all of my consciousness. The old consciousness I had held as a woman on Earth, where subtle judgments of others and myself, fears of loss or abandonment, and jealousies of others had affected me to contain my energy and not express my true nature, simply dissolved. A great liberation took place, and I became conscious of a whole new dimension of myself. A new being emerged, and I began to help others from a much deeper place of oneness.

This space I call Presence is the place of truth via one's direct access to the realms of enlightenment or our direct contact with God. Over a period of time, this energy connection grew within me to a level where I no longer could be just me, and I felt the loss of my individuality, but in a beautiful way. It just melted away as a larger group-consciousness began to merge with me, and I became aware of myself as much more than my physical reality. My thoughts no longer were so personal; they began to express a unity consciousness. This took place through the mergence of my Presence with the support of ninety-six Enlightened Masters that I had a contract with to activate the Divine Plan via the creation of advanced energy and consciousness programs.

This sacred work had not been part of my experience in this incarnation until fourteen years ago. In fact, twelve years ago when I completed cleansing my personal karma and became a spiritual teacher for the Enlightened Masters' work with humanity, I laughed inside deeply as this was the first job I had ever held responsibility for within my life. For many years, I had been searching for what I was meant to be doing, not knowing the plan for me on Earth, fearing responsibility, and as the Divine Plan activated for me, I was given a job so joyously easy, it was as if the job had been written for me. I became prepared through my energy body and consciousness for new forms of divine education to be birthed through me. Profound energy programs for students for the rapid recalibration of their consciousness were cocreated over many years. This I enjoyed immensely and found effortless, due to the great assistance I was given by the Enlightened Masters and the overlighting presences of many archangels and angels who assisted me to always be clear and to embody my Presence deeply. It has been this service work that has continued to facilitate the transformation of my family, community, collective, and planetary karma, to awaken new gifts from within me and deepen my embodiment of my Divine Presence so I could fulfill the next step of my service to the Divine Plan, the Earth, and humanity.

The truth I share as a result of my contact with the enlightened realms over the last fourteen years is that the Divine Plan for your life is unfounded on your present reality. In fact, if you surrender to the Divine Plan it may create all that does not serve you to transform, leaving you as a witness to yourself, as a completely new being who has evolved. Just as my reality now was not founded on my past experience in this life, so it may be for you as a soul. The truth will be known by you, for if you have found your heart calling or it has found you, you are already activated by the Divine Plan, and the journey has begun.

Presently your life may be fulfilling or not so fulfilling, but the truth is, circumstances always change and your life can transition and deepen through karmic clearing. If there is any karma that lies beneath your life experience, hidden away, know that this unresolved energy is draining you of your power, creating you to be less expressive, less true to your heart calling, and more involved in the past synergies or patterns of consciousness you held in other lives. Ultimately, it is creating false walls of protection around you that may create you to judge yourself and others, fear aspects of your life, deny wonderful opportunities for growth, and avoid embracing your spiritual responsibility and the personal empowerment you could receive by acknowledging, balancing, and clearing this karma. The almighty love of your soul addresses you to recognize the amazing opportunity life is offering you via your personal and family karmic challenges.

Whenever you find yourself feeling alone or unsupported, I ask that you remind yourself that your ancestors are with you at all times. On their passing into the other world they became angels, and they have returned to serve you and your family until every soul in your family has been liberated. Know that your ancestors are the angels that come to you regularly, deeply watching over you. Learn to trust their presence for they send messages through your conscience as helpful hints on your path in life, gently stimulating your inner guidance. These ones are always listening and only need to be asked to forgive all their unresolved experiences on Earth. Let them know that you are ready to choose to not carry the old consciousness of the hurts of your family, and that together you can choose to heal the karma of the family and your own personal karma.

Then call upon the Enlightened Masters to bless your choice in your awakening, spiritually and personally as a light seed of the Earth. Ask that they bring the dispensations to you that will open your path to purify the karma that needs to be balanced and cleared so you may take the next step and enter your quantum shift experience over the next year. Do not expect this to take place overnight. Give yourself the time to be with the karma and own it responsibly, so all the gifts and power may be returned to you via your heart opening and your embrace and forgiveness of the karma shown to you.

Spiritual Keys for Your Quantum Shift

The following simple spiritual keys were given to me fourteen years ago by the Enlightened Masters for my own quantum shift experience. May these words gently help you repattern your consciousness to reveal the larger nature inside you. What lies within you may be so magical and enlightening, creative and powerful, that you may feel a little strange as the transition takes place to allow more of you to stream into your body and activate your cells with the light frequency. Know your journey will be yours in all ways, and although you may feel no one understands your journey, know the Enlightened Masters are full of understanding and love, and they will hold you as you master your path in your unique way.

Take your time to be with your karma and learn to not make yourself wrong simply because you have life lessons. Do not rush to try to heal or fix yourself, as you will simply deny your light and wholeness if you approach your karma as something to fix. Instead, integrate it into your life as a part of yourself on the path of empowerment.

Learn to reward your most vulnerable self with kind remarks. Remind yourself how well you are progressing, how much you are growing, and how wonderful this is, rather than punishing the most sensitive part of yourself with self-judgment around not meeting impossible expectations you may have placed upon yourself. Let go of the outcome and simply practice forgiveness as an integrated spiritual practice in your daily life, for the journey of life to unfold in a simpler way.

Remember to enjoy the lighter elements of your personality by liberating your creativity and accepting that you have a wonderful ability to create with love all that you are destined to experience. Accept that you are on a path and you are assisted in all ways already, and that if you focus on expanding this truth through the power of your love, it will manifest in abundance and grace as God wishes it to be for you.

Allow the hand of God or infinite grace that lives within all of creation to guide you. Call on God's grace to flood into areas of your life that hold karma or struggle, and accept that there are some things you cannot do alone, so humble yourself and be willing to ask for help. Ask with an open heart and not from a space of being the victim, and the universe will hear your request far and wide.

Understand that there is always a divine timing for completions in your life, based on your ability to open your heart and surrender your personal desires for the greater good of your soul growth. Detach from wants and desires to release yourself from any struggle, and accept that if something is truly to be yours, the universal force in all of creation will return it to you without your need to be involved. Let go of any control patterns in your relationships so you may truly know God's love and grace in human expression, and allow the journey to be one of deep peace through surrender and detachment as your priority.

Contemplate the perfection of love and its true nature of giving. Let go of the belief that love will bring you fulfillment in life, and accept that love is for your bliss and oneness; it stems from within, and no other being can fulfill this for you. If you feel dry of your own love, contemplate the perfection of your love and your universal connection, and expand your consciousness beyond what is small and temporary.

Enjoy materiality, but without any attachment so you do not lose your spiritual essence and divine connection to the love within you. Let the universe bless you with material abundance so you can share it. Understand the nature of the universe and the flow of abundance, for it is to be shared freely and not hoarded. If you are hoarding, let go so the energy can flow in all aspects of your life.

Return to your true nature and your heart connection as your base frequency and truth each day so you may truly be guided in the highest way. Do not be concerned with what others think, as their perceptions may or may not be true for you. Honor other people's beliefs as you would wish yours to be honored, even if they do not resonate with you.

Be grateful for what you receive, and remember to always bless those in need. Accept offers of kindness and return them as your heart reminds you to give more each day, rather than hold on in fear that you will not have enough and not be supported here. Identify when you are in fear and speak with God immediately, asking for the grace to have this fear lifted and purified from your soul and body.

Finally, be sure to set the intention that you will have a beautiful life journey as you awaken each day. Blessed be!

INNOCENCE

Graceful pleasure
holds the space
for you, the beholder ...
She is ever-present with you
diamond and pearl in her innocence,
she is a part of you ...
Her highest wish is to rise up
take you away
from anything that may
not know the preciousness
of you ...
She stands by a gateway,
white golden wings above you ...
She calls your angels in
What do you need,
she whispers to you ...
Will you trust your innocence, she says
I am here ...
You are the beholder of such preciousness
and to acknowledge your grace
releases me to be free and happy ...
Through a child's eyes we shall see the world
renewed again, vibrant in all colors
as part of our preciousness ...
Take me in and let me breathe you too
I am your formlessness
I have no way or path ...
We are just the breath
know no mind, right or wrong
only that the dream and the song light our heart.
We are innocent ...

Giveth my name to your mind and soul
Let us fly in no blame or deceit that we are no more
of the shining light of love
Let me blaze your body and ignite your breath
to touch all in innocence
and wonder at the world she is . . .
Let me lift the veils of your old view
of majestic mother grace
and the life she giveth you
Let me take any old pain from you
Let us dance as the sun and moon set and rise
together . . . like brother and sister . . .
Can we walk hand in hand
trusting the grand plan
that we are innocent,
able to breathe
expressing our grace,
allowing all to just be . . .
I am your breath . . .

The Divine Plan for Our Earth

Generations of human beings have been living on the Earth with little awareness that the Earth herself is a Holy Spirit or divine being that has consciousness and full awareness, lighting up every cell of our being. In every living molecule of the Earth body, a great spirit is embodying and raising the frequency higher and higher, preparing to shift the energy field of the Earth into a geo-vortex, temporarily, for the transformation of her field to a new universal alignment that is her destiny.

This alignment is taking place through a system of universal centers known as the galactic core, the great central sun (Rakuna), great central moon (Lakura), great, great central sun (Sanura), great, great central moon

(Makira), great, great, great central sun (Kamura), and great, great, great central moon (Makina). These universal centers feed the Earth and all stars and planets within our universe with higher frequency currents for creation and for the development of consciousness.

Unknown presently to science, this alignment will also be creating the ignition of the Inner Earth and crystalline and plasma cores of the Earth, activating and opening them to higher dimensions, allowing the Inner Earth to draw forth a large amount of voidal energy or pure love from these universal centers. This will ultimately be released from the inner realms of the Earth and throughout the Earth's dimensional fields to bring the power and light of the sun more deeply into the heart of all beings as the Earth core reaches a specific level of universal frequency.

The Earth's structure and etheric field are undergoing great changes that may not be fully understood from our present human perspective, as the galactic sciences that describe this phenomena have no basis in any educational system developed on the Earth. The science presently utilized for most scientific understanding on Earth is based on a linear perspective, on time, and on a smaller dimensional bandwidth of energies than what is truly impacting the evolutionary process of the Earth body. Only one aspect of our brain is utilized to create this linear mapping and measurement, and until our brains operate as full hemispheres, our consciousness may continue to perceive through this limited dimensional bandwidth.

The galactic sciences of the universe utilized by the Enlightened Masters and other light beings of higher consciousness involve multidimensional understandings that create some aspects of our present-day Earth-based physics to be invalid as 100 percent truth. To be able to understand galactic physics, our brains must develop and activate to allow us to integrate the eighth dimensional consciousness needed for these higher levels of understanding. Both perspectives hold truth that is relative, but Earth-based physics is able to explain only that which is closest to the physical dimensions and reality. When we look at the Earth in its entirety, some of what is held as truth by Earth-based sciences is simply no longer valid.

What is proposed in this sacred text is based on the very basics of galactic physics, translated into a form that may be registered by our present level of consciousness. It is proposed that the Earth is a crystal and thus a generator, transmitter, and receiver in a much larger universal system. Her plate system, the facets of the crystal, is made of a highly concentrated, high frequency energy that has not yet been discovered by Earth-based science.

Within this plate system, streams of voidal, source, plasma-based frequencies, Christ light (crystalline), and pranic energies amalgamate to create the mirror of the twelve dimensions of this Earth Crystal. Within the field of the Earth, each of the portals—high-energy sites that may be seen as doorways for consciousness to be generated and created within—bridges each of these twelve dimensions of the Earth Crystal to the seven primary worlds within the Earth.

This plate system directs, integrates, and grounds all of the Earth's systems, including weather, atmosphere, biospheres, geological and biological changes, and growth within the process of evolution. It also directs the flow of the high frequency currents the Earth receives from the universal centers, some larger than the Earth's body itself, and orchestrates the down-stepping of these currents through dimensions of the Earth, which instigates the various dimensional worlds within the Earth to coexist.

These vast, high frequency currents stream from centers within galaxies and universes beyond our present understanding, building and empowering the physical and also other dimensions of the Earth that are not always presently recognized. The plate system lies within the Earth's body and extends through her etheric body into her celestial and universal bodies and also forms the basis of the many different layers of grids upon which all of life on and within Earth is fed divine energy and consciousness for its evolution. While the Earth as a source crystal generally operates through twelve dimensions, it will eventually evolve to establish twenty dimensions or planes of consciousness.

There are many dimensional worlds within the Earth Crystal, and living on Earth and within Earth are many races and species of life forms unknown to the majority of humans and invisible to physical eyes. Some of these worlds have eighth, ninth, tenth, eleventh, and twelfth dimensional light beings within them. Humanity primarily operates within three to four dimensions, although through the Earth's shift in vibration, humanity is being supported as a collective to shift into the fifth dimension as their base frequency and consciousness.

The wheel of karma held within aspects of the astral plane keeps the majority of humanity's perspective of life on Earth within a smaller bandwidth of dimensions and therefore unable to tap into the other dimensions consciously. This creates the limitation of a soul's experience of themselves and the Earth, but as a soul opens their consciousness to higher bandwidths of awareness as their brain chemistry and body increase in light velocity, they experience deeper states of oneness, love, and expanded consciousness.

Imagine that this wheel of karma is a vortex spiraling within all other fields of the Earth, and that this invisible field of consciousness is made up of veils. These veils cause the energetic locking of humanity's natural gifts, higher perceptions, psychic abilities, and some of the glands of the physical body. These veils cause humanity to close down their higher functions and believe that what they can see and experience physically is their only true reality.

The great spirit of the Earth, also known as Gaia, collaborates deeply with her own guardians and caretakers. These ones carry full knowledge and enlightened understandings of how the Earth Crystal gives life, form, and the power of creation and manifestation to an infinite number of beings, coming and going, incarnating and leaving physical form, translating from one dimension to another via their merkabahs or original lightbodies, experiencing their multidimensionality and cocreation.

Expand your consciousness with me and consider you live within one of seven worlds and have incarnated on Earth for a special reason. You also are one of the beings whom the guardians and caretakers are aware of. These ones are Ancestral Masters who live deep within the Inner Earth. They are the guardians of the libraries of the Earth, which hold all of her divine resources, and they communicate through the most ancient trees of the Earth. They guide the grounding of the Divine Plan for the Earth, and their wisdom is shared with all beings—animals, humanity, and spirits—through a group-consciousness known as the portal keepers, who work by their side. The portal keepers live within the portals of the Earth, high-energy sites that hold the plan of creation within them. The portal keepers also work directly with the Enlightened Masters who overlight the Divine Plan for the Earth and all other worlds of this universe and parallel universes.

The dimensional shift accorded by the Divine Plan has taken place three times on the Earth, and will continue to occur to allow the Earth Mother regeneration of her inner worlds and physical structure. When this takes place, the souls within the worlds of the Earth will ascend into a higher state of consciousness before returning to build a new world within her renewed and regenerated physical body. Many Earth changes have been prophesied, but the truth of how this will manifest has not been established yet, nor has the timing of the actual gravitational shift. The plan is dynamic and fluid, altering its direction as life responds and balances that which needs to be balanced.

Regeneration of the Earth body is essential, for the Earth Crystal has become hotter and thus drier, affecting the fluidity and motion of her plate system. Areas of the Earth that need more water for life to blossom are reflecting this phenomenon. The mountains are not only ancient wise portal keepers; they are also responsible for directing the currents of divine energy necessary for the plates to activate and unify to ignite the holy fire to feed all of life on Earth. They also direct energy through the ley lines of the Earth that feed the physical and etheric fields of all beings with light and prana.

If you imagine with me that the Earth Crystal is approximately twenty times larger than her physical body, you will begin to connect to the Earth Crystal I am describing to you. As you imagine this, contemplate the tectonic plates within the surface of the Earth's physical body. These are always shifting, but primarily they are rising in vibration due to the fact that the plates and dimensions of the Earth are receiving vast currents, more than ever before, for the Earth's evolution into the fifth dimension.

What this means is that the currents of the universe that feed the Earth are being directed by the universal field of All That Is to raise the frequency of the Earth Crystal to a base frequency of the fifth dimensional bandwidth. This is taking place in preparation for a restoration of the Earth's physical body as well as a regeneration of the seven worlds housed within the crystal.

The Earth is a jewel within our universe, and the resources it holds are very special. Some of these resources are being drained and not replenished by humanity. Some of the other species who live within the other worlds of the Earth are also freely using these resources and creating karma by not allowing regeneration. But this misuse is not the only reason the Divine Plan calls for a renewal of the Earth. The Earth simply holds natural cycles of regeneration, and the rhythm of these cycles is changing as the Earth rises in vibration, just as the cycles and seasons of the Earth are also naturally changing.

To understand the Divine Plan for the Earth, we need to recognize that the Earth is older and wiser than we know, a divine mother who nurtures and brings security to many. Her heart is so large that the true gift of our lives on Earth may not be felt until our hearts embrace Mother Earth and all within her as divine. She is part of the cosmic cycle of creation, just as we are part of a global, community, or family cycle of creation. Our understanding of these cycles can only be minimal, and in truth, it is not important for us to understand all details of the Divine Plan. What we need to understand is that the Earth has her natural cycle, which we are able to influence but not change, and which we are able to live in harmony with, and thus be supported with the energy to love and live while we are blessed to be incarnated here.

The Earth changes that so many speak of are occurring as the tectonic plates rise in vibration and the Earth Crystal releases stagnant energy that lies between and within her diamond plates. The effect upon the Earth body is presently at a minimal level. As all beings are connected to the

Divine Plan for the Earth, carrying it in every cell of their body, many acts are taking place to balance as much as possible so these Earth changes can continue to be minimal in their effect. Your acts toward the Earth and your higher awareness of what she needs to receive are an important focus. It is also essential that you hold faith in your fellow humanity as well as the Earth's organic systems to create balance.

The lightbody or crystal of the Earth still carries memories and consciousness from a realm that was anchored on Earth in the ancient time of Atlantis, so the portal system and grid of the Earth is presently renewing itself, and a fine-tuning of the Earth's meridian system is taking place in preparation for her regeneration. The beauty of the Earth is that she is always able to bring more life into any area and to activate creation with her special gifts.

The nature spirits, Earth spirits, elemental beings, *devas,* angels, and archangels are all aware of the mother's wondrous creation, and a deep respect is given to her. The light beings of the seventh dimension and above, known as the Family of Light, are specifically focusing on the areas where the Earth's resource needs to be held for the health and well-being of all beings living in all worlds within the Earth. There are giant pillars that extend from the universal centers beyond our sun and moon, through the star grids into specific areas of the Earth. These have been anchored into the Earth core through specific grids or plates to support the Earth's physical body during times when the field of the Earth or the plate system is not liquid enough for the gateways of life to all be open simultaneously.

There are seven primary worlds or levels of existence within the Earth's body of light, and all who live in these worlds consider the Earth their home. In ancient times, up through the time of Atlantis, these seven worlds cooperated and lived in unity consciousness; the Divine Plan calls for not only the regeneration of the Earth herself, but also a renewal of peace between these worlds.

Of the seven worlds, humanity usually experiences only one—the third world of physical matter—unless their higher cognitive abilities and chakras have activated and they are able to soul travel in their lightbody or merkabah to visit another world. These visits often take place during powerful spiritual experiences, dream states, out-of-body experiences, close encounters with death, and deep states of meditation. Soul travel is a form of consciousness expansion in which your central consciousness travels through the inner spiritual planes to another realm while you are simultaneously conscious within your physical body.

Working with the Enlightened Masters allows humanity to activate their consciousness and energy body to a level where they can experience connection with the realms of the ancestors, Earth spirits, star beings, angelic, Christ, and celestial and universal presences who share Earth as their home. Each soul incarnated as a human shares spiritual lineage with these ones from alternate realms, and great wisdom is stored in the establishment of a connection with the other worlds. This has been the path of many sages, saints, yogis, and initiates within all the mystical or esoteric traditions of all religions and disciplined metaphysical sciences for many thousands of years. We are now in a time when many more people are realizing this potential as their consciousness returns due to the increase in vibration of the Earth field. I share with you my understanding of the seven worlds of the Earth, gathered from visitations and journeys with the Enlightened Masters to these worlds over the last fourteen years.

The Seven Worlds of the Earth

The worlds of the Earth serve many purposes, but many of them exist primarily to stream new forms of life into existence. When you consider the concept that there is no real death, and that a soul or unique stream of consciousness can translate from one form to another via the incarnational process, the possibility of the existence of myriads of life forms begins to expand within your mind. When we consider also that there is no definitive end to the creation process, we see the possibility of the existence of all forms of life. If we consider each of the six other worlds of the

Earth as simply realms that link to our physical world, supporting the development of new life on Earth, the following short descriptions of these worlds may seem less threatening to our species.

The First World is held in the Inner Earth. The Australian aboriginal people who hold the connection to this world also know this as the *dreamtime.* The creation spirits who inhabit this world are often seen with the spiritual eye as giant beings, including giant insects, flowers, and other natural forms. The Inner Earth is filled with corridors that seem to grow larger and larger as you enter them, and you experience yourself also as being very large. This occurs because the realms within the Earth are larger than its physical structure and have the ability to expand multidimensionally. As you travel into the vast dimensions of the Inner Earth you experience a great magnetic heaviness. This is partially created by the voidal core center that draws all to it, and partially by the magnetic plasma cores, created by an infinite well of spinning geometries and liquid plasma conduits that envelope and surround the voidal core.

The Inner Earth is the world from which all other worlds have birthed, and it will continue to give birth as the Earth expands from twelve dimensions to twenty in accordance with the Divine Plan. Here live the original caretakers of the Earth, known as the Ancestral Masters. They have many different forms, but they are all giant, twelfth dimensional presences. Beings from other realms also reside temporarily within the Inner Earth, as this world is a doorway to the formless, voidal realms of pure love, where many travel to dissolve their form and return to their essence. Many beings from other worlds also travel to the Inner Earth to open their hearts or to change themselves, utilizing the power of this realm to harness their energy in service to Gaia. Humanity too is linked deeply to the ancestral guardians of Earth, and each soul within humanity has aspects of their own spirit housed in an ancestral form within the Inner Earth.

The Second World, or Middle Earth, is the home of the Earth spirits that at times share the surface with humanity. Animal spirits, elemental spirits, devas, nature spirits such as fairies and elves, and crystal guardians all share the Second World as a place of resource for their spiritual currents.

They also travel through the lightgrids or ley lines of the Earth to feed the physical with the spiritual current, which they draw from Inner Earth through the Second World. All animals and all of nature, including humans, are fed via the spirits of the Second World. Aspects of our own Earth spirit are housed in the Second World until our body, soul, and mind wish to receive its great wisdom and life force.

Other civilizations or star races also have bases within Middle Earth, which serves as a bridge between the Inner Earth and the surface of the physical world. The beings that live in Middle Earth all have the ability to travel through the Earth portals into the stars such as the Pleiades, Sirius, and other systems, and hold galactic knowledge of time, space, and energy. There are many cities made of a plasma frequency within Middle Earth. In fact, more souls reside within these cities than on the Earth surface. These beings live in plasma bodies that have a partial, crystalline matrix as a base, and they are highly evolved. Many have the ability to physicalize, but the majority of these beings are nonphysical light beings.

The beings of Middle Earth are mainly sixth to twelfth dimensional presences who have the highest respect for the Earth. However, just as humanity holds a mixture of soul groups, each with a different experience in consciousness, a smaller number of souls in Middle Earth have experienced a separation from their Divine Presence, and through their personal agendas have been misusing the resource of the Earth, as do some human beings, and simply need love and assistance to forgive and clear their karma. These souls base their consciousness and focus their power through the fourth dimension, though they may be able to access their gifts from the first to the ninth dimensions. More and more of these Middle Earth souls have also been experiencing a great shift in their consciousness, for as above, so below.

The Third World is found primarily on the surface, and it lovingly supports humanity, the nature kingdoms of the Earth, and humanity's known world. This world is a light-based existence and acts as the base from which beings from all other worlds often choose to incarnate in order to experience physical reality. Many beings from other worlds visit the

Earth's surface, as this is a passageway between the Inner Earth, Middle Earth, and the angelic, crystalline (Christ), celestial, and enlightened planes of the Earth. There is an immense amount of traffic occurring here, and many of the ancestral sites such as the mountains, sacred lakes, and waterways act as conduits for the portals, which anchor high frequency doorways, corridors, and even highways of light that these beings travel on between the worlds. Interactions between these beings are taking place continually within the Third World, and these interactions are felt by humanity even if we are not fully aware of them. Even souls who are shut down in their energy fields and have no awareness of anything but the physical are unknowingly experiencing the interactions between beings from other worlds. Many of these souls themselves are traveling to the other worlds in their sleep. The difficulty is that the astral plane, which lies as a belt between the Third and Fourth worlds since the time of Atlantean fall, often affects souls when they travel, for if their consciousness has been negatively focused throughout their day, they become caught in astral travel and the lower dimensional fields as they soul travel in their sleep.

The Fourth World is an angelic base of existence. Within this world, which is structured by pure light and geometry, beings live in group-consciousness and do not exist as individuals but more as streams of consciousness of pure light. This is the first world where there is no individualized consciousness. The plants of the Earth's surface are deeply connected to this world made from light geometries of living intelligence, as their spirits are sourced from this angelic energy and sacred geometry. The most beautiful plants, fruits, and foods on the Earth are originally gifts from this world for humanity and all others in the Third World to be blessed with. This angelic base responds to sacred sound and ignites through all of the worlds, through the beauty of sound being generated in harmony with the heart. The angels and the sacred geometries of light from this world are sometimes affected by other worlds, since all consciousness within all of the worlds affects each individual world.

The angels or streams of group-consciousness are at times affected by the cruelty, abuse, or control that has taken place in the Third World and that is also sometimes sourced from the Second World as they travel into these worlds. When this occurs, it creates imbalance in the Fourth World, and the angelic beings become fearful until they cleanse all they have experienced. Some angels lose faith and fall from grace into a state of "consciousness of self." Other group-consciousnesses have chosen to incarnate into the Third World to create change so the abuse, cruelty, and senseless violence found in pockets of this world can cease. Humanity's connection with the Fourth World is very important for the balancing and clearing of Earth karma. Many times humanity has opened the angelic portals and then lost their faith and closed them again. As humanity learns to love and accept aspects of their own spirit that live within the angelic world, they will ground their angelic consciousness and create peace as a collective.

The Fifth World is a crystalline base of existence. Within this world, which is structured through sacred geometry, light, sound, and plasma crystals, beings do not exist as individuals but more as crystals of divine consciousness. Our Earth portals and dimensional doorways located at sacred sites are made from the Fifth World's crystalline technology. Atlantis was a world within this Fifth World, and the crystals within the Earth body are connected to this world. The Fifth World houses the infinite intelligence of the unified field in a concentrated form, the blueprints of creation and all life on Earth, which are specific packages of power, concentrated and encoded into a crystalline form of living intelligence. Humanity also holds a connection to the Fifth World, as aspects of our spirit live in crystalline light or Christ bodies; as our chakras develop, humanity receives its fifth dimensional body, activating streams of Christ consciousness or crystalline rays of divine energy into the body.

The drying and heating of the Earth Crystal has been denying the Fifth World a powerful energetic resource. Mining on the Earth's surface and many miles into the Earth's body is one of the most disruptive activities that have been draining resource from the Earth and denying the Fifth World the currents of energy that concentrate and magnify to create new crystalline structures. Mining has disrupted some of the lines of power and the connection between the Second, Third, Fourth, and Fifth worlds, and has created a ripple within the doorways between these worlds and the Sixth and Seventh worlds. This world also houses the base frequency of Shambhala and many cities of crystalline light.

The Sixth World is one created purely from rays of sound or celestial light. The hemispheres of love and sound vibration within this world, also known as harmony spheres, are some of highest forms of consciousness on the Earth. These celestial spheres or presences of love often emerge from this world into other worlds in holy visitations, for the harmony spheres open doorways for the Holy Spirit of love to bless souls and all of life. Lemuria was created from this world in ancient times before the Earth physicalized. This world is liquid in its feeling and immensely expansive in its love. The highest dimensional angels, archangels, and beings of love come from this world to serve the Earth and bridge all the worlds with love. These higher dimensional beings work directly through the Holy Mother's field of love. When Lemuria was seeded and had partially completed its journey through the Earth realm, some of the beings from the Sixth World became trapped in other dimensions; their memories lie within the plates of the Earth. In the Akasha of the Earth lies the power of the love that wishes to return to humanity and the Third World to bring peace on Earth into manifestation, and humanity's connection to this world is through aspects of their own spirit that are living within this world.

The Seventh World is based on the creation matrix of the Earth and is home to the Divine Presences of all beings from all other worlds. This world is a gateway for the enlightenment of the Earth and all beings in each of the worlds. Enlightened beings travel to this world to make contact with beings of the Earth or to work with the Earth Mother in assisting the Divine Plan to ground through the Sixth World, into the Fifth World, into the Fourth, into the Third, into the Second, and into the First World of the Inner Earth. The Seventh World also carries the enlightened dispensations for all beings and for the Earth and is the source for all higher forms of creation that drop into the other worlds in accordance with the Divine Plan. One example is the sacred creation of the airplane, which manifested for humanity when a Presence of the Seventh World dropped this dispensation into the consciousness of a soul within the Third World. As each world is ready to receive dispensations for new levels of creation, the presences of the Seventh World gift these by merging their consciousness with beings from these worlds. All shared in this book has been sourced from many journeys into the Seventh World and visitations and dispensations given to others and myself take place via connection to this world. Many of the new creations for the future of our world are now being delivered to specific souls so they can be prototyped and developed. Only creations that benefit the collectives of all worlds are offered in this way from the enlightened presences of the Seventh World.

The Seventh World can be contacted consciously only through deep periods of meditation such as those mastered by the yogis and bodhisattvas of the Earth. Although divine contact from this world does bless beings within other worlds of the Earth, this is not through a conscious act of creation by any soul but is offered in service for a higher purpose related to the Divine Plan. The enlightened presences of the Seventh World live in strict alignment with the law of noninterference and do not use their power to intervene unless called upon for assistance. Humanity has a direct relationship with the Seventh World, through each individual's connection to their Divine Presence.

The resonance and the development of unity consciousness between these seven worlds is intrinsic to the Divine Plan for peace on Earth. The primary focuses of the plan are the restoration of the diamond plate system of the Earth Crystal and the reactivation of specific lines and currents between the seven worlds that have been mined, drained, or sealed by beings who have gathered the resource and not replenished the lines and grids that created it.

This karma of greed not only extends through the Third World, but also exists in the Second World. Beings from both these worlds are responsible for the gathering and storing of resource that in truth belongs to all beings of the Earth. Some of this resource has taken thousands or millions of years to form. As you become more conscious of your involvement in the karmic clearing of our collective, you are assisting your Divine Presence to support the balance and restoration of all on Earth.

Your Divine Presence invites you to become a worldbridger with the special frequency and heart energy you hold. You are invited to create your focus in life to be aligned to all that creates unity consciousness between your physical body and soul and your spirit that also lives with the First, Second, Fourth, Fifth, Sixth, and Seventh worlds. As you become the worldbridger, your spirit and your body also manifest unity and oneness in your reality, and this becomes your consciousness experience.

To understand the seven worlds of the Earth, understand that the vastness of your consciousness lives within them. As a spirit you are an ancestor, an Earth spirit, a star being, an angel, a Christ being, and a celestial and enlightened presence. You are all of these in spirit, and within the physical, you are human. To link your true spirit and your humanity as one, you bridge the worlds to create on Earth, for all beings.

THE CALL TO THE WORLDBRIDGER

Like the rain
a time just comes
blessing you, beloved one
to see beyond your world
as it is . . .
Into the formless
through the Earth Mother's great eye
through the wisdom of the great white whale
through the heart of Holy Mother
you are taken on a journey, beloved . . .
To see your world
as more than you know . . .

Your spirit bridge is forming
sounds of long ago echo, a calling
weaving a larger breath for you to live upon
so you may know the vastness in all . . .
The inner worlds of light
lie still, seeding your bridge of light . . .
Dreaming bodies coil and lie
contemplating being and expressing more . . .
A great gathering of light and love
expands as you accept your many forms
many ways, unique elements of self
and no longer judge any more any part of yourself . . .
Your cells charge with the light
as your spirit in each world ignites.
Tapestries of infinite possibilities
flow through your mind
as you accept yourself . . . as divine
And the many worlds
That weave the petals of your heart together
beyond all time and space
piece and unite your cells and heart with God's light,
through grace and forgiveness
A larger heart you now share . . .
Every particle, an infinite vessel for you
To share God's love and compassion
reflecting the sharing of your consciousness
and your divine relations between the worlds,
all races and species, all kinds of beings . . .
in love and forgiveness, and nonjudgment
in oneness
The depth of love and peace is yours to have
as you own the mirror of all parts of yourself . . .
Recognize those that forgive . . .

Love and embrace all that is . . .
And receive God's love within
Let your bridge to the world
your heart . . . fully open now
So you may know
Your Holy Spirit is a blessing
Accept the worldbridger within
That holds the life energy for your dream . . .
You are the dreamer, a creator . . .
As you bridge the worlds, you become your dream

The Enlightened Masters' Promise to the Earth

In the Seventh World, when I have been blessed to visit it, the greatest compassion and love and wisdom are shared in relationship to the Divine Plan of the Earth and to all that is creating slavery, war, greed, abuse, disease, fear, and poverty to occur within the Third World. The Enlightened Masters, who may be contacted directly through connecting to the Seventh World of the Earth, spoke with me as a group-consciousness and lovingly shared . . .

Blessed child . . .

The Divine Plan for the Earth carries forth through the heart of all of humanity as it is their world, and they are to reclaim their caretakership and take responsibility for the care of this great mother. The universal heart of humanity wishes to open and generate a new frequency connection between their human heart and their angelic heart. The Earth Mother is an enlightened soul and a great spirit that serves to host the life forms from over twelve thousand different worlds. Those that choose to live within one of the Seven Worlds of the Earth or visit in holy service or in learning come from many different realities originally, but they all share one thing in common, which is their willingness to earth their consciousness, for the Earth Mother is but a holy vessel for each soul and Presence to earth themselves.

We speak now of what the Earth provides for all beings. Within all of the beings from all Seven Worlds, their lightbody structures carry their consciousness into their new forms. This may be an incarnation as human as you are, or this may be the extension of one's consciousness into the angelic world, merging with many others to experience nonindividuality. This may be the incarnation into Middle Earth in a pranic or crystalline lightbody that shines and lives on the light frequency so one may truly experience the light, deeply. There are so many options that souls and presences may choose from to experience their incarnation on Earth, and each with the purpose of earthing something new within themselves.

What is it that you are earthing that is new to you? Within the Third World, you are a worldbridger and therefore able to travel between all of the worlds. As you travel you reclaim parts of yourself as your consciousness, and integrate and earth this new consciousness to return to you. Mother Earth is the home where all beings integrate and gather back into themselves the consciousness they may have left in other worlds, which they now need for the next step on their path of evolution. And so it is the same for all incarnated on Earth. Each one, our dear child, is here for the gathering back of their consciousness that they may have left behind within one of the Seven Worlds of the Earth. Their karmic clearing of the oldest fears of being their true self on Earth is the doorway they each are walking through, gently supported by their Divine Presence so they may integrate and carry this as new consciousness, grounded through their being and earthed through all dimensions of their consciousness.

A great awakening is occurring inside many souls unbeknownst to them, as it is occurring on the inner planes, we say. The inner planes of spirit within the Earth are the Fourth, Fifth, Sixth, and Seventh worlds of the Earth. The outer planes of the Earth are the Third World of the Earth where your physical body exists and where your soul primarily grounds into human form. The Source Plane is the First World from which all else is birthed and all returns to, to lose form and leave the Earth. The Soul Plane is connected to the First, Second, and Third worlds of the Earth. Here souls exist in different forms and live among spirits with beautiful forms. The Astral Plane of the Earth is connected to the Second, Third, and Fourth worlds of the Earth. Here, souls meet their other halves, mirrors of themselves in the past or aspects they have left behind, parts of their heart that were trapped or left in other lifetimes. This is the plane that is to transmute through the Divine Plan for every being of the Earth to live in peace, for the Astral Plane is felt by souls within their emotional and feeling bodies, and if a soul holds parts of itself within the astral belt of the Earth, they sense the temporary wound or illusion of pain or suffering or deep hurt. Beloved child, your heart goes out to these ones, but we offer you a loving prophesy from the Divine Plan of the Earth for you to know that these ones will be cared for; none will be forgotten or lost or ignored, as all will be found and assisted with love as they are ready to earth and ground.

From the Seventh World, a promise has been made to all beings of the Earth from the heart of God/Goddess, and this will take place through the grace and love and blessings being brought forth. Many are coming to the Earth to live in the Seventh, Sixth, Fifth, Fourth, Third, Second, and First worlds. They are returning to the Earth from far away and bringing with them the grace of God, untouched, unscathed, and blessed with peace, unity, and love, freely flowing from their wings and hearts of love. Many of these ones have only lived on the Earth in times of great peace and harmony, and others come with special skills needed to accelerate the shift in consciousness that is occurring. These ones are celestial and angelic children, mothers, fathers, brothers, and sisters who are incarnating on the Earth. For long ago the portals for the higher consciousness souls were closed, and only souls who lived on the Earth many times were able to incarnate within or between the worlds. These portals fully reopened through the healing focus and balance made over a one-hundred-fifty-year period, and a new alignment took place between the seven worlds during this time. The reopening of the portals in the field of the Earth between the Seventh, Sixth, Fifth, and Fourth worlds has allowed new souls of higher dimensional consciousness to incarnate through all seven worlds to create the balance between the worlds.

These ones have all agreed to cocreate peace on Earth, and a planetary shift is taking place in the global consciousness. This begins in the communities of the Third and Second worlds with the healing of their families and their relationship to the resource and abundance of the Earth. As many have come who have not specifically needed to be on Earth for their karmic journey, those who are completing the balancing of their Earth karma will receive the support and love they need. All those with personal agendas participating in the perpetration of slavery, war, abuse, disease, poverty, fear, and greed through the manipulation of DNA, control methods, or fear-based threats are to be supported to be blessed with safe passage to another reality based on love, so beings of Earth will no longer be abused or mistreated in this way. These ones will be supported with the greatest love, compassion, and wisdom to heal their hearts of all that creates them to be disconnected from the essence of their souls and hearts.

This sacred promise was granted and is now held by the Enlightened Masters until the absolution of the karma of slavery, war, abuse, disease, poverty, fear, and greed has occurred through all worlds of the Earth and the balance between the worlds for planetary peace is made manifest through the hearts of all beings. This will lead to a period of one thousand years of peace on Earth. The Presences of the Seventh World will then no longer need to be the enlightened guardians of the Earth and will be able to focus again on other worlds that need their assistance.

Beloved child, we will visit the Seventh World from the Universal Planes, and some of us will stay within this world, overlighting the Earth, offering our assistance until this is complete. This is God's plan, and through divine law, all obstacles to this will be removed. In accordance with divine will and So It Is. God's will is now done.

JOURNEY INTO THE SEVEN WORLDS

On ecstatic light rays, tenderly
we merge with you . . .
Golden filaments of your body rise

to meet the light that infuses you
deeply opening every cell . . .
We are communicating . . .
Consciousness awakening
like the sun warming the ocean . . .
A new day, a new dawn
as the golden eagle crescents above the world
every cell responds to our call
emanating murmurs, pulsating with love
from deep within the inner worlds
where we are . . .
Where I can be seen
but I may live in my hidden forms . . .
I may be unknown to you
always though, I will felt by you . . .
Will I be lost in the crack
between the worlds
forgotten by you
until you feel a pain inside?
But will you remember me
and the love I need to simply be one with you
As I call your name across the skies
I bellow like the wind, howling within
when you cry . . .
Do you not feel the others within you
their feelings and thoughts
the many parts of you?
Each one hidden in another world
dancing, playing, laughing
giggling, crying, rolling
feeling all that you can be . . .
Sometimes so beautiful

so painful . . . so joyful . . .
We are your feelings
we seek your love . . .
This is all we need . . .
Embrace your journey through the Seven Worlds . . .
Unite us within thee
and we will bring a light, deep from within
you have not known before . . .
It will awaken your remembrance
of all before
you were born . . .
Timeless realms speak to you
the silent wind links us within . . .
Your breath coils through our bodies . . .
The wings of your heart
ignite our heart . . .
We are one with you
worlds within worlds
as your spirit, we love you . . .

Journeying into the Seven Worlds of Light

As I received the discourse from the Enlightened Masters, a great wave of love, compassion, and divine wisdom came to me. Open your heart to receive this now, for it comes as a higher frequency to you. As you do this, I share from my heart an understanding about our release from the karmic wheel and how our consciousness can transform through simply loving, forgiving, and accepting all forms of ourselves.

I share this with you through the multidimensional journey of my soul as I met alternate parts of my consciousness from the other worlds. These were expressions that I met within my personality, emotions and attitudes until I journeyed more deeply within to acknowledge and love rather than judge. The true exchange of love, acceptance, and forgiveness is all that is needed to naturally shift our consciousness and balance any karma we may personally hold that lies between the worlds.

The Goddess came to me and spoke from inside me . . .

I am from the Sixth World, and I travel on the spheres of love to touch the hearts of those ready to open in love. I see the ones not ready yet, and only ask that you do not judge them. Let them be, as they need to be. It has been a long journey for them and a long time between sips of love, and they are very dry within. They are sensitive and protective of their hearts so they keep them closed, fearful of feeling what lies inside, hiding. They are not as strong as you although they may project their energy. Look more deeply and see how quickly they lose focus and the ability to truly see themselves. Take a breath and know the love is there inside them. Look a little harder behind their masks and see the soul inside, resting, hiding from the world, not ready to feel with their heart open wide. As you see their soul, bless them and know they will open when they are ready. No forcing, asking, pushing, pulling will create this. They must make the choice. Just know that in spirit, they have already said yes. This is a message I wish you to share with your world.

Quickly, she appeared in golden robes of light before me, and I was taken on a journey into a portal of light to remember and meet parts of myself. She shared there were three large aspects of myself that lived in the hidden worlds, which affected me in my everyday life as they shared my consciousness with me.

My feminine presence struggled with me deeply when I first met her in 1997 in the inner planes of the Second World. She was very tired from the sadness in the age of Lemuria and had stayed behind in the Second World, fearful that a powerful masculine force could hurt her. When I acknowledged her inside me and honored her, she felt my strength and love and forgave with me all she had witnessed in Lemuria through her experience of closing her heart and losing her feminine power. She forgave with me the feelings she had buried about the loss of soul family, and she forgave her masculine partner for leaving her and for the rage, violence, and anger he had repressed that created his lack of commitment to himself. Through acknowledging her karma and forgiving it, she reclaimed her feminine power and no longer held jealousy of other women. She opened her heart to soul family again, feeling young, in love, energized, and beautiful as a Lemurian Goddess.

This healing took place on a deep level within my being, as my beautiful partner at that time, Dreaming Heart, assisted me by holding me in his arms and loving me unconditionally. As my feminine shifted inside, I dramatically changed. I suddenly became gifted with sound, and a natural channel developed within me. My heart expanded powerfully, and it felt like every soul on Earth and every being from all worlds could now fit within my heart.

My masculine presence, when I met him within me, was very young, capable, fiery, and creative, and yet very bossy. He wanted to help others and guide them until they could guide themselves clearly. He was happy to learn with me as the Enlightened Masters visited me each day in my room. He was a part of my consciousness that had served in the councils of light overlighting Atlantis. During our training with the Enlightened Masters, he was able to release his fear of losing his power or being influenced by others and taken off his path. He was within the Fifth World as a Christ being, and following our two-year training, the first level of my mission on Earth began through his integration. Later, once he forgave humanity and their choices to hold on in fear instead of following the path of love, he opened his librarian nature again, and the Akashic records and libraries of light were suddenly accessible to me. I wondered how I was able to access so much detail in such a short time. I had simply become one with the Akasha and the libraries of light when my masculine spirit opened his heart and the understanding he needed to move forward on his path was communicated to me without any thought process or attunement, flowing out like a river of love and light when I was in his presence.

My field had changed dramatically and was now in vibrational resonance with the Akasha, in the same way the ancients of Atlantis had held resonance in group mind, via telepathy, with all others who shared the field. At this same time, the trees and nature were in deep communication with me as my telepathy expanded, and I could hear the spirits speak wherever I walked. I heard the plants sharing the truths of their medicines with me. This was in 1998, when I started to write and to create world-wide linkups based on the portals of the Earth, and to gift humanity with blessings for the evolution of all beings.

The Egyptian aspects of my Presence were a little more difficult to meet. They were very present, gifted, and wise, yet living as hermits, and it took me five years to meet all of them. They were parts of myself I had left behind from my only physical, Earth-based lifetime. Physically traveling to Egypt in 2005 was a deep part of this process. Mapping the primary portals of the Earth, the creation matrix, and reconnecting deeply with the ancestors and the rainbow serpent mother of creation that lived in the First World was another. Working with groups over one-year periods in mystery school trainings to clear the karma of the loss of the mystery school system from Egypt was another. Continuing to travel around the world to specific portals to offer the work of the Enlightened Masters to others who came as representatives of humanity and the collective was another. Meeting my source twin flame and uniting and separating with unconditional love, friendship, support, blessings, gratitude, grace, peace, healing, and forgiveness, supported the next stage of this, and healing the loss of my sexuality that had taken place when I united with my twin flame was another aspect of this karmic clearing. Finally, as I embraced and released the fear of financial responsibility and greed and fears of beings that carried a presence of authority, this completed the balancing of my Egyptian karma from this previous life where I had been a teacher.

These Egyptian aspects loved the work I cocreated with the Enlightened Masters during this period. It reminded them of the holy presence of God's love they had experienced in Egypt. They loved the innocence I held with the work and the love that was shared as many Enlightened Masters of immense power and wisdom would connect with others through me. They remembered the beauty and innocence of humanity and forgave themselves for closing down and for not completing their Earth mission.

They finally all let go, in divine timing. Over the five years as parts of the karma were forgiven, great changes would take place in my life and new gifts of teaching would manifest in my being. I had experiences of nirvana and *samadhi*, states of bliss and enlightenment. My multidimensional bodies would expand and I would enter deep bliss on a cellular level. The tantric energies of my body were activated through many higher centers. Whenever I returned from journeys into the other worlds where I met these parts of myself with the Enlightened Masters, sacred gifts would immediately open in my awareness, easily and naturally as if I had always known how to use them, even though they were a completely new experience in this life. I was on the Path of Illumination, a form of rapid acceleration that was granted to those who wished to benefit the Earth and experience bliss.

After these five years and the final creation and delivery of the EASE (Energy Attunement Science of Enlightenment) Program, I was able to birth the Divine University Project with others. I was able to feel supported in a deeper way to cocreate the first stage of this project, which would guide and direct my life mission. The founder in me birthed through the healing, release, and integration of these ones from the Second World that united with me in Divine Presence via the heart expansion of true, deep forgiveness.

It was through meeting these three very different parts of my consciousness that my life direction was clarified. Embracing these three aspects gently and choosing to love them allowed me to birth myself and allowed my puzzle piece in the Divine Plan to emerge. This experience prepared me for my work with humanity and birthed world compassion for all beings, which I had not known before in this life.

The Divine Plan for the Earth carries within it the Divine Plan for humanity. It carries the personal plan for your divine nature to open and birth, blossom and develop. This is known as the Divine Plan of your soul, and it naturally unfolds when you surrender to your heart and Presence and make clearing your karma your highest priority.

What other purpose do we have but to love, and how can we truly love when karma lies between another and us? We only truly love by embracing the karma and forgiving all that is bound by it. This frees our hearts and creates our hearts to expand and grow larger. Within the worlds of light, you exist in many forms, and the Divine Plan holds the keys to your liberation from all forms that bind you. These forms are held in Mother Earth's portal system for you, and each time you forgive and a heart awakening takes place, all in your soul family who have shared karmic experiences with you also receive their consciousness returning to them.

She spoke gently within me, whispering and blessing me. I was deep inside, simply present with her every move . . . this beautiful Goddess in her golden robes of light, shining by my side, so present with me, so loving, patient, and kind. She looked deeply into my eyes, into the oceans of my soul. She spoke her name to me, as Gaia. Tears flowed from my eyes as she spoke to me, and I felt her pure love hold me.

> You, our dear child, have helped many become free and open their hearts so easily, just through truly healing and lifting the karma of your soul, and this is the gift of liberty you have given to the Earth Mother, our child. For each time just one soul like yourself releases from the karmic wheel, families connected to them and souls who have also shared lives with them in other worlds are also lifted from the wheel of karma or given a wheel of grace to help them complete this task.
>
> The interconnection and oneness you hold is your power. Never forget that the unity you hold inside is the key to this planetary shift into the higher dimensions. It is this that is lifting the veils of karma from Mother Earth's body. As this occurs, her etheric body is able to support the regeneration of her physical body and the ignition of light in the deep pockets of the Earth and lines of light where she is lacking her natural resource and energy.

I overlight the evolution on Earth as Mother Gaia, and my role is to let the feminine light in to flow and support the Earth Mother. Take my hand and allow me to guide you into the sacred womb of the mother where I will always connect to you. There you may always bring any part or call to any part of yourself from any of the worlds within the Earth, and I will fill them with you and unite you as one again, heal any pain, and lift any suffering. This is my promise to you and all others who live on the Earth. I will be with you and guide your way to call these ones back into your heart and guide you with what you may need to forgive, and help them forgive. Know as you work with me in your own way, I will gracefully take these ones into the womb of the Holy Mother where they may leave their wounds or memories of pain behind. Guide your other selves, parts that may hold karma or feel they are lost spiritually, mentally, emotionally, or physically within your world of love and light. Know you are their guide. Guide their way into the light.

Let them know the grace is there. Trust them to care and want to transform and love again, to awaken to their truth again. This is all I ask of you, to gently call for them to meet you in the Temple of Divine Presence, where they may be blessed by my gifts, to shed the old energy and consciousness that may karmically bind them from experiencing love and oneness. Set the intention now within your heart and know I live within you and all of life on Earth. I am the Goddess inside the Earth Mother, her overlighting Presence or Holy Spirit. I am Gaia.

GAIA'S BLESSING

Tenderly I breathe
not to touch the wings of a moth
who so delicately lies still and asleep
dreaming inside
every fiber of me . . .
She travels like a free butterfly, inside the worlds I gift her
although her wings lie still, her soul so far away
she is conscious of me, my needs in every way . . .

She is like a dear child to me
her every wish is my wish . . .
As her spirit wishes for another body
it is my heart's blessing to deliver this . . .
As her wings crumble into dust and her body fades away
my soil enriched by her gift
a new breath, a new life form is given
her spirit reawakens . . .
She is but a small mouse birthing in a small house
children playing outside . . .
Bells are ringing
as this small mouse is being fed
a world through new eyes . . .
No longer a moth, she says . . .
How further she can travel now
how longer she can live?
A new paradise of opportunity
it is this life I give . . .
The blessing of life is mine to give and take away
only through the wish of the sweet child
each divine spirit . . .
Take me by the hand and allow our hearts to kiss . . .
Take me into your heart and allow your breath to be mine . . .
Take me far inside of you
so I may take you into my worlds of light
and astonish you . . .
The blessing is your life . . .
It is sanctuary for your soul
This is my gift of love
that which I bless your soul with . . .
Withhold none of your joy
let your life be your greatest gift
for it is only temporary . . .

CHAPTER FOUR

Our Potential: The New Human Being—
Our Evolutionary Path

Humanity is changing. This change begins within each soul's conscious-ness and DNA as karma is cleared via the conscious decision to make peace and love the highest priority. The universal wisdom of the ancients, utilized when humanity was at its peak in each previous civilization, is now returning to many on Earth. More and more people are accessing this wisdom as their higher self or super-consciousness is activated. The frontal lobe of the human brain, particularly the prefrontal cortex, is a center for higher awareness and is being activated again.

Your own brain structure is being rewired by the collective that you are energetically one with, via the unified field and the collective consciousness that lives within this field. All that occurs within the collective is affecting you whether you are aware of it or not. You are affecting it in the same way. It is altering as you alter your primary focus in life toward love and peace. You are extremely powerful. All choices you make during your life are either seeding the light into the collective or seeding fear if you give your power away to that which you find difficult to love or embrace with forgiveness.

As you make higher choices based on opening your heart, you activate your super-consciousness to ground as pure light into your brain chemistry. This ignites the codons of light in each cell, which switch on new centers of compassion, generosity, charity, humility, unconditional love, wisdom, intelligence, peace, and creativity. Each time this happens, the transformation of your mind and body is aligned to your highest potential evolution.

Your choice is the key. What do you choose? This is a question the Enlightened Masters asked me throughout my training with them. Whenever I was in a difficult situation that had the potential to bring back a large part of my consciousness to me and to anchor more love and wisdom, they would ask me to choose my reality, always asking me to receive from within what I was needing to acknowledge or needing to do to balance the karma and transform any situation. This training in activating my higher conscious state was very specific, and it involved never giving my power to the Enlightened Masters or to anyone, no matter how amazing they seemed. This enabled me to recognize God within as my Presence and to always seek all through my direct contact to Source within, via my own Presence.

Over the last fourteen years on this journey of awakening, my brain chemistry has shifted so that thought does not takes place in the same way it used to. There are no rushing thoughts, only stillness that opens at times for the voice of wisdom to speak from within. The inner voice is clear, and telepathic contact is now my major form of communication.

Over many years of soul travel and karmic clearing, a great void developed inside my mind sphere. The original thoughts and beliefs of my soul were transformed to love as both hemispheres of my brain began working as one. This transformation of the brain is also part of our collective evolutionary process.

This journey into a higher-conscious state is taking place for many light seeds on Earth. This book hopes to be a form of grace for these ones, for the journey can feel quite strange indeed. Some even close down their journey of evolution because they fear these deep experiences or because someone suggests they must be unbalanced. Our spiritual experiences bring the return of the sacred gifts we hold, as our vaster consciousness awakens our DNA and cells to the light of our Holy Spirit.

I remember the day when Spirit first contacted me. I was living in a tepee community on seven thousand acres with only twenty others. It was twenty years ago, when my daughter was only two to three years old. Our tepees were scattered along three miles of the river, in among the pine trees and she-oaks and the big boulders. Behind us a ridge of smoky quartz held us in oneness. It was in the autumn, a very beautiful time by the river and lush after the summer. Dreamtime was always special here, during the sunset. It was a time when Spirit was very strong, and the hum of the mountains was like a song, singing all in the valley, preparing all to enter the dreamtime. Often we were by the fire at this time. The fire guided a great deal of our daily life ritual.

I was in my tepee and lighting the fire. I heard many sounds outside that I did not recognize, and rustling or sounds of animals scuttling away. Then the wind blew up like something was coming my way. I was expecting a sudden storm, but outside there were no clouds in the sky. I went back inside to the fire and everything became very quiet. I could hear no sound. In the bush, this was not usual as there were always the cicadas or some sounds of life, night and day. From the power of the quiet, I became entranced by the fire. I felt time stand still. In these moments, a spirit man with an owl face crouched through my small tepee door and looked within. He saw me, came in, and squatted by the fire while staring into my eyes. It was like he had found me and was satisfied.

He was part owl and part man, an indigenous-looking spirit man with a part tawny frogmouth owl face and wings curling around his bare back. He was a beautiful being, but I was taken deeply aback. He was naked apart from a skin hanging around his waist, and a spirit who held a great deal of influence on the elements. Each time he moved, the wind responded loudly as if his movements directed the wind. I crouched still in awe for what must have been a few minutes. He did not speak out loud, although within my mind I could hear every word he wanted me to hear. This was my first telepathic experience. I was rigid, unable to move, crouched by the fire next to him. He made me feel safe with his words; he was loving and kind, yet strong. He had come to teach me and ask me to live in harmony with him.

He blew into the fire and I saw a vision of myself as a spirit woman of owl medicine, of wisdom. As I was suspended in time, unable to move, I felt my whole being change through the transmission he gave me. An amazing frequency ignited me to remember the owl wisdom. I was being prepared for something. This I knew. He had come to ask me to be aware I was living on protected land where the Yowie, a master of the dreamtime, did sacred ceremony. He shared that no woman or man had lived on this land before; not even the indigenous people stayed here, for it was too strong. To stay, I needed to use my owl medicine and tell others also to live consciously or else the land would release us and we would be shown that we had to go. Then like the wind he was gone out of my tepee and back into the trees.

I was unfrozen and freed to realize the shock I was in. I sat down and took deep breaths to integrate. Tawny frogmouth owls were on the land in large numbers, and I knew then that they were the totem or guardians of the land. I lived for another four years on the land, and from that day forth, I lived with the sense that the guardians were communicating telepathically with me, showing me the way to be in harmony. When I look back now, I know he was of Middle Earth, from the Second World. I am now aware these spirits travel from the other dimensions out through trees, which are sometimes energy vortices to Middle Earth or Inner Earth. The following year, after I had moved my tepee seasonally and was settled in another camp, I was blessed to have the veils open between the worlds again. In the distance I witnessed the Yowie doing ceremony not far from where I had been camped when the spirit man visited. The Yowie was giant and his hair was so long. I witnessed him dancing on the Earth and calling up the fire spirit, turning to a golden fire and then turning red as the fire spirit grew stronger and arose from the Earth. The Yowie showered the spiritual energy in every direction for healing and clearing the Earth. Nature was shining radiantly as the Yowie did his blessing.

More and more, these experiences of deep contact are taking place on Earth. The Earth spirit is waking up humanity and more and more people are sharing their otherworldly contacts with angels, archangels, Enlightened Masters, star beings, and Earth spirits. Often, of course, nobody believes this until they have an experience themselves, but then they can no longer doubt the authenticity of Spirit in nonhuman form.

I was speaking with a close friend recently who shared she had been blind and deaf to Spirit for many years, until she had an experience that opened her spiritual eyes. Her karma had held her in this state of blindness, and although these higher-consciousness beings had been helping her entire life, she had not recognized them until this day.

She was sitting in an early morning meditation, simply releasing the flow of energy from within her heart that would bring all she needed to live in the grace of her divinity that day. Her heart always glowed at the thought of the Earth Mother's love for all of humanity. As her own heart connection opened into the Earth's heart below, up through this doorway they rose—majestic mountains of varying heights, the physical mountains of Earth. Layers upon layers of mountain peaks grew and encircled her with great poise. She was in awe that she could see them moving, rising up all around her.

Tears welled up inside, for the mighty mountains had called to her through her entire life. Her heart had always opened at the sight of a rock face exposing the Earth Mother's heart. She had even shared with me the grief she felt that she was unable to commune with the spirits of the mountains consciously. Now she had been blessed in response to her prayers. Her soul wept deeply as a doorway opened into another reality.

The mountains took her back to the beginning of time here, when they had birthed from the void to bring form and structure to the Earth, for the Goddess to have her expression in a physical form.

This experience was truly beautiful but it was the loving service and the faith she gave to Spirit in her everyday life that prepared her to receive it. As she met her Divine Presence and the truth that she could experience her higher consciousness, she was supported to accept her power of Spirit more deeply as a human being, and to accept how loved she truly was.

As a spiritual teacher, I meet many souls; some are just awakening, some have been conscious of the presence of Spirit for some time, and others have been on the spiritual path for a very long time. They are all souls doing great work, whether it be in their own homes with their families, in their communities, or around the world. The truth I have noticed is that it does not matter how long you have been awakened as a soul to the self-realization that Spirit exists. In fact, the ones who carry the most innocence or nonattachment to having an experience, or those who simply open their hearts in the moment, are usually the ones who come to me with stories of amazing spiritual experiences.

Each journey has taken place either on a sacred site, in meditation, through sacred sounding, through a guided journey, healing, visitation, or teaching based on enlightened frequency, or after a deep emotional release. Each of these souls has wished to piece this part of their puzzle into their daily lives to give it meaning and to integrate the experience. They have shared stories of feeling the incredible energy of Spirit merge with them, of feeling tall and powerful inside.

Others speak of feeling their body go into ecstasy and filling with tingling energy inside every cell. Some describe their heart expanding with love for all beings. Others have felt themselves grow into giant spheres, larger than the Earth, and still others have the experience of levitating. Some have had visions of themselves in different lightbodies and in other realities, and through the Enlightened Masters' meditations and teachings have met and healed these different forms of themselves.

Others have met angels or received profound love from the blessing of an Enlightened Master or the Holy Mother. Others have received messages, wisdom, or downloads of divine truth through their inner voice. Some have experienced being heavy and feeling like they were giants, filled with rock or lava—ancestral and ancient, unable to move from the power of the energy. Others have flown through the galaxies as beams of light in their merkabahs, as angels and archangels took them to other realms.

Still others have described journeys inside the Earth, to crystal caves, temples, and cities of light, where they were met by beings of light. Some felt like they completely dissolved for a period of time, and when they returned they were different. Others entered deep peace, feeling the light like a pillar through their body, and yet others met the Enlightened Masters or their Presence on the inner planes. The list of spiritual experiences goes on and on, as our spirit is an infinite, all-expansive inner force.

Each of these experiences offers a soul a divine transmission or a new frequency that invisibly fills them. Such spiritual awakenings ignite the brain chemistry to liberate the higher centers of consciousness within the brain structure. This process can also occur in the dream state. Many have come to me over the years, sharing dreams they have had in which my Presence offered them a healing and describing how after the dream, things became easier for them. The transmissions offered by Spirit support chakra growth and ignite a soul to be deeply guided in life by their Holy Spirit.

These forms of spiritual experiences happen daily to people all over the planet, and the fact that more people than ever are interested and open to their self-development is a primary sign that the awakening is taking place. This is not a fad, but a revolution of the heart. There is a timing for everyone, which is related to the Divine Plan, the unlocking of the genetic code, and the shift to the next level of consciousness. The opening of the heart is the key, but without the clearing of the karma, the opening of the heart is created with great struggle and pain.

Our evolution is based on our contact with this super-consciousness, our contact with Spirit. This contact is being received at home, at work, in light centers, churches, or other spiritual centers, on sacred sites, while giving birth, while healing, while someone is passing over, and in all situations in life. There is no activity that Spirit is not utilizing to awaken humanity. Even the activities that seem to be of a lower resonance or unhealthy for self-development are being utilized by Spirit to awaken souls to the light. There is no doorway that Spirit will not go through. I remember some years ago a beautiful girl coming to me as one of my students. I was sad to hear that a representative of another spiritual organization, which was based on the Enlightened Masters' teachings, had rejected her from receiving their teachings. She had been told that as she had taken drugs in this life she would not be able to ascend. She was deeply distressed in my presence with this great worry. I shared with her that the power of forgiveness blazes through and heals all in life, and we are always able to return from any experience to our essence, truth, and love.

I continued to share, "There is no doorway you have walked through that will take you away from the path of your soul's ascension into the fifth dimension. Everything is connected, and even that which may appear to have been a mistake is no mistake. All is a learning. It is what you do with the learning that matters. Your past experiences with drugs may help others who now take drugs, when your learning is complete with this. There is a purpose for all experiences as all experiences can lead to wisdom." She was relieved, and I turned and saw through the spiritual planes Saint Germaine, smiling kindly, asking for the forgiveness of those who place their own truths upon the Enlightened Masters' teachings.

As you embrace your own path and your lessons in life and work with your super-consciousness through the awareness that a higher truth will appear to you, you are choosing to receive your super-consciousness as a form of guidance inside you. When we give over to this higher awareness, we choose to recognize that even though our mind may tell us one thing and our soul may feel another, there is a higher self that links our mind and heart in a unified view that serves not only ourselves but all beings.

What does this really mean? The super-consciousness is the higher spiritual awareness that carries a soul's living genius. It emanates as a higher frequency of light. Just as the sun emanates this higher frequency of light through its plasma rings and offers us a primary source of energy for all life on Earth, so does your spirit share the divine consciousness and light to create your soul growth. The sun supports our physical development as well as all levels of our growth. It is one of the doorways that our spirit travels through to anchor on the Earth. The sun feeds light to the cells of our body and into our eyes for cellular regeneration, and also delivers higher frequencies for the awakening of our super-consciousness if we connect our chakras to it.

Those with underdeveloped chakra systems are limited in their capacity to access their consciousness, as the chakras are the receivers, transmitters, and generators of our consciousness. The chakras act as doorways for our universal consciousness to ground into our bodies. Our spirit travels from universal centers such as the sun into our chakras in the form of light frequency. Anchoring your super-consciousness through underdeveloped chakras is like trying to squeeze a whole watermelon through a sieve. Just as a sieve is useless on a whole watermelon, underdeveloped chakras do not allow the free flow of Spirit through the body.

In our Earth-based sciences, human evolution has most often been described in terms of our physical development. The evolution of our consciousness and the awakening of our higher dimensional gifts has not often been explored. The human body is an amazing creation, yet the human energy field and its ability to evolve rapidly is the true source of all evolution. Universal energy science connects the physical body with the human energy field and fills in the missing links in our Earth-based sciences. The Enlightened Masters' description of the universal energy science of consciousness is based on the understanding that the universe is created from five elements, or specific energies and frequencies. These elements are prana, Christ light, plasma, voidal frequency, and source frequency.

The Enlightened Masters share that every form of life is made from these energies and frequencies and that our human energy field evolves through the interaction of these five energies within our chakras and the DNA chemistry within the cells of our physical body. Mother Earth feeds prana into our fields and this is then fed to each cell. The sun feeds us the

Christ light and this is then fed into our fields to create our minds, souls, and bodies to harmonize as one. The inner core of all stars and galaxies, our Earth, the sun, and the moon feed us the radiations of plasma, which is likened to a cosmic fire. This is then fed to our soul, body, and mind to ignite our personal power and increase the rate and amount of vibrational energy flowing through our body and field.

The moon and many celestial centers and the Earth core open us to receive the voidal frequency, which is pure love. This is then fed into our fields to create our minds, souls, bodies, and spirits to unite as one. Source frequency is received from the unified field of life when our hearts are open and the light within our heart chakra is activated. This is then fed through our fields into our souls, minds, bodies, and spirits to enlighten them. This frequency can only be received from within.

The unified field of life feeds us these five energies when our own field is open and receptive. Our evolution is based on how we connect to the universe via our human energy field. As these universal energies flow more purely through each one of us, our consciousness is released and our gifts are developed.

Life is a continual experience of energy exchange. Within every environment you enter, you are either exchanging energy and consciousness via your human energy field or you are being protective and closing down your personal energy field, which limits your receptivity.

The Enlightened Masters speak of the physical body as a living library of consciousness that temporarily houses the soul. They share that for those awakened on the path of conscious evolution, the body also enters a process of preparing to house the spirit in a more concentrated form. This is known as the embodiment of your Divine Presence. As this embodiment process occurs, souls experience divine energy transmissions and regular spiritual contact, and begin to consciously connect as a worldbridger. Extraordinary gifts begin to awaken, allowing these souls access to their spiritual power.

The evolution of our cells, minds, souls, and hearts is the true purpose of our lives on Earth. Once our chakras have developed to a level where our consciousness experiences itself as light, the embodiment of Presence can take place easily and freely. This manifests through the liberation of our karma and the raising of our vibration so the larger consciousness of our spirit may ground into the cells of our physical body and field. As this shift into a higher state of consciousness occurs, humanity becomes empowered with its true spiritual nature, with qualities such as kindness, generosity, charity, unconditional love, peacefulness, intelligence, wisdom, and creativity.

As children, we grow not only physically but also spiritually. Our chakras develop and form from the ages of zero to twenty-one years to support us to develop our consciousness as adults. Upon birth, our consciousness expresses through one large chakra—our heart chakra. During the ages of zero to seven, if we receive the love frequency from our mother's transmission to us, the crystalline nature of several new chakras develops in our field. Through this exchange of frequency, our base chakra begins to develop at three years old, our *hara* develops at four years old, and our crown chakra begins to develop at the age of five.

If we do not receive the love frequency from our mother, these chakras are not able to develop, and thus we are unable to access the holistic consciousness of our soul. We become more deeply influenced by the patterns of consciousness held within our genetic line, and we are more limited in our expression and the development of our personalities.

The Enlightened Masters share that during the time of our conception our energy field is blueprinted and begins to develop according to our parents' etheric-body blueprints. All that is held in our parents' etheric bodies at the time of our conception is passed down to us as they encode our newly birthing energy field with their consciousness and chakras. It is in this way that both parents weave a new energy body for their child during the process of conception. All star beings and souls of the fifth dimension are able to emanate unconditional love as their first response to life. They also carry this basic understanding of the true development of a child and its spiritual, emotional, mental, and physical formation into an adult. This grants them compassion for all souls, as they are aware that some souls received the blueprinting of a potent form of family karma and are therefore limited in their awareness, thoughts, and actions.

Our human evolution is initiated first by the frequency of love, from the time we are conceived and our physical body begins to form within our mother's womb. The period from zero to seven years is known as a child's journey through their divine mother initiation. Recent studies of the development of children's neural pathways within their brains are beginning to show us that our human brains develop most fully when we receive loving touch as babies and are in loving environments. As a child receives the love, they are seeded to ground the love or love themselves as beings.

It is this love that is needed to create the chakra development so a child can keep their heart open (heart chakra), ground themselves in their body (base chakra), stay connected and protected in their energy field (hara chakra), and hold their connection to their spirit (crown chakra). Each time love is exchanged from mother to child, these four chakras are seeded to grow and expand for the child's conscious development.

As the child grows older, they begin to enter what is known as the divine father initiation, from seven to fourteen years old. Through these years, as the light frequency of their father or a father figure activates their chakras, they develop their solar plexus for the grounding of their intelligence and mind, the brow for their higher vision and ability to link and unite all ideas and information together for a higher purpose, the throat for their communication, their Earth star and feet chakras for grounding their light, their sacral chakra for their creative power to ground, their thymus for their connection to soul family and relationships, their soul star for interstellar connections to the universe, and the link chakra for the integration of all parts of self during their life journey. If their father or father figure is honest, truthful, and positive in regard to his communication with his child, the child's chakras will develop to allow greater expressions of their consciousness.

The highest form of evolution for a child at age fourteen is to have twelve primary chakras activated and to be receiving the love and light frequency from both parents. If this is the case, the child will be multitalented and will have no fear of expressing their light wherever they place their energy, whether it be in academics, socializing, sports, or public speaking.

Between fourteen and twenty-one years of age, we enter our Holy Spirit initiation as we ground our spirit and develop our personas and our social connections with the world. It is at this time that we begin to come out of the arms of our parents and enter our community as individuals. During this time we receive our KA body, our merkabah, and our RA body, which support the grounding of our spirit and the loving development of our feminine and masculine energy and our mental, emotional, and spiritual bodies.

Our KA body, a spiritual body that activates at fourteen years old, offers our soul the ability to ignite our spiritual current and passion of creativity and access our soul gifts. Our merkabah is our light vehicle, activated at sixteen years old, that allows our soul and spirit to unite and travel interdimensionally. Our RA body, a spiritual body that activates at eighteen years old, offers our soul the ability to ground our spirit into our body and ground our higher self connection and personal empowerment.

Our fields expand deeply at this time if we have received the love from our mother or a mother figure and the light, wisdom, and truth from our father or a father figure. Our awareness grows, and our connection to the world is made through the spiritual qualities we begin to naturally develop. If we have underdeveloped chakras when our spirit begins to anchor, we often suffer from psychological, emotional, or mental fears, and instead of developing confidence, we develop insecurities about our life or ourselves.

Some children get lost on this journey, while others do well and reach their potential. Some find their way through but do not develop to the greatest potential that a full set of developed chakras would have offered them. These ones always feel like a part of them is missing. That part of them is simply their spirit, which just wasn't able to squeeze its way through their underdeveloped chakras.

As adults, either our super-consciousness has grounded and we feel passionate about life and deeply connected to the world, our community, our family, and our own heart, or we are still in the process of grounding our spirit. At the age of twenty-one, the blueprints in our chakra systems are set to a specific vibrational frequency and level of consciousness. It is this level of consciousness that many adults spend years healing or transforming, simply because as children they did not receive the love and light frequency transmissions from their parents.

In such cases the parents were often not able to be nurturing or emanate love because they themselves had not received these transmissions from their own parents, nor had their parents received the love, nor their parents' parents . . . all the way down through the genetic line. This is where the forgiveness is needed first: in the forgiveness of one's parents and ancestors for not being able to be honest and emanate the light. As we forgive this, we are able to forgive ourselves for not always being able to emanate light for our own children. This begins the process of clearing the genetic line as we honor the truth that if one did not receive the love, it is very hard to pass it along to others within the family line.

Karma is the primary force that limits the development of the chakras in childhood. When the parents carry karma with each other, or the child's soul carries karma with one or more of the parents, this blocks the heart connection and the sharing of light and love frequency. Imagine that your soul has large golden cords of light that extend from your heart to both your parents' heart chakras. These soul cords can never be broken, but when they are filled with karma or unresolved feelings, thoughts, and memories, they can feel very broken.

When two souls have a child together, their hearts are eternally connected by this soul cord, and they each have another eternal soul cord to the child. All that has occurred between two souls in all lifetimes is held within the soul cord; the love as well as the karma is held in the cord. If there is unresolved karma, it can affect every level of the relationship, because it blocks the soul cord from flowing with energy.

The family karma is held in the soul cords between all family members.

When there is a lot of family karma, the soul cords are blocked and the exchange of love and the expression of truth are limited. A blocked soul cord can also prevent the children from receiving from their parents the energy needed for full chakra development. When the soul cords are cleared of the karma, the child and parents will begin to establish a brand-new relationship based on unconditional love and acceptance.

The Enlightened Masters share that the super-consciousness can be received by every soul as long as they awaken their consciousness and begin to clear their karma. As the chakras grow to their original potential and the soul forgives their childhood, accepting that all experiences that limited them were their own karma, then the soul is freed to receive their higher-self connection and their spirit's power of light and wisdom. When the chakras begin to open, the great clearing process can create fear until the soul realizes that this is simply one leg on the journey of soul freedom. Once this period of fear is complete, the soul can begin to master living in their heart connection. The heart then becomes the central instrument for establishing intelligence, and greater light frequencies are attracted from suns, moons, and universal centers for the next level of the soul's evolution.

When we have these huge heart-opening experiences, our bodies begin to transmute the old storehouse of fears, jealousies, grief, and anger that have been repressed in the cells of the body due to the karma of our soul or our ancestors being trapped in our underdeveloped chakras. This process is known as the cleansing of cellular memory, and it can create fatigue in the body as the unresolved emotions shift from the cellular structure and the body opens to allow the flow of the light of one's Holy Spirit.

DNA activation and the ignition of a new brain chemistry are also a part of this awakening process. As our chakras grow larger, becoming conduits for vaster frequencies of light, our cellular structure begins to alchemize and initiate our DNA light codings, and our DNA filaments lengthen, allowing us to access and ground more of our higher consciousness through our body and energy field. This transformational process activates the original codings of God consciousness within our DNA and turns on a switch in our consciousness that creates the shift into the fifth dimension of light.

Receiving Frequency Transmissions— Opening the Higher Centers of the Brain

I was lying on the Earth, meditating with the sun, central sun, and great central sun by opening my energy body and aligning my central pillar of chakras to the Earth core and these suns. This had been my process for opening my consciousness to the Holy Spirit for many years. As I journeyed deeper inside, receiving the divine energy that the Earth core and suns provide, I began to feel embodied by my Divine Presence. A deep, blissful current ran through all my cells, and I felt the light and consciousness of myself from many worlds and dimensions concentrate within my field and physical body. I became aware of many beings around me beginning to gather in a circle to communicate with me. I was used to these experiences and knew there was a higher reason they were there. Tall and beautiful beings of light stood around me like a beautiful family. They were star beings, and they began to communicate to me.

"We have come from the great central sun. We are emissaries who work with the Enlightened Masters. We have been asked to support you to enter a new brain frequency or receive a higher dimensional field that will allow your brain chemistry to activate the new higher centers of consciousness you will need for your future work."

They took what appeared to me to be a small golden spoon made of pure light and carefully placed it in the core of my brain. One of the gifts that had opened within me some years before was my seership or ability to see into the dimensions and into the physical, cellular structure. I began to witness the rewiring of my brain chemistry. The golden spoon, which was made of a frequency I had not received before, opened a central vortex within the corpus callosum of my brain that linked my two hemispheres. This vortex appeared dark to me, but as the golden spoon merged into it, elixirs of source frequency poured forth, and the dark energy began to dissipate. The star beings shared with me that the dark energy was simply made of memories of the deepest trauma or fears that had been sealed away in my DNA by my ancestors. Apparently this dark energy had been blocking my hemispheres from truly communicating, and although I was extremely telepathic, there was a higher form of communication that humanity could achieve when the corpus callosum functions as a center of light within the brain.

As the energy within this central vortex began to flow with pure light, it began to emanate golden filaments. I witnessed these fine, hairlike filaments extend through both hemispheres of my brain, linking them. In four regions, connecting to the lobes of my brain, these filaments began to spiral together and braid, linking and twisting like fine fibers of silicon, forming conduits in spiral rotations. I witnessed each cell of my brain fill with light and the field it emanated turn violet, then golden, then magenta, then silver, then platinum. Platinum frequency instantly began to flood in from the universe, and a platinum liquid fire or plasma began to mold my brain into a new design. A higher brain was forming. My frontal lobe was opening, and the energy was so profound I was unable to move my body. I was held fixed where I lay on the Earth.

"You are having surgery, dear one," said the tallest emissary of the group. "It will take about another hour to complete. Just allow your breath to sustain you as you receive the energy and ground it through your body. You are receiving your platinum brain, which will gift you the higher communication you need for your work to take place."

I had already surrendered to the experience, but hearing how long it would take allowed me to surrender more deeply to the bliss. My brain was growing in every moment, as I was witnessing it. I found this profound, witnessing the evolution taking place. What a privilege I had been given. My eyes became sore for a moment, and a pressure built in the base of my brain and through my upper neck. I witnessed them place a golden disk in the base of my brain, and suddenly another central vortex opened. I could see the dark energy again begin to transform as the golden disk spun gently into the central vortex. The pain released, and a freedom was felt within the base of my skull and neck that was unlike anything I had ever experienced. He continued to speak to me, and I received this message through my inner voice. The loving, peaceful frequency he spoke with had become so much a part of my daily life that I simply accepted his gifting to me.

He was speaking about my cerebellum. "This is the center that holds the majority of a human being's unconscious memories. We are clearing unconscious memories that were sealed into the DNA by your ancestors. They have been stored in the cerebellum until they could be unsealed and released. You have unlocked the genetic code in your physical body through healing all with your family and through your clearing of your personal karma, our dear child. The unlocking of your brain chemistry may now truly occur. You will not drop into states of lower consciousness after this, and your brain function will be holding the higher communication centers open. There are four centers in the brain that coordinate the primary activations for raising consciousness. Other centers of the brain are essential, but these four are specifically needed to open for the higher levels of communication and the grounding of one's super-consciousness. They are the corpus callosum, the cerebellum, the prefrontal cortex, and the thalamus. You have been freeing your thalamus and igniting your prefrontal cortex through your karmic clearing. We are opening your corpus callosum and cerebellum to complete the transformation of your higher centers of awareness so you may travel and be a bridge for new forms of education and communication to ground from the enlightened realms."

I drifted into a state of sleep as the energy became stronger and their work continued. I awoke realizing that they had put me to sleep so I could receive the surgery more deeply by allowing my body to rest and my brain to enter a different energy cycle. As I woke, the streams of light between me, the trees, the grass, the sky, and the Earth below me seemed so large and wide. I felt like I had become interconnected to the universe in a way that I had not previously experienced. Sananda and Germaine, who were training me at the time, appeared and spoke to me.

"Your time has come. We will now take you into the world, and programs of new education and divine assistance will be created via this new form of communication that you have been given. We will share consciousness with you wherever you go, and the work we ask you to do in the creation of these new educational programs will carry the frequency needed to illuminate, activate, energize, and initiate the new human being on Earth. This frequency will be transmitted by you, as your bridge between the worlds is now fully open. The programs you will be offering and creating will be unique and specifically designed for one thing—the shift of your collective into the fifth dimension. The higher communication you now hold is with us in every moment, and you will walk the Earth with others hand in hand with you, and such love, we say, will be experienced by others and you."

As they stood in the paddock with me, I began to see the world of light and the physical world as no longer separate from each other. I began to see the physical world as simply an extension of the world of light, and humanity as one large group gathered around me in the world of light. I saw into their eyes and hearts, into their souls. I saw they were willing to enlighten their world, but some simply did not know how. I felt all of them speak to me from their hearts, saying three simple words: "We are ready." I looked into their eyes and felt them asking me to trust my fellow humanity. I opened my heart and chose on that day to trust humanity. This provided the foundation for my work of creating educational programs, delivering frequency transmissions and facilitating group experiences with the Enlightened Masters.

The experience of receiving higher frequency transmissions specifically designed for the evolution of our consciousness is an amazing opportunity we are given at this time. Yet, so much fear is releasing from the Earth's field that many light seeds become caught in duality, and many become frustrated or triggered by the smallest things. When a light seed is affected by the collective karma of the Earth, they start to take things personally, and all of the light that would otherwise have brought them great happiness is instead directed into life's dramas. When a light seed becomes affected by duality, their perceptions are based on beliefs about what is right and what is wrong. This can create a light seed to become very tired, and some will stop opening themselves deeply for fear they will be caught up in life's little dramas or dualities.

Receiving the frequency directly through your chakras shifts your consciousness, and you simply begin to start having self-realizations that naturally guide you to make the changes within. Without direct frequency transmissions, our cellular vibration will not rise, and we may feel like we have placed so much energy into clearing our karma and yet it never seems to fully complete. It is the frequency transmissions that create the transformation of our brain chemistry so our shift into the fifth dimension, where we hold unconditional love as our first response to all, can stabilize and complete.

The Brain's Energy Field and Consciousness

The brain chemistry of the human being is delicate and complex in its design, for humanity's brain holds the ability to establish a signal that attracts consciousness from beyond the dimensions of our physical space and time. As our brain's field raises or alters its vibrational resonance, we attract the consciousness of the more enlightened aspects of our spirit, and this lights up our brain chemistry and awakens new experiences within our mind. In accordance with the vibrational resonance of the brain's energy field, your brain attracts consciousness from your collective field of consciousness. This creates the linking of your mind to other forms of your consciousness in other worlds, also known as fractal selves.

Imagine your brain's field to be like an antenna in your own personal energy field. In accordance with the level of frequency the antenna is emanating, it attracts other signals carrying the same frequency of consciousness from the field of the collective consciousness.

This is how our thoughts are shared and psychic energy transfers through our collective. This is also how you share consciousness with your dimensional selves in other worlds. The strength of our brain's field determines what thoughts we attract into our minds from the field of our collective consciousness.

If your brain holds a higher frequency field, it attracts and integrates higher levels of consciousness and begins to integrate your super-consciousness from the more enlightened forms of your spirit. This takes place through your energy body's connection to Mother Earth's higher dimensional grids. If your brain holds a lower frequency field, and resonates to the lower dimensional grids of the Earth, it attracts and integrates lower levels of consciousness such as the unresolved unconscious thoughts or fears connected to your collective karma. Your brain is an integration station for the consciousness it attracts. As the higher centers of your brain ignite with light to their higher functions, your brain orchestrates your consciousness to shift dimensions so you may experience higher states of consciousness.

Your world, as you perceive it, is usually based on your physical space and time, but there is also a large part of your world that you are unable to see or perceive with your physical eyes that is multidimensional. Throughout each day and night, your brain is receiving the energy and consciousness from other dimensions of yourself and also from the collective consciousness of humanity if your brain's field is in a lower frequency.

Your brain continues to process this energy and consciousness even when your body sleeps and your conscious mind rests. Your dreams are connected to the integration of the consciousness your brain is attracting through its field. In other words, your brain is a synthesizer of your multidimensional consciousness from all worlds and realities, and as it emanates specific energy fields, it attracts different levels of consciousness through it to be processed by your mind or within your dream state.

To make things even more interesting, all that moves as energy through the cells of your body is directed by whatever consciousness you have grounded through your brain chemistry. If the consciousness within your brain's field is light and of a higher state of consciousness, this will be expressed through your cells as a higher frequency of energy that produces feelings of love, oneness, and ecstasy. If your brain's field is holding a lower vibration and holding fear within the field, these fears are transferred directly to the cells of your body and your body receives the lower frequency and fear-based energy directly into each cell. This produces feelings of anxiety, fear, worry, hesitation, inner conflict, and a dampening or numbing of your body's physical sensations to energy.

Your body is your temple, and it responds, reacts, and processes through its cells all of the consciousness that your brain's field receives. One person may receive consciousness through their brain's energy field that creates their personality and life focus to be energetic, happy, loving, and peaceful. Another person may receive consciousness through their brain's field that creates their personality and life focus to be depressive and unhappy, with a hopeless picture of the world.

The consciousness your brain receives is determined by three factors. First, the vibrational field of your brain influences what frequency of consciousness is attracted into your brain's centers. Second, the state or balance of your collective consciousness influences whether your brain receives a balanced or imbalanced energy. In other words, if your soul's relationship to your spirit is not in balance, your brain will receive an imbalanced energy or consciousness. Third, the nature of your own thoughts and the focus of your mind create a signal to attract a similar consciousness to the brain's field.

The witness or observer within your mind is known as your primary consciousness. As your brain's field receives lower levels of consciousness, your witness is influenced by this consciousness to begin to think more negatively, and as your brain emanates these thought forms, it attracts more negative thoughts from the collective field of humanity. As your brain's field rises in vibration, your thoughts no longer are affected by the collective consciousness of humanity, and you begin to process the thoughts and beliefs of your spirit. As these are processed and any karma is cleared, your super-consciousness is made accessible to you via the activation of the higher centers of your brain.

The librarians of light and the enlightened presences who hold the original keys, codes, and blueprints for the evolution of humanity's consciousness share the following words as their truth.

New foods of organic nature that vibrationally sustain your body and brain are needed for the biological and plasmatic regeneration of your brain chemistry. Your brain has become dull in some areas. Raw foods and foods carrying high amounts of life force will awaken the brain's chemistry to rise in vibration. Your brain has fallen asleep in some areas as a result of the entry of your ancestors into a great period of darkness. There was a time on Earth when all beings fell into this sleep. There have been many awakenings in pockets of your world, but never before has there been a completion in this way, where all have the opportunity to be awakened to the truth that they are not simply physical beings, but spiritual beings.

We share that this awakening is a spiritual emergence. It is an inner transformation that will, when it is complete, bring peace to the Earth and establish the mind's link to the fifth dimension. Those with brains holding lower frequency energy fields may presently be prophesying a negative version in relation to your potential future, sharing the energies of doom, and others with brains that are held by higher frequency fields may presently philosophize on the positive manifestations of your shift and may be inviting all to come together in groups to promote love, peace, and positive choices and actions. The fear-based perceptions are coming from the collective consciousness's field, where the memories of past devastations are held as the collective memories of your ancestors. The light-based perceptions are being sourced from the planes of light and from the higher selves of souls.

Your role is to recognize the energy of karma in all that humanity is doing, saying, or feeling and to recognize what is sourced from the karmic plane or from fear so you do not give your power to it or create your reality through the influence of fear. To discern what is loving, kind, charitable, peaceful, and wise within all that humanity is doing, saying, or feeling will support you to rise in consciousness and activate your brain chemistry. Giving the power of thought to fear-based projections upon your world will only attract the collective memories from the astral plane that were left over from traumas that your ancestors experienced or that you experienced in ancient civilizations.

This is your role because as humanity you are creating your planetary experience with your conscious intentions. You can no longer afford to place faith in negative perceptions. Your planetary experience of peace can only take place through love if you discern which truth is based on karma, and which truth is truly based on the vibration of light and invokes your heart to open in unconditional love. No matter how truthful something may appear, if it has not lit up compassion, love, and wisdom within you, this truth is still veiled by karma and old perceptions. If a situation is true for you, there will always be a deeper truth for you to discover, one that reveals compassion, love, and wisdom about any situation. As you penetrate this hidden truth, the switch within your brain will ignite to illuminate your brain chemistry with a higher frequency.

It is also your faith in your fellow humanity that switches on the light in your brain chemistry to allow your consciousness to link into the universal matrix via the unified field shared by the collective. Without this faith, the light that ignites the brain chemistry to activate the higher centers will not be received. This faith in your fellow humanity is received as you clear and balance your collective karma as a being.

Your own light may be activated through one hemisphere of your brain, where it is circulating and depicting your reality as the base reality for all beings. This is the left side of your brain. It may also be activated through both hemispheres, if your brain has been awakened and both hemispheres are communicating to you, sometimes from an individual point of view via "consciousness of self" and sometimes from the higher overview or "we consciousness," the group-consciousness mentality.

Your evolution as a being and as a collective takes place as new frequencies are relayed to the cells of your body and your DNA is activated, releasing the old consciousness from your physical body and your lightbody. This is a cycle that no being can avoid, although the release of the old consciousness sometimes creates an experience of karma, a sense that one's energy is trapped in a lower dimensional expression, or a manifestation of illness, unhappiness, pain, or suffering.

When the old consciousness is locked in the physical body, the manifestation of disease is increased in its possibility. The codons of light that stream through your being from the unified field for the purpose of creating evolution for all beings are unable to be received when the physical body is locked in a state of fear and therefore the healing of disease is unable to take place. The old codons of light may activate inherited patterns or precursors to possibilities that have been blueprinted by your ancestors. Even in the physical body, this only manifests if the old consciousness is locked inside in a state of fear, or what is known as unconsciousness.

Many have discovered this truth in the realms of healing, new medicine, and the new sciences that are developing or being rediscovered. The old consciousness must release its fear for the completion of the natural cycle of transformation, whether this is your body's cellular structure entering the fifth dimension, or your mind's or the collective's. It makes no difference whether it is within the macrocosm or microcosm of your reality. The fear must transform for the shift to take place within your physical form.

Karma can be expressed in subtle ways, not only through the great crises, struggles, and sufferings of our communities. Karma is found in the underlying, unresolved energy that lives between the super-consciousness and the consciousness of humanity, also known as the unconscious nature. Karma can influence a soul to step aside from their highest potential in life, away from that which will give them love and peace, and away from that which will reignite their empowerment as a divine being.

Every second that you are not aware of your karma, you are unconsciously giving your power to it and living in a state of partial sleep. This sleepy state keeps you from experiencing the gifts that your Holy Spirit holds for your soul's amazing journey of oneness with your Divine Presence.

Your perception of yourself may not be true, and if your soul humbles itself to receive the Holy Spirit, the path ahead is lit with light and faith and you are led in a direction in which you are asked to embrace your karma so the true gifts of your light, your life, and the Holy Spirit may bless the Earth Mother.

You are each a vessel of love, and you are each endowed with gifts beyond your present knowing. You may have inklings of this, you may sense what is possible, or you may have no idea presently of what these are. As your brain chemistry awakens, as you receive the transmissions of pure love and the higher frequencies of light that are needed to turn the switch from fear to unconditional love, your gifts awaken so you may experience yourself as a vessel of love here.

This is the potential for your soul, and a very large group of awakened souls, as a collective, are presently working toward this goal. Your own soul may turn the switch at any time by asking to be shown your karma with grace and ease and by asking for your spiritual eyes to be opened with love, compassion, and kindness. It may be difficult at first to own and take responsibility for your karma, but if you work in group-consciousness with your spiritual family, and stay willingly open to receiving assistance from your Divine Presence, the angels, the archangels, and the Enlightened Masters, all that you need to own the karma, forgive it, and bless it will take place easily.

YOUR POTENTIAL

In the timeless days gone
trepidations passed
miles of path walked
worlds crossed . . .

You spoke . . .
Dreamed . . .
Created . . .
Yourself . . .
Painted your world to be
filled with those you now love . . .
Many more who are still to come
and those gone and passed by . . .
No window was closed in your mind . . .
The tapestries of light you wove
so concentrated and fine . . .
But did you forget your dream
from long ago?
Awakening your remembrance
is the golden butterfly
the spark of light within your eye
that I see within the shadow
Behind the night curtain drawn
the sun rises to light the sky
and dreams may have passed you by
yet you are still within the dream . . .
The sun is your source
your heart holds the way . . .
Will you remember all that you
dreamed yourself to be?
Touch upon your skin
sends ripples of light
blissful sensations, textures of ecstasy
ignite rainbow spheres and geometries
weaving away your fears
that you are no more than you know
yourself as, here . . .

The tears are wiped away from your eyes
so you may see yourself in the beauty way
a new mirror is raised before thee . . .
Storms and showers have rinsed off the old ways
trials and tribulations passed long ago
dreams awakened and your heart paves the way for you to know . . .
The dream you painted
in all their glory
your soul embraced in its full divinity
The passion of your lips . . .
Your breath awakens the spirit of your life to be unveiled . . .
Your spirit dances, expanding beyond
and into a journey of depth, a breadth
that fills and expands your heart
so large . . . all in one breath
You no longer know yourself
as one mind, one heart
as you grow wings from your heart, head, and arms
your journey is ignited
by the dreaming of your spirit long ago
that cannot be denied . . .
Rivers upon rivers
and ancient mothers of the mountain come . . .
They sing your body, your bones
to remember your dreaming journey
what you painted as your heart's desire
etched into the sky
and through the crevices of the mother's smile
it ran deep into her body
woven through the fabric of space and time
through the trees, blossoms, in nature . . .
Your dreaming travels on the winds of time . . .

Horses run wild upon the mountain
toward the sky, crystal mountains sing
following you into the dreaming . . .
Strong waters coil, she snakes through the Earth
piercing your body and heart, shaking your bones
so you may remember more of . . . the painting of your world
Celestial spheres spinning your dreaming within Earth
into the passageways of the void . . .
She rises from the heart of all of creation
out of the Earth and into your heart . . .
She calls to awaken all within you
that has been forgotten or left behind . . .
It is a time of trust, innocence and love
gateways of your Holy Spirit and dreaming come to you now . . .
Soon you will see the world as you originally painted it to be . . .
Remember your inner spark . . .
Speak the truth . . . Reveal yourself . . .
And all will be as you dreamed your world could be . . .

The Earth's Activation of Your Brain's Energy Field

Imagine that the Earth's lightbody or Earth Crystal behaves like a brain, giving direction to the new energy and consciousness and grounding into Mother Earth's body from the universal centers. This brain orchestrates an energetic transformation within a sphere that is twelve times the size of the physical Earth. You may hold a specific view based on what you can see of the microcosm of your reality, but from the Enlightened Masters' perspective, all appears very differently. I share with you a little more about how they see the Earth Crystal and how it works.

The Earth has an *antahkarana,* or primary spiritual current, that streams all consciousness through the internal fabric of its body and into the Inner Earth. The Earth is held dimensionally through a diamond-plated body. The dodecahedron, a twelve-sided geometry, is the base geometry that these plates begin to grow from to receive the currents of energy from the universe for the Earth's body. The icosahedron, a twenty-sided geometry, is the base geometry that these plates begin to grow from to allow the transmission of the Earth Crystal to activate and regenerate the life, consciousness, and energy within all seven worlds of the Earth. As these base plates within the Earth Crystal activate, they draw the currents from the Inner Earth's core, and this continues to expand and ignite life within the worlds of the Earth.

The antahkarana of the Earth is not anchored through the north and south poles, as Earth-based science's understanding of magnetic fields may suggest. The Enlightened Masters offer another truth related to the Earth's axis in its principal spiritual form. They offer the awareness that there is a seven-sided prism located in each one of twelve areas within the Earth, and each of these twelve prisms allows a magnitude of twelve pillars to ignite and interconnect to form an axis which is multidimensional in nature and not centered linearly via two points. These twelve pillars and twelve prisms hold the Earth's field in rotation cycles with the universal and galactic cycles.

These pillars oscillate at different frequencies. Three pillars oscillate to a harmonic, which is aligned to the magnetic field of the Earth's body and the core of the Earth. These three pillars hold the Earth in the dimension where her lowest base energy is held. This base frequency of her body's structure is presently rising, as her body's vibration is to enter the fifth dimension in accordance with the Divine Plan. These three pillars also offer a containment field, which is slowly weakening due to the dynamic, internal changes in the Earth's field, but which will strengthen again once it allows the release necessary for the vibrational and dimensional shift of the Earth.

Another three of these pillars sustain the power of creation and the flow of creation currents throughout the Earth Crystal and all seven worlds. Three more pillars sustain the gravitational field from the core of the Earth and accelerate, repair, and regenerate the Earth Crystal's dimensional and grid system that feeds all of life on Earth.

The last three of the twelve pillars hold the Earth's positioning and also coordinate what seems to be the Earth timeline, which is experienced only by those within the Earth's living system. As these three pillars are initiated to a higher frequency, they will lift the Earth out of the timelines and karma of Earth's story.

Each of these last three pillars operates on a plasma band of frequency. This plasma force forms conduits through the Earth Crystal. This white plasma or cosmic fire is a resource that many of the advanced species utilize to power their technologies, which supersede the technologies humanity is presently working with. As these pillars receive more powerful currents from the universal centers, the Earth's field rises in vibration, delivering this white cosmic fire or plasma into our energy field and activating the neurons in our brain to ignite with light.

Over time, as humanity shows to its elders of light that we are responsible and peaceful in our nature, these advanced forms of technologies will be released to our collective. The evolution of our brain chemistry will allow us to be ready for these discoveries. The super-consciousness of individuals will receive them when the greater collective of humanity is ready. Just as the world was once considered flat and was eventually discovered to be round, so will the axis of the Earth be discovered as a twelve dimensional axis. Field dynamics will progress to a new level, and it will be accepted among scientists of Earth that consciousness exists within all of life.

Your present consciousness may not be aware of every energetic experience taking place within your being. I ask that you open your mind to the possibility of fractal realities. Within every aspect of your awakened self, you have a parallel fractal self. A fractal part of you is not a fragment broken off from the whole of your nature, as the linear mind may perceive it to be. It is simply another dimensional reflection that is living in an alternate reality, another aspect of your vast spirit expressed through alternate bandwidths of energy.

The alternate realities of the Earth are sevenfold, and you also hold consciousness within these fractal worlds. When the consciousness of your spirit is united in all seven worlds, your being is enlightened on Earth.

The cosmology of human evolution is linked to more than 1,011 species that live within the seven worlds of the Earth. All that you see, experience, and create within the Third World is directly connected to the experiences of your consciousness within these fractal worlds.

The elders of many of the traditional native peoples who have carried the stories of their ancestors across time, in some cases long before the written word, share in common stories of humanity's star-seeding. Many of these stories speak of beings we do not see with our physical eyes walking on the Earth with us. They speak of worlds beneath or above the world of humanity. They speak of a mother who birthed all beings of a supreme creator, of great water, of the creation of animals and the first human beings. While each story is unique, all depict how their ancestors experienced Earth, with their inner eye open to many beings from all seven worlds of the Earth.

To begin to link your consciousness to the vaster nature of your being, and to the Earth Crystal or lightbody of the Earth, you are being asked to accept the possibility that you are not only genetically linked to your ancestors but also connected to some of the beings that have been described in these creation stories. Also consider that members of our collective are linked not only to each other but also to other species who originally star-seeded humanity.

Within your brain are higher centers that may not have yet evolved. The codons of light you need to receive for your evolution are activated through the invisible conduits of white cosmic fire or plasma that are formed by three of the pillars of the Earth's axis. As your karma releases and your consciousness expands, your brain's energy field begins to attract this cosmic white fire from the field of the Earth. As your consciousness receives the new codons of light, your brain chemistry alters to create your shift into the fifth dimension, beyond the limiting nature that the cycle of time placed upon you.

Your body is integrating more of your consciousness and may need assistance to allow the integration to take place. Cleansing the body allows this integration and also facilitates the regeneration that your new brain chemistry is directing to take place within your physical, emotional, mental, and spiritual bodies. Calling on the cosmic white fire to flood through your brain will support the process of raising the field of your brain, the most important field for the human evolutionary process to feel smooth and organic.

The field of your brain is so powerful it can close down your heart chakra and seal you in another world if it is polarized and holding fear-based illusions. This is known as mental disease. The field of your brain can initiate the great shift in your consciousness, or it can limit it and create you to feel small and trapped in your physical body. The enlightenment of the human brain's field is the key to humanity's shift into the fifth dimension. What is so special and divine about the plan for humanity is that every human brain that changes its brain chemistry and activates both hemispheres is serving to activate a new collective mind based on unconditional love through the balance of our Earth karma. Because of the energetic link between all of humanity, as one brain creates the shift in consciousness, it allows the super-consciousness to be shared throughout the collective. As another, then another, then hundreds and thousands of brains make the shift, the hearts of humanity are opened, and the super-consciousness of streams of higher intelligence is accessible by the collective.

Your spiritual eyes fully open when your brain chemistry has activated the higher centers of your consciousness, and you are also fully receiving all streams of your super-consciousness, which grow from only one power source. This power source is unconditional love. The acts of unconditional love you create in your life empower your consciousness to receive streams of your super-consciousness. This is the blessing that you receive through your evolution.

The Human Brain and Our Dream State

Have you ever wondered why you dream? Your dreams are simply your process of integrating with your ancestors and your collective consciousness all new information you have received or generated through your brain's energy field.

Imagine that your consciousness is always streaming. Know that you truly let go to this when your body is sleeping and you enter the dream state. As you sleep and your brain state changes, the central communication between your hemispheres begins to share rapid downloads from your energy field as a form of processing the consciousness that you received through your experiences during the day. The Earth's field is the great conductor for this activity, as it holds a specific magnetic pulse and electromagnetic grid, as well as a plasma conduit system that creates a field where all of the consciousness of your whole lineage is held as you integrate it.

These streams of consciousness are formed from thousands of filaments that link through the brain. Sometimes the braiding of these filaments is disrupted when they are broken into derivatives. These fractals in the chemistry of the brain create difficulty for the children on the Earth whose consciousness has come in at a higher velocity to ground into a small, human body. There are misunderstandings within the education system regarding what creates a child's difficulty in learning, behavior, and creative endeavor. The source of their difficulty often does not lie in the structure of the brain but in the brain's field, for it is the field of the brain that allows a soul's consciousness to ground into the physical body.

The children who have difficulty with learning, behavior, and creativity all have three things in common. The first is that their brain's field is oscillating at a frequency that is much lower than their soul's consciousness. Second, their energy field is not resonating to the Earth's energy field, or, as many in the healing world would say, they are ungrounded in their energy. Third, there is a part of their consciousness living in between the worlds and not grounding into the Third World.

A child's consciousness naturally travels more freely between the worlds than the consciousness of an adult. Children's brains have a higher content of plasma flowing through them, which creates them to enter the lucid state of dreaming more easily than adults. Many children live half in the physical world and half in the dreaming or spirit world. They have not created filters strong enough to close down their conscious awareness of soul travel between the physical and nonphysical worlds of the Earth.

These children are calling to adults to create new choices in regard to child-rearing and education. Without guidance for their consciousness, some of these children have become lost on the Earth. When a soul's consciousness is traveling between worlds and they hold karma between one world and another, it manifests in physical symptoms such as disease in the body, learning or behavioral difficulties, or mental disease. These are some of the hardest experiences to witness, and of course with children, the question always arises, Why do they need to suffer? It seems so unfair.

It is true; there is no fairness in any form of pain or suffering. There is only karma and potential to complete the learning. Young children in these situations may be thousands of times more sensitive than adults to all forms of energy. They react to energy before anything appears in the material world, whereas most adults react to appearances before they experience the energy of a space. For children with learning or behavioral difficulties, the energy field of their brain needs to be balanced and earthed so they can experience groundedness in the material plane.

When the brain's field is holding the clear light frequency that resonates to a soul's consciousness, the soul can always be centered and connected to their heart. This is a sign of a soul's shift into the fifth dimension. When the brain's field is not holding the clear light frequency that resonates to a soul's consciousness, the soul is unable to be centered and connected to their heart. This is sign that some form of karma may be affecting the brain's field to hold a lower vibration. As a light seed, you can always ground your consciousness when you are deeply in your heart.

Our Spirit Journey into the Fifth World

In ancient civilizations, humans held a more activated brain where the conscious awareness of Spirit and all of the worlds was possible. The cause of humans' higher brain activity was the celestial and earthly portals enlightening the spirit of a soul to infuse their brain with light. These souls were interconnected with the others worlds consciously, and in one of the seven worlds there was a great development of their spirit and their light.

Throughout all of the Earth's development, one of the seven worlds of the Earth has been the primary world of consciousness development. The Earth switches her dimensional fields to a new alignment for the purpose of serving the development of consciousness to focus through a different primary world. All of the stories, legends, and myths that humanity has received from their ancestors as well as all of the stories that souls have connected to through the Akashic records are connected to the Earth's shifts in dimensions that allow a new primary world to develop powerfully in consciousness.

We are presently in the stage of development where our spirits are being called to enter the Fifth World. There is no set time period for this, as this is also connected to our collective shift in consciousness into the fifth dimension. The Fifth World is where our spirit unites its heart in Christ consciousness in the experience of unconditional love. For our spirit to enter the Fifth World, a bridge is opening through the higher dimensional grids of the Earth and parts of our consciousness are returning into the light and merging back with our source. The journey into the Fifth World is assisted through clearing one's karma until one is approaching all situations in life from a place of unconditional love.

This fifth dimensional shift is an inner experience that is to be made first by our spirit, and then by our soul, our mind, and our body. These forms of our consciousness are simply merging to resonate to the vibrational energy of the Fifth World. All aspects of our spirit are called to eventually unite and travel from the First, to the Second, to the Third, to the Fourth, and into the Fifth World.

This is an aspect of our eternal journey where our souls will be able to ascend into the Fifth World upon death as easily as all souls presently are able to ascend into the Fourth World of the angels. This spirit journey is occurring on the inner planes in the spirit world, and once it is complete, it creates a soul's consciousness that is incarnate in the physical world to hold a fifth dimensional consciousness.

The development of consciousness has been taking place primarily in the Second World, the Middle Earth, but as this cycle completes, and the Earth empowers a consciousness shift, the Third World (the physical plane) will become the new primary world of consciousness development. The energetic and spiritual events of 2012 and the completion of the Mayan calendar relate to this transcension of consciousness development accelerating within our physical reality and accelerating our spirit journey into the Fifth World.

The Third World is to be the new primary world where the greatest shift in consciousness will take place, and 2012 is one of the points where these cycles of consciousness switch. Spiritually, our world is granted more power for this shift. As this occurs, all of the consciousness within our physical world is preparing to unite itself with a higher consciousness.

The animals of Earth are already aware of what is to occur, as they receive this information in their dream state, when the shared consciousness of their spirit in other worlds communicates higher truths to them. Many humans have prophesied a new age, but this proposed new age is not the completion of a millennium or a period in history. It is the completion of an old consciousness through the generation of a whole new consciousness, the mergence of our spirits into the Fifth World and the fifth dimension.

Each soul is moving through a completion of a cycle with their eternal spirit, which is synonymous with their birth and death. Birth on Earth begins the journey of a soul. Throughout this journey, all souls travel between the worlds. Each evening as we enter dream reality, we travel on a light bridge that connects our physical body to the plane of the spirit, which is unbounded by space, time, or dimension.

In the physical realm, the senses are extraordinarily enhanced by the containment field of the Earth. As a soul releases from this containment field and is freed from their concentration on the material world, they experience what is known as the oneness or heaven. Out of this state of spiritual bliss arise gifts that allow these souls to be conscious of their travels between the worlds.

This access to our spiritual body may seem extraordinary, but in truth it is an ordinary function of the human brain. The hemispheres of the brain support the field of the brain to oscillate at specific frequencies to create this sense of oneness, and as more souls are awakening within the Third World and their brain chemistry is changing, more and more people are having these experiences with Spirit. Their consciousness meets itself in other forms in the other worlds. This soul travel was originally the work of the secret societies of the Earth. Those high initiates within the ancient mystery schools and within the mystical orders of all religions, as well as yogis, sadhus, and monks, gave away their focus on the material world to focus on the spiritual. They were the first to change their brain chemistry and meet themselves in altered states in other worlds, uniting their consciousness and enlightening their cells.

We are now blessed that this process of evolution is everybody's journey, and anyone may choose this path. The process can be subtle at first, and if fits of anger arise, they are a sign of a genetic mutation or a manipulation of the original codon of light within your stream of consciousness. This manipulation of the genetic code occurs when one gives one's power to a force or god outside oneself. This is the very source of humanity's manipulation of their DNA within the body that they carry today. Of course, not every human being holds this genetic mutation, as either their ancestors or their own soul may have met this anger and traveled through the worlds to heal the source of this karma.

The anger is very deeply buried and can manifest as rage within, linked with deep anxiety or terror. If it arises, it comes from this genetic manipulation that was created by one's own being or by one's ancestors. Many see this as an aspect of their ego or unconsciousness, which is correct. Yet what many do not understand is that the anger is not personally held but is held within the collective of humanity.

When a soul has a genetic mutation within the stream of their consciousness, they are unable to shift into the fifth dimension until this karma is cleared through their ancestral line. The unlocking of the genetic code clears the whole genetic line, freeing all who share the DNA chemistry from this original anger. Mothers and daughters are linked, as are fathers and sons; consciousness is partially passed down from mother to daughter, or father to son. As the genetic code unlocks and the ancestral line is cleared, mothers and daughters become closer, and fathers and sons open their hearts more than they ever could before.

Your evolutionary process is naturally occurring whether you wish it or not. There are only two paths to embracing this. One path is the acceleration of your consciousness, which occurs through the alignment of your choices, actions, and words to your heart frequency and your brain's energy field, to receive the clear light frequency. The other path is the acceleration of your karma, releasing the old consciousness and activating your brain chemistry to integrate your present consciousness, then opening to receive your super-consciousness. This process occurs through the exchange of new codons of light between you and others, between you and the sacred lands of Mother Earth, or between you and your fractal selves from other worlds, beloved. Both of these paths are accelerating you, yet one is presently accelerating your growth more deeply than the other.

There is an outer and an inner cycle of soul growth. When you are integrating more and your karma is accelerating, you are in your inner cycle of soul growth. Your consciousness is focused on receiving and is more present in the other worlds. When you are expanding and creating more, your consciousness is accelerating, and you are in your outer cycle of soul growth. Your consciousness is focused on transmitting and is more present in the Third World, which is your outer world at this time.

Dreaming and being also constitute a cycle of consciousness and creation. As you dream and the two hemispheres of your brain integrate all information you have received through your field, your soul is liberated to travel between the worlds and integrate other parts of self within your fractal worlds. As a being, you feel what other parts of you in the other worlds feel. As a soul experiences grief in the physical world, there is also a part of them in grief in another world on Earth. The source of the grief is not held only in the circumstances of your known world.

You may ask yourself if you are dreaming your present reality from another world. Are you creating your reality as a divine being on the Earth not only through your choices, actions, thoughts, feelings, and words but also through the fractals of yourself in the other worlds? This is a possibility, depending on how much of your karma has been balanced and cleared, for your karma lies between your consciousness in this world and your consciousness within the other worlds.

A Visitation from Hunab Ku— Our Dreaming Pathways of Creation

I was meditating one morning, very early, and received a visitation in the form of a Presence called Hunab Ku. He came as pure light. He invited me to journey with him into the galactic core so I could integrate a new awareness. This filled my heart with immense love, so we merged and became one.

We entered a blue crystal doorway leading to many paths. I became aware that I was standing on a rainbow path. I was shown that this rainbow path is the path I am presently on, the path that directs my life experience. I looked back, and I could see many other paths. On these paths I could see many different life forms that ran beside and behind me.

Hunab Ku said these were all original forms of myself that I had dreamed into existence, potentials for me to experience.

"It is wonderful to see," I shared, "but I do not understand it fully."

Hunab Ku explained it to me. "Humanity's brain function became limited thousands of years before your history books begin, even before the time that your archaeologists date the Great Pyramid or ancient temples and ruins. The higher brain functions hold derivatives or probabilities for a soul's path. All is not destined, even though the Divine Plan directs a soul's highest potential path, for the soul must also choose this. The other choices are the myriads of probabilities, and they are all based on these original forms you are seeing. These are your dreaming bodies."

I looked at them more deeply, and there were so many. I asked him how they affected me in my daily life. He said they carry my dreams. "You have dreamed of much from the vast consciousness you are as a spirit. These dreaming bodies are your probabilities on your life path. You can attune to these, and if you follow one dream, the dreaming body that carries that dream will activate and connect to you within the physical."

I was amazed. I looked at these life forms again. He said that this is how our consciousness is stored for us, in bodies of light. "Your soul has incarnated in human form, but you have extensions in other worlds. You may have a dream that you are aligned to, but if your extensions in other worlds fear this dream, then you experience the fears, and this can self-sabotage the manifestation of the dream in your Earth reality. Your rainbow path is the path you resonate with now, and the dreams on this path are very beautiful. You have been clearing your karma, old emotions and beliefs held between you and your fractal forms of the other worlds. As you have done this, your dreams have become more and more your reality on Earth, manifested in an earthly form. What is most important is that your heart is clear, my child."

He walked with me on my rainbow path, and I saw many beings I knew: my daughter and my grandson, my closest friends, and a very large group I call my soul family. As we walked toward them, they surrounded me.

Hunab Ku spoke. "And you dreamed all of these ones into your life, too."

We continued to walk, and they walked with me, and the path widened to allow hundreds of beings to walk the path. The rainbow path became like a streaming highway or a great bridge.

He said along the path, "You will meet everything you have dreamed."

I replied, "What if I do not like it?"

"Then you must ask yourself, why did I dream it? Did I dream it from fear or love? If you dreamed it from fear, you must embrace the fear and release the karma and the belief empowering it. As you do this, this part of your dream will release."

He looked back, and the dreaming bodies and other paths were far behind us now. "See how you have left your old dreams behind and are now only focused upon this one. Inside all of the bodies, no matter which one you may have chosen to resonate with, is the consciousness of the dream, but for it to become a reality, you must believe in yourself and the dream. No one else can do this for you, no matter how many people you dream on your path with you."

We continued and came to a large golden tree. I felt truly magical in its presence.

Hunab Ku spoke again. "This is the tree you dreamed you would be married under."

I was surprised to hear him say these words to me.

He continued, "You have dreamed of an amazing partnership for your future. You will know him through the sound of his voice and through his connection to the trees. It is a part of your evolution to meet this love again. He will come with much that is not simple, as you have dreamed him to be an equal in all ways to you, a resonance through all chakras. You will see the mirror of your love, and it may create a part of your consciousness from another world to react and withdraw in fear. An immense journey lies ahead, but you must embrace yourself in all worlds for the dream to be made manifest."

I asked, "How will I know if my other selves are reacting?"

He shared that I would change inside and feel different, and that I had states of consciousness in the other worlds that held thin layers of fear. I was astounded to think that any time I felt a sudden change inside, it had been created by my other selves in other worlds.

"Your partnerships have all been a mirror of your growth, and as your partnerships have completed through keeping the heart open and exchanging deep love, forgiveness, and honesty, your previous partners have become some of the most important friendships in your life. Each one has gifted you a gift of growth that could not be received in any other way, a blessing that you are deeply grateful for. This blessing each time has been the return of a part of your self, your higher consciousness.

"A deepening of your oneness through a new relationship will be experienced, for you have chosen this dream as a stream of consciousness to integrate and manifest on your path. The timing of this takes place only as you embrace all that may arise within your consciousness, as these experiences manifest opportunities or doorways that will lead you to your self-discovery. Your self-discovery is based on your willingness to surrender any feelings that are fear based. As you walk your path, know the true feelings you meet inside yourself are signposts that your other selves are communicating to you."

I asked if my other selves were on the same rainbow path as me, or if they had chosen their own dream. He shared that only those in the Third World manifest their dreams in the physical and that my other selves experience the same dreaming as I do, simply by sharing consciousness with me. My dreams would download to them as feelings. If I were hurt in this world, they would also feel this hurt. If I felt deep love, they would share in this and feel deep love.

I asked, "How do I know if I am individually creating the love or if another of my selves is creating it?" He said that I and all my fractal selves created our experiences in group-consciousness, as we could never be separated. We were linked forever by our vast consciousness, our Holy Spirit.

We continued along the path, and we came to a beautiful land, which carried a deep peace for me. It felt like I was home. There were many books around me that I had written.

He said, "This is your life where you dreamed yourself to be a writer."

I smiled and looked through the glass windows of an adobe home to the beautiful nature surrounding me.

"You dreamed of creating deeply with your Presence and living in peace and beauty, within nature."

I knew this as my truth.

We left the house through its back door and walked upon the rainbow path again. It twisted and turned, and I could see that it connected to many other pathways. He said, "This is where all of your other dreams meet you, and you have another chance to choose from your many dreaming bodies. When you have manifested your present dream to become your reality, then you may receive a new dream."

I looked at the paths ahead and asked, "Where do all these dreams come from?"

"You dreamed them as the vast spirit you are. You created them in the First World, which is the source of all of the other worlds. They come from the void through the dreamtime, from the core of your infinite nature, a place of pure love, and when you have completed with them, the dreaming bodies will return to the void as you become the dream. Each dream gives you a part of yourself. As the dream is manifested through your experience, it becomes no longer a part of you, but lives inside you forever."

I thought for a moment about what I had dreamed in my life and could see that a part of myself had been returned to me through each leg of the journey, just as Hunab Ku had described. Each time, a new gift or power had been integrated that I had not expressed before. I realized I had sometimes been confused between two dreams and had to make a choice at a crossroads on my path. I remembered asking myself, What do I really want? I remembered thinking I wanted both dreams and attempting to follow two paths, trying to please others, afraid I could not make a decision. I realized this avoidance had led me to feel split and had caused my energy to be unfocused. I would then manifest situations where one path seemed to be taken away from me, or where I would be forced by circumstances to choose one dream. I remembered feeling the loss for the other dream.

How much easier it would have been to know that only one dreaming can be followed at any one time. Other dreams can be experienced later. I could see the waste of our life force when our energy is placed into lost dreams, the deep disappointments that block us when we hold attachments to our dreams. For the first time, I could see my path clearly; I could see how opportunities would come, offering an expansion of the path, or how I could go in a completely different direction and step onto another potential path.

The many paths that linked to my rainbow path were calling me. I could feel them pulling on my energy.

Hunab Ku said, "Be careful, as this is how a soul can lose their connection to their Presence, by allowing their future potential dreams to take them away from being fully conscious with their present experience. Many do this unconsciously, wanting to have their minds map out their life experience for them. Many wish to know which path to take in the future before they come to a crossroads of true choice. Many wish to do this before it is their time to do this.

"Your path is set on this dreaming path you have already chosen, and it will be some years before your path shows you the new potential directions you may take. Your partner will be with you by this time. You will be married and you will have written many more books. You will have evolved through all the experiences you will have had between now and then. You must stay present at all times, for those that take their consciousness into their future in this way experience only fear. They are not yet the person they need to be to meet their new dreams or new possibilities.

"We will now return through the blue crystal door. We have been traveling the corridors of time that exist between all dimensional realities, known as the dreaming paths. Time is not a measurement of seconds or minutes. It is based on the rotation of the galaxies, the Earth, the sun, the moon, the planets, and all celestial spheres. It is illusory in some ways, for consciousness cannot be bound by time, yet it can be bound within a dimensional form. Time is the difference between the frequencies or the velocity of radiations that each dimensional form emanates as its uniqueness. It only exists from the perspective of being a life form or a unique being. When your consciousness leaves form and you disperse and merge with your Holy Spirit, time no longer exists, and you are everything and simultaneously nothing. In truth, time does not exist, as all is one, and yet time exists within the differences between dimensional forms and their uniqueness relationships to each other. Both realities about time are true.

"Therefore some say, 'It is all here now.' Others perceive that all is connected to the past and the future, and their journey through timelines is also an acceptable belief system. The dance between dimensions can create you to perceive that time is in control of your reality, yet the truth is that you are the dreamer and creator. You even dreamed the timeline of your reality and its shifts and changes."

As I traveled back through the blue crystal, I saw myself as a giant winged rainbow serpent. We flew spiraling from the center of the galaxy where I had been taken to be shown this higher perspective, and I now felt like I was plummeting toward the Earth at high speed. As I came closer to the Earth, I became a long beam of light or pure consciousness. Entering the Earth's atmosphere at a much slower speed, I could see the blue and green of Earth below me. I gently traveled toward my physical body. As I merged with my body, it felt like it fitted me perfectly—a strange but beautiful feeling that I had not felt before so deeply. I felt like I was coming home to a new reality of loving my body and our Earth in an even deeper way as I embraced that I had chosen the dreaming path of my life creation.

Receiving the Codes and Our Completions for the Release of Our Karma

As a golden child, Buddha lies on his side in many temples around the world. Statues of Buddha or other enlightened consciousnesses represent humanity's choice to anchor a specific stream of consciousness on the Earth. For thousands of years, prayer wheels have been spun to cleanse the wheel of karma. Many chant the ancient sounds, not only in monasteries but also in homes and light centers all over the world. The intention is to anchor the clear light frequency on the Earth and bring peace to all on Earth.

Souls travel as they are guided to sacred power sites, mountains, glaciers, volcanoes, the oldest forests, canyons, rivers, oceans, and deserts to receive the frequency they need to activate the next level of codon sharing with their family, their community, and the planet. Many sacred places on the Earth are transceivers of currents that flow through all seven worlds, and others are transceivers between the Third World and another of the seven worlds. Often people are deeply drawn to these places because another part of their consciousness is calling them from another world. In these specific places they have been guided to, they are able to link with their selves in other fractal realities, either through their dreams or through spiritual practice.

The everyday reality of a soul on the Earth, although it may appear to be self-guided and self-determined, is not always the truth of a soul's reality. Choices made within the other worlds or the karma lodged between the worlds also predetermines a soul's journey on Earth in any given incarnation.

Surrendering one's fear of otherworldly experiences can be frightening unless one is held by love and able to trust one's own spirit. Your spirit carries only the highest intention for you in life. Your spirit is the consciousness between the "you" that you know, see, and hear yourself to be via your five senses, and the "you" that is unseen and unknown and is a mystery to you. Your other senses activate when your brain's energy field begins to oscillate at a higher vibration and the two hemispheres begin to conduct the super-consciousness and ground it into the electromagnetic field that flows through and surrounds your body. As these senses open and activate as clairsentience, clairvoyance, telepathy, and clairaudience, you are able to have clearer contact if it is needed with your selves in the other worlds.

Every soul has something to complete that is connected to their selves in other worlds, their karma, and their family, their community, or the planet. Whether their circumstances lead them to be a caretaker for their mother or to write a book to encourage others, to journey to the north pole or to spend their hours feeding their family and others, they are working toward freeing their karma from between the worlds.

Even a heroin addict is on the path of completion, and there is a part of them in another world holding the karma of the experience until forgiveness can be made and this soul and spirit can detach from the heroin. Even a man who struggles with the physical pain in his lower back is completing an aspect of his journey, and somewhere he also lies in another form, in pain, and this is feeding into his lower back. As a part of his spirit in the other world forgives, there is no pain in his back. Every part of your life is interconnected with your self in an alternate world. The karma of your life experience may be very light, and you may not suffer, for the interconnection between your heart and your self in other worlds is a clear, free flow of consciousness.

When a nurse in a hospital saves a man's life, this is a part of her completion process, a key to her personal evolution. When a man gives every night to the care of his elderly mother, this is a part of his completion process, a key to his personal evolution. Another woman sponsors children in poverty-stricken countries for many years, and this is part of her completion. Another consoles her friend who is grief-stricken by the death of her partner, and this is part of her completion. Another hugs and cares for her children and leaves her work to have more time with them. This too is a part of her completion.

Forgiveness, acts of inspiration, and acts of service to others are all acts of love. All acts of unconditional love, expressed and guided by the heart, are part of a soul's completion and a key to their personal evolution. Why specifically these acts and not others? A soul intrinsically knows what they must do and where they need to go, for they are intimately linked to their other selves through thousands upon thousands of filaments of consciousness.

If a soul is guided to the north pole, they are guided not only for themselves. Invisible energies are exchanged, invisible filaments of consciousness are enflamed, and invisibly and inaudibly, a connection is being made between the soul and another part of self. What is the purpose of this? The truth is that you are all working together in group-consciousness to complete something you need to complete. There are invisible parts of you working with you to expand your heart for the shift into the fifth dimension.

You may ask, How can those who seem to have no heart make it through the shift with us? Our answer is that every soul is building the heart. Even those souls who seem heartless, who seem to have no love inside, are building their hearts in another world. Parts of their heart are simply held in the other worlds of the Earth. For those that appear to be heartless, all of their heart lies in the other worlds, beloveds. As the brain chemistry is ignited, your heart chakra is able to interconnect with the streams of consciousness of yourself in other worlds. Each time you meet karma and practice forgiveness and a part of your consciousness in another world forgives with you, a part of your heart returns to you.

Around the central region of your chest is a vortex made from an invisible plasma or cosmic fire. This vortex, which is often meditated upon in spiritual practice, is the central stream of your consciousness as a soul, also known as your soul's inner flame or inner heart flame. This vortex has the potential to build powerfully over your lifetime.

When the brain chemistry activates your heart vortex to open and expand, building a higher frequency heart chakra, you may become unrecognizable to your oldest friends and family members. Some on the path of evolution transfigure in this significant way up to five or six times in one lifetime. What once took a soul a lifetime to complete can now occur within seven years. Shifts in DNA and brain chemistry are activated now by more people than throughout the last one thousand years. The Enlightened Masters share that the number of people investigating new possibilities of thought, experience, and creation has almost quadrupled just in the last ten years. They also share that the number of people having unusual feelings and experiences has almost doubled in the last twenty years.

This increasing vibrational activation of the consciousness of humanity manifests within every aspect of life on Earth. Even acts orchestrated by individuals with an intent to harm others actually awaken the collective consciousness to share more love. The karmic events of September 11, 2001, are an example of this. Although shock and grief was felt around the world as people witnessed this event on television, it also released a karmic blueprint held by the collective. Some people were involved personally, through their community or family, but all were involved on a collective level. Karma was clearing as hearts opened to release the grief and shock. The karma would be complete when forgiveness could be created, even though this was a tragedy.

Events like this affecting the collective, such as the bombing of Hiroshima and Nagasaki, leave karmic imprints. Even though time acts as a passageway for healing and forgiveness, the energy of these events also needs to be balanced. The many karmic blueprints held from the wars on Earth, carried over and triggered at specific times, cause individuals and groups in positions of power to create war. Just as America, Australia, England, and Iraq, as nations, hold a karmic blueprint together that presently creates the war in Iraq, so can our families and communities hold karma that may play out and create isolation, violence, separation, and abuse.

Yet there is promise of a kinder way to release the karmic blueprints. When enough people gather together as representatives of humanity, all focusing on the release of the collective karma, when enough people forgive the experiences of war, abuse, violence, poverty, greed, slavery, and disease, then we will heal the collective, simply because all are connected in a living light matrix. As enough people forgive, it ignites those in other worlds to also forgive, and then balance takes place between the worlds and peace on Earth is made manifest.

Our True Reality

Each time I come to a crossroads in my life, I experience some trepidation, some excitement, and great inquiry. I also feel a great change occurring within. This great change is produced by my internal body chemistry as it is being activated by a new consciousness streaming from alternative dimensions into my field. This is a delicate time, for we do not have a road map, and we have yet to choose the direction of our future journey. Although our life lessons are chosen by us before incarnation, much of our journey is shaped when our soul makes contracts with our Holy Spirit while our bodies are peacefully sleeping.

Our journeys as light beings take place more often than we know. Have you ever noticed how on some days you are as bright as a button, and on other days you are not quite here? In the moments when we do not feel present, our soul is journeying or connecting more deeply with Spirit.

As your body's basic functions or actions do not need all of your soul's consciousness, there are times during the day or evening when some of your consciousness travels or connects with Spirit in order to receive all that it needs energetically. Your soul is large and made of pure light, and there is no boundary to where your consciousness can travel, as your soul is eternal. You travel in your dreaming bodies as your body sleeps, and at times you also travel in your spirit body when you are awake, gathering codes and energy, making connections with others in the spiritual planes.

Many years ago, not long after I had completed my two-year training with the Enlightened Masters and my period of hermitage, Sai Baba appeared to me. I was in my living room, and he suddenly appeared and shared I would be traveling to India. I would not be coming to visit him specifically, although I would be in his field of energy. I would enter a large creation portal where many would be gathering for their reconnection to their eternal journey. I was being called there for the sealing of my higher lightbodies.

Sai Baba explained that this land in India carried a highly intensified current of the Holy Spirit, as the light there acted as a generator for Spirit to fill the souls of the Earth. It was a special land that carried a spiritual portal so large that all of the mirrored reflections of humanity's karma would be visible. The intensity of the light velocity moving directly from the spiritual planes into this physical land would not allow anything to be hidden, and all of the karma would be unveiled.

In the next moment I was in India, in an ancient cave in the north. Sai Baba showed me how many yogis, sadhus, and sages had drawn their energy from the spiritual current of the Himalayas for their enlightenment and universal service. I was shown that through the Himalayas and other sacred mountains of the Earth, there were passageways of spiritual energy where the veils between the physical and spiritual worlds were very thin. He showed me the giant serpents of creation that lived beneath these mountains, and the portals that were opening all over the Earth.

He shared that these portals are continually changing and growing. Old ones are closing and new ones are birthing. He shared that I would be working with these portals for the next twenty years as part of the path I had chosen in life. I would witness great changes in the people I met as they built their energy fields to become like these portals, with a great light and spiritual current rising through them.

At the end of this spirit journey with Sai Baba, he showed me my plane ticket to physically travel to India and shared I would spend one month in hermitage there.

Some time later, all of this did unfold, and I ended up in India for a month. I was in the south and spent most of the month in meditation in Sai Baba's ashram with thousands of people who devoted their path to his teachings or were seeking something from him. I was in a very deep space, and the Enlightened Masters were visiting me each day, so I was very fed spiritually and had no sense of seeking anything from Sai Baba personally. I could sit very deeply in meditation though, and journey into my heart to be with God. I had extraordinary experiences there in the field of Sai Baba, as my higher lightbodies were sealed to allow me to complete my initiation in training with the Enlightened Masters.

Light from every direction, from within me and all around me, began to concentrate in every cell in my body. Every cell began to burn as if it had a hot flame inside. This heat grew and grew, and I could see the light coming through from the spiritual field, but also from within me, like two different frequencies. A rainbow light from the field and a pearlescent golden light from within me were uniting in every cell and activating the great flame, and I was burning.

The meditation hall gave me very little physical space, so I was used to dropping beyond the pain or feelings of my body. They would melt once I dropped through in complete detachment from them. As I burnt in a raging hot fire, I let go and dropped in deeply and melted through the holy flame. Golden rivers of plasma filled me as I melted. I felt myself become golden lava, ancient as the volcanoes of the Earth, ancient as fire. I grew wings and became a tall, golden plasma being. In an archangel's body, I stood twelve feet tall.

I flew with great power in every part of my form; I could feel my muscles, as if I had the body of an Olympian. I felt heavy, as if gravity were still affecting me. As this archangel, I placed a golden disk inside every cell of my physical body, and I witnessed my body turn to white light. My body suddenly was cool again. The heat had released.

A voice inside my mind lovingly spoke and said, "We are about to release you from your brain's version of yourself. You will see your true nature in spirit, and then you will reenter and see the version your brain creates."

My breath became very still and almost nonexistent. I could sense a slight movement of my nostrils, but all sensation and awareness of my body completed at that time. The field of light grew all around me and within my archangelic plasma body, and a brilliant sun shone out of my heart. The sun in my heart expanded until it became larger than my plasma body, and golden streams of light poured forth from every direction to fill me until I felt as if I could not be filled any more.

I heard a voice inside. "Surrender, our dear child."

I dropped inside and melted, and no more was I. I was no more. Dissolved into the light. I had no eyes, no voice, no words, no story, and no reality. I was formless, a sea of love, infinitely expanding. I was bliss, ecstasy, freely flowing through All That Is, expanding until there was no more to expand into. Then I was everything inside of everyone, inside of everything. There was no ending. I was beyond the stars, beyond the moon, inside of all beings. I was within all. I was the Earth. I was the galaxy. I was the universe. There were so many eyes I could see through, simultaneously. I could see all, know all, feel all, and be all. The love and bliss expanded and expanded. I was a jewel within everything, waves of bliss. I had no body but all bodies were mine. I felt the bliss through all bodies and time.

There was no mind, yet I was within all minds. I was within all of nature. I was the breeze. I was the ocean. I was the animals. I was the children. There was no place where I was not, yet I was not anything, or anyone. There was no separation. All felt in peace and love. All felt grace. All I felt was me. I was feeling the world within me. Yet I was not me any more. I was everything. I had no need for anything.

Pulsations of light flooded into me, and I began to see that although I was in everything, I was also concentrated in one physical body. The light spiraled and took me as I became aware I did have an identity. Suddenly, I could feel and remember my body. Spiraling again through the tunnels of light, I felt my breath, my nostrils move again. I was alive. I was me. I was looking out of my physical eyes and could again see through my singular reality. I was incarnate in the physical body.

A voice inside spoke. "You are back with your brain now. It has coordinated your consciousness to see your individual reality. Releasing from the brain, there is no singular reality, only oneness with all. This is your true reality. You experienced your God Presence. Your brain is now able to harmonize and open your spiritual eyes. You have just received the last activation of your brain, and now you may share the codes of light with others so they may also receive the new brain frequency of the super-conscious mind."

When I picked myself up to leave *darshan*, my body was like a rag doll, and I wondered whether I would be able to walk. Within moments, I felt my brain activate, and my body began to fill with energy and pure light.

As the light streamed in, I began to feel the muscles of the archangelic body. I stood up with great power and felt very tall, much taller than my physical body. As I walked, I could see the wings of my plasma body expanding. I had received a connection to my archangelic body. I suddenly had so much physical strength and energy, I felt like I could run miles.

The voice, my Presence, spoke again. "You are now able to do anything! You have received the transformation. Many have received this and many more will transform. You carry the codes of light for others, and you now know your eternal self and the truth of your soul. Let this be your guide from this day forth, so you may not forget the true reality and that your incarnation is only temporary."

CHAPTER FIVE

Humanity's Call to Transformation and Illumination

You may wonder how your life and all that you are doing could possibly be aiding the human spirit to rise to the call of transformation and illumination on Earth. Your ancestors who dreamed of a better future for their children set this path long ago. Their call was so strong that the mountains of the Earth, the rivers, the largest trees, the birds as they fly south for the winter, the great wind that rises to sweep away the old, and the glaciers that hold the records of time all carry the truth of this call. We may feel small in comparison to these great mountains and glaciers, the oldest trees, or the spirit that lives within the wind that carries this timeless message—but then Spirit comes and fills our body, and we feel our potential, our power of creation, our love for our humanity.

Our pain as a race of not loving each other and our ancestors' repression through a hierarchical system have left their karmic blueprint, but we are being called to forgive and enter our true sovereignty with love and to create peace. Your small acts may seem unimportant to you, but to your ancestors they mean a great deal. Your ancestors are still watching over you and guiding you to aid our collective to balance and clear the collective karma that we have inherited.

I have worked with the ancestors for many years and found them all willing to forgive for the freedom of the children of their family tree. In a family tree I worked with, I found that none of the ancestors had ever experienced receiving love. I was introduced to an openhearted young man who had a remarkable ability to share love with others. He was a beautiful spirit, yet he shared with me that he would enter dark spaces of depression and anger that seemed to arise for no reason. It was easy for him to give love, but he could not receive it from others. He became shy and protective when he was on the receiving end.

As none of his ancestors had ever received love directly through their heart chakras, he could feel their ancient distrust when others openly focused on giving him love. He did not like being the center of attention; he would break out in sweats and try to shift the focus to someone else. His DNA held the memory of his ancestors, who at some point had chosen not to receive love. An original experience seven generations before him on his father line and five generations before him on his mother line had taken place. This created his consciousness to be locked into an agreement not to receive love.

As I was connecting with him, he sensed from his great-great-great-grandmother that as a young child she had been abandoned by her father when her mother had died, and that she had been abused for most of her life. Because of her fear of being abandoned again, she was unable to open her heart, and she was cold to her children as she got older and became unforgiving and angry a lot of the time. Her husband loved her deeply, but she could not receive the love. She had made the agreement to never let anyone love her, not even in her own children or husband.

As the young man met the spirit of his great-great-great-grandmother, he simply opened his heart and gave her the strength to forgive all she had been unable to forgive. As her heart opened, and as he broke the agreements she had made through speaking a powerful decree, all the ancestors in the lineage began to be freed.

A great circle of his ancestors gathered around us at this time. His ancestors from seven generations back, from both his mother and father lineage, surrounded us. I saw the light in their eyes spark each time this young man sent love and compassion to them. How willing they were to forgive and allow all they had left unresolved be brought to a state of peace. The young man sensed his great-great-great-grandmother's presence thanking him, and he felt something lifting something from him also, something he could not describe but could feel inside. He felt her arms or wings around him. I shared that future children of his line would no longer carry the old consciousness that stated it was better not to receive love.

I explained to this young man that his ancestors were angels. Over 90 percent of them upon death had accepted their next soul contract as an angel to serve all on Earth in their family tree. I explained how this contract extends for 250 earthly years. He gently cried, as he understood that these ones had been around him and others in his family as silent witnesses, helpful hands, and angels in service. I shared with him that they had been at his birth, visited him regularly as a child, and watched over him as he grew into the young man he was, and that many of them would again be at his death. I shared that he may be joining them upon his death.

As I spoke more deeply to him, he understood that it was the compassion and love he held for his ancestors' journeys on Earth that would release some of the angels who were 250 years of age or older to ascend into new forms or to return to the Earth with the ability to receive love through their human form. I also explained to him that he would now attract a relationship where he would be able to receive love. When his children were born, he would be able to both give and receive love from them. This would be the next unfoldment in his life that his ancestors also blessed.

The young man was deeply touched by the depth of peace he had found with his whole mother line. This included his own mother, who was still alive. As a child, he had always wanted to be held by his mother, but the family consciousness inherited through his ancestral tree dictated that the mothers of the lineage were too busy for affection and were cold and unforgiving of their children. He understood now that his own mother had been influenced by the same inherited consciousness that had been formed from his great-great-great-grandmother's traumatic life experience.

I asked him if he was willing to connect to his father's ancestors now, as they were very sad. He shared with me that his father was also very sad. I shared this was to be expected, for when the ancestors are sad, so are their children. He broke into tears, and when he raised his head, he said he had always cried as a small boy and wondered why. He asked me what his ancestors were sad about.

I explained it had all begun with a traumatic experience shared within his great-great-great-great-great-grandfather's lifetime that led him to blame himself, not trust others, and fear that he would lose what he loved most, his family, unless he did what he was asked by his commander. The command he was given was to kill or punish others with torture. This had taken place over two hundred years ago. The young man shared that his father's line came from Europe.

I explained that his ancestor had been involved in some activities he felt were unforgivable. After the traumatic experiences, as a broken forty-year-old-man, he had rejected his family because of the shameful memories he could not bear to live with. Each night when he slept, he would have visions of the abuse he had been party to, and his soul would not rest. He lost trust in his brothers, his wife, and his children, and feared he might become violent toward them. He could no longer live, so he committed suicide.

As I shared the story, the young man began to sense his ancestor's deep pain. He realized his ancestor was more than sad; he was a broken soul who carried the burdens of all the family members of the ones he had hurt or killed. This was his karma. I explained that his ancestor, although he was an angel, would not be at peace until the family members of all the souls that had been killed or tortured could forgive and that parts of his soul were still trapped in pain in the portals of the Earth until this forgiveness was made.

I explained that we could call on his ancestors to offer up this karma and that he and his ancestors could receive karmic absolution. If he held compassion and love for this ancestor who had hurt and killed others out of fear that he would lose his family, and if he helped this ancestor trust himself again, enough to forgive this after more than two hundred years had passed, then the sadness would begin to clear from his whole ancestral line.

The young man sat in silence for some time, deeply feeling his ancestors.

I said, "You can feel them, can't you?"

He could, and this surprised him. I explained he was an empath, one who could feel the truth of others, which was another gift he had received through his ancestral line. I shared with him that some people feel their ancestors' emotions while others are more affected by their ancestors' thoughts, and everyone can learn to connect to their ancestors, as they are always sharing their streams of consciousness.

He breathed a deep sigh from the well of sadness and said his ancestor was hurting and needed healing. How could he help him? I shared that it was best to ask his ancestor to receive healing from his Divine Presence directly. I suggested that he call on all of his ancestors' Divine Presences, and on his own as well, to bring the divine energy into his ancestors' hearts and to ask them to choose together to forgive with this older ancestor.

He shared that he felt his father had never been emotionally present. His family was not close; everyone had gone their separate ways in life and hardly saw each other. He felt sad when he was with his family, specifically with his father. He had felt controlled by him as a child, yet his father always spoke about how important his family was to him. He thought his father felt he may have failed the family and possibly this was why he was so sad.

I shared that all of this was connected to his ancestor's choice to commit suicide. I suggested that the young man ask his Divine Presence to assist him by repatterning his DNA. In order to clear the family karma, he would have to break the agreements his ancestor had made by declaring the following: "By divine decree, in the name of my Divine Presence, under the laws of grace, love, divinity, oneness, forgiveness, grace, and liberty, I now break all agreements made, held through my DNA or consciousness, to never forgive myself for hurting others, creating great sadness for others, or disappointing or failing my family, or leaving my family. I now call for karmic absolution for all of my ancestors and family and ask for this family karma to be lifted."

As he spoke these words out loud, as a representative for his family and ancestors, a great light flooded through him as his Presence filled him with love. I became aware of a larger group of Presences, the archangels who had come into the space, arriving to assist his ancestors to complete their forgiveness.

Archangel Michael stepped forth and shared with me that a great healing had begun not only for the young man and his ancestors, but for the other members of his family, specifically his father. Michael was calling on this young man to spend time with his father to bring him out of his sadness. I explained that it only took one member to begin the karmic clearing of the family, and when three souls in a family are awakened, it is a sign that the clearing of the family karma is close to being complete.

I told him about three women I knew, grandmother, mother, and daughter of the same mother line. They were all at different levels of spiritual awakening, and this was a sign that the mother line was clear of its family karma. I shared that the mother had begun doing the work of clearing her family karma with me, and this had ignited her mother and daughter to join her. As she continued, her son also became involved in the forgiveness process. Then her ex-partner, the father of her children, had started to open to spiritual practices such as meditation. This was unbelievable to her as many years earlier she had chosen to meditate in a small walk-in closet in her family home to keep her spiritual life away from her partner's eyes and ears, as he had been so reactive. I explained it only took one to start the chain reaction. All the rest took place through the karmic clearing.

I shared with the young man that there are only two forms of family karma. One is held in the mother line and the other in the father line. I explained that clearing the family karma is more difficult for those at the end of their line, that is, those who have no children, as they are left alone with the responsibility. The young man sensed this deeply and we said prayers for these souls. I also explained that if someone cleared both the mother and father lines of their ancestral wounding, the karma would be lifted from all children so they would no longer carry it through their DNA and pass it down to future generations.

I explained that his father needed one of his children to bring love to him, to truly forgive him, and to wish to develop a relationship with him again. This young man had the power to create a broken man to come alive, and this was the work of an angel. I shared that two hundred years ago he had watched over his great-grandfather and family as a guardian angel, and when his contract had ended, he had chosen to incarnate again, carrying a higher vibration and consciousness. I shared that souls choose to incarnate into the same family until the love is truly flowing, and that if he balanced his personal karma with his father from his previous incarnation when he had judged his father, they would share love again.

I explained how blessed he was because he was so young, and that if he did this early, he could live karmically free and enjoy the love between him and his father before his father passed. Many men wait until their parents are on their deathbeds, and then sometimes it is too late and their parents take a lot of their karma with them. We completed with a big hug and thanked each other for the experience.

As he left, I caught a glimmer of his soul, of the faith he held not only in himself as a man who could receive love, but also in his father. I could feel his prayers, with my heart, that his father could also receive love again, and I sensed how empowering it felt for him that he could have a hand in creating this. Later that week, I received a call from him. He was going to return to the area where his father lived and study at the university there. He felt at peace with this decision. His heart was overflowing, to be able to receive as well as to give.

I already felt in my heart that his small acts and the grounding of his humanitarian spirit would not only assist him and his family but also affect the collective. As his ancestors witnessed his small acts and forgave, some of humanity's collective karma would also be balanced and released. Know your ancestors are also with you, witnessing your life, and all your small acts of compassion are aiding our collective in a powerful way. Your vastness of spirit cannot be measured through these acts; only when you see the shift in another will you truly know the result that each of your small acts delivers.

Our Collective Responsibility and Our Spiritual Power to Absolve Our Karma through the Open Heart and Forgiveness

What is amazing about our humanity is our ability to bend and change according to our circumstances. Adapting to our environment has been one of our greatest gifts, and a major contributing factor toward our evolution and the survival of our species. The basis of our energy field, its design or lightbody structure, gives us this ability to adapt to new circumstances. Our field structure is in a continual state of evolution and is dynamic in its ability to integrate different forms of energy and consciousness. In truth, our fields are switching frequencies throughout our day, and when our body rests, we have the ability to regenerate not only our physical energy, but also our consciousness.

Just as the tectonic plates facilitate the evolution of our landmasses or Earth's shift over millions of years supported by the Earth's crystal and its many plates, our lightbody supports our physical body as well as the integration of our consciousness. As the lightbody of the Earth charges to a higher vibration, it receives new forms of frequency and consciousness from the universe. As our lightbody charges to a higher vibration, it receives new forms of frequency and consciousness from the Earth and universe and feeds them to our physical body and soul to raise our level of consciousness and our power to create new experiences.

Our lightbody is designed to adapt, and when we enter a new environment, it begins to resonate to the dimensional band of frequency that is most present. This is called the law of resonance. The only way you can alter this is to enter a higher state of consciousness than what your environment holds.

Sometimes when you enter a new environment, you will notice the presence of unbalanced karma or unresolved energy, particularly when emotional issues are being hidden, or when experiences of unloving exchange in communication are carrying an abusive, violent, or insensitive energy into the environment. You may ask, When is it my responsibility to work with the karma hidden underneath any life situations I may witness or experience?

Through universal law, you are unable to interfere energetically with another individual soul regarding their personal karma without their permission or you begin to create karma with this soul. A soul's personal karma is held within their soul, physical body, chakras, and energy field or lightbody. It is not your responsibility to work with another soul's personal karma or to transmit healing energy into their field even if you feel you are helping them. If this is done without permission of the soul, it is interference with another's free will.

While you may not interfere with another's personal karma, you do have certain responsibilities with regard to family karma, community karma, or planetary karma—the unresolved energy that lies between individuals, groups, families, communities, or the Earth's body. If you have personal involvement in a situation and you are not simply a witness, and you have negatively directed your energy, words, or actions toward another soul or toward the Earth, you have the responsibility of the personal karma you have created through this. If you have no personal involvement and are simply a witness, you are only responsible for the karma if this is a family or global situation. If you are personally involved in the situation and you are unable to hold your unconditional love and nonjudgment for others, you are responsible for any judgment you may have projected on others.

Every situation shown to you with your spiritual eyes grants you the opportunity to reclaim a part of your consciousness by taking a few moments to honor your responsibility. It is not your responsibility to take any person's world upon your shoulders. Yet when we live blindly, believing everything we witness outside of our personal sphere is not our responsibility, our spiritual empowerment weakens and our physical body also loses energy. We each carry a spiritual current that has the potential to energize our body, enlighten our mind, and bring joy and peace to our soul. This spiritual current is sourced from our hearts but lives within our lightbody. Your journey of empowerment comes from receiving this spiritual current from your Divine Presence and coming to a place of self-realization where you choose how you will use your energy and consciousness.

As your lightbody switches frequencies according to the environmental energy, you also experience yourself differently within each environment you enter. When your lightbody switches to a lower-based frequency, your lower consciousness is more active in your personality. When your light-body switches to a higher-based frequency, your higher consciousness is more active. At times you may experience your consciousness at a variety of different levels within one day.

Our feelings are directly related to the level of frequency our lightbody is holding a resonance with. Emotions of joy, sensations of light, and experiences of love and peace accompany the environments that hold a higher frequency and consciousness. Emotional projection, sensations of fear or pain, or experiences of isolation accompany the environments that hold a lower frequency and consciousness.

Your spiritual current, when grounded, has the ability to release karma from the environment or from your own lightbody. Grounding our spiritual current is an act of spiritual empowerment that can resolve not only our personal karma but also the karma that is held in the environment. For the truth is, beloved, that when a soul is unconscious of their karma and what they create, they often leave old, unresolved energy in their environment. This creates a dampening in the field that lowers the vibration of all who enter it. As a member of the collective, we may take responsibility and raise the environmental field by simply opening our hearts, forgiving all that we have witnessed in the environment, and calling on our Divine Presence to ground our spiritual current through our lightbody and physical body and into the Earth.

As karmic absolution floods the environmental field it lifts any unresolved energy and the environment lifts in vibration, and those sharing the space are no longer triggered by family, collective, or planetary karma. Once the environment is no longer holding stagnant energy, members of a collective or a family who personally share a mirrored version of the old karma will be supported by the environment's new energy to raise their consciousness as well, rather than be triggered into an energetic or physical struggle with each other.

Our collective responsibility is to hold the field of nonjudgment in any karmic situation. If we are unable to do this and find we are judging, then we are being shown our own personal karma as a mirror to us. If we open our hearts after we judge and are able to love and truly forgive, and not hold someone else responsible for the creation of the experience, a part of our personal karma will be absolved.

Our Communities and Families—Our Role as Peacemakers

Our role within our families and communities is to be the souls who are willing to hold the frequency of light for all others until they are ready to receive this light directly through their own heart and spirit. The Enlightened Masters teach that in every situation there is the potential to have peace, and the primary manifestation of peace comes from a process of detachment, forgiveness, and acceptance of all in life.

As light seeds, we are asked to make it our daily priority to create peace within our energy fields, not only for our own evolution but for our families, for our partners and children, and for all of our collective. When one person grounds this light frequency and creates peace within their own energy field, they are able to be a peacemaker of the Earth and hold the field of peace for all others.

As a child, I went to school in a very small town, and my community consisted of mostly quiet and peaceful country people. I was blessed with a family that was very loving. My father held a strong integrity, and my mother held a beautiful sense of service to others. I witnessed these qualities throughout my childhood, and it created me to learn to be at peace.

I was an emotional child, very talkative and interested in the world and specifically other people. The smallest things would upset me. I remember the first time I saw a grasshopper die, how it shattered my sense of peace. Whenever I felt others not open in their energy, I would feel sad for them. Whenever I felt others angry or disappointed when I did not do what they wanted, I would also cry. When I felt my teacher angry or stressed, I would cringe inside, feeling her pain. I was often unbalanced by other people's energy, as I had no boundaries and lived in a sea of consciousness. I was wide open with my energy field, open to new ideas, new discoveries, and new people, but because I was still a child, developing my chakras and conscious awareness, I was not grounded in my light frequency, so I experienced the feelings of everyone around me, from the grasshopper, to my teacher, to my parents, my brothers, and all others I met.

Because children are still developing their chakras from zero to twenty-one years of age and learning to ground the light frequency of their soul and spirit into the body, they have no choice but to feel whatever energy enters their field as if it were their own. As adults, we often continue to assume that we have to either feel whatever comes through our field or else close down our field altogether. Yet, as adults we have the ability to be aware of our own energy and thus filter the energy of others that comes our way without closing down our fields. When we open our heart and refrain from judging what another person is experiencing, it creates our field to filter the lower-vibrational energies or unresolved feelings connected to the other person's experiences. This state of nonjudgment is the highest gift we can give to our families and communities, and it is the essence of our role as peacemakers on Earth.

Often I hear from friends or students that they are feeling energetically misaligned due to changes in their personal field and in the collective field as we shift into the fifth dimension. The truth is that aspects of each of us still reside in the fourth dimension while another part of us already lives in the fifth dimension. When our lightbodies are switched to the level of frequency that resonates with the fifth dimension, that part of our consciousness is able to express unconditional love. When our lightbodies switch to the base frequency that resonates with the fourth dimension, our hearts become more protective and closed, and our consciousness becomes centered in the mind. Our mental consciousness will be the more active consciousness creating our experience at this time.

The frequency that unites all to enter an energy field of peace can only be transmitted in a state of nonjudgment and love. This is a fifth dimensional state of consciousness. As we are all shifting into the fifth dimension together, and a part of our collective is still operating from the fourth dimension and third dimension, we cannot expect ourselves to always be holding unconditional love in every moment.

The Enlightened Masters encourage us to see ourselves in a transition. Our aim is to love unconditionally, but at times we may oscillate in our energy bodies and resonate to our old consciousness in the fourth dimension. This is a part of the peacemaking process also. If you experience a shift from a space of peace and love to a space of judgment and uncenteredness, know that you are learning and you have not failed. You are in a process, and each experience you have offers you the opportunity to bring a part of your consciousness from the fourth dimension into the fifth dimension.

When you drop into a space you do not enjoy, know it is so you may embrace a part of yourself that wishes to come to peace, that wishes to enter the fifth dimension but does not know the way. Your role as a peacemaker is first to recognize you are always love, whether or not you feel it or enact it or transmit it, beloved. This is your essence, and you are asked to return to it. Each time you return to this truth, it deepens and strengthens your heart and your ability to bring the field of peace to others.

You are not being asked to take on the burden of other people's suffering. You are simply being asked to hold the field of peace when you can, and when you cannot, you are asked to go on the journey inside and embrace the part of you that needs the field of peace. Some students share with me that at times they feel they are moving backward three steps as they take one step forward in their embodiment of love. Yet, it is actually the embrace of your own aspects of consciousness that need unconditional love and nonjudgment that will open your heart and truly allow the shift into the fifth dimension.

The key is to not expect yourself to always be in the higher state of consciousness when you are still in the process of clearing your karma. You have a great gift as a peacemaker no matter how much karma you have, if you are willing to be a conduit for pure love by simply calling on God, Great Spirit, or the Universal Heart to assist you to hold the field of peace for others, beloved.

Recognize that a great universal field of love does exist, even if humanity does not always know of it or receive from it. This field, which some call the Holy Mother, is abundant in its love and forever willing to shower a soul with more love than they would ever need to raise the field of peace in an environment. As this field of love opens in an environment, the angels and higher evolved consciousnesses that hold nonjudgment and immense love are able to enter the environment and support all beings. As peacemakers, we can choose to be supported by the universal field of love with our work. The belief that humanity is solely responsible for our world limits our field's connection to the realms of light and creates our separation from our lightbody and from the light of our consciousness in the other worlds.

I often meet such beautiful souls here on Earth. I do not believe I have yet met one who is not beautiful or holding something inside them that touches my heart. I truly hold faith in the law of divinity, which teaches us that every soul is a divine being.

I am especially blessed to receive many long, heartfelt hugs from those I meet. My experiences with hugs are often extraordinary. So many souls have angels in their field, which means their consciousness is also expressed in angelic form in the Fourth World. Other souls have many ancestors around them, and their consciousness expresses through an ancestral form that they hold within the Inner Earth.

I am always blessed when I hug all these souls, for I am left radiant from the exchange of love with them. As our hearts connect, I am able to see into the other worlds of their consciousness and meet their soul on a deeper level. As we hug, the exchange of codes of light takes place through our hearts. Everything I am holding from my latest shift in consciousness is exchanged with them, and everything they hold from their latest shift in consciousness is received by me.

What is so beautiful about the code exchange is that so much is lifted from our soul that we no longer need to carry. The code exchange also releases karma, but in the most loving, gentle way. As you receive another's codes into your heart, they dissolve karma held inside your lightbody that is a mirror of the karma they have shifted through their love and forgiveness. This is one of our most important roles as peacemakers, linking hearts, soul to soul, and sharing our codes of light that we carry inside.

Our World Cities—Our Role as Representatives of Humanity

Our cities have been holding aspects of our collective karma, woven through the etheric structure of their energy fields. These sites on the Earth carry much of our history as well as a great source of our collective power as a species. The transformation of the etheric field structure of our cities is also a part of the Divine Plan for our shift as a collective into the fifth dimension. These great structures that we have built to serve our civilization to expand also have a Divine Plan.

Germaine stepped forth to me one day and spoke of our world's cities and how the Divine Plan was to activate them to ignite a new energy that would be more supportive of our collective, specifically the souls that live in the cities. When he came, a great violet flame surrounded him, and he took me through a portal of pure white light. As we traveled from city to city, he showed me souls that were suffering, unable to fully open their energy fields to receive any comfort or love. He explained to me that the etheric fields of the cities were partially responsible for the suffering of these souls, for the karma held in the cities' etheric fields made it difficult for souls to open their energy fields and chakras.

One of our last stops was Tokyo, where I was shown many grey buildings stacked together, packed with people who had no personal space yet were trying to live in harmony. Germaine shared that the collective consciousness of the Japanese people was different from the collective consciousness of the Australian people or the Balinese people. He said that every nation on the Earth held its own stream of consciousness, and there was karma between the races that would need to shift. When the karma between the races shifted and the city's etheric fields were cleared, humanity would experience peace on Earth.

We looked into a small flat where a young man who appeared to be about twenty-seven years old was lying on his back, very depressed, thinking about committing suicide. Germaine shared that the young man would not take his life if he could receive love at this time. My heart filled with mixed emotions, from great compassion to a deep wish to hold this man. My own partner had committed suicide, and the tears were welling up and rolling down my face.

"How can I stop this?"

Germaine said, "Say a prayer for this soul, and you will make the difference. Prayer will open a gateway above his heart so the flow of love from the angelic realm can begin to gently hold him through his field. It can be the difference between life and death."

As Germaine spoke, I remembered that at twenty-one, I had not had the strength to say a prayer for my partner. I had been so overwhelmed with my feelings of responsibility that I had not known how to ask for help. I felt inside that if I had known to say a prayer for Little Owl, it would have made the difference, and he may not have committed suicide.

All of this flashed through me, and Germaine said, "Your partner is fine."

I had met my partner Little Owl very powerfully in spirit six or seven times since his death, and for many years I had felt his spirit with me as I raised my daughter without him. I knew he had forgiven and become an angel and was watching over my daughter, which deeply comforted me. Germaine opened a portal, a window into another world, and I saw my partner there. He had reincarnated and was not in despair.

Germaine spoke to me. "Upon his death your partner went through a great journey of meeting his fears, and this led him to forgive all. He watched you for eight years, crying to sleep, feeling your guilt, and it took him some time to heal. His angelic form ignited and you were both freed. You also forgave yourself at a similar time, beloved. At this time, although he was holding a soul contract to be an angelic guide, a part of Spirit extended and also reincarnated as a small child."

In this moment I realized deeply that consciousness is not bound in one body, as so many in our society seem to believe. I understood that my partner who had died was an angel in the Fourth World, watching over my daughter, but he had also reincarnated.

I felt my heart and his heart connect for a few moments, and I felt great love and peace inside. Germaine closed the portal of light that gave me the window to my ex-partner, and my heart felt again for this Japanese man who was in difficulty as a soul and so close to the edge. I could feel the fine balance of life that the Enlightened Masters often spoke of. We could not intervene but we could send love. But what if a soul is closed in their energy field, so shut down that they cannot receive? I felt a deep pain inside.

Germaine said to me gently, "You are feeling the pain of this soul, and you must not take it into your heart. It is important that he experience this."

I asked him, "Why is it important that he experience this form of mental and emotional suffering?"

He spoke to me gently and said, "It is his karma, my child, and we cannot take this away from any soul. They have the free will to find their way home to their heart. This discovery is like a new flower on the Earth, growing, that has never before been known to exist. He is a new flower of the Earth, a child discovering himself. Only through his own discovery will he birth. You must hold faith that he will do this. You must ask him to be assisted, as he cannot ask. You must have patience to know his spirit is with him. You must trust the nature of his free will."

I spoke telepathically with the heart of his soul, and even though his personality and mind were not aware of my contact, as I spoke to him his body moved and he sat upright as if someone was in the room.

Germaine said, "He senses your presence as an angel but does not understand in his mind what this is."

I called to him as a soul and began to speak to him from my heart. "Hold my hand. Take my strength and know I am with you, even if you cannot see me. Trust there is another way. There is not only one door in your life at this time. Let the thought go at this time and be held by the love. You deserve so much more than death. Life awaits you. It is not your time. Let your death come after you have lived and done all you need to do. You will meet another here and the pain and this blackness will be a memory of the past. This one will love you, but you must love yourself first. Do not despair that you are not enough, for this an old belief that you no longer need to give power to.

"Let go of the thoughts of your death. It is your emotional pain that offers you no other solution, but you can let go and surrender your pain. It will be a journey, but life will hold and sustain you. Open your heart to me, and I will fill you with love. Do not blame yourself. She is not blaming you; she is angry inside and has her own journey in life. Blame not yourself for another's choice. Do not take it personally. Make the choice to live through this and grow stronger as a man. You have so much to give."

I was speaking to him of the young woman he had fallen in love with who had rejected him. She worked in an office. All of this came to me as Germaine opened the portal for me to see his life of the last twelve months like a movie projected before me. I saw everything that had led him to this moment: how he hated the job he was expected to do for the rest of his life, how he had to force himself to lift his body each morning, how his mind thought only of ending his life.

Then the movie stopped, and Germaine said, "You now know why he wishes to let go of his body, for he knows no other way to release the pain he is experiencing, beloved. This is why your partner suicided also. He knew no other way, and neither did you. Speak to this young man now, and you will help on a soul level. This is all you can do, trust and hold faith in him."

I spoke to him gently, whispering to his soul. "You have to forgive yourself. It is not your fault. She does love you and would not want you to suffer."

I was speaking now of his mother. The movie of the last year of his life had shown me six events that had synchronized to push him over the edge. First he had lost the love of a young woman, who had pushed him away when he became too needy, relying on her love to help him through his depression. Second, his mother had died, and he had not seen her or spoken to her for many years. He came from a broken family and had left home at an early age due to his father's temper and tendency toward domestic violence. He did love his mother deeply and felt guilty for not ever contacting her. Third, the young man's job was disempowering, and he was often criticized for being too slow and for daydreaming. And then his sister was angry with him for not returning home for his mother's funeral; she said he had shamed the family.

The fifth event was his realization that he had nothing in life to live for. He believed he had no family and no future. The sixth was that he was being evicted in a month, and he did not have the energy to find another place to live. They were selling the block of flats, which was very old and would be torn down for a new building; every tenant had to relocate. He felt the collective consciousness of his ancestors and race, and held great expectations of himself in honor of his heritage. He was deeply ashamed of himself.

I could relate to some of his pain, for in my youth I had experienced homelessness and despair after leaving university at eighteen years of age and not knowing my path in life. I had chosen to opt out of reality by numbing myself with drugs instead of entering society. A part of me held an unconscious death wish, and I had many close encounters with death and thoughts of suicide at the time.

The young man stood up in the room and opened a small window. There was no breeze, so he closed it again. He picked up some books and flicked them back down. It was as if he was looking for something but could not find it.

Saint Germaine spoke to me. "He can feel your presence, beloved. Soothe him. He is on a dangerous path, but he can be supported with love to gently move to another path."

A book fell on the floor, and a photo fell out. It was a photo of his mother from when she was young. He picked it up and lay on the bed again. I heard him think of her, and his mind sensed that she might be in the room. Saint Germaine opened another portal of light, and the young man's mother came forth. The spirit appeared as an older Japanese woman with white light all around her. As she entered the space and saw her son, she moved to his side and placed her hand upon his heart and said, "Forgive me, my son."

He was in a deep place inside. The photo had brought up all of his memories of his childhood and how his mother had hid him from his father so he would not be hurt. He missed her and could feel her, yet he did not know she was there in spirit with him. He just stared blankly into the wall, feeling numb.

She wished she could hold him. He turned and curled into a ball on his side, and the photo crumpled in his hand. Thoughts raced past, and then he came to a memory of being very small and holding his mother's hand as he took his first steps.

She filled him with her love and said again, "Forgive me, my son. I could not protect you, but you are grown now and you can protect yourself. You can learn from this and love yourself."

He felt her love in that moment as if she were really there. The memory was strong and beautiful and filled him with love.

She said, "I am still here with you my son, and I will help you."

It was beautiful to see them reconnect, even though he could only do it through a memory. I felt his light grow stronger, and I knew he was going to be okay; he would not take his life now. He had received his mother's love even if he did not know how. I was relieved.

Saint Germaine spoke to me and said, "It only takes a little love. It does not matter where it comes from, but once it is received, the light and spirit within is always lit again."

I could see the light coming back into the young man's eyes. He was beginning, in his own way, to surrender. He stayed coiled up in a ball on his bed in that memory of love from his mother, and she stayed with him.

Saint Germaine said that she would stay until he had moved through the grief. "Just as your partner did with you," he said. I remembered being coiled in a ball on my bed, lying and simply staring, the memories of my partner coming to me. It was so long ago, before my spiritual awakening and heart opening. My surrender had been a long journey. As I honored this and thanked Germaine, we traveled together through the portal of light and I was taken to another city.

We were in Stockholm this time. Germaine shared that he wanted to show me one more thing before we returned from our journey. This time he showed me many groups of people gathering together all over the city. We came to one group of about thirty people from all walks of life, focused together in a large room. They were all interested in humanitarian aid. I could see their lightbodies glowing and their passion to assist others in need.

Germaine said, "God has created everything to be placed on the Earth that humanity needs to create balance with the Earth. Every soul, every gift is here already. It is the true power source of humanity."

He shared he wanted to show me the city's connection to this power source we hold. He said the power is only available when we gather together for a common purpose. He shared that there is more power living inside our bodies than the power that generates all of the electricity on the Earth. A city of people could power our whole world for generations if we could just learn to access the power of our collective.

I watched carefully as a silent witness as Germaine showed me the group gathered together. They were unaware that many were waiting in the wings of spirit to help them. Their plan was to create the humanitarian aid from their own energy source, as they were unaware they could tap into the collective power source. I was not sure what he meant exactly at this stage, but I could logically see that every city held a lot of people, and this was obviously a huge power source.

At that point, there was a discussion between three or four people about a situation in Africa that needed humanitarian aid more quickly than they could arrange. They spoke of other organizations they were working with, and considered how it would be possible for them to work together. All of the people gathered were either volunteers or paid staff of a nonprofit organization whose focus was mainly on Africa and its children. My heart immediately felt these souls who were suffering in ways that felt deeply inhumane.

Saint Germaine spoke to me and said, "The hand of God is within everything, my child, but the karma at times is so deep. It takes a great deal of time for change to take place, beloved. Change occurs from within, beloved. All change in your outer world must first take place within."

I understood what he meant, but it did not make it easier when I felt for the people in Africa who needed assistance to simply have their most basic needs met. He said I needed to put aside my personal feelings and again to have faith in my fellow humanity. He shared that the people gathered in this room had found their calling; their karma was linked to the need to aid this human suffering.

He said, "In the field of the city of Stockholm, there are ancestral memories of all that was left unresolved by the Swedish people's ancestors. This collective karma is always held in the etheric field of the largest cities or communities."

He shared that every race has karma to resolve connected to their ancestors and is working to resolve the karma that creates pain and suffering. The Swedish people were being called by their ancestors to bring equality to all. "It is their role as a race," he shared, "to begin to move the collective in this direction, specifically in regard to the equality between men and women. They are holding this puzzle piece as a nation within our world."

I listened carefully, absorbing all he shared. I gently asked him how the nation's ancestral karma, and the individual gifts that arose from it, was connected to the city's etheric field. He placed his hand of pure light on my third eye, and I saw the field of the city as a pulsating energy. Parts of the field were flowing with divine energy, and other parts were heavy and appeared stagnant and dark. Above the city's buildings, high in the heavens, I could see a vortex of light.

Germaine spoke to me and shared, "This is the heart chakra of the city, and every soul in the city's heart is connected to it. Imagine all of the people in the city merging their hearts as one power source. You are witnessing the collective heart of all souls in the city, beloved."

The vortex was filled with light, but it appeared to be struggling to fully open. Germaine shared that the heart chakra was only partially open. I could see fine filaments from the etheric field of the city and its huge heart chakra connecting to the etheric bodies of each member of the group

I was witnessing. Their fields all became light as I witnessed Germaine fill the collective heart chakra of the city with an immense light. It was flooded with divine energy and burst open for a few moments, and I witnessed a waterfall of divine energy flow from the heart chakra through the whole field of the city.

He said, "I can do no more than this, for it is up to humanity and its representatives to transform the etheric body of their cities."

As this wave of immense love and light flooded the city's field, I could see each person in the group before me receive this energy. In that moment, one person became excited and shared a new idea. It was a profound idea of how they could deliver the humanitarian aid in a quicker way, without too much effort. The others were excited too, and asked him how he had come up with this idea; he shared it had just come to him in a flash. I knew that the energy released from the opening of the heart chakra had brought a great wave of light and love that had supported him to access his super-consciousness in that moment. He had accessed the Divine Plan, which carries the win-win solution for all problem solving.

I realized in that moment that the power source of our collective was stored in our collective heart chakra, and that together, we create a field of great power that we are not consciously accessing. I understood more deeply what Germaine had originally meant by our collective power source. Germaine shared that the etheric body of humanity and the etheric body of the community had great impact on each other, as they were the fields of energy that held the closest connection to the physical body.

He shared he was not able to clear the collective heart chakra of the city, but I and others who chose to be representatives for humanity could do this if we wished. I could see that even though this work may not be understood by all of humanity, it was deeply needed, and it was a puzzle piece of mine to assist the collective karma of humanity to gently be transmuted in divine timing.

This experience led me to work with Mother Earth's energy portal system for many years and to then cocreate a four-year worldwide karmic clearing project called the Celestial Project. This project began in September 2009, when I invited others to join the Enlightened Masters and myself in sacred linkups as representatives for humanity, for the clearing of the collective karma held in primary cities of our Earth.

SPIRIT INVITES YOU

Eyes quietly open ...
Will I be brave today and awaken
or curl my body into a ball
feel the smoothness
peace and comfort some more?
Harsh light and sounds
break me into thought
awaken me to wonder why,
where, who, how it shall be?
Is it any wonder
I toss the blankets to the floor
and arise ever so tall
yet feel so small inside of me?
Will it ever change
or is this all there will ever be?
My body sighs
wet with desire for more ...
The small voice echoes wisdom
beloved, giveth over and into you I shall come
speak no more of loss ...
You are a vessel of love
for all your wish to create
but have you left your wish
behind you?
It liveth with your heart
The home of your soul ...
Rest within my arms
I shall carry you

returneth all . . .
and we will feel as one . . .
your eternal nature is calling
Drop your name, all concepts of your form
and know spirit holds all you may wish
and all you need
will whish itself into a new form . . .
Your door must never close
your heart must hold a glow
for your vessel to accept me
allowing your special wish to ignite
our eternal heart connection's light
To bring special gifts to your life
will you let me into your heart?
Will you give away that which I show you
no longer serves you?
Will you swim the oceans of love with me
let me sound through your body?
Will you dream of another day
awakening as one with me
allowing me to fill your day?
Will you let me move your world
show you what you have not imagined can be
give you a holy life, filled with more than you
can imagine to be wonderful, powerful, and beautiful?
This is my invitation . . .

The Divine Presence of the Many,
Waiting in the Wings to Assist on All Levels

Mother Gaia calls your name through her mountains, rivers, forests, and
fields of flowers. You and your spirit are to meet each other on Earth and

allow a healing to occur not only for yourself but also for your family and community and for Mother Earth. Why are you called, you may ask, and what is this calling? It is a calling to meet our hearts, in Divine Presence.

Long ago, before humanity had birthed, before the flowers were in physical form, the Earth was a gaseous, radiant star, housing many worlds, none of them physical in form. This was the time of Lemuria, the original angelic and archangelic world of the Earth. The angels and archangels were developing their consciousness as the outer, primary world of the Earth. You may have been one of these winged beings. The Enlightened Masters Kuthumi and Sanat Kumara share that every being in incarnation now has returned to the Earth to complete something from long ago when they were within the world of Lemuria.

They came in blue robes one day, and many of them came, thirteen or more Masters in a group merkabah. Kuthumi stepped forth to me, as my relationship with him had become one of great friendship, over many years of contact. We often joked with each other, and he would sometimes appear as a miniature being sitting before me on a small violet cushion, appearing only as large as the crystal on my altar. It was his joke, for in the beginning of my relationship with the Enlightened Masters, I saw them as superior to me, not yet realizing that truly there is no hierarchy in spirit, only oneness; this was his way of humoring me.

On this day, they took me to the pinnacle of a high mountaintop that I recognized as Mount Kilimanjaro in Tanzania. We entered a spiritual doorway and walked through a long passageway that led into the portal under the mountain, deep in the Earth. I had no idea why I was there, but it felt important, and I could feel a large gathering was about to take place. It was a gathering of ancestral Masters, with the Enlightened Masters and many representatives from between the worlds. I asked Kuthumi why I was there. He said, "You are to witness this for humanity."

We entered a very large temple structure, larger than I would have expected, inside the mountain. He heard my thoughts and explained telepathically that the inner dimensions are larger in spatial awareness than the outer because the frequency of the inner dimensions is much higher. I accepted this and continued to be fascinated by what I was witnessing, as hundreds then thousands of beings of light came into this immense grand hall to gather together.

I wondered what this gathering was for. Kuthumi heard my thoughts again and instantly explained.

"You live in many bodies of light, my child, without full awareness, and this is a gathering of all of your consciousness, your Divine Presence and all other Divine Presences who have a connection to Mother Earth and humanity. These Presences have returned to the Earth and are waiting in the wings to assist humanity in its process of shifting into the world that will develop the most consciousness. All members of humanity have a connection to the Earth from long ago, from Lemuria, and they are all here to complete something so they may evolve."

I continued to see streams of beautiful presences of light enter and find their place in this great temple and was fascinated by how loving and peaceful all of these beings were. I was filled with light and entered an ecstasy, and every cell of my physical body began to tingle as a magnificent blue crystal in the center of the temple began to radiate its light to me. I realized we were all gathered to commune with the Holy Spirit of Mother Earth, and the blue crystal was a part of her consciousness. I felt my heart and chakras connect to the crystal, and I felt the field between me and all of the others expand and ignite in a deeper level of oneness. I was unable to witness any more, for the power of the experience was lifting me into an ecstatic state. I felt myself rise in vibration and expand to a state of bliss beyond the psychic field, and all of my psychic abilities dissolved as I dissolved into the immense love of Gaia.

I felt myself floating in the sky above Africa. Mother Gaia appeared as a dark-skinned woman in the heavens with me. Her face was beautiful, and her eyes shone the light of thousands of stars, covering the whole sky. I felt like I was swimming toward her eyes. They twinkled at me, and she said she was the mother of the dreamtime and of all creation on Earth, and if I allowed those waiting in the wings to assist me, I would see my dreams come true on Earth. She smiled at me and shared she would hold me whenever I needed it, and asked me to tell all the children of Earth that they are loved by Mother Earth.

Gently I came back to Earth and was returned into the temple again. Kuthumi handed me a small crystal and asked me to look inside it. I touched it and instantly saw many people on Earth, each waiting for their Presences, and in the portals from the physical world to the spiritual world, their Presences were waiting for them to be ready to receive the new frequency and divine assistance.

I realized that the "wings" Gaia had been speaking about were the portals or energy doorways of the Earth that link the physical and spiritual worlds. Kuthumi shared that many people on the Earth were traveling to these sacred sites to receive the frequency they needed and prepare themselves for their evolution. He shared that the beings from other worlds utilized the portals of the Earth to travel between the worlds.

He invited me to call on my Divine Presence to merge with me, a practice I had been doing every day since I first met the Enlightened Masters, and as I did this, I felt my energy subtly begin to shift.

Kuthumi said, "But you must open yourself to receive your Presence more deeply."

I sounded in ancient language and took my consciousness into my heart chakra with the intention of opening my energy field. A light began to fill me, and I felt myself gently lift in a nonphysical way into a more expanded, peaceful state. My chakras began to fill with more energy.

He said, "You just experienced your Presence fully when the blue crystal connected to you. Your Presence, all of your consciousness from all dimensions and worlds, merged with you, and you entered bliss and ecstasy. This is the nature of your Presence; it is your enlightened self, formed from all of your energy and consciousness merging as one. It offers you an experience of enlightenment."

I acknowledged I had felt enlightened in those moments and had felt I could access all the love and ever-present wisdom of the universe. He said, "This is what is waiting in the wings for humanity. It is their enlightenment."

The nature of our Divine Presence had never been explained to me before. Many pieces began to click into place. I realized that this consciousness was accessible to me whenever I wished to embody it. Kuthumi heard my thoughts and shared that assistance from our Divine Presence comes in infinite forms, and it is available to everyone. They simply need to ask for their Divine Presence to merge with them each day, and the process of assistance will take place in the highest way.

The Grace That Wishes to Be Provided to the World— Visitations of the Enlightened Beings Who Are Guides for Our Process of World Peace

I looked into his heart and saw a soft glow of light. He was still alive. A small baby kangaroo in its dead mother's pouch, lying very still and frightened. Its mother had died on the road when she slammed into a car, obviously blinded by the headlights. I picked up the baby and let it know I would look after it. Its mother was with Spirit now, and it was time to let her go. Its eyes opened, and although it struggled at first as I said this, it settled into my arms, surrendering sweetly.

I felt it was letting go of its mother, yet was still in deep shock. I filled it up with violet light and all my love for five or ten minutes by the side of the road. I felt its heartbeat change and become more normal a few minutes after I began injecting it with light. I was sad for the baby kangaroo that had lost its mother, but I felt if it was filled with love it would integrate even this great loss and shock. I wrapped it in a blanket in my car and placed it snugly in a bag so it would feel like it was in a pouch again. I got in my car and drove the remaining thirty miles to my home, where I was able to relocate it to a specialist who cared for young kangaroos.

What guided me that day to get out of my car and check a dead kangaroo's pouch to see if there was a baby? I could not tell you, as there was no voice asking me to do this, and I had not seen any movement of the kangaroo as my headlights flashed directly on the body. It was a feeling inside I just had to follow. When I saw the kangaroo directly in front of me, freshly hit but clearly not moving, I stopped without thinking. My spirit simply opened the door, and the next thing I was out on the road and noticed it was a mother with a bulge in her pouch. This saddened me until I placed my hand inside and it wriggled about.

The hand of grace is ever-present, and sometimes we are blessed to be in tune with it. It guides so many hands and hearts of our humanity to deliver the kindest deeds in support of others in need of assistance.

Grace comes in many forms, not according to what is needed but to what will be received. Animals, insects, plants, crystals, the great trees, mountains, and rivers, our seas, and the birds are all aware that grace is a part of nature that ebbs and flows according to what can be received.

Humanity has a narrow perspective as a collective and sees grace as either being a miracle or a blessing of good fortune or a gift for being good. Many beliefs held by our ancestors around being good so God or the gods will favor us are still held within the DNA of our collective. These beliefs take us into unconscious thoughts that share that we are not deserving enough to receive grace. Humanity is currently in a process of evolution that began long ago but accelerated less than 100,000 years ago. Since that time, humanity has moved through the ebbs and flows of receiving and not receiving grace via the human lightbody structure. Some in our collective have no problem with receiving grace; others are still opening their DNA to unlock the unconscious beliefs our ancestors may have held from their consciousness.

When we are clearing our karma, we need to receive grace in our lives, as our karma can sometimes take us to painful places where we do not feel our wholeness. Difficulty in letting go due to death of a loved one close to us, the loss of a partner, a deep separation or argument with a close friend, or deep illness are just some of the examples of our experiences of karma on Earth.

The grace that truly wishes to be delivered to humanity comes from the enlightened realms via visitations from the Enlightened Masters or archangels. This grace may be needed so a mother can continue to care for her children, even though she is grieving the loss of her partner. This grace is so a woman does not become bitter and distrustful of other men, simply because she experienced difficulty with one man. This grace is based on the dispensations that the Enlightened Masters hold for all beings—dispensations that absolve the original source memories held within the karmic plane of the Earth.

If you call on your Divine Presence to merge with you each day and invite the Enlightened Masters to assist you in your karmic clearing, the original core consciousness of your soul will be slowly peeled back, layer by layer. Your Divine Presence is all you need to work with to enlighten your consciousness more each day, but the Enlightened Masters hold the mantle for all dispensations and divine gifts that can be given to humanity to bring ease and grace to their journey as they evolve. Through becoming close to an Enlightened Master, you begin to enter new levels of initiation within your consciousness, and many things are arranged for your life to flow in the direction of your highest potential path.

The difficulty some experience is that they activate their spiritual path but do not realize that their DNA and ancestors play a role in their journey, and that it is not until they do the healing work with their family that their genetic code can unlock and truly free their consciousness. The process of unlocking one's genetic code so one's Divine Presence can be received is powerfully assisted by the Enlightened Masters. Through calling on their names or simply inviting them as a group into your life, you will begin the process of being assisted, and the greatest grace will become available to you as you unlock your genetic code so you can fully receive all you are meant to.

Awakening Your Super-consciousness and Wisdom through Releasing the Tape Loop from Your Mind

Each journey you take is a potential doorway to reclaiming a part of your consciousness so the super-consciousness of your soul can be released and accessed by you in your everyday life. Finding yourself clearly moving in a new positive direction on your life path signifies that you have just completed reclaiming a part of your consciousness and you are now ready to access a little more of your super-consciousness.

This super-consciousness is not just the wisdom and gifts you may hold, but the living genius of your soul. Every soul has a living genius or inner wisdom, yet it is not always accessed, due to karma or unwillingness. The wish to access one's higher reasoning is a journey that involves the transformation of consciousness within the body via the activation of centers within the brain. It is also the doorway for a soul to begin to receive the higher frequency of their Divine Presence. This is not every soul's wish, but many are choosing this as they are awakening to the truth that this is no longer only a possibility for those that live a life in sacred chanting and prayer, or within a cave in deep meditation.

The veils between the realm of Spirit and the physical world have been pierced to such a level that many on the Earth witness Spirit, feel and hear Spirit, or experience Spirit in their body. The Presence is birthing from within, and as this occurs, the heart is activated as a generator and harmonizer. The heart chakra of a soul who has evolved beyond their personal and family karma will generate peace and harmonize all environments the soul enters.

To be able to access your super-consciousness, you need to have a frequency flowing through your chakras that will raise the vibration of your energy body to allow your mind to rest in a higher state of consciousness. Our lower thought forms are a sign that our mind in that moment is not resting in a higher state of consciousness. When your energy field is raised, your mind naturally connects into the collective's higher band of consciousness through the law of resonance.

None of our thoughts are personal to ourselves. This may seem strange to you, as many people identify themselves with their thought forms and their beliefs, which are their strongest thoughts formed into a philosophy. When I first met the Masters and surrendered to my training, one of the first tasks I was given was to discipline my mind and bring it into a state of clarity. Every day for a period of four or five months I awoke and began my disciplined mind training that the Masters had given me to open my mind to my super-consciousness and my Divine Presence. I had no idea how long this training would take. I went about my normal daily activities and simply incorporated my practice into all I experienced. It was a very funny, intense, amazing, challenging, eye-opening experience that took my mind into a state of awareness, chaos, release, cleansing, emptiness, and then bliss.

The Enlightened Masters shared that I would need to do this exercise from the time I woke to the time I went to sleep every day, until it was complete. They would not give me a timeframe. They simply said I would know, as I would discover clarity and a completely empty mind that was filled with love and with no thoughts flowing through it. They shared that the way I saw the world would change, and the way others saw me would change. My larger triggers or attachments in life would also release.

They explained that the unconscious mind was made of three forms of energy. The first was our own collective consciousness; the second was all of the imprints of thought we had collected from our environment; and the third was the unconscious beliefs our minds formed from the relationship between these first two forms. They explained that until all the old imprints release from our mind through a cleansing, there is a tape loop of collective consciousness that is not our own, running in the background of the mind, and this filters our true access to our own collective consciousness.

They explained that our own collective consciousness holds the super-consciousness of our spirit, yet this is unable to be received if we carry this old tape loop within our minds. The tape loop veils the mind and holds it in a lower vibration, and therefore we only receive the lower dimensional thoughts of our spirit, based on our karma instead of the wisdom of our Divine Presence. It amazed me that clearing this busy and sometimes unloving or irrational mind could be a possibility. My mind was mostly busy with its attitudes and judgments, but sometimes I was fortunate for it would just be a witness.

They simply asked me to witness my mind at work, and if in any moment my mind had a thought that was nonloving and negative about others or myself, I would immediately offer this to be released into the light and apologize for any judgments I may have made. I did this by saying within my mind, each time I noticed a lower thought form, "I release this into the light." If my mind was also projecting on another, I would say within my mind, "I apologize to . . . [insert the name of the person] for this. I forgive myself."

This began quite smoothly, with thoughts popping in about myself, my relationship, my partner, and the world, and at first, most of the thoughts were incredibly loving and positive and I simply let these ones flow. I soon noticed that underneath these kinder thought forms there were some gnarly, subtle little judgments.

Sometimes the thoughts were guilt or anger or blame or other forms of emotional judgment. I became aware how many there were, and it was like a can of worms had been released from underneath the beautiful, loving thoughts I held on the surface of my mind. The Masters came each day and explained that there was a tape loop of consciousness within my mind, and if I went beneath the surface of my mind and simply witnessed with no judgment and offered these thoughts into the light every time I noticed them, eventually the tape loop of the unconscious mind would dissolve.

It had been about a week, and my thought forms were no longer just a little judging or subtly negative. They were downright rude to others and myself. They were demanding, and in the third layer of my mind I found all my demands, my list of expectations on myself and others, my judgments on others if they disappointed me. Each time I met these thoughts I felt a commander or demanding authority inside me. The Masters said it was all a reflection of my ego and these thoughts were a part of my consciousness, but they were also a part of the collective. Within the unconscious realms there is no separation between the individual and the collective. They explained to me that we do not have individual egos, but in truth there is one band of collective consciousness that is unconscious, and the ego nature is shared.

This was extraordinary for me to hear, that we do not need to personalize our egos. How freeing for us as individuals, spiritually, to not have to own a personal ego and to recognize this state of unconsciousness is collective. The part of me that was the witness of my whole journey was able to receive peace, yet I was also feeling the pressure of being unable to stay present with so much reaction within. Once I arrived to the fourth level of mind and witnessed the thoughts held there, everywhere I went there was only a barrage of abuse coming through my mind. It felt like the garbage of humanity.

During this phase, the thoughts seemed to have no self-awareness that they were even abusive, and I felt they stemmed from memories of deep abuse held in the collective. No more politeness or kindness was present as my witness dug deeper, honoring and releasing the thoughts of the subconscious of my mind. It seemed to take a week or two to get through this level of my mind for the thoughts to change and present a new personality to me.

During the fourth level, the thoughts were nonstop, and I was going crazy. No matter what I was doing, it was as if I had five very broken, rude, and angry people in my head, having a relationship with everything I met. I was continually praying to God and offering these thoughts into the light, apologizing telepathically to people who were around me. I remember one day a woman walked past, and I heard my mind say, "You fat pig." I was so shocked by this abusive comment, but the archangels showed me that I was simply on a journey through humanity's consciousness, layer by layer. It was hard work.

Once I got through to the fifth level, there were only thoughts of poor me and how everyone else was better off than me. The victim within our collective really came through at that time. These thoughts had the energy of resistance in that they did not want to transform but would rather remain as victims than have to change in some way. They seemed to carry no real energy, whereas the others had been very passionate thoughts. I felt the broken spirits from our collective with these thoughts. This took three weeks to shift. I honored and witnessed each thought as it arose and offered it into the light with a blessing and thank you for the journey.

Once I got through to the last level, the thoughts were very anxious and worrisome. They were full of the most negative projections about the future. They projected that even the process of witnessing my thoughts would go wrong and I would get stuck in the tape loop forever. The thoughts during this time also seemed to be fixated on other people's negative viewpoints, worries, and difficult situations, while positive people seemed to be strange or false, faking life in some way. As these thoughts released after many months of coming in and out of my mind, I felt a great peace. This peace and quiet lasted for at least two weeks, and I thought the process had completed. I had just begun to feel this peace of mind was going to last forever when I began to have thoughts of killing people and destroying things.

This came as quite a shock, and with it a voice of rage was met inside. It screamed at God, how dare God control us in our lives. This voice I called my Goddess; she was trying to cleanse herself of her old tape loop around hierarchy, disempowerment, the trap of duality. I would call upon God/Goddess each day, and this voice would rage as I said my prayers; in between I was offering these thoughts to the light. I would meet with the Enlightened Masters, and this voice was even angry with them.

In between every thought that emanated as this voice, I would offer these thoughts to the light and apologize. For many months I had two realities running parallel in my head. The first reality was what was occurring in my life, and the second was my training to honor, acknowledge, witness, love, and release all negative thoughts into the light. This took all my focus, and there was no moment when I had a break except for those two weeks of deep peace. As my raging Goddess dissolved, she became quieter, less vocal, and less angry. She eventually was dissolved into the light.

My mind's inner voice was clear, and all I could hear was the tranquillity of the Earth Mother's heart beating and the inner sounds of her loving nature. This was new to me, and my mind felt interconnected with nature. It sang inside, and no more thoughts ran through it. A void of love was felt inside and an emptiness but oneness with the nature realm was experienced. It was then I truly knew peace in my mind.

My attitudes to all of life completely changed. I was no longer in deep need for others to fulfill my expectations to prove they loved me. Through the journey, I saw the games that my mind had played unconsciously with my partner, trying to get him to do what I wanted rather than allowing him to be free to do what he wanted and trusting that this would resonate and give me what I needed.

My attitudes to my partner changed, and no longer did I see myself as reliant on him. I could feel great love and oneness no matter what he chose and did. He and I were now truly able to express the depth of our passion as light beings together.

The Enlightened Masters came and said, "Now you can open your mind, beloved, to the universe and to the truth we wish to share with you."

No longer did my mind question eternally why this was occurring, or react even when the most beautiful things took place within, or react to the little things in life occurring each day. Within my mind I began to hear the symphonies of sound as I was drifting to sleep. I felt my mind weep inside like a beautiful child whenever I witnessed something sad, rather than analyze it. My mind just experienced life as it was, in all its beauty and sometimes in its sorrow. It felt as if the moon and sun had married within it and merged to create a field of unity. My mind had united with the world.

This was my personal journey of opening to my super-consciousness and Divine Presence. The journey of clearing the mind of the collective consciousness tape loop, or collective ego thought forms, is the quickest way to receive one's super-consciousness and activate one's natural, creative genius. The mind simply needs to move out of the old bandwidth of thoughts that emanate from the collective. Then the mind will become completely still, filled with love, empty of thoughts, but full of one's Divine Presence.

As this completed, Saint Germaine, Maitreya, Sananda, El Morya, and Metatron, the primary Masters that were offering me visitations, came and congratulated me. They said that the journey, even though it was very focused and disciplined in every moment, had also assisted others in the collective. The energies I was releasing were from the collective mind of humanity. They explained that our minds were linked in a group-consciousness, and the concept of having personal mind space was an illusion. They shared that many people's thoughts are either transferred from one mind to another or are simply drawn from the collective memories of humanity.

They shared that all thought forms that travel from the left side of the brain's field to the right side, or flashing thoughts, are thoughts that have been picked up from the environment. Humanity's thought forms emanate from the field of the brain into the field of the environment and imprint the environment with the emotional energy that accompanies these thoughts. If a person is more emotionally charged, they will leave stronger imprints in the environment, and others will receive these energies as they enter the environment. This is how our humanity often unconsciously exchanges energy and thought forms.

The Masters explained that our thought forms are the smallest radiations of consciousness emanating from the fields of our brains. When a person clears the field of their mind as I had done, all the imprints and thoughts from the collective that they have received over their life are released, and the mind is then free from the collective consciousness of others. The field of the brain then rises in vibration, and the super-consciousness is able to ground through a person's mind.

Metatron took me to Sirius for many months after this, and I listened to hundreds of discourses in the auditoriums in the realm of light on the Divine University. Each discourse held a different focus on the emanation of consciousness. Thought was described as the lowest form of consciousness unless it was sourced from one's super-consciousness, and then it was described as wisdom. Between thought and wisdom lay intelligent awareness, cognitive reasoning, and intuitive recognition.

Metatron explained that humanity was learning to let go of the belief that their thoughts were absolute truth, and to step into a higher awareness where wisdom could be accessed through the process of mastering intelligent awareness, cognitive reasoning, and intuitive recognition. He shared that many had already accessed their intelligent awareness, cognitive reasoning, or intuitive recognition, but the majority had not cleansed their mind. which was needed to evolve to the level where the mind emanated deep wisdom. It was beautiful to hear about the evolution of our minds from Metatron's mastery, and it helped me develop higher level programs of education that assist the activation of the brain chemistry and the development of the heart and the mind for the illumination of one's consciousness.

CHAPTER SIX

Your Contribution to Your Family, Your Community, and Our World

Just as a flower blossoms over the course of its life, every day that we become older we are moving toward our greater peace as spiritual beings. The completion of our lives is the moment when all begins to truly integrate and we are shown exactly what our life has contributed to the world, to ourselves, and to others we may have affected—how we have made a difference.

My grandpa passed on some years ago, and he was a lovely man that all of my family loved deeply. Upon his death, I spiritually contacted him.

I was shown by the Enlightened Masters to meditate with him each day at 6 p.m. and attune to him and assist him in any way he needed as he moved through the veils and into the light to leave our world behind.

The first day I meditated with him, I found him floating above his body. His soul was not distressed but had not fully realized he had died, and he could still feel the connection to his body. He simply felt like he was when he was asleep, not realizing his body had no breath any more. I spoke to him, and he recognized me. I shared he would need to let go of his body, for he had passed, and he was now on the journey of moving to the other side to be with my grandma.

He detached, and I saw him smile as his silver cord between his body and soul began to coil back inside of him. His spirit had already left some time before and had opened a spiritual portal in his energy body for his soul to also travel into the spiritual planes when it was ready. It usually takes three days for a soul's complete release from the physical body connection.

The next day I meditated with him I found him floating in a sea of memories of his own consciousness, and he did not realize who he had been in the incarnation he had just left behind. The unresolved memories from his life's experiences were floating in his field, and these confused him.

I called his name and spoke to him. "Grandpa, you have just passed from the world of Earth, and you are on your journey into the light now."

I told him the age he died, who he had been, and where he had lived. I explained that he had had a good life of helping others and had a beautiful family who loved him deeply, and that he was greatly missed. He then recognized me as his granddaughter and began to remember his life and to realize he had died.

I shared that if there was anything that he needed to forgive, he could let it go now, as he would not be able to take it with him into the light if it was left unresolved within him. I shared with him that all parts of his consciousness that could not forgive would need to stay in this realm until they were ready to forgive and enter the higher light realms. I explained that his soul would travel into the light when he was ready and merge back with his spirit through his lightbody. He would experience his Divine Presence filling him with light and unlimited love, and he would be free of pain or karma. I explained he was in a place between the worlds that allowed him the time to forgive anything he may wish to so he could take more of his energy and consciousness with him when he met his Holy Spirit in the realms of light.

As he embraced this, I asked him if there was anything he would like me to share with other members of my family. He gave me some personal messages for my family, sharing that he loved everyone and asking me to spread his message of forgiveness to one family member. I shared he would be staying in this place for a short time to allow this forgiveness to take place. Each day I returned, he had a new message, and he had entered a deeper level of forgiveness and was in a fuller state of peace.

On the fifth day I meditated with him, I found him not far from a great bridge of light, yet he was fearful of it. This surprised me, as my grandfather was a strong Christian who believed in God. He was a man of high morality based on kindness and a very gentle spirit. As I came to him, he reached his arms out to me. He was grateful to recognize someone, as the nonphysical world was so different to him. I felt I was grounding him as we connected. I was in a spirit form also in my communion with him. I saw many angels with him and the bridge that was blinding in its light, so I understood how it overwhelmed him.

I said, "Grandpa, you are ready now." As I spoke these words he looked into my eyes, and I could see the fear in his eyes and a sense he might be judged. I said, "Grandpa, there is no need to fear the light."

I realized then that he was fearful of God, as he did not understand that God was simply the love and light and creation energy in all of existence. He did not understand that he was simply entering a realm of light where he would see the beauty and truth in all. He had ideas in his mind that he might not be worthy, or he might be judged for sins unknown to him.

I looked into his eyes and sent him all my love and said, "You will experience only the most beautiful reality in the light realms. There is no judgment in these realms. You will meet grandma again and be able to share love on a much deeper level than you even shared on Earth. You will become light and leave any heaviness or fear behind."

I could see into the light bridge, which arched into the heavens, and the angels showed me all of my ancestors and my grandmother waiting for him, preparing to greet him. My heart was filled with such love. I took his hand and said, "Grandpa I will take you part of the way."

We walked into the light together, hand in hand, and he could see the bridge arching further. I walked about one-third of the way across the bridge into the light realms, which held the frequency I was able to receive, which was similar to the Enlightened Masters' energy.

Soon the frequency was too strong; it would take me out of my body and I would leave the world if I continued, so I said to my grandfather, "You will have to walk the rest of the way by yourself; otherwise, I will also be taken. It is not my time, so I can walk no further. Grandpa, know God walks with you and we are all in your heart. God is simply this light, and you will be safe for there is only peace within the light. It is your time. She is waiting for you on the other side."

I could see my grandmother and a beautiful rose archway of flowers that she was standing under, looking our way. Clouds of white and soft pink light flowed between us. My grandfather had already started transforming; he was no longer a tired, old, fearful man. His radiant light within was returning, filling his soul, and his spirit was merging with him.

I stood and witnessed as my grandfather crossed the bridge and turned into pure light, his whole form glowing with white light. I saw my grandmother and grandfather as pure light beings embracing each other, and as their arms and hearts connected, the whole world lit up. Their fields expanded in rainbow energy, and great wings formed from their arms as if they were angels, merging hearts. As they connected, the light and love of their souls were fully ignited, and colors expanded in every direction, flooding across the bridge to me. I wept at what I saw and felt as their hearts connected.

I cried for my whole family at the joy of my grandparents' reunion. They had spent their lives together in sacred marriage, and the love they held for each other could now be freely shared. Their upbringing and the times they had been born into had restricted this deep expression of love in their physical lives. I felt deep peace and the beauty of death, finally. This was a great healing for me personally, after having my first life partner also cross over to the other side. At this time, my spirit traveled back and I completed my meditation, wiping my eyes of the tears that my body had wept. I knew he was now at peace and had returned to be with my ancestral family.

My grandfather taught me something that day that has been an important influence in my life. How he walked across the bridge and transformed into his lightbody, turning to pure light as he crossed, was an amazing blessing for me to witness as I realized that I was doing was exactly this. I realized that every human being has the potential to ascend into their lightbody; not everybody has to wait for their death. The only difference between me and my grandfather was that I had chosen to do this before death by receiving the higher frequency of my Presence through my chakras and body. I also realized that my grandfather and all of my ancestors had paved the way for me, as the veils on the Earth were so light now compared to when he was my age. I realized the legacy he had left me and all future generations.

When I witnessed him merge with his spirit and become light, before he met my grandmother, his whole being changed. He turned to light. It was in this moment that I realized this was our evolution. Now that the Earth's field is of a higher vibration and so many veils have lifted, we as a race can evolve into our lightbodies and embody our spirit before death. My grandfather, through his kindness and charitable acts in life, had left me a legacy of being able to open my heart in charity and be kind. He had left me the legacy of a lighter world.

The Difference You Make Can Change
Many Lives as Well as Your Own

The universal path for our collective is one of love. Love always holds the potential to unite us through any experience, even experiences that reveal our karma to us. So often on the path, challenges can hold us in a state of uneasiness. Maybe we do not know our direction, or we cannot feel our love and joy, or we do not trust our hearts and we fear the worst will occur as our karma is released. Often, karma can feel so large and painful it can break the human spirit, creating us to lock into the rational mind as a form of protection and a false sense of being in control. This is why so many choose not to change some aspects of their lives even though they are essentially very unhappy. Yet, they are unaware of the great assistance available to them from the realms of spirit. They have forgotten that the laws of love, oneness, grace, forgiveness, divinity, karma, and liberty will bring them the assistance they need to evolve and change.

When we enter the belief that we are alone and must rely only on our own energy in life, we then respond from our rational mind and are unable to experience our heart connection. One hemisphere of our brain switches on and jumps into the control seat, and we are unable to truly respond to the situation with love. In this state we have limited access to the frequency that brings trusting and peaceful feelings out of us. Our reactions become based on what other people did to us, how or why they chose to hurt us, or how they took something from us.

Our rational reasoning always finds others as the source of our challenge. This includes the projection of blame and the belief that we are victims of circumstances. Until we are ready to acknowledge that we hold the key to our lives and everything we experience is manifested by our consciousness for our learning, our left brain analytical function will continue to hold us in victimhood and we will hold the patterns of thought that disempower our creation.

It is important to acknowledge that you are here to create with love and that on your journey of challenge, every act you create that heals or brings wholeness to your own life benefits your family, the collective, and Mother Earth. The acknowledgment that you are part of a collective and there is no true separation between you and others, even though you may seem to have your own individual consciousness, is also needed, as the light of our collective is far more powerful than our karma. Your oneness with the collective is a great empowerment for your individual consciousness.

The difference you make in your own life through karmic clearing is in itself immense, but when you choose to clear your karma as a representative for humanity, the difference you make has a planetary effect. If you walk this path, willing to open your spiritual eyes to the karma if it does arise in life, you will always receive the greatest assistance to integrate, evolve, and accept what you must forgive to receive a larger part of your heart back to you.

Accepting Your Personal Karma as a Representative for Humanity

Your personal karma is unique to your soul and is specifically connected to your last three incarnations and your present life. Your personal karma is held within the chakras or energy centers of your body, and it arises as your energy field rises in vibration and energizes your cells. Your cells, your organs, and all within your physical body ground your consciousness, and sometimes your consciousness carries karma as unconscious memories. As your chakras develop, your spirit is able to ground more love, passion, wisdom, consciousness, intelligence, compassion, and creativity. Simultaneously, as you move forward in life, your karma can arise, offering you an opportunity to reclaim a part of your heart and consciousness so you may evolve to new levels that you did not believe were possible. Through karmic clearing, you manifest your deepest experiences of evolution in this life.

By becoming a representative for humanity, you are able to meet your personal, family, collective, and planetary karma and clear it simultaneously. You can do this by simply asking for assistance for yourself when you feel you are in a karmic situation, and saying the following prayer to support your family, the collective, and Mother Earth to release any aspect of karma that may be connected to your personal karma.

Prayer for the Clearing of Your Personal Karma

Mother, Father, God/Goddess, or Divine Presence of Love and Light,
I call for the highest form of love and assistance with the clearing and balancing of the karma I hold with_____
_____ (insert your karmic issue here). I accept and embrace this karma now as a part of my consciousness and ask that it be supported to heal through all time, space, and dimension. I ask that I be guided to be in self-realization of all I need to forgive and of the truth I need to share. I ask for karmic absolution for any acts, deeds, words, energy, or consciousness that I may have projected on others or myself to create this karma and close my heart, mind, body, or spirit in this life or in any of my last three Earth lives. I ask for all karmic cords between myself and other souls to be cleansed as I own and accept this karma as a part of my consciousness that needs love and forgiveness. I call for the karmic clearing of my soul and of anything that may block my heart from feeling the love and spirit of my light.

I call on my Divine Presence to merge with me at all times when this karma is present. I ask for the Enlightened Masters' assistance and ask for my ancestors to forgive with me all that we may hold that may block our happiness and sense of wholeness as beings. I acknowledge that I have attracted this situation to me and ask that all obstacles be removed so I may open my spiritual eyes and see the truth of what I need to forgive within myself, my family, my community, and the collective so I may learn my lessons in life. I ask that this clearing benefit all of my family, the collective of humanity, and Mother Earth. I call on the laws of love, oneness, grace, divinity, karma, forgiveness, and liberty to flood through me and to clear any karma that lies between me and any member of my family, the collective, or Mother Earth. I give thanks for this.

The next step is for you to trust the process and to be as honest as you can with yourself so you may discover the truth that lies beneath your feelings. Karma evokes deep feelings, and our oldest program is to repress them. This is held as an old program in our bodies until we have learned to freely release deep emotion. Karmic clearing is based not only on the acknowledgment of these feelings but also on the recognition that our deepest, unresolved feelings are accompanied by unconscious beliefs that lock our consciousness from streaming through our hearts.

As you realize how karma creates you to feel and think, you are able to begin the karmic clearing by breaking agreements you have made to hold onto these beliefs as your truth in life. It is important that you recognize that you are in a karmic clearing process and that what you think and feel is sourced from the karma and not from your clear light consciousness. As you recognize these beliefs without giving your power to them, an unlocking takes place in the chakras, and the first veils of the karma are released. It is important to offer the old beliefs that no longer serve you to your Divine Presence in a process of surrender and to ask that these veils be lifted from you and your DNA filaments of consciousness.

As soon as you accept what you are experiencing and stop judging it, the first veils of your personal karma are released, and you can begin the journey that allows your mind to recognize what you truly wish to create. This is the time to feel deeply into your heart and be honest with yourself. What is it you truly want as your reality? What is this karma blocking you from creating? This heart wish that you feel inside, underneath all of the belief and emotion, is your soul's truth that you must access to clear the core of the karma. You must accept this truth, even though the thoughts and emotions may not agree with it.

This karma will also have a connection to a part of your consciousness that holds the belief that you cannot have this as your reality due to an experience where your soul used its power to close down your consciousness in this life or in one of your last three lives. To complete the karmic clearing, you will be guided to forgive yourself for having closed down your consciousness.

Every form of blockage in your life is sourced from a blockage in the flow of your consciousness. Heart chakra blockages occur when a soul's consciousness is not streaming through their heart, and can manifest as heart disease, depression of the mind, a marriage breakup, or an unhappy relationship. The experience of being an unhappy soul or the mind forcing itself to do something that the soul does not want to do is connected to the specific form of karma that creates heart blockage. Personal karma locked in the heart chakra is the most common form of karma on the planet, and as enough souls awaken and follow their hearts, this karma will clear for the whole collective.

Healing the Heart through Personal Karmic Clearing

Mary came to me as a client with three chronic issues in her life. The first was that she found it difficult to trust other people, and this created her to be very lonely. The second was that she was fearful around communicating her truth to others, and she often found herself holding back and entering shyness. The third was that she experienced depression and would find herself on her bed, spiraling into a black hole.

She was a beautiful soul, but her true beauty was unable to be expressed in the presence of others. She had many qualities that could endear her to others if she could share them, but her fear of speaking and lack of trust made it hard to initiate relationships. Having very little heart-based contact with others triggered her into depression, where the sense of failure and the feeling of not being wanted would arise as emotions and beliefs held unconsciously between her body and her mind.

When she came to me, I shared that the Akashic records of her last three lives and this life, where she had not been able to forgive certain experiences, were creating a heart chakra blockage, and it was her time to embrace this, as her soul could not grow or feel free within her relationships until she did. She did not understand what this meant at first, so my Presence explained to her how her energy worked.

> Your body is like a magnet and your brain is like an antenna. Your heart is the link between your mind and your body. Your true self will only be experienced when you forgive all that you have been unable to forgive that lies between your mind and body, beloved. Your personal karma is with relationship, and you have all the gifts you need. You have felt abandoned by people in your life, but the source of this comes from you, from closing your heart and not forgiving others. You need to forgive yourself.

As my Presence spoke this, Mary broke down in tears and shared with me how lonely she was as she felt she could not connect to her family in a deeper way. Her mother was very beautiful but did not understand her and wanted something different for her than what she wanted for herself. In her mother's presence she felt guilty, as if she was doing something she shouldn't be doing. Her father had never been a force of love in her life, and she had isolated herself as a child so she would not be affected by his dominant, angry energy. She loved her children but worried about them constantly and felt responsible for every difficulty they experienced. As she shared her story, she revealed she had not forgiven her mother and father, and therefore was not able to forgive herself for not being a more loving mother.

I shared that this was blocking her heart, and that all in this life was only a part of her consciousness, trapped as Akashic records in her heart chakra. My Presence continued to share with her.

> Your relationships with your mother, father, children, and husband go back through your last three lifetimes, and the source of the fear that is held inside you that overtakes you as deep depression comes from your

Akasha. You are reliving the journey that you experienced three lifetimes ago when your father was your son, your mother was your sister, your daughter was your daughter, your son was your son, and your husband was your husband. You were the mother of many. You cared for many more than your own family; there were many in difficulty in your village and you took others in and fed and cared for them until they could travel again. Many were looking for work and you held your heart open. You blamed yourself for depriving your own children, as they did not receive as much care as they would have had you not been attending to others in need.

As I was speaking, her body responded. It was as if her body knew this story, and it started to breathe more deeply to prepare for an energy release.

Your body is holding all of the memories, for you have come to a point in your life again where you have your family, but there are also others around you needing help, and your spirit is guiding you to move beyond your personal karma that disempowers you, holding you in a state of lone-liness, regret, depression, and noncommunication. In that lifetime, the sadness was not that your children could not be loved more by you, it was that you blamed yourself and felt that if you had not helped others, maybe you would have stopped the experience your children went through. The truth is, though, that whether or not you had given to others, you would not have stopped your child from experiencing his own karma, for this was the nature of his personal karma.

She asked my Presence what this meant. My Presence continued:

Long ago, you had three children, two of whom are your children today and one who was your father in this life. You lived in comfort for the first ten years of your life as a mother, and then war changed your country and your people. Your village became a war zone, and your family experienced many difficulties, from lack of food to losing their shelter to losing mem-bers of the family and then losing you. While you were alive, you shared your shelter and food and all that you owned with others in the village who were in need. Your heart could not say no.

She listened carefully to the story of the memories held inside her body, which I was receiving from the Akasha held in her chakras. Gently she sat up and took a deep breath, wiped her eyes, and said, "Yes, this is story of my ancestors too. My family has had this experience in the last few generations."

I shared that until she could forgive and assist her ancestors to forgive, the consciousness of this experience would sometimes overtake her field. My Presence continued to share.

The karma is about generosity, for you left this life believing your generosity had hurt your family. You left the Earth believing that through giving to others, you lost everything. This belief was strong, for you witnessed the war progress and your family lose their home. Your elder son, who was your father in this life, became a very bitter and angry young man. He tried to care for the whole family when your husband died in the war. Your sister came to live with you and she did not like that you gave food and shelter to others, although she was generous in her care of the sick and would visit others and care for their wounds, beloved. Others gave to you as they knew how giving you were, but when your elder son became hateful, you felt you could no longer be generous to others without them being hurt by his words, beloved.

Your children were of most importance to you, yet as they grew, you lost each one in a different way. You lost your elder son to bitterness, your younger son to fear of abandonment, and your daughter to fear of trusting you. You blamed yourself for the loss of your children's father. You closed your heart and thought that if you had never opened your home to others and shared what you had, your children might have been protected from the disasters of the war. You were not able to forgive humanity for destroying your home, your village, and your family, and instead you blamed yourself and closed your heart to humanity, promising that you would never again share what you had, promising that you would never again listen to your heart.

You now need to break the agreements you made to never again open your heart or share yourself with others. You need to break the agreements you made to never trust humanity, to never speak your heart's truth. You need to break the agreements you made to hold onto the belief that through giving to others, you will lose everything you love. Sit with me in deep forgiveness of yourself for making these agreements and giving up on yourself. This is your depression, our dear one. As you forgive yourself, a part of you will let go of something very old, and you will feel the freedom of your generous heart return to you.

She shared that this explained a lot in her life, as her father had been so angry. Her daughter loved her but was not always willing to listen to her. Her son again was affected by the loss of his father, and it did make her feel guilty. She had difficulties sharing with others and difficulty listening to her heart and receiving what she could do to make herself happy. Often she felt her heart wanted to give, but regret would run through her mind when she was generous. I asked if she wanted to receive karmic absolution from the Enlightened Masters, and shared she could call for karmic absolution and their Presences to assist her with this karmic release from her chakras.

I invited her to call for the frequency of the universal laws of forgiveness, love, oneness, divinity, grace, karma, and liberty to flood through her energy body, soul, and chakras until the Akashic records in her heart dissolved and her heart blockage released. As she did this, she felt a great pain in her chest region, and I guided her to place her tongue out and sound "Ahhhhh" for five minutes, so the old energy could physically release. I explained that if she placed her tongue out, this would allow the energy to flow through her meridians and her heart chakra would open to support the release.

As she made the sound, she felt flashes of the old memories lifting from her—thoughts and feelings that had been buried in her heart, keeping her from connecting with others. As this completed, she shared that she was tired, but her heart felt lighter. I suggested that for the next few weeks she stay in this awareness, continuing to forgive herself and to break these old agreements to allow the full shift to take place.

I shared with her that if she wished for her journey of karmic clearing to benefit her family as well as the collective of humanity and the planet, she could call on the Enlightened Masters, her ancestors, and the angels and archangels and ask that her healing and forgiveness journey be supported to also help her family and the collective. As I spoke this, I saw one of her European ancestors from over one hundred years ago, and this spirit shone its light upon her. It lit up her energy body as she was speaking her prayer. I shared that her ancestors were with her and watching over her. They would forgive with her as she forgave the war and all it had created, for they carried the same guilt that she carried. They would heal as she forgave more of this each day.

ANCESTRAL TEARS

Golden embers of fire dance
upon the memories
our ancestors hold . . .
In each flame lives their breath
their wisdom, eyes of gold . . .
Through the worlds
where there is no time
their flame flows back into the void
to awaken you at this time . . .
Ancient roots through your mother's tree
expand the breath of love
within you . . .
Precious joy to the children
before you . . .
The Holy Father breathes your soul

tapering back into the night
As grandfathers root themselves deeply
with wisdom, integrity into your body . . .
The death of no man, woman, or child is lost . . .
Wisdom is only gained and shared
as the ancestors of your soul
return through your heart flame
to ignite your source again . . .
Let their breath be an anointment for your great journey
let their hearts unite, opening you to the light . . .
Let them take the old ways from you
let them bring the greatest blessings to you . . .
Let them breathe through you
so your body may keep its wellness
and know the Earth Mother
through an ancient old creation tree
timeless . . .
Your family tree . . .
Through the roots and branches
let the new seeds fall upon the ground
flower into new families, founded upon
their wisdom and love and with your innocence
in sacred marriage . . .
Let the new shoots of light
streaming and opening
bring new ways of being
sourced from their strength
inside your being . . .
They are here inside of you
their hearts as one breath, one tree . . .
Ancient golden wisdom
will always guide you . . .

A path of love awaits
those who honor the great strength
of all that has been before them ...
Embrace the mothers and fathers
who came before you ...
Let their blessings
not be lost upon the world
or their wisdom be buried
in ancient times ...
Take the gifts of love
from your family tree ...
Forgive their misfortunes
so they may live with integrity ...

Clearing Your Family Karma

The living light that threads between your heart and soul and each of the hearts and souls in your family forms an amazing matrix called your Family Heart Tree. The lines of light are like roots that ground the love of your family into the Earth and anchor the love in your own heart.

On the Earth, some families simply have more karma than others; their Family Heart Tree looks wilted, and its roots do not tap deep into the Earth. These families have had traumatic experiences on Earth and have lost their love and heart connection. They usually have broken relationships and difficulty with communication, and when they are together at family gatherings, there is no peace felt between them.

Some families have a lighter family karma, and they do experience love and peace, but they may have issues that stem from their ancestors where they have not forgiven each other or themselves. The lightest karma can create these families to not speak their complete truth with each other. Members of the family may share many aspects of their lives but keep some details completely personal and separate.

Every family has a guardian angel that may be called upon for the healing of family karma. This guardian angel has the ability to move the invisible energy that lies between different members of the family so the karma can gently shift. Some family members spend years without talking to each other, yet when there is an energy shift created in the Family Heart Tree, even members who have spent twenty years apart will be linked again through the energy shift generated from the karmic clearing of one member's heart.

You are this family member, and as a light seed, you have the power to make a difference not only to your current family but to the future generations within your family tree. This can be done simply through saying a prayer and asking for assistance when you experience family karma in the air.

Family karma feels like a little stab in the heart, a pain that will not go away as you witness something with your family that makes you close your heart. This may be the way one member communicates to another, or it may be the lack of communication between you and a close family member. Whatever it is, it is based on the consciousness your family shares as a group that blocks their heart energy from grounding on Earth and blocks them from enacting a space of love and trust with one another.

If there is anything you cannot express with your family, then you presently have family karma blocking the clear light from flowing from your heart to theirs. Know your family is one of your closest soul groups, and by opening your heart to them you are becoming more embodied by love. Your family carries one piece of your heart, and unless you open your connection to them and clear the karma, your heart will not be able to truly give unconditional love to your own children or to your partner in life. For some, the karma can be so strong that it can even prevent them from ever attracting a life partner.

The unlocking of the genetic code is the key to truly opening your heart and allowing the development and growth of your brain chemistry and chakras. This takes place as you take gentle steps toward the recognition of your family karma and make the heart connection with each of the primary members in your family. To hold a heart connection with them you will need to accept them as they are and look at what they trigger in you as your divine reflection.

The law of reflection simply states that all you close your heart to, judge, or project negatively upon is your mirror and will continue to be attracted into your life as your reflection until you recognize that you hold this consciousness inside. This means that until you accept that there is a part of you that is just like the person you are judging, you will continue to be trapped by this reflection, triggered into a state of separation each time you meet the mirror.

The law of grace states that whenever you call for assistance, you will receive all you need as soon as you are willing to surrender. Sometimes you may hold contracts inside that need to be broken; grace will be delivered in the package that your contracts allow. There will always be a messenger sent to deliver this grace, so once you call for God's grace, be open to all potential offers.

The law of love states that whether your heart is closed or open, love can flow through your energy field and support you until you choose to forgive, fully open your heart, and accept the gift that your heart expansion delivers you. There is an infinite amount of love available to you through the field of life, but you need to attract it to you by loving yourself and forgiving yourself so your heart can receive the universal love.

These three universal laws have the power to deeply transform family karma. If you call on these three laws regularly for yourself and your family, your family karma will gently lift and your family's guardian angel will also be able to clear some of the karma your family holds. You may say the following prayer to support this, when family issues arise.

Prayer for the Clearing of Family Karma

Mother, Father, God/Goddess, or Divine Presence of Love and Light,
I call for the highest form of love and assistance for clearing and balancing the family karma I hold between my heart and my parents,

ancestors, brothers, sisters, and my children related to _____
_____ *(insert your family issue here). I accept
and embrace my family karma now as a part of my consciousness and
ask that it be supported to heal through all time, space, and dimension,
not only for myself but also for every member of my family and for all
of my ancestors. I ask that I be guided to be in self-realization of all I
need to love and forgive to create this to take place and be guided to the
truth I may need to honor and share with unconditional love to transmute this. I ask for karmic absolution for any acts, deeds, words, energy,
or consciousness I may have projected on my family or myself that created this karma and closed my consciousness and heart to any member
of my family in this life or any of my last three Earth lives. I ask for all
karmic cords between members of my family tree and myself to be
cleansed as I own and accept that this karma is a part of my consciousness that needs love and forgiveness.*

*I call for the karmic clearing of my family's heart chakra and any-
thing that may block my heart from feeling the love and spirit of my
light in the presence of my family. I call on my Divine Presence to merge
with me at all times when this karma is present and to guide me on my
path. I ask for the Enlightened Masters' assistance and on the assistance
of all my ancestors, that they forgive with me all that we hold that may
block our happiness and sense of wholeness and receptivity of love through
our family dynamics.*

*I acknowledge that I have attracted this situation to learn from and
ask that all obstacles be removed so I may open my spiritual eyes and see
the truth of what I need to forgive within myself, my family, my community, and the collective. I ask that this clearing benefit not only me
but also all of my family, all future generations, the collective of humanity, and Mother Earth. I call on the laws of love, oneness, grace, divinity,
karma, forgiveness, and liberty to flood through me and clear any karma
that may lie in my field or between me and any member of my family,
the collective, or Mother Earth. I give thanks for this.*

The Preciousness of Love Returning into the Deepest Level of Your Heart

My pearl or greatest gem in my life has been the gift of my beautiful daughter. She is the closest soul to me and has spent the most years with me in this life, seeing all sides of my being, from my happiness and joy to my moments of misery. She has seen me grow from a grieving young woman who was unable to be present in society to a grandmother who is thankful for all gifts in life that God has bestowed upon her. Throughout our journey, my daughter has taught me unconditional love, bringing to me exactly everything I have needed to open my heart and not only give love, but also receive it.

Although my daughter is the most precious gift I have received, my family karma blocked me from receiving her fully during many of the years I spent raising her. I had lost her father, and I had also been disconnected from my own father. The same feeling of loss that had blocked my heart energy from fully developing when I was a child blocked my heart energy as a young mother.

As a child, I never had enough time with my father, as he was always busy at work or with other things at home. As a young girl entering high school, I yearned for my father as my older brother stepped in to help me with my homework and all the things that I wanted my father to do with me. I remember resenting my brother for this even though he was helpful and kind in offering to be there for me. I simply needed to make a connection with my father's soul, and my brother could not replace him.

My family karma was passed down through me and it affected my daughter in the same way. As a young single mother, I struggled to put food on the table, keep a clean home, and play the role of two parents. My daughter received half a mother and half a father, and the feeling that I was not doing either job well enough created me to hold deep guilt inside. It was not until I forgave myself and let go of the guilt around Little Owl's death that I was able to heal my family karma and become the mother I wanted to be.

This karma lay as energy corded between my heart and my daughter's heart and between my heart and my mother's heart and my father's heart. This is the essence of your Family Heart Tree. The trunk of the tree is composed of the soul cords linking your heart to your parents' and your children's heart chakras. Unless this trunk is healthy, the divine energy of your Family Heart Tree is unable to provide love, and you end up feeling unloved by your family or feeling you are not enough.

In other words, if your soul cords are not flowing with divine energy, no matter how much your family may love you, you will not receive it. I knew both my parents and my daughter loved me, but I could not feel the love in my heart fully. Looking at our soul cords and the family karma of loss, I could see why my trunk was not strong enough for me to receive their love. My heart chakra was blocked with the family karma I carried from the loss of my father. This same karma had also compounded when my daughter lost her father.

No matter how much I tried to nurture my child, I knew it was not enough, for she also carried the same family karma in her heart. Sometimes she would feel my love, but there I felt a distance between our souls even though we held so much love for each other. I knew I had created this karma, but I also knew that if I did not judge or criticize it, it would heal through the laws of reflection, love, and grace, and the depth of our relationship would return to us.

I began to call on the universal laws to help me to have the courage to own my family karma and all connected to it, layer by layer. This was a call to the universe to also heal the distance I still felt with my father. There I was, forty years old, and my father was almost seventy, and we still had not had a decent conversation in our lives, although it was what my heart yearned for most when I was in his presence.

At a two-week retreat I was facilitating, I received the deliverance of the enlightened teachings on the development of children's chakras and the initiations that a soul moves through from the ages of zero to twenty-one, and this activated within me a healing process with my family karma. It took me back into my own chakra development and supported me to clear the soul cords between me and my mother and father on a much deeper level. I was shown that my father had not received the light frequency from his father, nor had my mother received the love frequency she needed from her mother, nor had my ancestors received the love they needed from their parents due to our family karma. As we sat in retreat, receiving the divine energy and teachings as potential mentors of the new generation of children, my ancestors forgave the lack of presence, light, and communication from their own parents in their earthly lives.

All of my ancestors were present during this healing, and this created a great release in my being and a powerful clearing of my DNA. Many of the aspects of my consciousness that were living in ignorance were awakened during this retreat. My spiritual eyes were opened to see my daughter's chakra development and to see what I needed to do to support her to become an empowered twenty-one-year-old woman with a healthy set of chakras. I realized she had not received the frequency of her father, and I had been alternating roles to try to sustain this for her. She was just about to turn eighteen at the time, so I knew I had three years before she would complete her childhood initiations and enter adulthood.

I realized that if she was going to be truly nurtured through the next leg of her journey of self-empowerment, I would have to step back and trust God and the universe to provide her with what she needed instead of trying to be both mother and father to her myself. I finally saw that trying to be both parents did not allow me to completely fulfill myself as her mother or to sustain the higher love vibration. After that retreat, I came home to be only her mother, and I let go of all that was not my role as a mother. Beyond that I just had to trust that she would be guided by her own Presence and Holy Spirit.

At school, my daughter encountered some major initiations with her heart, first when she entered a relationship and then when she became a young mother herself. I released my fear and simply sat in my heart as her loving mother, allowing the Holy Father and Holy Spirit to do her father's job. As the most blessed gift in life, I witnessed my daughter evolve and open to her own experiences of deep love. I felt the depth return to our relationship and watched her become the most wonderful, present, and loving mother who no longer carried our family karma.

The birth of her boy child, my grandson, and the sweet love between his parents, healed something in our family tree, and becoming a grandmother healed something very deep within me. It was beautiful to witness the next generation no longer carrying the karma. I felt my ancestors cry with joy and with the release of the pain they had carried of being separated from their fathers. Not long after this, I had the most beautiful experience, a deep conversation with my own father. I finally felt the connection with him that I had longed for as a child. I realized that I had feared I might not have this connection with him before he passed. This conversation was a sign that the family karma had shifted. My heart had healed, and I could finally feel the love of my family warming my heart and soul. I knew my chakras had now completed their development, and no longer did I carry my childhood memories as woundings inside me.

TRANSFORMATION

Wildfire breath

pierces her eyes

tears stream down her face

rain blesses her skin

wind washes away memories

as she walks the land and sings . . .

No more, she says to their fears . . .

Time fades away

massaging into her core

generations lost

loved ones

feeling the coolness of her breath

flowing home on her song

crying no more . . .

Glancing into the light

her body rises and remembers

celestial cities in the Earth
their frequencies expand
healing her ancestors . . .
Glancing back, all who walked behind
no longer hidden in the shadow
now walk beside her
resonating, pulsing, activating
magnifying, energizing, igniting
her to restore
all that she is . . .
Rainbow wings expand
encircle the world, comfort all beings . . .
Her eyes filled with pearls
peach crystalline fields
diamond light penetrates within
her celestial heart fire ignites
she expands her wings wider . . .
From her heart
geometries of love
spin within
birthing new codes of light
into the worlds beyond
where time stands alone
and the mists of our ancestors' tears
formed the ice ages
of long ago . . .
She gathers all of her spirit
in a bundle of love
births through her heart
into the womb, woman
born again
shining and radiant in her form
she has found her truth, her core . . .

She will continue
until she rides the wildfire
all the way home
to ignite her ancestors
to remember
that they are the blessed
doorway keepers
of Earth . . .
They are her doorway home . . .

Our Collective Consciousness as a Matrix of Golden Light

You are becoming aware through the concepts I have presented that you are not only incarnate as a soul through your physical body but you are also incarnate as a spirit via other dimensional bodies within the nonphysical worlds of Earth. A matrix of golden filaments of light links your physical body to all of these dimensional bodies through a fine field of consciousness known as your collective consciousness. Through this matrix, your spirit and your soul share consciousness. The significant events in your life are not formed by any choice of your own, but by the nature of your relationship with all aspects of your consciousness, including your fractal selves in the nonphysical worlds of Earth.

Imagine yourself standing on a great mountaintop. A golden cord of love and light extends from your heart deep into the Inner Earth to the heart of a body of light where your spirit is held incarnate in an ancestral form. This is a very powerful connection that opens the lower chakras beneath the feet to allow you to receive the power of the inner core of Mother Earth.

Know that as you clear your body and mind of your ancestral fears, your connection to your First World self becomes stronger, and you begin to receive the frequency from the Inner Earth as an empowerment in your life. You also begin to receive the consciousness you hold from the First

World. No longer do you fear that you cannot create what you wish to in the physical world. For this power of creation is the gift of your First World self.

As you imagine yourself on top of the mountain, call forth your ancestors and ask them to join you in the clearing of your collective karma that may block the flow of your creation current. Consider this as a river of light and love that extends from the Inner Earth into your heart and that it is the source that ignites the tantric energy and kundalini within your physical body to feed your physical body with light. This golden cord regenerates the physical body and fills each cell with pure light to create bliss in the body and pain to dissolve.

The collective karma of disease is held between the consciousness of a soul incarnate in the physical world and the matrix of the collective consciousness held through the Second and First World. In other words, beloved, clearing the collective karma of your soul and the cords between your soul and your spirit in the First and Second Worlds will support the process of healing the consciousness that creates your physical body to carry any disease.

Imagine with me now that you are standing on this tall mountaintop where your ancestors bless you, and the golden cord extends not only from you, but from your spirit in many forms in many worlds that center their reality underneath you. The golden light matrix will either be clear of fear or it will be holding contraction through any fear that your spirit holds in these other dimensions.

Have you ever wondered why you have fear in your life and why some things trigger it and others do not? Have you wondered about the irrational fears you may experience that your logical mind finds silly? Have you wondered why you have sudden flashes of ideas and inspirations? Have you wondered why you are so connected at times, and at other times are not quite yourself?

This is your collective karma influencing you, which generally arises as negative thoughts, doubts about yourself or others, and feelings of distrust.

Fears that feel trapped in your mind or body often source from the collective karma held between humanity and the Middle Earth, the Second World.

To accept you are multidimensional may be a stretch if your brain chemistry has not yet switched and ignited both hemispheres to begin to illuminate. The perceptions you hold are primarily influenced by your brain chemistry, and then by your state of consciousness, as your brain chemistry can unfortunately limit your access to your consciousness until you have unlocked your genetic code. Yet your brain chemistry is not something that is simply inherited; you create your brain chemistry through your own choices and through your acceptance and willingness to clear and balance your karma.

Understanding Collective Karma

Collective karma lies between the hearts of all souls within the seven worlds until peace is made manifest on Earth. It is the unresolved, invisible energy that causes people to live in either a state of unconsciousness or self-consciousness and to be stuck in the karmic wheel, living out repeated experiences of their karma. Clearing your collective karma creates your heart connection in the physical world to grow more powerfully so you may attract the love of soul family. When you clear your collective karma you begin to receive love not only from your closest friends and family members but from all people you meet, and you are able to expand your heart's energy and embrace every soul and spirit without judgment. Clearing your collective consciousness creates your heart to open to all of humanity, rather than to selected people only.

You may wonder why you are responsible for the collective karma, especially if you do not relate to it in your present life experience. You may ask, How am I involved in this and why do I carry this?

The golden cords that carry your collective karma and connect your heart to your spirit in its many forms were created through all of the incarnations you have chosen and through all of the dreaming bodies you have dreamed. Your complete nature beyond its current physical form is known as your Divine Presence or your Holy Spirit. You have come to experience the Earth, and you shall continue to travel and ground yourself on the Earth. Yet there is always more of you held as potential in the body of your Divine Presence.

Collective karma is sourced from incarnations in previous civilizations on the Earth where you were in a larger energy body with a larger consciousness and personal power. Although your memory may not now be able to access your incarnations in Atlantis, Lemuria, Ancient Egypt, or other civilizations, as your brain chemistry begins to alter and you receive your super-consciousness, events may occur to activate your memory around your original experiences within these civilizations. Significant events in your life at this time may also create you to be forced to accept and forgive your collective karma so you may continue to break your spirit free of any self-imposed limitations to the creation of your reality.

The purpose of these recollections is not regression, self-glory, or ownership of your past-life identities, for in truth, you were not incarnated as the individual consciousness you may now believe yourself to be, but as a group soul that is a group-consciousness. Your group soul is also known as your monad. Your monad is the collective of your alternate dimensional selves incarnated in spirit, also known as your soul extensions.

You are guided to these moments of remembrance only so you may open your heart to your group soul again and share the gifts of all you are, from all worlds and dimensions. This revelation will propel your heart to expand beyond your own limitations and truly embrace every other soul you know. As your collective karma clears, your heart begins to attract your soul family back to you, and you begin to physically meet those you knew before this life and to connect to many who have held great love for you.

All moments of guarding your heart are over and done with when your collective karma is cleared and the matrix of light expands through your energy field. As the lines and cords of light between your soul and spirit are freed of karma, fear, and limitation, a significant piece of similar karma is also lifted from the grids, portals, and plates of the Earth, as your collective consciousness is wired into Mother's Earth energy field and extends through all seven worlds. Through clearing your own collective consciousness of collective karma, you also serve the greater collective by offering a partial lifting of this same karma from Mother Earth and her grids.

The seeping of collective karma can become the deepest manifestation of pain and suffering within the body and mind. The body, as an integrator of your multidimensional consciousness, will reflect the flow of consciousness between the heart of your soul, incarnate in the physical, and the heart of your spirit in the other worlds. Your mind is also formed by the shared consciousness of yourself through all worlds. Those who have mental imbalance or disease often directly experience themselves as these spirit forms in other worlds and do not have a clear connection to our physical world.

Souls who have a great amount of collective karma are unable to establish a clear connection with their Divine Presence, as the matrix of light of their collective consciousness needs to be purified for them to receive their super-consciousness. Through meeting this collective karma, their hearts purify so their consciousness can expand. When our spiritual eyes open, the Enlightened Masters share that we are powerful in our creation, for our collective karma can be transcended simply by many in our collective coming together for the clearing of the collective karma between all peoples, species, and beings of the Earth. They share this karmic clearing will increase as the Divine Plan guides more souls to offer their puzzle pieces toward the manifestation of world peace.

Prayer for the Clearing of the Collective Karma of Your Group Soul

Mother, Father, God/Goddess, or Divine Presence of Love and Light,
I call for the highest form of love and assistance with clearing and balancing the collective karma I hold between my heart and my spirit within my collective consciousness related to _____
_____*(insert a positive description of your*

collective karma here). I accept and embrace my collective karma as a relationship between different parts of my consciousness and ask all forms of me to be supported to heal, through all time, space, and dimension, the cause, core, and Akashic records that hold this karma within me. I ask that I be guided to be in self-realization of all that I need to love and forgive to create this to take place, and to be aware of all unconscious beliefs I may need to recognize in order to release the control mechanisms in my consciousness that may create me to experience this karma.

I ask for karmic absolution for any acts, deeds, words, energy, or consciousness that have created this karma and for all I may have projected upon myself or the collective of humanity that has closed any of my consciousness down in any lifetimes I may have held in ancient civilizations on Earth such as Lemuria, Atlantis, and Ancient Egypt. I ask for all karmic cords between myself and members of my collective consciousness to be cleansed as I own and accept this karma as a part of my consciousness that is in need of love and forgiveness. I call for my Divine Presence to begin to clear the spiritual cords between my heart, mind, and body and parts of my consciousness in the other worlds. I ask that this take place every day until this collective karma is balanced and has cleared from my energy body and physical body.

I call on the laws of grace, love, forgiveness, wisdom, divinity, truth, karma, sacred resonance, liberty, oneness, faith, compassion, charity, service, communion, reflection, expansion, divine bliss, creation, and manifestation to flood through me and all of my collective consciousness to create balance in my collective consciousness. I ask for all of my chakras to be balanced and for my energy field to be balanced as this takes place. I ask that all of my selves through all worlds be protected and given grace, and if there be a blockage in our collective heart and mind, may this now be gently released with grace and ease.

I call on the assistance of all my ancestors and ask that they forgive all with me. I call on my spirit from all other worlds to also forgive as we receive the universal laws and ask for karmic absolution. I call on my Divine Presence to merge with me at all times when this karma is

present and to guide me on my path. I ask for the Enlightened Masters'
assistance and for my ancestors and aspects of my spirit to simply accept
what is taking place in life and to enter deep forgiveness.

I ask for karmic absolution for all of humanity regarding this form
of karma, and as a representative of humanity, I offer to forgive all souls
connected to this experience so this karma can be lifted from our whole
collective. I call and pray for the healing of all other members of my soul
family who may have their own collective karma with this. I acknowl-
edge that I have attracted this situation to me to learn from and ask
that all obstacles be removed so I may open my spiritual eyes and see the
truth of what I need to forgive within myself, my family, my community,
and the collective so I may learn my lessons in life. I ask that this clearing
benefit not only me but also all of my family, all future generations, the
collective of humanity, and Mother Earth and that it be lifted from the
Earth grids, the Earth Crystal, and my lightbody and DNA. I give
thanks for this divine assistance. So be it.

The Five Most Common Forms of
Collective Karma Experienced by Humanity

There are many forms of collective karma, but five in particular have a
powerful effect on our collective and are currently creating the largest problems among our families, our communities, and our nations. As it is the
oldest karma it has been deeply woven through the fabric of our society.

As you attune to the collective karma, may you be clearly guided by
your heart to know which of these five forms are held within your own
collective consciousness. When collective karma is active in your consciousness, it may negate the positive actions you take in life and you may
feel as if you are taking one step forward and three steps back. Collective
karma creates the experiences we label as self-sabotage, which are sometimes our most powerful learnings, yet also often are the most challenging
experiences that can create us to feel we are a victim and hold no power
to transcend our life circumstances.

Our collective karma holds a greater effect on what we choose to do or not do, as it affects us to hold nonresonant feelings with potential activities and choices that may in truth be positive for us and lead to our greater liberation. Our collective karma can also create our most limited aspects of consciousness to guide us with fear and negate positive experiences of growth from occurring in the specific areas of our lives linked to this karma. This karma can create control mechanisms to be held in our etheric body, creating our unconscious beliefs to control our lives and personalities if our heart chakras are not activated and open and we give our personal power to the belief in these fears.

The five most common forms of collective karma can be found within our intimate relationships, our sharing of resource, our sexuality, our use of power, and the well-being of our physical bodies.

The Collective Karma of Love, Friendship, and Ownership—Collective Karma of Loss

When the collective karma of love, friendship, and ownership is present, exchanges within relationships are not made with love. An example might be a broken marriage where a divorce suit is filed and both parties dispute the ownership of all belongings and children. Or perhaps two souls who have been very close part ways and hold blame toward each other and sever their heart connection. The collective karma of love, friendship, and ownership can create jealousy and dishonesty and may breed revenge and hatred between friends who originally held a loving connection. Codependent relationships are created by this karma. Nations also carry this karma with each other, and it can cause them to either bond together in trust or see each other as potential threats.

If you feel the need to own someone, this may be sourced from the collective karma of love, friendship, and ownership. It is this karma that creates the loss of friendship and the loss of love between souls, and it is this same energy that, among nations, creates the belief that one nation must control the ownership or caretakership of another nation.

As a representative of humanity, you may clear the karma of love, relationship, and ownership by inviting your ancestors, your soul, and your spirit from all incarnations within the seven worlds to join together and make a choice to forgive all experiences where your heart closed or friendship was rejected.

What follows is a story of my journey into the light and truth of my soul as a clearing of the collective karma of love, relationship, and ownership took place within my collective consciousness.

About twelve years ago, some of my soul family came together to travel to Uluru, the Divine Mother's ancestral creation portal based in the center of Australia, to work with the Earth grids and travel to other dreaming sites on the creation lines between Eastern Australia and the Red Center that surrounds the great red desert rocks Uluru, Kata Tjuta, and Atila. There were around twenty in the group who journeyed in convoy from Eastern Australia to the Red Center and back. As representatives of humanity, we joined in ceremony at different sites along the road. The rainbow serpent, Mother Earth's creation spirit, had been a large part of my personal journey, and we were following some of her creation lines through various power sites. I had just completed my training in hermitage with the Enlightened Masters and had begun to facilitate groups, ceremonies, teachings, and healings according to their guidance. I was also in relationship with Dreaming Heart, and we had come to a place of deep peace, honesty, truth, love, and union. We could easily have spent the rest of our lives together; this was my personal life plan at the time.

One day I was writing in my journal when I began receiving messages about a change that was to take place in my relationship and home. This was the first time I was shown by Spirit that another man would come into my life. The messages shared that this man would be a partner to me for the activation of my Earth mission. I resisted these messages and decided to ignore them. I was already with the man I loved and had chosen to be my life partner.

The next time I was shown this message, I was halfway out on the road to Uluru, traveling with my soul family. My partner was not with me. I began to have unusual experiences with a man in the group. My body would vibrate into ecstasy when he walked toward me, and this great magnetic energy would be felt inside, as if my body wanted to merge with him. This was strange as I was not romantically attracted to him. At first, I tried to simply avoid making contact with him so it would happen less regularly. This continued until we were in the center of the desert and I started to have very deep experiences in the dreaming with him, as I slept. Finally I was in the actual portal of Uluru, and I had an experience that proved to my mind, soul, spirit, and body that this man was one of the closest souls to me on the planet. He was a mirror to me, and we carried something together that was beyond my present understanding. He was my mission partner for the next step of my journey.

In the first couple of years of our relationship, Dreaming Heart and I had often found ourselves in sensitive places of sharing our truth as we entered a deeper union. Usually these intimate moments grew out of an emotional experience where I initially felt hurt. I was on a fast path of emotional clearing at that time. Dreaming Heart would run a bath for us to share or we would spend time holding each other in sacred space in heart connection. Whenever this took place in the early years, I would have visions of a white knight, tall blond man accompanied by a small blond boy. He sometimes appeared on a horse, and the vision would always be in the sky, as if he was a spirit coming to visit and bless me. This spirit would comfort me, but I also felt he was witnessing Dreaming Heart and me, healing us and bringing our karma to a place of love and oneness. This occurred so regularly when I was in a deep sensitive space that Dreaming Heart had a bit of a joke about the white knight coming to save me.

Our soul group had planned the journey out to Uluru by gathering a few times before we left. Now, out in the middle of the desert, I suddenly remembered something that had happened after one of those planning meetings. I had just gotten into my car to drive home when I realized I had left my car lights on. A tall man with blond hair, Golden Phoenix, walked toward me, and I explained that my car battery was dead. He went to his car and returned with jumper cables. Looking into my window and staring into my eyes, he said, "I am your white knight."

At the time, my mind refused to register what was occurring, and I simply pushed it aside until the Enlightened Masters shared with me in the middle of the desert that Golden Phoenix was my twin flame and we had a lot to create together, not only for our own enlightenment but also in service to the planet.

This was insane to my rational mind, as I was very attached to my partner and my present lifestyle. I loved Dreaming Heart and adored him so deeply that I would never have thought of anyone else. Yet the power of my spirit and my Divine Presence overtook all of my rationality and attachment, and over the next few days I experienced a knowing of the truth of my relationship with Golden Phoenix from the core of my being, even though all other parts of my mind and personality were very confused.

I was in the biggest karmic jam I had ever experienced, and my life felt completely out of control. My heart and love belonged to my partner, yet my spirit and soul were connected to this other man. When I received that this man was a twin flame to me and we held a planetary mission together, I was shocked, but another larger part of me knew it was true and this was the path I would eventually be lead to.

The heart of my soul split in two directions. I felt my spirit and my soul look toward this new life that was unknown, magnetically attracting me, and simultaneously I felt my soul, mind, and personality hold onto the life I already had of beauty, love, and grace, in fear of it being taken away.

It was Dreaming Heart who finally helped me. Even though I was out in the desert, he knew that I was feeling a powerful connection with Golden Phoenix. When I phoned him, he shared with me that he could sense another man was in my field and asked me what was occurring. I shared the truth with him. As I had been confronted by Dreaming Heart's attraction to other women in the beginning of our relationship and supported him through his experiences of feeling attraction to others, Dreaming Heart felt compelled to return the favor, and his heart held unconditional love for me as I spoke my truth to him. I was truly held by the hand of God through this.

My rational mind wanted to control the situation, deny what was occurring and push both men away, it was all so overwhelming. The karmic clearing process took place as I met myself and sincerely owned my truth within the experience while choosing not to cut off my connection to either man. The depth of my love for my twin flame was not apparent at first. It was very different from my experience with Dreaming Heart, where we dated and fell deeper and deeper in love and bonded our lives together. This was a love from the unseen worlds, from my vast consciousness, as if it were a source remembrance. With the ownership of each feeling, layer by layer, I gradually became free enough to acknowledge my truth and share it with Dreaming Heart. This sharing of truth slowly lifted the veils of karma for my path to clear a little more each day.

Of course, Dreaming Heart was also experiencing his mirrored journey and was held by his own spirit to recognize he may need to let me go. As we came together and shared our truths, we chose to complete our journey. We were deeply saddened and held each other. We promised that we would give ourselves three more months to love and experience each other, knowing this would be the completion of our relationship as life partners. I would then move to another home where I could begin to connect with Golden Phoenix as a potential new partner. Dreaming Heart and I would keep our deep friendship, but we would also need time to let go of each other. We had both been in partnerships before where our relationships had ended suddenly, with no resolution. Mine had occurred through Little Owl's suicide, and his had occurred through his previous life partner leaving him. We both still had unresolved karma with partnership, and by making this decision to not complete with bitterness, anger, resentment, blame, or projection but instead to choose to complete with love, a great healing took place not only for ourselves but for the collective. As we paved a new path where love was not lost through the completion of a relationship, our collective karma of love, relationship, and ownership was healed.

What allowed us to move through our initiations together, rather than separate in anger and pain? We both did feel these emotions at times, for our passion and spirit were deeply entwined in our union. Yet, it was our responsibility to love each other and embrace our truth with the awareness that there was always a win-win solution if we were willing to be responsible for our karma. This was our promise to each other, and it was our ability to accept each other's truths that allowed us to forgive the separation rather than carry pain. Dreaming Heart gave me away, freely, through the power of his love for me.

The Collective Karma of Resource, Finance, and Greed—Collective Karma of Control

Humanity's collective karma with the Earth's resource and with finance is based on the karma of greed and the fear of losing control over what one believes one needs to survive or succeed in life. This karma is non-personal, yet it affects one's personality to be controlling of others or to manipulate situations for the benefit of self. The essence of this karma is held in the conscious aspects of the mind and unconscious aspects of the spirit that fear a loss of control of the environment. This karma is evidenced by selfishness and disrespect for others and for the Earth. The building up of personal wealth is placed as a priority over the conservation of nature and Earth's resource. This collective karma can be found as a core issue between most governments and the original native peoples of the land, as the indigenous ways were not based on placing personal wealth over care of the Earth's resources. Their connection to the land gave them the sense to take what they personally needed for their families and to leave the rest as a form of respect for life.

This karma can also be found in the environmental movement, where people are struggling for the protection of our wilderness, and in smaller ways in our communities where there are challenges over use of land or resources. This karma can also be seen when valuable resources go unused or wasted because of people's fear of sharing with the collective. This kind of collective karma is in evidence when people lack the resources to create their life to be sustainable on all levels of their being. It is this collective karma that influences the creation of poverty in our world.

As a representative of humanity, you may clear the karma that your collective consciousness holds with resource, finance, greed, and control by inviting your ancestors, your soul, and your spirit from all incarnations within the seven worlds to join together and make a choice to forgive all experiences where acts of selfishness took place and more resources were taken than were truly needed, leading to an eventual closure of your heart connection to Mother Earth, to sharing her abundance, to finance, or to your own worth.

This collective karma of greed may be held between your heart and your spirit in relation to any aspect of your life, from your relationship to Mother Earth and the land to your own abundance, including finance and all your material resources. If you sense that you hold the energy of greed or control around the material resource you have acquired at this time, no matter how small or large this feeling is, this is sourced from your collective karma and the beliefs that it is greedy to be prosperous, or that you do not have the ability to attract abundance. It is this that creates a lack of growth in the sharing of your abundance in your life. It is this same energy, when magnified by the heart of those who have control over the world's resources toward those that have less control over it, that creates poverty to spread and continue to grow within our world's communities.

The Collective Karma of Union, Sexuality, and Abuse—Collective Karma of Violation

Humanity's collective karma with union and sexuality is held in one's collective consciousness if there have been instances of abuse and violation during incarnations within the ancient civilizations of Earth. These unresolved experiences can attract repeated occurrences of mental, emotional, physical, and sexual abuse into a soul's life.

This form of karma affects a soul to be hesitant to surrender to deep loving union and intimacy through heart-based sexuality and a fear of being violated or abused. This kind of collective karma is present in all experiences of abuse, from self-abuse through drug, alcohol, and sexual addiction to domestic violence, rape, repetitive verbal abuse, or acts of aggression and violence.

As a representative of humanity, you may clear the karma that your collective consciousness holds with union, sexuality, and abuse by inviting your ancestors, your soul, and your spirit from all incarnations within the seven worlds to join together and make a new choice to forgive all experiences that led you to witness or be party to mental, emotional, and physical forms of abuse and violation of others. This collective karma of violation may be held between your heart and your spirit in relation to any aspect of your life and may affect you subtly or powerfully.

If you sense you are being violated or have the need to destroy your sacred space or another's at any time, this is based on the karmic act of interference of another's energy upon your will, or of your energy upon another's will. This collective karma may block you from experiencing intimate union with another or expressing your heart-based sexuality, due to fear of abusing another or of being abused. It is this same energy, on a larger scale, that causes grave infringements of human rights to take place. All violent crimes against humanity such as torture, rape, genocide, and persecution are sourced from this collective karma.

The Collective Karma of Power, Responsibility, and Righteousness—Collective Karma of War

Humanity's collective karma with power and responsibility is held in one's collective consciousness if there have been experiences of righteousness or acts of war during an incarnation in an ancient civilization of Earth. These unresolved experiences can attract the recurrence of righteousness or war into a soul's life and can also create a being to deeply experience power issues and battles within themselves, their family, their community, or their nation.

This form of karma affects a soul to be fearful of using all of their power in the fulfillment of their responsibilities in case this leads to a misuse of power. They may become protective of their power and fail to use it responsibly, or they may become locked into a perception that they are right or that their path is the correct way, and give themselves permission to act without the engagement of their heart.

As a representative of humanity, you may clear the karma that your collective consciousness holds with power, responsibility, righteousness, and war simply through inviting your ancestors, your soul, and your spirit from all incarnations within the Seven Worlds to join together and make a new choice to forgive all experiences where a closure of power and rejection of responsibilities led you to witness or take sides in an argument, battle, or war, in the belief that one side was right and the other wrong.

This collective karma of righteousness may be held between your heart and your spirit in relation to any aspect of your life. If you sense righteousness within you at any time, this is sourced from your collective karma, and it is this that creates arguments with others, the rejection of your responsibilities, and the misuse of your power. It is this same energy, when magnified to the scale of one nation toward another, that creates war and the revenge and killing mentality to be released into our collective.

The Collective Karma of the Energy Body, the Physical Body, and Disease—Collective Karma of Separation

Humanity's collective karma of the energy body and physical body is based on disease and the fear of separation through change or transformation. When this karma is present, disease takes place within the energy body and seeds itself into the physical body, creating a blockage between specific cells of the physical body and the light held within the energy body. This collective karma may manifest in any specific form of disease, such as Parkinson's and Ménière's disease. Each unique manifestation stems from a distinct, fear-based belief system. Through opening our spiritual eyes to the fear of separation we may hold, not only on a cellular level in our body but also through our energy field sourced from our collective consciousness, we may begin to embrace this karma and release it from our physical body.

As a representative of humanity, you may clear the karma that your collective consciousness holds with your energy body, physical body, and disease through inviting your ancestors, your soul, and your spirit from all incarnations within the seven worlds to join together and make a new choice to forgive all experiences where they chose to separate from their light through a process of change, transformation, illness, or death and to deny their faith in themselves.

This collective karma of separation may be held between your heart and your spirit in relation to any aspect of your life. If you sense a fear of change, transformation, or evolution at any time, this is sourced from your collective karma. This form of collective karma creates one to repress one's feelings and thoughts and deny one's faith in self. It is this same karma, magnified, that creates the majority of illnesses that lead to painful death or to long-drawn-out experiences of physical suffering.

Golden Phoenix's Journey

This is a man I will never be able to separate from, as although he is no longer my life partner, he is always in my heart, and wherever I go I feel him with me. I feel our oneness daily.

About six years ago, as I have shared, I was in a karmic situation that was very confusing for me, as Golden Phoenix and I were completing as life partners. I found it very difficult to let him go for three reasons: my deep love and fear of losing him; my collective karma with union, sexuality, and abuse; and my fear that he was getting older and may not be supported by another to heal. He was not in very good health. He was fifteen years older than me and in need of a great deal of assistance, and I was concerned about how he would manage by himself.

We both knew the karma he was experiencing extended through his collective consciousness and was not simply based on his soul's choices or on finding the right Western medicine, doctors, herbs, nutrients, diet, water, acupuncture, and exercise for his body. We were aware this was very important, but the karma creating the disease would not lift simply through lifestyle changes and good medicine.

Golden Phoenix was receiving many treatments and doing everything he could to assist his body, but Parkinson's seemed to be lodging more deeply. He felt like he was losing control of his physical reality, and he could no longer take care of himself without assistance. He was in a deep process of surrender, and a part of his path of surrender was guiding him to let go of me and our life partnership. This was not an easy choice for him as not only did he love me deeply, but also I was the primary support in his life, emotionally, mentally, financially, and spiritually. What was missing was his primary physical support, and although we had people helping us, we had not managed to find the right formula so he felt fully cared for and supported in all situations.

My life with the Enlightened Masters was leading me to spend more and more time overseas, traveling, working with the Earth portals and many people around the world. I had many creative projects, and he knew I could not put these aside at this stage in my life. His life was taking him into a deep inner process of healing where he needed to be very still in his being and to live in a stable environment. My lifestyle and career did not provide this for him, as it was too active and creative, filled with many projects and people. He was deeply guided that for his own soul growth he needed to complete with me, even though it scared him to walk this path on his own. He needed to do this to strengthen and empower himself. His heart also had feelings for another, and this assisted him to make this choice as it gave him a potential new romance to explore. As he left, I simply had to let go and trust he would be supported.

One of Golden Phoenix's deepest difficulties at the time was that he could not stabilize his energy enough to feel physically supported by the Earth, and this sent him into deep anxiety in his mind and strong pain in his physical body. At other times, he would appear radiant in his being, his body and mind shining in oneness with his heart, and people could not believe he had even been diagnosed with Parkinson's disease. This radical switching back and forth between states of amazing radiance and periods of extreme pain and anxiety did not support his health.

He had had three deep, long relationships before I met him, which created him to have a broken heart. During our years as partners, he healed and developed the most beautiful heart through an immense amount of forgiveness for all that had occurred. A huge amount of anger arose through him at times, and I witnessed as he bravely humbled himself and forgave. His deep karmic journey involved four forms of collective karma, and his collective consciousness felt controlled by this karma as it manifested in most areas of his life, including in his relationships with his friends and family and in our partnership. This collective karma specifically manifested as the fear of losing all that he loved, the fear of being controlled and the need to take control, and the fear of not being able to have union with another—all deep fears lodged between his heart and his spirit forms in the other worlds, creating his consciousness to be locked in this deep, paralyzing fear of separation.

The first form was the collective karma of love, friendship, ownership, and loss, which he cleared through our intimate relationship and his subsequent one. He is now able to access the personal power of his own love for himself, and it is from this place that he has been able to lift other forms of collective karma and is continuing to heal his physical body.

The second was the collective karma of union, sexuality, abuse, and violation, which he also cleared through meeting his karma with me as a twin flame. He went through a deep process of releasing feelings of guilt around his sexuality and fear of not having union. Sexuality had been a deep attachment in his life, an important part of his manhood and his worth. He was an extremely beautiful and caring lover, and losing this power for a period was like losing his manhood. Yet, he was able to heal aspects of himself that were obsessive around sexuality that felt the need for sex to sustain a connection in his life with the feminine energy.

Through meeting this collective karma, he opened up his feminine energy and became more gentle, patient, and compassionate. His anger dissipated, and his consciousness became more open and less rigid. As he cleared this collective karma and his feminine power of receptivity finally opened, not long after the completion of our relationship he manifested a full care package from the Australian government. Now he would be supported financially to employ experienced caretakers and cooks, who were his friends, to come to his home for thirty-six hours a week and create all his meals, take on domestic duties, and spend time supporting the rehabilitation of his mind and body. He would receive this care package for as long as he needed it.

Leading up to this, our business, which was held by a trinity of three dedicated beings, was not doing well financially. As business partners, we were at our wits' end as to what direction to take. We had spent many years building the business, and it had served many people well, but it was no longer serving us as individuals. We all were aware we had created this through some bad choices we had made that were influenced by our collective karma with resource and finance. We came together and made some big changes that supported us to begin to clear our collective karma with finance and resource.

Through the support of many who offered assistance, we were taken on a journey of releasing control over our finances and were able to allow others to take care of this aspect of the business. The immense resource of educational material that had been created over the years had supported the birthing of the Divine University Project, and many students held great love for the work. As our karma with finance began to clear, a new organization began to take shape.

Golden Phoenix was released from many responsibilities at this time that related to being a business partner. As business partners we donated some of the educational resources we owned to the new organization, and then Golden Phoenix's care package manifested and he knew that this support was a sign that his collective karma with resource, finance, greed, and control had also begun to shift.

I share this story with you so you may understand that some forms of karma are held on the cellular level and also within many dimensions of our consciousness. These forms of karma take much longer to clear and balance. Patience, love, compassion, and trust must be reclaimed and developed. Karma that manifests in diseases that have no known cure must shift from the mind before they can shift from the body. Consider that your state of mind is simply shared consciousness. The Enlightened Masters share that as the mind releases the many layers of unconscious beliefs and the physical body and energy body are purified, a soul's consciousness is gently released from the deepest levels of karma that cause disease.

The feeling of being unable to control his reality has been the underlying theme of Golden Phoenix's experience with Parkinson's disease. Any inner struggle evoked by the feeling that he is being controlled by the disease only creates his symptoms to worsen, and he is aware that his only choice is to surrender, accept, and even love his disease, the part of his consciousness that manifests the Parkinson's. All of his ancestors are witnessing him and forgiving with him as each day he meets with love all that he needs to embrace to be at peace with what is occurring.

At some point, he will have cleared this collective karma to 51 percent, and it will begin to unlock from his genetic code. Until this occurs, when his collective consciousness feels the fear of being controlled, he experiences pain or the locking of his physical body. His greatest shift in health has been through developing a loving relationship with all parts of himself. He has experienced that when he generates love for all parts of himself, he has the power to unlock all of his pain and physical symptoms and feel his full health return to him. This is a very deep healing process, and he has dedicated the next few years to healing the body through the power of love, by bringing love to all parts of himself when the symptoms of Parkinson's arise.

His brain chemistry is being asked to receive what his ancestors did not receive and what he did not receive as a child. Golden Phoenix had been an undernurtured child who did not receive the love he needed to develop his brain's neural pathways. As an older man of fifty-five, he began his journey of opening his brain centers so he could experience compassion and no longer be overtaken by aggressive instincts. His brain is presently building its field of light so further healing of his body can take place. As his mind develops trust, the field of light around his brain will stabilize and strengthen his brain's chemistry so it can direct the physical transformation that needs to take place on a cellular level.

The Enlightened Masters share that Golden Phoenix developed Parkinson's disease due to three factors. The first was the collective karma of separation, arising from his lifetime in Atlantis and Ancient Egypt, where his spirit was separated from his heart and his spirit became very controlling. The second factor was his twenty-eight years working with high-energy currents, installing telephone cabling systems in North Western Australia. His energy body was depleted of its natural ability to produce life force and to regenerate and heal the physical body. The third factor was his body's chemistry, which was unable to assimilate the light that he needed to have health within his physical body.

The collective karma of separation first began to affect him when his mother and father split up. His own divorce and separation from his two young children were also left unresolved and drew more of these karmic experiences to him as he grew older. His third separation from a partner and the loss of his homes, family, and wealth in his late forties finally triggered all of the karma to arise, which began the process of the formation of Parkinson's disease in his body.

It was not long after this third separation that I met Golden Phoenix, and we entered our journey of discovering his disease and finding a road to recovery. We met at a time in his life when he needed the deepest love and support to find his way back to his heart. Through our relationship, he began to heal his relationship with his mother, his family, his children, his ex-partners, Mother Earth, and himself. This was an immense journey of moving through fifty years of unresolved energy, but he opened his heart and developed the inner strength to meet the larger journey he had manifested with his body, which threatened his quality of life more deeply than his separations in relationship.

Golden Phoenix is now on the path of embracing all he meets with love, and once he has completed the clearing and balancing of this karma and released it from his mind and body fully, he plans to share with humanity all he is learning about Parkinson's disease. Say a prayer for him and others like him who are doing all of us a great service by embracing the karma of our collective and releasing it from the Earth.

Your Relationships, Soul Family, and Collective Consciousness

Attracting your loving soul family and having healthy relationships and deep loving experiences are manifestations that take place when you clear your collective consciousness. Attracting others to you that love, accept, recognize, and enjoy being with you takes place more deeply as your collective karma clears. As you meet your collective karma in life, you are taken on a journey to restore your faith in your fellow humanity, and this is reflected back as others have faith and trust in you.

This clearing takes place through forgiveness and through the creation of powerful new life choices. When we make completely new positive choices in our life, we dissolve the old emotional control mechanisms, and this creates us to hold a new consciousness. Our control mechanisms are created by all of our unconscious beliefs that falsely attempt to protect us from our deepest fears, when in truth, these beliefs actually create the manifestation of our fears.

Collective karma is very tricky, as it is more hidden and unconscious than personal and family karma. It arises in the areas where we trick ourselves into believing in our fears that are connected to our most repressed emotions. When we make powerful new choices in our life and take ourselves beyond our oldest emotional fears, the control mechanisms we have created simply dissolve. The release of our control mechanisms from our etheric body is an important and natural part of our human evolution. It is this journey that truly opens us to our power of attraction as souls and to the recognition that we have wonderful things to share with others.

As we open our hearts and minds and embrace any collective karma that we are shown, we begin to meet souls who have been very close to us in our other lives. These souls are known as our soul family. With our soul family we share new codes of light through our heart exchange, and this supports us in our evolution. It is for this reason that the Enlightened Masters guide all light seeds to take responsibility should any karma arise to block our heart from trusting another soul from our soul family.

Our relationships allow us to express different aspects of our consciousness. They also allow us to see the mirror of ourselves, both the hidden or darker forms as well as the more loving forms of ourselves reflected from the other worlds. You may have noticed that when you are in the presence of one friend, one part of your personality may light up, and in the presence of another, a whole different aspect of your personality may activate its expression. We are attracted to souls who carry qualities that we have not yet ignited in ourselves; these are the very qualities we often seek to experience with our friends or partners.

I remember my first love in life. One of the reasons I was so attracted to him was because of the art he created and his freedom of expression through it, as I so wanted to be an artist when I was a child. I had been raised in a family of engineers, and I was naturally very good at math and science and less confident with expressing myself through art. It felt like another world I could not relate to, so I attracted this learning into my life, and creativity began to flow around me when I ended up living with artists, musicians, and other creative souls. These people reflected parts of my consciousness that I needed to integrate within myself or gifts I needed to awaken. To find my own connection to art and music and my creative self, I unconsciously surrounded myself with creative people. As I was stimulated by this new environment, the power of art, music, divine voice, and performance ignited through my spirit, and I found myself creating a lot of performance art, writing songs, and creating works of art with Spirit.

The Enlightened Masters teach us that we can access everything within us through tapping into the vast consciousness we are, our Divine Presence. We share consciousness with ourselves in the other worlds, but we also share consciousness with all people who enter our energy field. The artists, musicians, and creative souls I spent time with over the years shared their consciousness with me each time they came near me. I received the codes of light for creation from them, something that was blocked in me, that I originally feared. This is the power of forming a group and working together.

Our collective consciousness is so powerful that when it is unbalanced, it can create our body to feel unwell, our energy to be out of balance, our hearts to close, and our thoughts to be very limited. If at any time you feel physically, emotionally, or mentally unbalanced and you sense there is an energetic reason for this, the energy in your collective consciousness simply needs to be balanced.

To do this, all you need to do is ask yourself three questions. How are your emotions tricking you to give your power away to unconscious beliefs? What choice do you need to make to change this? What is it you need to forgive? Once you have discovered the answers to these three questions, the energy will rebalance itself within your collective consciousness. Your collective consciousness can then be guided to release any control mechanisms you hold in your etheric body so you can come into the self-realization that you and only you are creating your reality.

The Control Mechanisms We Create within Our Consciousness to Falsely Protect Ourselves

I remember lying curled up in a little ball in bed after being triggered into an emotional experience through a sharing of truth with Dreaming Heart, who was my partner at that time. As I lay isolating myself, my thoughts wondered whether he truly loved me. Dreaming Heart came to comfort me with all of his love, yet my wounded self pushed him away. I watched myself as he wandered away, feeling rejected yet feeling he was doing his best for me by leaving me alone, as this is what I wanted. As he walked away, another part me was already beginning to judge him and had decided that he did not really love me as he had left so easily. This part of me was angry with him for giving up so easily.

In my heart I yearned inside for him to return, yet another part of me didn't want to receive him into my field. In that moment as I witnessed the different parts of myself, I realized the manipulative game I was playing with all my feelings and their various rules. I realized one part of me was trying to make Dreaming Heart prove his love to me, while another part of me was giving him no possible pathway to do this. Another part of me wanted to punish him and make him feel guilty. Another part had already decided he did not love me. I saw each part of my consciousness at work and how together they were manipulating the energy of the situation between us, and this shocked me.

All these parts of my collective consciousness were affecting my mind to play games with his energy and mine. It was subtle, but I could see it clearly was not loving. I sought him to love me, yet parts of my consciousness were not willing to love and trust him. What I wanted from my partner I was not willing to provide for him. This is how I was manifesting a partner who at times did not act like his love for me was a priority. Everything I was experiencing with Dreaming Heart was a reflection of my consciousness. Some parts of me adored him and would do anything for him, and other parts had judgment, rules of engagement, conditions, and fears he did not love me. Dreaming Heart played out the reflection of both parts of me perfectly, being an adoring partner but also with his own fears of commitment and conditions that would arise.

He returned to the room to bring me a cup of tea, and I sensed he felt guilty and sad also. I saw that I had projected my emotions to make him feel this, and I knew if I continued to allow my consciousness to play these games, we would not truly meet the reflection of sacred union with each other and our relationship would hit a dead end. I made a decision on that day never to play emotional games to get what I wanted. I shared this realization with Dreaming Heart and told him I truly did want him by my side. I shared how sorry I was for all the emotional games of control.

As I looked back at my past relationships, I could see that I had always unconsciously used my emotions to control the men in my life, and I was horrified by what I saw. I could see how this pattern played out between many men and women as a form of control of each other. Once I discovered this control mechanism, and honored that it was not needed any more to protect my feminine energy, I no longer felt this form of unconscious manipulation expressed in my relationships. My relationship with Dreaming Heart changed, and our sexuality, heart connection, and deep sharing went to a completely new level.

Looking back on this experience, I can see that as I became more honest with myself, I was able to share my truth more easily with others. This was an aspect of my collective karma with love, relationship, and ownership that was being cleared. As Dreaming Heart and I continued to live together, many more of these aspects were cleared to allow our relationship to be deeply loving and harmonious. I learned to witness what was occurring within my mind and what choices I was making. Each time I needed to make a significant decision in my life that affected my relationship and my heart, I would simply ask myself if I was making a choice from love or from the place of control.

Your Human Energy Field, Your Collective Consciousness, and the Earth

Many in the world of energy science, consciousness, esoteric studies, healing, and human evolution understand that the human energy field has many dimensions. The source of energy has been a mystery to many, but recently, more and more people are becoming aware that the dimensions of the human energy field are directly connected to the energy and consciousness of our spirit in the other worlds and fed by the greater field that connects us all, known as the unified field.

It is the exchange of energy and consciousness between our soul and our dimensional selves in the other worlds that creates the flow of energy within our auras as human beings. You may ask why one soul is so open, loving, expressive, forgiving, and trusting, and another seems so angry and bitter and finds blame where compassion needs to flame. The answer lies in the flow of their energy and consciousness within their energy body. The forgiving person is harmonious with the essential nature of their soul, whereas the bitter person is in a state of disharmony in their energy field.

The grounding of the spirit into the physical is a task that your ancestors may not have achieved. Because our energy bodies are woven from the fabric of our parents' etheric bodies upon our conception, many of us live in energy bodies that do not really support us to express our true spirit as human beings, and this can be the cause of every difficulty in life.

The map of your energy field is based on twelve dimensions, seven of which are switched on as you move through childhood, between the ages of zero to twenty-one. The higher five dimensions of your potential field begin to be switched on within your energy field once you fully awaken spiritually and accept the power of Spirit as a major element to the experience of wholeness within your being. Therefore, some souls are operating on less than seven fields of consciousness and others are building seven to twelve fields of consciousness. Those operating on less than seven fields are unawakened and either living in a state of unconsciousness or living a state of consciousness of self.

Our human energy field is directly connected to Earth via her lightbody or the Earth Crystal. This is our collective field while we are in incarnation on Earth. Our personal energy fields are wired into the Earth's field via our collective consciousness.

The majority of your collective consciousness is very light and free of all forms of personal, family, or collective karma, yet this is not experienced unless you have balanced your personal, family, and collective karma. Just as your collective consciousness extends into the First and Second worlds, so do spiritual cords extend from your heart into the angelic, crystalline, celestial, and enlightened worlds of the Fourth, Fifth, Sixth, and Seventh worlds of the Earth. Your consciousness within the Seventh World carries no karma and knows only oneness with all of life.

Your consciousness from the Sixth and Fifth worlds is free of personal, family, and collective karma but carries your planetary karma. Your consciousness from the Fourth, Third, and Second worlds carries your puzzle piece of collective karma. Your consciousness from the Third, Second, and First worlds carries your personal karma.

In truth, the consciousness you hold between your soul and spirit carries more wisdom, love, peace, and super-consciousness than karma. Your collective consciousness holds only a small veil of karma compared to the super-consciousness it holds, yet when we are not living in alignment to our soul's truth and love as our chakras are closed or blocked, our karmic challenges always seem overwhelming and too much for us to deal with in our lives.

You may ask, If I hold such an amazing super-consciousness within me, why can't I feel it? The answer is that your energy body may not be holding enough frequency for you to attract the super-consciousness you share with all parts of yourself through all worlds. Your consciousness may be stuck in the lower dimensions of your energy body, and your chakras need to be cleared of your old Akashic records.

Mother Earth's body is a powerful source for raising our consciousness out of the lower dimensions. Through learning to connect your energy body into the Earth's energy field more consciously, you are able to receive divine frequency that expands your chakras so your consciousness can rise out of the lower dimensions and flow through a larger dimensional field. I have worked with many students and clients over the years, and in every case I found that major transitions took place in their lives once they had shifted the karma that kept their consciousness locked in the lower dimensions of their energy body.

The seven dimensional fields that affect humanity's everyday life and determine their quality of life are known as the soul body, the genetic body, the physical body, the etheric body, the emotional body, the mental body, and the spiritual body. These seven lower bodies form the reflection of light around the body known as the aura. Each of these seven lower energy bodies is fed the awakened consciousness from your fractal selves within the seven worlds.

Once a soul opens to their spirit via a powerful heart awakening and develop their chakras and brain chemistry to a level where they are able to ground their super-consciousness from the five higher dimensional lightbodies into their lower seven bodies, they begin to experience their divine consciousness as a human being. They then begin to operate from a larger number of dimensions within their energy body and to build the twelfth dimensional energy field, which is needed for the embodiment of their Divine Presence. Those that are awakened as light seeds are evolving and developing their energy bodies to eventually hold twelve activated dimensions. All have chosen their own path and will find the tools, people, and energy they need to manifest their consciousness to ground for the purpose of peace and their own evolution.

As each light seed opens to Mother Earth as a mother and spirit and to connect their heart into the First World of light regularly, they begin to receive the first form of light transmission needed for their evolution. As they learn to bring this light up through their lower chakras and receive assistance from their Divine Presence, they are freed to raise their consciousness into the fifth dimension, which is simply the Christ consciousness state of unconditional love.

Once a soul's consciousness has transformed and their energy fields have cleared, significant events begin to take place that are signs for the soul to continue on their path. In 1993, I was in England at Glastonbury Tor, and I met a wonderful man who was an author, seer, and spiritual healer who had many amazing gifts. He invited me to dinner as an opportunity to enhance our connection. My collective consciousness at this time was not balanced. I still held fear inside me about beautiful men, and I carried a fear that I was not as beautiful as this man. I had not yet learned to love and fully accept myself.

This man was one of many people that Spirit placed on my path to show me the mirror that would lead to my future, even though I could not accept it at the time. Even though at the time I had no conscious access to the gifts I hold now, my spirit was showing me what I held inside as my potential, if I was willing to make the choice. Looking back on this, I see my karma within my collective consciousness was blocking my lower chakras at this stage in my life. My consciousness was trapped in my lower dimensional bodies and I was living in consciousness of self.

I loved the idea of having this man in my life and had attracted him to me, but I could not receive him fully as I was unwilling to recognize myself as his equal. Because of my fear I let go of some powerful opportunities to grow. I lived for many years with this blockage in my chakras that created my consciousness to perceive myself as small or to experience situations in a fear-based way. My connection with Mother Earth and the Family of Light truly changed my life. As my energy field recalibrated, a new dimension of myself opened up that I had no idea existed.

I share this with you as miracles can occur for all beings when they are ready. When our hearts are not in energetic connection with Mother Earth's heart, we experience the veils of karma as very large and we begin to embody the collective karma. But this does not have to be our experience if we are willing to transform our energy bodies. Miracles can occur through a clear energy body for a soul who is willing to open to the greater field of light that holds infinite love and blessings for our lives.

The Miracle Story of EASE (Energy Attunement Science of Enlightenment)

One of my students who received the EASE Program for eighteen months in Australia with me experienced two miracles in her life. These miracles took place for three reasons. First, the high frequency transmissions and consciousness teachings of the EASE Program had cleared her energy body and opened her chakras. Second, she was willing to be a vessel in service and chose to receive high frequencies from the unified field now that she had a clear energy body and an awareness of how to draw the power of God into her body, mind, and heart. The third reason was that she had cleared her karma through the program, which enabled her to have an experience of the power of her Divine Presence.

The following is an account of my student's miraculous story written by Sue Short and published in *Living Now* magazine.

When the medical team had left the operating theatre, as the patient was proclaimed dead, nurse Leilani Jamesersuin felt compelled to stay with the patient. It had been scheduled as a nine-hour operation and Leilani had known on the drive to Sydney Hospital that it wasn't going to go smoothly. Halfway into the operation, the patient's heart had begun to waver and beat erratically. While the medical team tried frantically, they were unable to do anything and the patient's heart stopped beating. As Leilani stood in the theatre all on her own with the patient, she was told what to do.

Leilani explains, calmly.

"I was told by this little voice ... you have got fifteen minutes. I put my hands on this person's heart and prayed. I asked for the EASE emissaries, my EASE healing team, I asked for Mother Gaia, the archangels, the angels, my ancestors and my own self-mastery to help me with this person. I had already connected with heavenly prana, Earthly prana ... breathing, and time just seemed to fly. I felt pulsations underneath my right hand. My hands felt like they were sinking into their heart and my feet were so heavy I was sweating profusely. I felt more pulsations and more pulsations. I took my left hand off and with my Jupiter and Saturn finger I placed them on the perineum and within 10 minutes as I connected to the sun and moon, I opened my eyes to look and I could see the hair on the crown, waving on the patient's head. I thought, wow, the life force is there."

Time stood still for Leilani and the palpitations became more rapid. One of the surgeons came in and asked her what was happening. The machines were still on and the heart monitor was starting to wriggle. Leilani told him the heart was beating again. The patient lived and when he recovered he told Leilani she was his angel. At the time of the operation, Leilani, a registered nurse for twelve years, had completed all levels of the EASE Program, an eighteen month training program and was studying advanced practitioner training and mentor teaching training with her teacher, Qala Sri'ama Phoenix.

She had been doing all these trainings without being able to hear one word that Qala was saying because she was deaf, due to a horrific accident 10 years earlier when she was working as a paramedic, driving an ambulance. She was in a coma for six weeks after the accident and suffered multiple factures in the head and body, was unable to walk and had to have massive reconstructive surgery. Not long after her experience with the patient in the Sydney hospital, Leilani was attending a weekend training for EASE with Qala in Byron Bay, Australia, and at the end of the workshop she suddenly found she could hear again. She can now speak on the phone without a hearing tool and can sit and listen to her teacher without having to lip-read.

CHAPTER SEVEN

Assisting the Clearing of Collective Karma or Humanity's Burdens

The greatest way each one of us can assist the clearing of collective karma, which carries humanity's deepest burdens, is through simply acknowledging the potential we each hold in our hearts to transform our own collective consciousness and our life experience to a place that creates our soul's inner peace and happiness. As our ancestors are watching over us and they forgive as we forgive, and we embrace all we are shown to be our personal, family, or collective karma, we are able to be held by our Divine Presence and the Enlightened Masters to truly transform our life experiences.

The Enlightened Masters teach that the most important aspect of our work as representatives for humanity is the work of our own evolution, for as our genetic code is unlocked and the filaments of our consciousness begin to grow, we transmit this to everyone who shares our DNA. As our light vibration continues to grow, all we hold is radiated through our communities as our etheric body transmits the higher consciousness into the field of our environment. This light is then transferred into the group heart chakra of all who share this environment and back into their etheric bodies to create a chain reaction of transformation. Our highest work is this journey of evolution based on embodying the principles of love, wisdom, divinity, faith, service, communion, and charity. But what blocks us in this journey more than anything else is our attachment to those we love.

Germaine and Mother Mary came to me one day and asked me if I was willing to allow my daughter to grow and fully develop as she needed to, without my taking on her struggles. My daughter was eighteen, and I could see her life was taking a direction she had not planned. She had many choices to make and held fear about which path to take. I asked them what they meant, as I felt it was my responsibility to share in her struggles and help guide her way. As I questioned them, a great light shone above me and my Presence merged with me. I entered a higher state of consciousness where I was one with my daughter yet could also see myself in my daily relationship with her. I silently watched myself engaging with my daughter's soul in a situation in which she was struggling within herself.

I could feel the pain she held inside and the fears affecting her, and I wanted to take them all from her. I wanted to protect her from experiencing her fear or feeling pressured in any way. I wanted her to have this perfect life with no struggle or challenge. I realized that I did not hold complete trust in her and her own relationship with Spirit. I wanted to intervene and take on her learnings and make them my own. In a way, I wanted to do the journey for her so it would be easier for her. I wanted to take on all of her burdens and place them in a bag and carry them for her.

I wanted to hide the bag from her. This was creating me to help her make her decisions rather than trusting her to receive her own answers from her spirit to meet her fears and transform them. My own unconscious fears were preventing me from trusting in my daughter's heart to guide her clearly through her journey.

Mary came and stood by my side, and many angels were around my daughter, sending her light. Mary said, "As a mother, you need to give love in an unattached way. This serves our children to truly know their own power of love, for their learnings offer them the pathway to grow and experience love in their own way. Your daughter is amazing, and as long as you bring her love with nonattachment to the outcome, she will flower and shine through all of her own experiences. Know she is already perfect and everything she experiences she has called into herself to learn from so she may experience her spirit. Detach from her fear and pain, and you will truly share your unconditional love and this will be her greatest support as she trusts her own spirit to guide her way. You will see your daughter's spirit rise through her being as you do this, beloved. Be aware of the unconscious fears you may project on her reality and be responsible for your own energy. Offer it to the light so you can be unattached and provide her with all of your nurturing wisdom.

Germaine placed his hand on the back of my heart and I was lit up again and felt myself levitate higher and higher until I could see the world below, Mother Earth and her blue hemisphere of light surrounding her body. I levitated higher and the Earth became a very small, soft, blue-white light in the distance, and I felt myself enter a giant heart, a field of plasma. I recognized the plasma frequency from my deep experiences of embodying this through the EASE Program, and I sensed the plasma of all suns and galaxies were drawing me into them. My heart expanded into oneness when I was filled with the plasma. The field was heavy, like liquid lava, and everything began to slow down. I felt as if I was a giant being and all the suns and galaxies were within me, and I felt layers upon layers of voidal frequency flood through me. Through each new layer I traveled, a part of me melted. My mind melted as I became filled with the voidal frequency, and I could no longer recognize myself as me, as I had merged with Source. My whole being dissolved as I was filled with the source frequency, and all melted into a state of bliss. All was light. There was no form, no body, no mind, no individuality, no thought, only pure vibration, a pulsating light that extended forever. This was the infinite nature, or the infinite nature of All That Is.

Held in this state, an abyss of love where all emanated from, consciousness was created; all knowing, yet no mind; all loving, yet no heart; infinite in creation, yet no body. Boundless, infinite, all-expanding light. I am not sure how long I was held in this state, but eventually my consciousness returned to become an individual awareness again; again I was myself standing in the presence of my home, with Mary and Germaine, feeling very altered. I realized then that my body, mind, soul, and spirit were simply one form of consciousness, and that within our source, our consciousness exists purely as light, and this is all we truly are. This light is infinite, and if we choose to access it from the core of our beings, we are able to cocreate with God, our source of infinite power, love, and light.

Germaine and Mary shared with me that the reignition of source connection was taking place for many souls on Earth, and I too was reigniting my direct contact with what many call God. They shared that humanity has many burdens, and only as we learn to cocreate with God's Presence again will we dissolve the burdens we carry as a collective.

I asked what they meant by "cocreate with God." Germaine shared that if I traveled through the heart of a soul, I would find this same core that I had just traveled into, and that this source, or what many call God, lives within all of life and all of humanity. It is not a force outside of us. He explained that this source can be tapped into for the greater good of all beings.

Germaine shared that there are three forms of creation. The first is God's creation, where the light comes directly from this source energy I had just traveled to. Mother Earth is an example of one of God's creations. The second is a Divine Presence's creation. This is a creation that has been made from the power of many souls accessing this source and cocreating with God. He explained that the new education, the EASE Program, the GRACE Program, and the Self Mastery Program I had created with the Enlightened Masters were creations from a Divine Presence. The third form of creation comes from the mind of a soul, or the combined power of the minds of a group of souls. The collective mind is the director of these creations. Most organizations and businesses of our world are an example of this form of creation.

Germaine continued to share with me that all of the angels, archangels, Enlightened Masters, Ancestral Masters, and true guardians of the Earth had made a sacred agreement to create only from this source energy. He shared that each member of the Family of Light had consciously chosen to live in service to all beings by only using their energy and consciousness to benefit all. He explained that my journey through the plasma field into the voidal field and into Source was known as the journey of enlightenment. He had given me this experience as this was a journey I would make in the future, from my own power of creation.

He shared how important it is for every soul to become aware of their power of creation and how they affect others with their choices, words, and actions. This is the basic work of every light seed on their path of evolution. He completed his teaching by sharing that if we give our love in an attached way, we actually block those we love from creating their own source connection in life. He explained that sometimes we trick ourselves into believing we are helping others by giving them the solution to their problems. But this is a manifestation of our attachment, and this only creates others to be reliant on us. He shared that every soul has their direct contact with the source of power, love, and light, and the journey through the heart, even if a soul is in pain, is the journey of the reignition of their direct contact.

He shared that this is the truth that allows the Enlightened Masters to witness atrocities occurring on Earth, hold the unconditional love for all beings as this occurs, and bring grace to those that ask, and not break the universal law of noninterference even though they may have the power to stop atrocities from continuing. For if they did this, they would block another soul's evolution and journey they had called in to experience, and they would also de-evolve through the misuse of their own power and therefore be unable to help those that were asking for assistance. They would also create further imbalance, as they carry such vast consciousness and light, and through an act of intervention to save some from atrocities, they would create harm to others simply by breaking the universal law of noninterference.

Germaine said that even the deeds you may believe do good can do harm if they are not aligned to universal law. He shared that in the times of Atlantis, there was a fall in consciousness within some Presences as they did not abide by universal law, and they used their power to intervene where others did not give permission. This is why humanity today stills carries the collective karma of power, responsibility, and righteousness, which creates wars on Earth. Many souls have learned from this lesson and are now ready to embrace their power and trust their light again. These souls realize we are not here to save others who are suffering, but are here to love them and support them to be true to themselves by being true to ourselves and listening to the wisdom of our ancestors, Mother Earth, and our own Divine Presence.

Becoming a Clear Representative for Humanity in Balancing Our Collective and Planetary Karma

Specific frequencies have the ability to transform energy and consciousness at a rapid rate. Celestial frequency is sourced from beyond our known fields of experience and is generated from great hemispheres that link the stars, planets, and galaxies within our universe. As you may be aware, many of the stars in our heavens are many times larger than our sun, and our small planet Earth can seem like a minute dot in comparison to these heavenly bodies that direct energy to us through the Earth's field. If you choose to receive this frequency, you will evolve at a rapid rate as it has the power to dissolve karma in your energy field and activate your consciousness to awaken on all levels of your being.

Imagine that linking each of these immense celestial bodies we call our stars are hemispheres made from voidal, source, and plasma frequencies and sound currents. From these hemispheres, rays of Christ light emanate as grids through All That Is, and as life forms are ignited, clouds of this light feed life force to all. These hemispheres emanate specific celestial frequencies and sounds that hold great love and power for all in our universe, and each connects as a portal to alternate universes. Each hemisphere is mirrored by another that extends into alternate universes through the presence of a larger sphere made of pure sound. These spheres of sound are portals to worlds beyond the Earth and hold within them the same power that originally seeded all life on Earth. This power is known as the power of creation.

The celestial hemispheres emanate the sounds of the spheres, which orchestrate the cycles of our universe and the rotation of the stars and planets within our galaxy.

As the Earth receives these celestial frequencies, her new etheric body is being created for the higher purpose of her shift into the fifth dimension. As we receive celestial frequencies, our new bodies and new consciousness are activated. We are carriers of specific codons of light that only human beings are able to receive, and this gives us a role as caretakers of Earth, a role that only humanity can fulfill. We are supported in our evolutionary process through these celestial currents more deeply than any other energy. We have the power to clear the collective karma of humanity simply by transferring these frequencies into our cells. This activates our remembrance of our true selves as Divine Presences.

I met with a beautiful woman the other day, and she asked me, "Qala, what is the fifth dimension?" I shared with her that it is simply the place within our consciousness that provides us with the divine energy we need to stabilize to a specific energetic state based on unconditional love, forgiveness, compassion, and nonjudgment. She shared with me that she felt she had a fair way to go with this, as she was sometimes experiencing this, but also at times would revert into old patterns.

I shared with her that what she described was a very important part of the journey. Every time she felt herself revert, she was simply experiencing a part of her consciousness that was in need of her love so it could travel all the way into the fifth dimension. I asked her not to judge this part of her spirit, for it would shift into the fifth dimension as she was able to open her heart in unconditional love again. The shift is gradual, and all it needs is for light seeds to stay grounded in their love to the best of their ability.

Your evolution is the key to our collective's evolution. As the temporal and parietal lobes of your brain receive specific frequencies, your multidimensional awareness is activated to ignite your ability to sense the higher frequencies of energy moving through the world in which you live. As your brain chemistry is altered through its receptivity of high frequency transmissions of light, you have access to the greater potential of being a spiritual representative of humanity with the ability to transmit vast frequencies from your own energy system, chakras, and DNA filaments of light. This experience of receiving vast, high frequency transmissions into your brain, aura, dimensional fields, and body is what the Enlightened Masters offer to all souls who wish to be representatives for humanity in the clearing of humanity's collective karma. When you work directly with the Enlightened Masters, these transmissions are delivered to your being. Through receiving a specific quantity and quality of the divine transmissions from the enlightened realms, a soul will lift from the wheel of karma, develop their consciousness and chakras, and build their twelve dimensional fields so they can experience their Divine Presence.

Many in the physical world are controlled by what lies in their etheric bodies. They may have unclear thoughts, lack of wellness in their bodies, codependency in their relationships, and power struggle with others, for the etheric body holds the unconscious beliefs of a soul's karma. Unless the etheric body transforms, the physical, emotional, and mental bodies cannot evolve either. The etheric body is the base energy body that holds all the blueprints and is a storehouse of information within your field. This body lies closest to the physical world and your physical body, and seeds the energy, intentions, blueprints, and consciousness into all that creates your experiences in the physical world.

If your etheric body is bound by karma, it links your energy body into the lower aspects of the fourth dimension and connects you to the collective karma of humanity and all that is unresolved from your past. When you have cleared your karma to 51 percent, your etheric body no longer resonates to the karmic wheel or karma of the collective consciousness of humanity. When your etheric body is cleared of 51 percent of your karma, your vibrational field can shift an octave through the fourth dimension and begin to rise into the fifth dimension, and you will no longer be affected by astral energies.

Your etheric body carries your Akasha, and the Earth's etheric body carries the Akasha of all beings on the Earth through all seven worlds. Your etheric body is also the only energy body that can hold a direct connection with the astral plane through the lower aspects of the fourth dimension, as it is the energy field that weaves your dreaming bodies and also supports you to soul travel. It is also the energy body through which your chakras seed and generate new consciousness. You may always call on your Divine Presence and the Enlightened Masters' assistance regarding your etheric body and its clarity, and you may receive the light technologies that transmute and activate your etheric body to serve your journey of evolution.

The light technologies held in the higher dimensions are able to support our etheric bodies to transform for our consciousness's shift into the fifth dimension and for our true nature as vast spirits to ground into our physical form. When the etheric body holds the blueprints of unresolved karma via the activation of our Akashic records, our consciousness either embraces our karma or rejects it by projecting it on others or on our outer circumstances. It is recommended by the Enlightened Masters that as a representative of humanity, you learn to work with universal law and to recognize how all consciousness is created in alignment with our free will and the universal laws.

The universal laws of grace, love, oneness, divinity, karma, forgiveness, and liberty are encoded, high frequency waves of God consciousness that move through the fabric of our universe, supporting creation to be sustained and balanced. It is the relationship of the universal laws to one another that forms our worlds and creates the unique dimensions within our worlds.

The universal law of grace provides all souls grace when they ask for it. The law of oneness holds the unified field in place and ignites all in oneness. The law of divinity ignites the spark of God within all beings. The law of karma holds the balance of all karma with the balance of all creation.

The law of love provides an infinite supply of love throughout our universe. Love is the essence of a soul, and as a soul accepts love from the universe, their original essence is ignited through their heart so they experience the love they are. The law of forgiveness ignites the transformation of all in darkness or suffering. The law of liberty frees all consciousness that is bound when it chooses free will. There are many other universal laws, but these seven, when called upon, will balance your energy so you can be guided to transform a situation and complete your learning with success and a sensation of unconditional love.

Universal law translates into your life in a very simple way when you recognize that universal law is the greatest influence on your reality, and when you align to it, rather than fearing or living in ignorance of it, you empower your reality. In other words, whatever your thoughts, words, feelings, actions, and choices are, universal law will interact with these and the resulting experience you have will be your consciousness interacting with these immense forces that form all in nature.

Universal law is the force that many call the "hand of God," the innate force that holds a greater power than we each hold individually. The concept of divine will does not mean that a soul gives away their power, for each soul has been granted free will to use in the highest way, and each soul is an aspect of God. Divine will is simply your alignment to universal law. When you align your will to universal law, the universe empowers all that you do with divine frequency.

When you are experiencing challenges in life, it is a sign your karma is calling you to align yourself with universal law to transform the cause of the situation. When you align yourself with universal law, the rearrangement of your thoughts and feelings will take place quickly, and the result will be an experience of wholeness and oneness. From this new place of deep connection with yourself, you are then able to create your life with awareness.

Many on the spiritual path speak of Spirit, yet the embodiment of Spirit in its clearest light does not take place unless the energy body of a soul has risen in vibration powerfully, and the old etheric body has been released. So many on the spiritual path seek this, but do not know how to reach this potential. So many do not know that through the doorway of their karma they can reclaim the light of their spirit into their physical body. Many feel free at times, less centered in their mental body, or less emotional and lighter in their attitudes, yet so many believe that this means their spiritual embodiment process is complete.

In truth, this sense of freedom and lightness is the only the beginning of the journey. A part of one's consciousness has shifted into the fifth dimension, but it is not the complete shift. The complete shift is manifested by the illumination of the soul and physical body, an experience of bliss and ecstasy within every cell of the body. It is not simply a process of feeling lighter and freer. It is an experience of the body being directly fed by the unified field of life and no longer needing to sustain itself only through food, sleep, and other sustenance from our physical world.

Those sincerely on the path, who dedicate themselves to consciousness evolution, have the potential to evolve into plasma bodies, which allow a higher consciousness to live permanently in the physical body. Souls who have developed to this level live with their Presence fully in their bodies. Some beings that are Divine Mother embodiments have developed voidal energy bodies to experience life on Earth in holy service. Each of these developments has its unique chakra, vortex, and grid system based on a unique energy. Although it has been very rare in the last eight thousand years for humanity to develop plasma and voidal bodies on Earth, there are more people now developing these bodies than ever before.

Our collective is presently evolving into our crystalline lightbodies made from Christ light. The Fifth World of the Earth is made from this substance and energy. As we shift into the fifth dimension, all of us as a race are evolving from a pranic-based energy system to a Christ-light-based energy system. Our chakras are no longer only developing pranic cones, but the core of each chakra, which is created from crystalline light geometries, is being activated by the new codes the Earth is receiving. As the Earth is shifting and her crystal and the diamond plates of her light are being cleared, she is activating the crystalline nature within all of life on Earth.

According to the Enlightened Masters, there is no possibility of any soul living within a pranic energy body in five hundred years' time. Over this period, our crystalline structures will have developed to a level such that the pranic fields we hold now will become pure light frequency. Mother Earth's crystal will have activated to a much higher intensity of light, creating more complex geometries of light and crystalline bodies for all life forms.

How will this change us? Our consciousness will become brighter, our heart more radiant, our thoughts will instantly manifest, and we will live in a deeper union and experience group mind more than individual thought, although we will still know our individuality. This is the vision that the Enlightened Masters gave me of our world in its evolution as we receive more Christ light, plasma, and celestial frequency into our fields. The Christ light is the pure spectrum of energy that brings clarity and purification and creates integrity. The plasma is the power current that we receive to cocreate with God and activate our collective empowerment. The celestial frequency is what links our hearts to Mother Earth and the universal centers, the suns and moons that open us to our infinite vastness, our Divine Presence.

There is much in our world that will transform and much of it we may not understand, but we are being asked to live in unconditional love with nonattachment so we can stay present within our evolutionary process. This will not be an overnight experience. It will take generations, but you are the light seeds, seeding this for the future generations who know this is their birthright. The Enlightened Masters share it will take one thousand years to create this new world where only peace is experienced.

This is the truth that the Enlightened Masters have given me to share with humanity. Know that your ancestors and the ancestors of all beings will witness this as it occurs on the Earth. When this world of peace is created, you could very well be an ancestor witnessing it yourself, or you may have chosen to reincarnate on Earth, or, if you clear your karma and evolve, you may incarnate within one of the other worlds of Earth as an angel, archangel, Christ being, or celestial or enlightened presence.

The Etheric Structures of Our Collective and Our Planetary Service

Holding faith and trust in our collective's positive path of evolution can take place only if we are individually enjoying our own personal journey and our energy body is emanating at a higher vibration. This can be difficult if our etheric body is resting in a lower vibration than it needs to be. It is even more difficult if we are living or spending time in an environmental field where the etheric body is held in a lower vibrational field.

Our cities' etheric fields are created through the mergence of every soul's personal etheric field, linked through a collective matrix of light that is empowered by a group heart chakra. This group heart chakra rests above the city, and if you are spending time in a city that has a blocked heart chakra and you have an etheric body that is emanating a lower vibration, then you will experience your heart partially or fully closing in a state of protection, veiling you from your truth and clarity while you are in that city.

The etheric structures of our collective are very powerful, and unless we have an etheric body that is emanating a higher vibration than the collective etheric body, these structures can influence our energy bodies to close. Consider how you feel when you enter a city, and how you feel when you go to the country. Yet you are the same being with the same energy body. For many people, the environment of the city influences them to close down their energy body, and even though they may love what the city offers, they do not feel their true self when they are in the city for long periods. Many have shared with me that they feel drained when they are in an environment that is not their home or when many other people are around them.

My experience is no longer like this, although I spent years in deep sensitivity to all energies and was only able to be in nature in some periods of my life. My etheric structure has altered and has been recalibrated by receiving large amounts of higher frequency, and now I feel the same energy flow in myself wherever I go, and do not feel negatively affected by any of the environments I enter. I love the exciting opportunities of the city, and I love the peace and nature of the country.

The etheric structures that are our collective fields of light also hold our Akashic records. Whenever a group gathers, they bring their etheric fields together, and each individual begins to experience the energy of the collective. If your etheric field is of a lower vibration than you need, you experience a heaviness as your etheric field connects to the Akasha in the collective etheric field, if the collective carries heaviness within their Akasha. If your etheric body is holding a lower vibration, it connects only to the unresolved energies or karmic energy within this Akasha.

Sometimes when groups connect and the exchange of Akasha and karma occurs, those with the lowest vibrational etheric field take on the karma of the collective or receive the Akashic records of the collective into their etheric fields. This only takes place if a soul's etheric body is weak and their own personal energy field is not strong enough to filter these karmic energies, and only if the soul has been attaching to another person's chakras through the creation of psychic cords.

These forms of attachment are also known as astral cords. They are created through psychic thoughts about others that are not truly unconditionally loving. Psychic cords or attachments are made to the chakras of any other person that one's mind becomes fixated upon through the projections of thought forms from one's brow chakra and central consciousness. You may simply ask Archangel Michael to clear these for you. So you no longer create astral cords, become aware of your thoughts, and if you do find your mind projecting desires or needs onto another person, then apologize to their soul within your mind and offer these thoughts to be lifted into the light. When you no longer attach to others, no others will mirror this and attach to your chakras.

Two of the most important lessons with energy are learning not to pull on another person's energy psychically through energy cords and learning to stay connected to your heart and ground your energy into the Earth core. These two lessons allow you to care for your own energy body so it does not continually fluctuate and create mixed emotions that make it impossible to ascertain your true thoughts, feelings, and energy.

When your energy is pulling on another person's chakras, you find yourself thinking about them all the time, or they simply pop into your head every so often. This is a sign that you need to get clear in your energy with this person. You are pulling on their energy, and spiritually you are not being clear with your use of energy. This can be a one-way experience, or it is possible they have also reacted and are corded to you from their psychic energy.

If you are clear psychically in life, you will be able to raise the vibration of your etheric body. If you have created psychic cords from your etheric body to another person's etheric body, they will feel you draining their energy. This is the pull some people feel from others when they are in groups. The truth is, you will only feel this if your etheric body is weak and you have created psychic cords to another member or some members of the group.

When we come from a place of unconditional love, we place everyone as an equal valuable member in a group. If you are not empowering yourself to see yourself as equal to others in a group, your psychic energy may want another to give you something to make you feel equal. You may witness yourself with thoughts that you are not worthy and unconsciously you may also be emanating this belief to the group. As this occurs, your psychic energy may send out cords to others whose qualities you admire, and you may attach to them, wishing to receive some sign from them that you are truly equal and worthy.

This occurs on a subconscious level, but these subconscious feelings direct your primary consciousness to seek in others what you feel is missing within your own being. What often occurs, though, is as you attach cords to other people's chakras, they do not respond in the most open way, as unconsciously they are aware you are seeking something from them. This can create you to experience the very thing you feared, a feeling of inequality or unworthiness.

You may feel these pulls on your energy as undercurrents in your relationships. Control mechanisms form in the etheric body when you attach to other people's chakras as a regular pattern. These mechanisms anchor into the etheric body as a series of unconscious beliefs that set rules for how you will relate. For this reason it is important to be aware of how we use our energy with others, so we may become clear in our etheric bodies to allow our spirits to ground into our physical bodies in the presence of others.

The etheric structure of any collective carries the Akasha for all that has occurred within that collective. Within the etheric field of a group that has gathered, the Akashic records of all that has taken place are held between all souls present, so sometimes when a group forms and spends time with each other, the karma of the group can arise for all to forgive, to bring them closer together.

When our personal etheric fields are weak, though, we can become a representative for the group karmic clearing. Usually the karma of the group will play out through members of the group that have the weakest fields. This can create the soul who has the weakest etheric field to feel the Akasha of the group and embody it into their chakras, creating them to experience the karma as a reenactment of what lies unresolved in the Akasha. If you witness someone in a group you are in experiencing karma or reacting to it, it is best to support them to release their psychic cords and attachments, for otherwise they will continue to embody the old Akashic records of the whole group, and this can create a soul to enter suffering. Call on their Divine Presence and say a prayer for their karma to lift and for their Akashic records to be cleared. This will bring assistance to them when they are ready to receive it. If you feel blame toward this person, this is a sign that you have cords attached to their chakras. These cords will always create you to react in a negative way to their actions and choices and block you from experiencing unconditional love as your first response. Attachment creates a great deal of suffering on Earth, and whenever you are in a group and karma is felt, all you need to do is simply open your heart and detach from all your own desires and forgive, and this will release the karma.

Every etheric field of a collective holds immense truth and knowledge within it, but until the old Akasha or karma is cleared between the hearts of all in the collective, this great resource of wisdom, truth, love, and knowledge is not accessed. The true power of any collective is released when the karma or old Akasha between members of the group is absolved, purified, or transformed.

If there is discord in a group you are in, to assist with the clearing of the group's etheric structure, you may wish to simply call for the Divine Presences of all souls who form this collective and ask for karmic absolution for the group through the following prayer. This will begin the process of karmic clearing, and as all participating have the opportunity to forgive, the karma will be cleared from the etheric body they share and the power of the group will ignite and the manifestation of their purpose will flow without blockage. Saying a prayer for a group is one of these special acts that orchestrates the clearing of karma, as all transformation is initially activated through the law of grace that states, Ask and you shall receive.

Prayer for Karmic Clearing of the Etheric Body of Groups or the Collective

Mother, Father, God/Goddess, or Divine Presence of Love and Light,

I call for the diamond light frequency of love to fill the etheric body of my collective consciousness and the collective field of _____

_____ (insert name of family, group, organization, community, or city) and for the clearing of all control mechanisms, grids of duality, old hierarchy, or polarity held within these fields in divine order for all beings. I call on the universal laws of love, forgiveness, oneness, grace, divinity, karma, and liberty to flood through the etheric body of my collective consciousness and this collective, _____(insert name again). I ask for Archangel Michael and the Divine Presences of humanity to activate a field of protection and a fifth dimensional field of unconditional love as my collective and the collective of_____ (insert name again) embrace all karma and enter a deep state of forgiveness and peace. I call on the Divine Presences of every member of this collective to overlight this clearing and healing and guide each member to a place of forgiveness, love, and acceptance with regard to the clearing of this collective karma. I ask for the clearing of all psychic cords that bind me or this collective karmically. I call on the grace of all of the angels, archangels, and Enlightened Masters to bless my collective consciousness and this collective, _____ (insert name again). I ask for all obstacles to now be removed from all paths, so love and peace can blossom and all can link hearts, minds, and souls in unity. I ask that if there be any collective karma that I share from my collective consciousness with this group, _____ (insert name again), that I be shown this so I may ask for karmic absolution for this collective karma as a representative of this group. I call for karmic absolution for all karma I may recognize is linked between my collective consciousness and this group. I ask for the Enlightened Masters to bring forth all dispensations to this group and to my collective consciousness in *divine order for our beings. I ask we be placed on a karmic clearing program in divine order for our evolution and in accordance with God's grace for all beings. I give thanks for this and ask that the diamond light frequency of love continue to clear our etheric fields of all collective karma. I call on the blue celestial frequency to saturate our fields until the karma has been lifted or dissolved or balanced. So be it.*

Working in Super-consciousness Connection with the Divine Presences of Humanity and the Earth

In the world of spirit and unseen worlds, the vast consciousness that you are lives within the field of oneness as your Divine Presence. Your Divine Presence has no one form, but is in fact able to infuse God consciousness into anything, including your body, mind, soul, and all dimensional forms of your spirit. As you choose with your free will to evolve, more of your Divine Presence sourced from this immense field of oneness focuses on you.

Every human being has a Divine Presence, and their connection to their Presence is held through the source flame inside their heart chakra. Every soul has the potential to evolve powerfully, if this is what they wish from their hearts and they apply their free will toward working with their Divine Presence.

To ignite this in your own life, you have the opportunity as a representative of humanity to work with the super-consciousness of every soul on Earth by calling on the Divine Presences of all souls on Earth when you need the support personally, or for your family, your community, or our world. When you call on the Divine Presences of all on Earth, it links your soul and your collective consciousness to a greater field of enlightened support. When you create this connection, everything that you do is magnified by the frequency of this vast connection. Imagine that this field is abundant and ever expanding and that when you call for assistance in this way, a great consciousness of love, presence, and light focuses on anything you ask it to focus on if it is for the highest good.

As a soul, you are always connected to your Divine Presence, whether you are conscious of it or not, so connected, in fact, that the power of your Presence supports the creation of your reality. Your Presence, though, has no preference for what you choose to create, and therefore you may create wonderful things or you may create your own suffering. Your Presence is a force of unconditional love and therefore will not break the law of noninterference with you.

When you call on the Divine Presences of humanity, it needs to be for a sacred purpose, as this force of infinite love and enlightened wisdom is able to influence a situation only when permission is given or the law of grace is called upon for the highest good of all beings and you. As you have the ability to give permission to your Divine Presence and the Divine Presences of humanity, you can be the first to receive the support and divine energy they offer as assistance when you call to them.

When you are in a situation with others, you may need to call on their Divine Presences, and although these ones will not interfere with the free will of anyone else, they will fill the energy field with love, and just this will influence all to flow in a positive direction.

Every Divine Presence of Humanity has the permission to open an Earth portal for the greater good of all beings. This can take place only with the assistance of one's Divine Presence and the ancestors of the Inner Earth. This is a powerful process that helps evolution and specifically the grounding of all situations, which includes completions. Opening an Earth portal supports the release of karma or old energy and consciousness that has become blocked or is unable to release from the Earth or the physical world, or even from your body.

Sometimes karma can be trapped in the physical world, and an Earth portal needs to be opened so the blocked energy may travel down into the inner core of the Earth where it is transformed instantly into its original form. This can specifically help groups that have become stuck and cannot complete their focus in a clear way. Opening an Earth portal supports the release of the oldest karma and assists the physical to receive light and clarity. Opening a heavenly portal brings in the new consciousness and frequency needed for creation.

The Enlightened Masters will assist this process, but in truth, they simply watch over as the Ancestral Masters open the Earth portal when you ask for this to take place for the highest good of all beings. The portal keepers and guardians work with all representatives of humanity for this purpose. They support the Earth portal to stay open for a short period of time so the energy and consciousness can earth as the transformation completes, and they also open the ley lines and song lines so they too may be freed of any old energy. The ley lines and song lines connect to the collective field of all beings as well as to the Earth's field. As they are opened, all aspects of the collective and planetary karma held within the Earth's field and the collective's field can also be transformed.

The greatest transformations for groups and individuals take place when an Earth portal and a heavenly portal are opened simultaneously and at least one representative of humanity opens their heart beyond any karma present and forgives all connected to this karma. This empowers a soul to lift karma from their closest collective, their family, and this imprints as a benefit to our whole collective. When three representatives join together in this, it creates a permanent shift of an aspect of collective karma from the Earth's body. It takes three representatives of humanity working in an Earth and heavenly portal to shift karma from the Earth herself and from the collective. This form of service also lifts planetary karma.

The currents that open up through both an Earth portal and a heavenly portal have the ability to heal a heart completely within one hour. When an Earth and a heavenly portal are both fully open for two hours one can become empowered to be able to clear the field of a soul who is in such distress, terror, or anxiety that they cannot sleep. When both an Earth and a heavenly portal remain fully open for an entire day, one can be empowered to regenerate a part of the Earth that has been mined or disrespected in a deep way such that the link between the resource and the spirit of the land has been severed. This of course only takes place if representatives do the karmic clearing and forgiveness work within the portal.

As representatives of humanity working with the Divine Presences and Mother Earth, when the Earth and heavenly portals are opened, we have the potential to transform all situations and balance all forms of energy. There is nothing that cannot be balanced through the opening of these portals and our hearts coming together in forgiveness, compassion, and love, as brothers and sisters. When a collective tries to do this alone, without the assistance of their Presence, the karma they hold as a collective can arise and create the group energy dynamics to either collapse or weaken the group's focus and clarity in fulfilling their purpose.

Every group has a great resource from the source of love and light of each member. This resource can only be accessed when every member of the group is seen as an equal and when every member of the group links their heart together to create from their shared greater resource. This greater resource is the super-consciousness of each individual, and this connection can only be made when the heart is open and the brain's field is generating light frequency.

The super-conscious connection with the Divine Presences of humanity and Mother Earth creates us to think compassionately, be considerate of others' feelings, and see life from many angles. When we listen to others with an open mind, when we share without deciding that our viewpoint is the only viewpoint worth hearing, we see from a greater overview, and this viewpoint is the place of connection with Divine Presence or the Holy Spirit.

You will find the Divine Presence of every soul who is with you is waiting in the wings of spirit, in the portals, and if they are called to be present with you in the physical world, a great wave of love and light will begin to transmit into the field of the physical space you are in, and this will support the energy to change for the better so eventually a win-win situation can manifest. Whenever you find yourself in a karmic situation with others, simply call on Mother Earth and the Divine Presences of all souls who share this situation with you, and ask for their assistance to move the positive energy through the group. It is amazing how quickly things will begin to shift when you begin to do this.

There are three primary methods a representative of humanity is given to work in super-consciousness connection with their Divine Presence and the Divine Presences of all beings on Earth. The first is prayer, invocation, and asking for assistance. Communicating with Spirit through prayer and intention is one aspect of the higher work of an activated light seed or representative of humanity. The Enlightened Masters share that as a representative of humanity, you need the highest form of assistance when clearing your personal, family, collective, or planetary karma; otherwise situations can become very sticky. Through living life in alignment with the law of grace through communicating with Spirit via prayer you attract the highest form of assistance into your life circumstances.

The second method for working in super-consciousness with your Holy Spirit is to receive specific light frequencies for your evolution. Your own evolution can be your highest service to all beings if your heart is clear of personal and family karma and you only need to balance your collective and planetary karma. If you have no personal or family issues that create your heart to close or contract, this is a sign that your personal and family karma has cleared to a level of 51 percent in your energy body. This simply means that your heart is empowered by more than 50 percent of your consciousness to stay open in the presence of your own life situation and in the presence of all of your family.

When the deepest karma that blocks the heart is present, there is usually still one major challenge in your personal life and one major challenge in your family life. My major challenge in my personal life stemmed from my wish to escape society and isolate myself in my own little world. I loved people, but I could not love our society. My heart connection to the world was blocked by my personal karma when I was a teen and into my early twenties. My major family challenge was around my inability to feel loved fully by both my father and my partner. My receptivity in my heart was blocked through my family karma. As these two issues in my life cleared, it was a sign that both my personal and family karma had cleared to at least 51 percent in my energy body.

After the 51 percent is cleared, you may still experience other side issues or personal and family challenges, but you will find they all source back to one Akashic record that you could trace through all your lives to the first incarnation you held as a human being where you closed your heart to your Divine Presence. By receiving the specific light frequencies for your evolution, you can gather back the consciousness that closed down in that original lifetime. This second method of working in super-consciousness connection with your Divine Presence raises your vibration and shifts the old consciousness that is ready to simply dissolve into the light.

The third method of working with your super-consciousness and Divine Presence is based on receiving clear guidance. Clear guidance comes via a dedication of prayer and communication with Spirit and through your frequency activation, which generates and opens the portals in your consciousness to receive your guidance.

These three activities are essential to any person who wishes to be a representative of humanity offering planetary service to Mother Earth and all beings. To pray and communicate with Spirit opens the gateway in your collective consciousness so the transmissions and frequencies can flow through your brain's field and into your body. When you receive the divine frequency into your being, new energy centers open inside you. Transformation takes place within you, and you receive the guidance to support this process to be a complete shift rather than a partial shift. This is the nature of being within an Earth and heavenly portal, for they open for one purpose only: as a planetary service, to support the shift into a higher dimension.

Setting your intention is important before beginning the ceremony for this portal work. Even when traveling to sacred sites, it is important to recognize that these portals are not open in all dimensions and they are safeguarded and protected by the guardians of the Earth. The ancestors and guardians will open the sacred sites and portals if your intention is of the highest and if you do ceremony and make the sacred connection with them.

Any time you are aware of karma being enacted, you may simply say prayers to begin the first step of the shift. If you also call on your Divine Presence and the Divine Presences of all humanity, you can begin to receive the divine frequency through your heart, chakras, and energy body and ground it into the Earth, and this will activate the second stage of the shift. If you receive your guidance from your Presence and follow it, it will complete the shift needed to absolve this karma. Through these three simple steps, you will have done your work as a representative of humanity. You may always call on your family, community, nation, and world and the beings of all worlds to receive this with you, and they will also benefit. If you sit in a deeper place of heart connection, many will hear your call and come into the portal to assist.

The following prayer may assist you in your work as a representative for humanity, and in the opening of an Earth and heavenly portal for a specific purpose that benefits you and all beings in divine order for all.

Prayer for Opening an Earth and Heavenly Portal for a Higher Purpose of Planetary Service to All Beings

Mother, Father, God/Goddess,

I call on Mother Gaia and the Ancestors and ask that they open an Earth portal in this sacred space for the benefit of all souls and all life forms on Earth. I call on my Divine Presence to merge with me. I ask for the platinum and golden spheres of love to ground into Mother Earth and through my body, chakras, and central pillar to open the light connection through all dimensions of this sacred space and my being. I call on all of the angels, archangels, celestial presences, and enlightened presences to assist and overlight the portal as it is opened.

I call on Archangel Michael and my Divine Presence to overlight this and to create all aspects of divine protection so this sacred work may take place in the highest way. I ask for a heavenly portal between the Earth and the great, great, great central sun and great, great, great central moon to be opened so divine grace may flood into this space and ground into the Earth. I call on all of the divine frequencies of love to fill me and this space in divine order for all beings. I call on the Divine Presences of humanity and my Divine Presence, and I ask for this portal to be opened for _____ (insert the name of the higher purpose that is a planetary service to all beings). I call on my collective consciousness to free itself and forgive all that may need to be forgiven to ground this grace.

I ask for the grace to _____ (insert that which you are calling for assistance with) and ask for this for all beings and all souls on the Earth who may need this. I ask for the grace and special frequencies to fill me as I offer to surrender all that is not serving me. I call on the violet flame to blaze through and the holy power of forgiveness and love to ignite all aspects of all within this portal now.

I call on all of my spiritual, soul, and blood family to receive these special dispensations with me. I invite my ancestors to forgive all that they may need to forgive so this grace may truly be received by my whole being and by the heart of all in need. I call on the Earth and heavenly portal to stay open for as long as I am in sacred space here.

Once I have completed my sacred work or received this, I ask that the portal be closed, and I ask for all that has been received to be blessed, consecrated, and sealed in divine order for my being. I give thanks! Blessed be, blessed be, blessed be!

The Old Etheric Grids of Our World

The following information is given to you to assist you to understand the nature of a worldwide karmic clearing project that was initiated by the Enlightened Masters in 2009 and will complete in 2013. This project is known as the Celestial Project, and it is part of the implementation of the Divine Plan for the Earth and humanity. This project is focused on gathering people together in linkups as representatives for humanity in the karmic clearing of humanity's collective karma held in the etheric fields of many primary cities and portals of the Earth.

As a soul learns to receive divine frequency and to work with the heart chakras of the cities and communities and clear the grids that hold the collective karma of humanity and their ancestors, their own heart connection also clears and expands, and this benefits the clearing of their personal, family, collective, and planetary karma. Their work as a representative of humanity becomes empowered when they join and link up with others who are also assisting this project's purpose.

Each of our world's cities where there is a high density of population or high level of world affairs being managed has within the etheric planes of light an etheric grid structure that affects the level of awareness of all who live in or visit the city and affects whether they can easily raise their vibrational field in the vicinity of that city. This etheric grid structure is formed by the combined etheric field of all souls that live there or travel within it, as well as the energy within the land and all that the city has been created from. Consider a city's etheric structure as carrying the story of the city from its birth and the story of all souls within it. It also carries the karma of the collective of all souls within the city.

All of our cities are overlighted by the angelic guardian of the city, an archangel who is the primary caretaker of the city, and the Divine Presence of all souls who live in the city. This is also true for the communities in our world, although our communities are usually overlighted by an angel. The divine frequency and purpose of a city or community is held by these oversouls, and when a soul releases from the three veils (or old grids, explained below) they are able to access clear guidance from these overlighting presences who carry the higher truths of all related to the city or community.

The etheric structure of a city or community also holds within it the karma of the ancestors of the members of this city or community, and the karma of all who have died upon the land where this city or community is built. As individuals choose to represent the collective, in the clearing of their karma and in the clearing of the three old grids of control, duality, and old authority from their etheric bodies, the oldest karma of our ancestors can be released from the Earth and the collective consciousness of humanity. Through this powerful form of ancestral healing and planetary service, Mother Earth and humanity will be deeply supported to move into the fifth dimension.

The Three Etheric Grids That Carry the Unresolved Karma of the Collective of Humanity

Imagine an etheric grid system that rests above all of humanity as they walk around and live on the Earth. This etheric grid system is very beautiful, but it also carries three very old grids within this beautiful system of divine energy. In the etheric realm of the Earth, many grids or energy fields lie in different dimensions. In the fourth dimension, the three old etheric grid systems that carry the collective karma of humanity weave from above each city or dense population, connecting city to city and town to town, community to community and family to family. Imagine this network of light now. Visualize above each city, community, and family a large heart chakra made of pure golden light, and call on your Divine Presence and all of the Family of Light to begin to clear each of these group-consciousness chakras—the heart chakra of each city and community as you send love to them.

As you do this, recognize that you have the power of love and light to work with the Celestial Guardians of the Earth to dissolve these three grids that run from a city or community's heart chakra, affecting the chakras of all souls within the cities and communities. The collective karma held in these three old grids can influence souls to give their power to the belief in duality, control, and hierarchy.

Recognize that you have the power of light and love when you sit in your heart to simply love and embrace this network and see it in a form where it is transforming to golden light, using your own gifts as you are guided. Following the three steps of your work as a representative of humanity will always lead you to being instrumental in creating a shift in karma to take place.

These three grids center from the city's heart chakra (beginning at 380 feet above the center of each city and expanding sometimes to heights of 12,000 feet) and expand out from the heart in different directions, connecting to the heart chakras of other cities and towns. The three grids can sometimes appear as veils, likened to darker pathways of light energy. Sometimes these veils are dark and sticky in their energy and at other times they are black or grey. When ignited and illuminated and cleansed, they take on the appearance of golden pathways. When they are cleansed and built with celestial frequency, they create the etheric field of a city or community to become crystalline and light in nature.

When these veils are cleared via the transmission of blue celestial energy and diamond white light frequency as humanity and the Celestial Guardians work together in connection to the planetary portals of the Earth, golden wheels of light as large as the heart chakra are then anchored above the city, surrounding and protecting its heart chakra. The etheric grid linking all cities of the world is then fed with Christ consciousness and the golden light frequency, and this in turn raises the vibration of the etheric field of the city and the three grids that carry our collective karma. The transformation of the etheric structure of a city allows souls to open their heart and liberate themselves from the wheel of karma.

Activating Our Angelic Body and Grid of Light by Clearing the Human Grid of Duality

The Angelic Grid of humanity's collective consciousness carries within it, in the lower dimensions, the old fourth dimensional grid known as the human grid of duality. This grid presently carries the density of humanity's ancestral or collective karma created from any time period between one hundred to twelve thousand years ago. When this grid is cleared and dissolved over a city it opens the etheric doorways for the angels to be able to fully bless the souls in that city or the communities connected to the city. The clearing of this grid opens our physical, Third World to the angelic vibrations and light frequency of the Fourth World, the angelic realm of the Earth.

For example, in New York City, 21 percent of souls presently come from the angelic planes, so the clearing of this grid would allow 21 percent of the population to awaken their light frequency, which supports them to know their truth and guide themselves clearly. In other words, 21 percent of the souls presently in New York came from the angelic realm before their present incarnation as humans. If twenty light workers met as a group for two hours of energy work once a week for a year and worked deeply with the Celestial Guardians, Mother Gaia, the Enlightened Masters, and the Divine Presences of all on Earth in a heavenly and Earth portal, they would be able to fully clear this grid of 51 percent of its karma so the grid could activate clearly. This would deeply support all souls in New York to release their duality issues when they were ready. This would be a wonderful service project for a group of light seeds to manifest in New York City in service to humanity and Mother Earth. More angels would be able to travel to assist others through this portal, and all of the angelic souls would be supported to open their hearts.

In many cities, the grid can be very dark and sticky, which makes it difficult for the angels to work through the heart chakra to help humanity on deeper levels. So that the angels can access the city and assist humanity, light portals must be opened by light workers through prayer and ceremony. Once the angelic lightgrid is cleared, the angelic doorways into the city are opened, and the angelic higher selves may guide or merge with their souls.

The Angelic Grid of Light wishes to transmit pure, golden white light so it can be healthy. It calls for each person working with the Celestial Guardians to own their own duality belief systems so they may clear the old grids of duality-based beliefs from their own etheric body. This is important, for as each person works with the Celestial Guardians to clear the grids, they also need to unhook themselves from this grid.

The following examples of duality give power to the belief in two opposing truths, canceling out the positive benefits of any of the truths.

- I wish and intend our world to be at peace, but first, I need to argue, fight, and sometimes even hurt others so we can achieve this.
- I deeply love my partner, but I need to deny him my love as I do not feel he truly loves me.
- I intend to create all in my life with love, but I need to analyze, criticize, and judge others and their creations before I can create with total responsibility and love.

If you find duality belief systems like these playing out in your life, then simply say the following decree to unhook yourself, your chakras, and your energy body from the human grid of duality and activate your connection to the fifth dimensional Angelic Grid of Light and your true connection to the angelic realm and the Fourth World. You may need to do this a few times to discover all of your duality beliefs that are connected to your personal or family karma.

Prayer for Release from the Old Grid of Duality

Mother, Father, God/Goddess, or Divine Presence of Love and Light,
I call for the divine laws of love, grace, oneness, divinity, forgiveness, karma, and liberty to flood through me and all of my energy centers and energy bodies and into the Angelic Grid of Light to purify and align and activate my truest connection to the angelic realms. I call for the love of my Divine Presence to infuse me and all aspects of my angelic self and my soul extensions within the Fourth World. I call on the flame of forgiveness to blaze between my soul and all forms of my spirit self in the Fourth World. I call on karmic absolution for all forms of myself and my ancestors for any collective karma held between my souls and the Fourth World. I call on all dispensations and divine assistance now to liberate my energy from any dualistic perspective and from any energy connection I may hold from any time, space, or dimension to the old grid of duality that may block my angelic connection on Earth.

I call on my Divine Presence to bless my energy body, matrixes, consciousness, and energy through all time, space, and dimension with this clearing, and I ask that this be gentle and easy for me in divine order for my being. I ask for the clearing now so my angelic connection may open with love, grace, oneness, forgiveness, divinity, and liberty as I call for any of my personal or collective karma to be absolved if it is blocking my angelic connection from grounding clearly on Earth. I call for my angelic connection to be opened, purified, cleared, energized, activated, and grounded on Earth and ask for the angels to work with me night and day until I have clearly established my connection to the angelic realm of Earth, so I may live without fear or need to project fear toward others.

I call on the overlighting Angelic Presences and Angels of Love and Light to clear any of my chakras or any level of my energy field from grid of duality affecting humanity's collective consciousness and ask that my energy be purified in divine order for my being. I ask for all attachments of my energy and consciousness to the old grid of duality to be dissolved now with celestial blue light rays and for my energy to be unhooked from any aspect affecting me that holds any source of duality.

I call on the full activation of my fifth dimensional angelic body of light and ask that I be guided deeply when I may be hooking into the old energy of duality so that I may choose not to do this. I give thanks for all divine assistance with this. I call on the archangels and Enlightened Masters to assist me to open my angelic heart with ease, peace, and harmony, in divine order for my being. I call on my Holy Spirit and the spirit of love to flood through me and all dimensions of my being to complete this healing and transformation. I call on my ancestors to forgive with me all that may have created the duality issues of_____ (insert your list of issues). I ask for karmic absolution for my ancestors, all of humanity, and myself, regarding this. I give thanks for all assistance I receive. I ask that this healing take place and all I receive benefit Mother Earth and all of humanity's collective, my community, my ancestors, and my family. Blessed be, blessed be, blessed be.

Activating Our Archangelic Body and Grid of Light by Clearing the Human Grid of Control

The Archangelic Grid of humanity's collective consciousness carries within it, in the lower dimensions, the old fourth dimensional grid known as the human grid of control. Until this grid is cleared of 51 percent of the fear within it, or 51 percent of the collective karma of control is dissolved, the full activation of the Archangelic Grid of Light and your archangelic body is unable to take place. The activation of the Archangelic Grid supports humanity's collective consciousness to rise into a state of consciousness that emanates the frequency of grace and ease, as well as supports their masculine and feminine energies to synergize, harmonize, and unite within their energy body.

The full activation of the Archangelic Grid of Light will only take place through the clearing of the collective karma that creates this old fourth dimensional, fear-based grid to veil humanity's connection to the archangels. This grid presently carries the density of humanity's karma from their last three lives on Earth and also from incarnations which may have occurred any time between one hundred thousand to twenty-six thousand years ago. When this grid is cleared over any city, it opens the etheric and Christ doorways for the archangels to fully bless the souls in that city or the towns that are fed by the city. As a soul's etheric body is cleared of control mechanisms and this old grid in their consciousness is dissolved, they connect to the super-consciousness they hold in the portals between the Fourth and Fifth worlds, between the angelic and Christ realms of Earth.

As this grid is dissolved, all in the city will have more connection with the souls from the archangelic realms, including their higher selves from the stars and the star emissaries from the Pleiades, Andromeda, Venus, Chiron, Arcturus, and Sirius. The star-seeds or starry souls incarnated within the city will awaken and begin to do their archangelic light work with sound, light, love, and creation, working in group-consciousness to assist unity consciousness to develop and blossom.

For example, in Los Angeles, according to the Enlightened Masters, 12 percent of souls presently come from the archangelic planes of the stars, so the clearing of this grid would allow 12 percent of the population to awaken their love and light frequency. This would support them to open their hearts and do their sacred work in group-consciousness with others who may be in their soul family. These are the souls that incarnated directly through the portals that lie between the Fourth and Fifth worlds and link to the archangelic realms of the heavens, who naturally hold the gifts of creativity through working in group-consciousness.

The Enlightened Masters also share that if thirty-three advanced light workers met as a group for two hours once a week for a year, working on the Archangelic Grid, opening an Earth and heavenly portal, and working deeply with the Celestial Guardians via connection to the planetary portals, they would be able to fully clear this grid of 51 percent of its karma. This would activate the Archangelic Grid, open the archangelic doorways for Los Angeles, and unlock many souls from the old grid of victim consciousness.

Groups may be guided to work with the grids that extend from nearby cities to accelerate all within the North American grid system or cities on another continent. Clearing between the Archangelic and Angelic Grids from the heart chakras of more than three cities would create a powerful shift and doorway for humanity to step through, unlocking many souls from experiences of control dynamics.

In some cities, the Archangelic Grid can appear dark and sticky, which makes it almost impossible for the archangels from star bases such as the Pleiades, Andromeda, and Sirius to work through the heart chakra of the city to help humanity or for star-seeds to feel themselves. Love portals must be opened by light workers, and once the grid is cleared, the archangelic doorways into the city will open easily. The starry higher selves that are merging with their souls, as well as an immense number of archangels or emissaries from the stars working through the Galactic Federation or Ashtar Command, will then be able to assist souls in that city.

The Archangelic Grid of Light is wishing to transmit pure, golden white light so it can be healthy. It also calls for each person working with the Celestial Guardians to own their own control dynamics. This is important, for as each person works with the Celestial Guardians to clear the grid, they also need to unhook themselves from the grid and choose not to give their power to control dynamics.

Control dynamics are more subtle than duality issues. They create the greatest loss of individual empowerment, though. Control dynamics cause shutdown or separation when one gives power to the belief that they are a victim of a situation and others are to blame for whatever they are experiencing. When a soul believes they are sole creators of their reality, they begin to break the effect of the control grid that is formed in the lower dimensions of their collective consciousness, which initially formed from both their personal experiences and their collective karma related to humanity's experience of control. The belief in victim consciousness denies the universal law of karma, which states that all souls receive all they have given or created, to maintain universal balance. One reaps what one sows.

The following are some examples of control belief systems.

Example: "I create my financial freedom in life by forgiving myself for all the debts I have not been able to pay others, but I am very angry with my friend because she owes me $333. I did not really want to lend this money to her, but I felt obligated. Now she is ripping me off, and it is unfair. I feel controlled by her choice not to pay me back, and she is to blame, not me."

This soul experiences a closed heart and closed soul star chakra in the presence of her friend. Her friend, when speaking with her and receiving her anger, feels controlled by her. Neither of these women feels free in their relationship. The more this soul thinks about this friend, the angrier she becomes. She will not be free of her control drama until she has truly forgiven herself for not repaying her own energetic debts and until she sees this is karma playing itself out and she has created this to learn from. The control belief system for this situation is, "I must always lend my money, otherwise I will be seen as greedy. But I cannot trust others or I may lose control of my finances." The fear deep inside is fear of losing control of finances and fear of poverty.

Example: "I create my relationship with my partner with love by allowing him to have sex with me whenever he wishes as I love him and want him to be fulfilled, but I get upset when he does not kiss me or show affection. I am being abused when he makes love to me as it is simply a physical release for him while I am numb inside, waiting for him to finish. It is unfair he does not truly connect to me as a woman and fulfill my needs. I feel controlled by his need for sex all of the time and his dislike for deeper communication, and he is to blame for this, not me."

This soul experiences a closed heart and closed soul star chakra when making love, and sex becomes a lower dimensional experience due to the victim consciousness she emanates. The projection of blame on her partner closes her heart and her soul star chakra. When her partner comes toward her, she feels resentful and afraid that she will need to fulfill her so-called duty of love, and she feels numb as her heart and her soul star chakra do not allow her to receive or transmit love during lovemaking.

This numbness may cause her to seem like an empty shell by her partner, yet she blames her partner for the lack of connection. In truth, what is creating her blockage in sexual expression is her own lack of connection to herself and her sexuality and sensuality, as well as her fear of speaking her truth and guiding the lovemaking in a more sensual direction. During lovemaking, her partner will feel controlled by her inability to be present, to engage on a physical and emotional level and orgasm with him, and she will feel controlled by his need to have a pleasurable release and orgasm without her enjoyment of their lovemaking. She will not be free of this control drama until she forgives herself for not connecting to her true needs as a sexual, sensual being and recognizes that her blockages are her own karma.

The control belief system for this situation is, "I must give sex to my partner any time he wishes so he will continue to love me, and I cannot be sexually open or fulfilled in my life or I may lose control of my reality." The fear deep inside is fear of losing control via sexuality.

These forms of belief systems create all control dramas for a soul, and if a soul becomes attached to blaming others and being the victim, they begin to connect with the human grid of control. When a soul's heart is closed, their mind can become hooked into this grid and they can be affected by the control beliefs of the collective of humanity that are also held in this grid.

When we are attached to our control beliefs, we blame or envy others as we hold onto the old, unresolved beliefs of our last three lives. This creates us to deny our responsibility for our feelings and to reject our need to forgive ourselves first and then any other soul that reflects this karma to us. Until forgiveness is made and all blame and envy is released, our chakras will be hooked into this old grid of control.

Our heart chakra is the first chakra we close down whenever our controlling beliefs are questioned by another. Our brow chakra is the second chakra we close when we feel deep emotions about a situation that creates us to blame another for our experience. Our soul star chakra is the third chakra we shut down when we experience fears connected to what were unable to forgive in our last three lives.

If control belief systems seem to be playing out in your life, know they emanate from your last three lives and arise when you blame others and see yourself as a victim. Simply say the following decree to unhook yourself from your control belief system, release from the human grid of control, and activate your connection to the fifth dimensional Archangelic Grid of Light, which grants a soul the frequency of grace and ease in the area of life that the old energy of control has been held within.

Prayer for Release from the Grid of Control

Mother, Father, God/Goddess, or Divine Presence of Love and Light,
I call for the divine laws of love, grace, oneness, divinity, forgiveness,
karma, and liberty to flood through me and all of my energy centers and

energy bodies and into the Archangelic Grid of Light to purify and align and activate my truest connection to the archangelic realms I call on all dispensations and divine assistance now to liberate and free my energy from the perspective of being a victim in life and from any energy connection I may hold from any time, space, or dimension to the old grid of control that may block my archangelic connection on Earth. I call on my God Presence to bless my energy body, matrixes, consciousness, and energy through all time, space, and dimension with this clearing, and I ask that this be gentle and easy for me, in divine order for my being.

I ask for the clearing now so my archangelic connection may open with love, grace, oneness, forgiveness, divinity, and liberty as I call for any of my personal or collective karma to be absolved. I call for my archangelic connection to be opened, purified, cleared, energized, activated, and grounded on Earth and ask for the archangels to work with me night and day until I have established my connection to the archangelic realm of Earth, so I may live without any control or need to be controlled here.

I call on the overlighting Archangelic Presences and Archangels of Love and Light to clear any of my chakras or any level of my energy field from the grid of control affecting humanity's collective consciousness and ask that my energy be purified of old control energies in divine order for my being. I ask that all attachments of my energy and consciousness to the old grid of control be dissolved with celestial blue light rays and that my energy be unhooked from any aspect that holds a source of control.

I call on the full activation of my fifth dimensional archangelic body of light and ask that I be guided deeply when I may be hooking into the energy of control due to old patterns of communication, so that I may choose not to do this. I give thanks for all divine assistance with this. I call on the angels, archangels, and Enlightened Masters to assist me to open my archangelic heart with grace and ease in divine order for my being. I call on my Holy Spirit and the spirit of love to flood through me and all dimensions of my being to complete this healing and transformation. I call on my ancestors to forgive with me all that may have created the controlling beliefs that _____ (insert your list of beliefs). I ask for karmic absolution for my ancestors, for all of humanity, and for myself in regard to this. I give thanks for all assistance I receive. Blessed be, blessed be, blessed be.

Activating Our Christ Body and Christ Grid of Light by Clearing the Human Grid of Authority

The Christ Grid of humanity's collective consciousness carries within it the old fourth dimensional grid known as the human grid of hierarchy, authority, and polarity. Until this grid clears 51 percent of the fear, or 51 percent of the karma is dissolved, the full activation of the Christ Grid of Light is unable to take place. This grid presently carries the density of all of humanity's karma from the civilizations of Ancient Egypt, Atlantis, and Lemuria, from anywhere between three thousand to millions of years ago.

When this grid is cleared over any city, it opens the etheric doorways for the Enlightened Christ Presence of all Souls, the I Am Presence, to fully bless the souls in that city or the towns that are fed by that city. As this grid is dissolved, humanity is able to have more connection with their Divine Presence, and all souls from the Christ realms will awaken in the city and begin to do their divine work. As your etheric body is cleared of this grid, you are able to connect to the super-consciousness you hold within the Fifth World of Earth, the Christ realms or crystalline realms of the Earth.

For example, in Mexico City, 8 percent of souls come from the Christ planes, so the clearing of this grid would allow 8 percent of the population to awaken to their full power and access their spiritual and soul gifts from all dimensions. In other words, 8 percent of the souls presently in Mexico City were originally incarnated in the Christ realms before they incarnated into physical form, and their gifts would be supported to awaken if the etheric body of Mexico City released the grid of hierarchy, authority, and polarity.

If forty-four light workers met a group for two hours once a week for a year and worked deeply with the Celestial Guardians and planetary portals, they would be able to fully clear this grid of 51 percent of its karma so the Christ grid could activate clearly. When this grid is dark and sticky, it is difficult for Divine Presences to work through the heart chakra of the city to help the humanity on deeper levels. Enlightened portals must be opened by the Divine Presences of light workers; once this grid is cleared, the Christ doorways into the city will open, allowing the Christed or ascended higher selves to merge with or guide their souls, and allowing an immense number of Christ Masters to assist the souls in the city.

The Christ Grid of Light is wishing to transmit pure, golden white light so it can be healthy. It also calls for each person working with the Celestial Guardians to own their own power belief systems. This is important, for as each person works with the Celestial Guardians as a representative of humanity to clear the grids, they also need to unhook themselves from this grid and choose not to play power games.

Power games are the greatest cause of the deep wounds of all souls on Earth and stem from the belief that no matter what, one must hold more power than another or one will lose the game of life. When a soul believes they need to be on top, they begin to hook into the grid of hierarchy, which carries all the collective karma of humanity related to power and authority. The grid of hierarchy is held in the lower dimensions of the collective, formed by the collective karma of humanity's experience with power games within the old civilizations of the Earth.

The following is an example of a belief system that creates power games:

"I am a very prominent person in the community and people look up to me because of my position and standing. I cannot afford to be seen as weak or others will begin to disrespect me and I may lose my place in the community. I expect everyone to submit to me unless they are a higher authority than me and will cut another down if they question me. I am in control at all times and expect people to do as I say. I do not encourage friendship with those who are weaker than me. I may seem coldhearted but I am just protecting others from taking power from me."

This soul cannot experience the opening of their heart or mind, as they use power to limit their heart connection with others. This sort of power belief system will create power games with others. This soul will do almost anything to another in order to reinforce the belief that they are the one in power.

Humanity's power belief systems usually stem from unresolved experiences in Lemuria, Atlantis, or Ancient Egypt. The beliefs left over from these lives can create power issues to be played out in one's life. If a soul becomes attached to seeing a hierarchy around them, these beliefs can lead to acts of ruthlessness and to the destruction of other people's dreams and creations. A soul that places their power in power-based belief systems begins to hook into the old human grid of hierarchy, authority, and polarity. Those that are connected to this grid have collective karma with the use of their own power, and this attracts hierarchical situations to them, which they then judge or reject as false.

When we are attached to authoritarian beliefs, we project on others as being evil, as we hold onto the unresolved beliefs from our lives in Lemuria, Atlantis, or Ancient Egypt. This projection can create us to deny our personal responsibility for the situation and may create us to reject our need to forgive ourselves first and to forgive any other soul that reflects this karma to us. Until forgiveness is made and our need to project upon others is released, our chakras will be hooked into this old grid of hierarchy and we will continue to be affected by the collective's ego-based dramas.

Our heart chakra is the first chakra we close when we believe our power is being questioned. Our brow chakra is the second chakra we shut down when we see ourselves as less powerful or we believe others see us as evil. Our soul star chakra is the third chakra we close when we experience fears connected to the use of power in our other lives. Our *hara* is the fourth chakra we close down when we sense unresolved memories of giving away our free will in other lives and losing our true power connection.

If authoritarian belief systems seem to be playing out in your life, and you begin to see others as holding authority over you, or you see yourself as the only authority, know that these beliefs emanate from your past lives in the civilizations of Lemuria, Atlantis, and Egypt. Simply say the following decree to unhook yourself from your old authoritarian belief system, release your chakras and energy body from the grid of hierarchy, authority, and polarity, and activate your connection to the fifth dimensional Christ Grid of Light and the Christ realms.

Prayer for Release from the Grid of Hierarchy, Authority, and Polarity

Mother, Father, God/Goddess, or Divine Presence of Love and Light,

I call for the divine laws of love, grace, oneness, divinity, forgiveness, karma, and liberty to flood through me and all of my energy centers and energy bodies and into the Christ Grid of Light to purify, align, and activate my truest connection to the Christ realms. I call on all dispensations and divine assistance to liberate my energy from the old hierarchical or old authoritarian perspective and any energy connection I may hold from any time, space, or dimension to the old grid of hierarchy, authority, and polarity that may block my Christ connection and I Am Presence from grounding on Earth.

I call on my God Presence to bless my energy body, matrixes, consciousness, and energy through all time, space, and dimension with this clearing, and I ask that this be gentle and easy for me, in divine order for my being. I ask for the clearing now so my Christ connection may open with love, grace, oneness, forgiveness, divinity, and liberty as I call for any of my personal or collective karma to be absolved if it is blocking my Christ connection from grounding clearly on Earth. I call for my Christ connection to be opened, purified, cleared, energized, activated, and grounded on Earth and ask for the Christ Masters and Emissaries to work with me night and day until I have established my connection to the Christ realms of Earth so I may live with full clarity in my power and no longer need to give away my power or fear other people's power here.

I call on the overlighting Christ Presences and Christ Emissaries of Love and Light to clear any of my chakras or any level of my energy field from the grid of hierarchy affecting humanity's collective consciousness, and ask that my energy be purified of authoritarian energies in divine order for my being.

I ask for all attachments of my energy and consciousness to the grid of the hierarchy to be dissolved now with celestial blue light rays and for my energy to be unhooked from any aspect that holds a source of the old hierarchy. I call on the full activation of my fifth dimensional Christ body of light and ask that I be guided when I may be hooking into the energy of polarity, authority, or hierarchy due to old patterns around power, so that I may choose not to do this. I give thanks for all divine assistance with this. I call on the angels, archangels, and Enlightened Masters to assist me to open my Christ heart with love and wisdom, in divine order for my being. I call on my Holy Spirit and the spirit of love to flood through me and all dimensions of my being to complete this healing and transformation. I call on my ancestors to forgive with me all that may have created the authoritarian beliefs that _____ (insert your list of beliefs). I ask for karmic absolution for my ancestors, for all of humanity, and for myself. I give thanks for all assistance I receive with this. Blessed be, blessed be, blessed be!

Accepting Your Power as a Soul to Transform the Old Akashic Records with the Assistance of Your Divine Presence

The Akashic records of our collective hold all of humanity's gifts and higher consciousness as well as all of humanity's personal karma, family karma, collective karma, planetary karma, and karma of the ancestors. All of these forms of karma are linked. They are simply held in different layers of one's energy body, and some of these forms of karma are more deeply lodged in the chakras.

The Akashic records are held in the etheric body of the Earth and within your etheric body. As your consciousness evolves and your chakras develop, your etheric body begins to connect to more of your super-consciousness and to new levels of your Akasha. It is as if a new door in your energy body opens to levels of your consciousness you have not experienced before. Always when this occurs, a significant event takes place that opens us to new possibilities in our life.

Sometimes this new level of Akasha takes you to heights of joy; you may meet a new love or rediscover your love. Other times it may renew a sense of confidence in you. Always the gift is in the strengthening of some quality you may have locked away. Sometimes a new learning or challenge or old karma greets you on the way through the door. This is when you truly need to remember what is on the other side of the door and the power you have to transform the Akashic records for the highest good of all.

Your Akasha is made from consciousness and energy. It is stored in a crystalline form of light within your etheric body and is activated by memory, experience, and frequency that are triggers for unresolved aspects of your consciousness. It holds all of your gifts, truth, wisdom, and super-consciousness, and it also holds the original core memories that were left unresolved by you as a soul or spirit.

With the support of their Divine Presence, every soul is able to transform their old Akashic records and balance and clear their karma. The key to this is accessing your core truth, the truth that lies beneath the surface of your thoughts and feelings. This is found by journeying inside, beyond what your mind may believe on the surface of your consciousness, and beyond that which your feelings and circumstances may project is a possibility for you. Your karma is a doorway to your discovery of this truth as a soul, and although the journey through the door may sometimes feel like something you would prefer not to embrace, as you do embrace it a manifestation of a great love takes place in your life.

Akashic records are sometimes frozen in the chakras, and this creates a soul's chakras to close. As a chakra closes, so does a potential experience in life. I experienced my sexuality closing some years ago. My body instinctively moved away whenever my partner touched me or came to have intimacy. I simply was a witness to my body's experiences as this took place. My sacral chakra was closed, and it was filled with Akashic records through all twelve dimensions of my energy body. These records held the memories of my experiences of being abused in this life and also of sexual abuse that took place in a previous life in Egypt, where I became paralyzed from the waist down. As the pain I experienced had been so deep, I had built layers upon layers of belief systems to protect myself from opening to intimacy in union again.

My Akasha led me back to the source where I had witnessed others being sexually abused and had chosen not to intervene due to my own fear. I had the power speak out and stop the atrocity, but I let my fear overtake me and simply witnessed it. In this life, I was unable to speak about the sexual abuse that had taken place, and this was a reflection of the karma which kept not only my sacral chakra closed but also my throat chakra contracted, due to the secret I kept hidden inside of me. It was this karma that created my own sexual abuse to be attracted as a learning experience, for I carried the guilt about allowing others to be sexually abused, believing I had cocreated the abuse by not stopping it.

It was not until I accepted and owned that I had karmically attracted sexual abuse to me that I could truly forgive myself for carrying the guilt of others being abused. This deep forgiveness cleared the Akasha that blocked my sacral chakra through many dimensions. It allowed my true passion as a being to ignite again. It activated my creativity and in fact opened my sexuality to a new experience that I had always dreamed would occur, where the tantric currents rose from my kundalini through my sacral chakra and up through my spine to ignite my ecstatic bliss. I began to feel sensations I had thought were only possible through physical orgasm with a partner, and these experiences began to take place regularly. The rising of the tantric energy often ignited every cell of my body into bliss and created my body to experience great oneness. These experiences are phenomenal.

As my transformation took place over a period of a few years and I met new truths inside me and embraced layers of old beliefs, I felt new levels of my sacral unlock and open to new dimensions. I knew that this karma was very deep and it may take time to heal, so I accepted this and allowed myself the space by choosing to not have sexual intimacy for some time. It was not until the last piece unfolded and the tantric activation occurred within me and I forgave the old hierarchy I was a part of in Ancient Egypt that I was able to release the guilt of it all. I felt my renewed womanhood return with an abundance of sexual feeling and immense divine energy in my body. The next few years of my own spiritual practices of circulating and expanding the divine energy in my physical body in holy communion with my God Presence eventually led me to train others in the Self Mastery School of Tantra.

The Akasha is our instrument that brings us back to our truth, aligns us on our path, and opens our eyes to the possibilities of creation we originally dreamed of. Accepting your power as a soul and your Presence is simply created by honoring the deepest truth underneath all else you think and feel. As you meet this deepest truth and you complete the karma of an experience, you carry the teachings and higher truths that will help others birth through your experience.

My Seer Journey into the Akasha of Union and Sexuality

I was in a cave in my own heart, in meditation one day, and I was determined to change my situation regarding my sexuality. My sexuality had been an important part of my life, and I missed it deeply. It was a part of my feminine energy and my passion for life, a way to ground my love through my body joyfully.

I had accepted and forgiven a great deal concerning my karmic situation with sexuality and realized the karma was involved with three influences or events in my life.

One was that I was in partnership with my twin flame, Golden Phoenix, and everything in our lives was spiritually and physically magnified because of our holy relationship. We had come together for love and to support each other's healing of our deepest karma. As twin flames, we carried the partnership connection not only between our soul's hearts but also between our spirits and all of our dimensional selves. This power of two entwined flaming hearts created the love to be amplified, but also magnified the karma that lay unresolved between us. My karma with divine union lay in my energy field in the lower chakras, specifically my sacral chakra.

The second aspect of karma was related to the sexual abuse I experienced as a child. This aspect of the blockage in my energy field was held in the higher chakras that were still developing when I was thirteen, and in my sacral chakra, my etheric body, and my DNA. The older boy who had abused me had left a lot of anger inside me, and this was deeply repressed as guilt and anger in my body.

The third aspect and most powerful influence was related to the guilt I held in my body due to my choice to close my lower chakras as a form of protection when I was in the middle of tantric union with my partner in my last physical life in Ancient Egypt. This was a life where I had been a man. This had occurred when I was in union with my partner, and my lower fields opened to the astral plane and were saturated with polarized light or fear. This experience led to the loss of my partner in that life.

This created some of my lower chakras and my physical body to be filled with the astral energies of the collective, and the more our tantric serpent energy rose and entwined up through our chakras, the more the DNA filaments in my lower bodies were filled with dark, astral energies. I closed my lower chakras so as to protect my consciousness and soul from being influenced by the astral energies. This created my spirit and soul to be able to experience life only through the higher chakras.

As my light increased in my field in this life, I became aware of needing to clear the energy that was held in the back of all of my chakras, my brain's cellular matrix, my spine, nervous system, glands, etheric body, genitals, and uterus, and the front of my lower chakras that carried the memory of this experience.

The truth in my life at that time was that parts of my consciousness were refusing to open my sexuality to my flame, as their most recent memories of union in relationship were painful and scary. These parts of my consciousness were coming from the other worlds where my spirit was incarnated in alternate forms. Holding all of this cellular memory in my body and field, my spirit chose to never allow sexuality to take place again, as it was simply the safest option. My spirit feared I would be embodied by astral energies again through this form of union, as the memory was still strongly held within my being.

It felt as if a sticky, black net of light were attached to some of my neurons and braided into my etheric body. I did not feel the anger as an emotion, but my body reacted angrily in the presence of my twin flame, as if it were shouting, "How dare you touch me." It was a strange experience for my body to have a different voice than my heart, mind, and soul.

I could see this net clearly, and I could clear it easily, but then in the presence of my twin flame, it would reappear and my body would have the same reaction. This black net of sticky consciousness, made primarily from anger and guilt, overtook my body. I knew this was an aspect of my twin flame karma as well as my collective karma of union and sexuality. It was triggered by my loving partner, Golden Phoenix, and the vision I had during our lovemaking of being abused by him and others.

On this day, I was feeling frustrated with how long it had been since I had been able to make love, so I decided to spend one whole day receiving the highest assistance for this. I decided to do a seer journey to discover and heal anything that I was ready to heal so some energetic movement could occur toward completing my karma with union and sexuality.

I sat in council in the cave of my heart. I meditated on my heart flame and took my consciousness on a deep journey. I called in all of the parts of myself that were scared of opening our power of sexuality in the presence of our twin flame and invited them to come and share what their fears were, receive the love, and open to receiving assistance. Very gently, a beautiful golden mermaid came out of my heart. She was crying and said she was very sorry. She said she was desperate to heal it, yet so tired and had tried so hard. I knew her to be a part of me, as I experienced what she shared as feelings and experiences inside me. She lay down by my side and said she was ready to surrender. I cuddled her and filled her with love. She was so beautiful yet so tired of trying to heal a wound that seemed unable to be forgiven. As she received love, she gently cried. She missed the ocean, so I went for a walk down to the beach and sat by the ocean so she could experience this through me.

As I sat in meditation by the sea, a second part of my consciousness showed itself to me. It was my thirteen-year-old self, lying on a rock, unable to move. She had given up on herself. She felt violated, and any display of aggression from a man reminded her of the older boy who had sexually abused her. She said she was closed to Golden Phoenix as he sometimes showed signs of aggression; although he was deeply loving, she could not trust him fully. I realized in that moment the reason that my sexuality had not closed to any of my previous lovers. None of my previous partners had displayed an aggressive energy toward me.

She went and lay with the golden mermaid on the beach, surrendering to the love with me. I melted more deeply into the sand and lay back listening to the waves and sounds of the birds and ocean. As I melted, I found myself dropping down through the sand into the Earth, and spiritually I began traveling through the worlds down into the Middle Earth. I saw lakes of beautiful colors and found myself with Sananda, Archangel Gabriel, and Archangel Chamuel. These two large, winged archangels and Sananda, in golden white robes with long hair and a beard, looking like a radiant version of Jesus, came toward me, and Sananda held a crystal scepter in his hand that glowed as he offered it to me. He spoke to me with great power and love.

"We have taken you into the other worlds, for the source of your pain is lodged in the other worlds and in your higher dimensional bodies more than in the energy body you hold around your physical body, our dear child. You have come a long way, and you have grounded much understanding, but you are not yet aware that your outer bodies are carrying the fear of tantric union. You are not yet aware that healing the wound of your sexuality is a preparation for tantric union, which you will have for many years as you grow older with a partner. You have chosen this initiation for this very purpose, our dear one.

"It may feel difficult to embrace this loss, but know that what you will reclaim from meeting this will fill your heart as you grow older and bring great joy to you as a woman. This is to support your patience. Take the scepter from me now. It has the power to dissolve the memories of what occurred when your physical body closed, while you were in your highest state of ecstasy in tantric union in Ancient Egypt. You lost a great deal through this experience and you were unable to forgive it in that life. You are in this situation now to allow you to forgive it.

"The memories of this experience are held in your spiritual bodies, your feminine rainbow serpent body, which carries your feminine tantric energy, and within your sacral chakra, beloved. Your serpent body was the spiritual body you experienced tantra within for many years in Egypt. This is one of your most powerful bodies of consciousness and energy. Your rainbow serpent body is presently twisted through your antahkarana and blocking the natural flow of tantric love through your physical body. It is keeping your sacral locked, and your feminine energy is unable to be expressed sexually. Do not be concerned as you will heal this as your soul and spirit forgive, and your sexuality will return so your tantric initiations can begin.

"You need to break the many agreements you made in Ancient Egypt to close down your power of tantric union, shut down your sacral chakra, and take on the fears of others. In that life, you sacrificed yourself to help others as you found yourself in a situation where you felt you could not abandon them. You will need to heal all that you closed down as your sacrifice, and then many blessings will come to you and much that you gave to help others will return to you."

He placed the scepter in my hand, and suddenly I was back on the beach again. I placed the scepter of light that Sananda had given me into my sacral and ran it through my brain, my nervous system, and up my spine three times, then placed it into each gland, then into my higher chakras, and into my genitals and uterus. As I did this, I saw filaments of light opening, growing, and glowing with golden light.

I could see the dark memories in my cells, blocking the light from flowing in certain parts of my body, and I saw the source of the unconscious memories in the back of my chakras, feeding my cerebellum in my brain. I could see my cerebellum feeding this polarized light through my brain and my brain directing it into my cells via my nervous system. I placed the scepter through the back of my chakras, and the golden mermaid by my side squealed and rolled around like she was being tickled. It was amazing to see how simply moving the old energy and consciousness stuck in the back of my chakras affected this part of my spirit, which was from the Fourth World and also from Lemuria.

I could feel my Divine Presence assisting me deeply as I continued to move the scepter through my field and body, clearing and dissolving the ancient memories. I was guided to place the scepter, the piece of light technology Sananda had given me, into the heart of my thirteen-year-old child spirit who was still holding the shock and horror of my original experience. I placed the scepter in the sacral chakra of my thirteen-year-old self and ignited the connection between the heart and sacral and immediately felt a huge release as old energy from my physical body flowed down into the Earth beneath me. I saw this energy disperse and become rainbow light. I felt a shift in my lower chakras, and my physical body felt lighter.

I could see my rainbow serpent body inside the Earth. She was huge and coiled up. She was giant and beautiful, yet she was isolating herself. She was protecting a wound in her body. It was blocking her heart and sacral from flowing with divine energy.

In this moment, I recognized she was my most vulnerable self, and asked if she would receive healing. I shared I could see the Akashic memory in her heart and sacral that created her pain and wounding. She agreed to receive healing as long as I did not speak about what had occurred. She did not want to remember. "It was too painful," she said. "I do not want the full, conscious remembrance."

I shared I did not need to talk, but she would need to forgive at some point to allow the healing to complete. I placed the scepter in her heart and sacral and brow chakra where I saw the wounding was held. At that time, I felt a great pain in my chest and in my sacral. It was a pain I had felt only when birthing my child. I realized how deep her pain went, to all dimensions of my fields and all the way to the core of each of these chakras. I realized that not only was her consciousness influencing me but also her energy body was influencing the golden mermaid and my thirteen-year-old child spirit, and this was the true cause of my closure in sexuality.

Sananda arrived again and said, "This will take time, beloved. This is unable to be healed overnight as it extends through twenty dimensions of your field and is also held by your DNA, as sexual abuse is held in your ancestral lineage also, beloved. You will need to work with your rainbow serpent body for many months. You will also need to travel to the portal where this wounding took place, to reclaim the parts of your heart that were lost from the experience. Know beloved, as you complete the healing with your feminine rainbow serpent, you will then be a carrier of the codes for all who need this same healing."

It was true, what Sananda shared. It did take time for me to heal this. It was another two years before it was complete. It was my initiation, and in truth, it was just what I needed to grow into more of my heart. It was a challenging yet powerful transformational experience, which I do not regret, as the benefit of receiving tantric energy flowing through my body again was a great gift I received from this deep healing.

My message to you is that no matter how deep or painful your loss, do not give up. Allow yourself to receive the highest form of divine assistance. If you do not know where to find this, ask for it and you will attract it. If you have your own difficulty in sexuality, I send you all the codes on a stream of love. Simply ask for them now to flood to you, and it will be done in accordance with God's will, as a blessing. Know the codes will heal this, but you will still need to forgive. Forgiveness is the power you hold inside, to love again beyond that which you closed your heart to originally.

Our Deepest Forms of Karma

The deepest forms of karma are humanity's deepest burdens. The pain of this karma is often hidden. In women, the deepest form of karma with regard to union and sexuality creates numbness and neutrality and a lack of presence with their sexuality. The freezing of sexuality is a very common experience among women, and it sources back to Ancient Egypt, where more than thirteen thousand years ago there were experiences of great abuse that took place in the deepest states of union between men and women. Many women stop making love regularly as they grow older, simply because of the ignition of their collective karma of union, love, and sexuality.

During this period, thousands of years ago, humanity lived in very different energy bodies than those we live in today. Their energy systems were based on a larger chakra structure, and the experience of union was a spiritual meeting with their higher selves and a profound exchange of love through all chakras. When two souls shared union with each other, their energy bodies merged and dissolved into a larger united body. Their experience of being two separate beings was released, and they merged into a field of oneness together. Great healings took place for all beings in this way, and the planetary field, the collective, and families all benefited from the lovemaking of individuals.

As humanity evolved and made choices, many began to give their power to the belief that an outside force had more authority, spiritually and on all other levels, than they did, and the karma of slavery began. At this time, many began to worship something that they felt was greater than them, and they began to give away the power they held in their chakras.

As these souls gave more power to those who somehow seemed more holy than they saw themselves to be, they experienced less of that original experience of divine union with partners. They experienced less of their higher self or Presence, and they believed that a force outside them had created this change. As they no longer felt the connection to their own divinity and felt overpowered by another force, they sought the union they were losing even more deeply. Some became obsessive and sexually overactive, others emotionally needy and controlling; others were angry, which led to violations, and others just felt pain as they closed down their power of sexuality. They continued to merge chakras and enter union with each other, but the relationships they continued to develop began to be built around control mechanisms.

As this occurred, many souls made agreements which they felt would help support their unions to work. They made agreements based on the needs of the alter ego of their partner, such as, If you love and respect me, I will always give myself to you sexually, even if I am unable to be fully present or enjoy it. Or, I will learn to live without affection in my life as long as you claim me as yours only, and you own me. Or, If you give me sex, I will feed you, but if you do not want what I want in life, I will not feed you or have sex with you. I will deny you myself until you obey my every want. In this way, thousands of years ago, humanity closed down their open-hearted spirit with each agreement they made from their alter ego rather than out of the genuine love and trust of their heart.

Sex became a form of exchange, based on controlling tantric energy, or the sacred serpent current that travels from the base of our body to our crown for the grounding of our spirit and our experience of ecstasy in the physical body. Those ancient agreements created the control mechanisms that still lie today in the etheric field of our collective, affecting our intimacy in relationship.

Our collective is needing to release a deep fear of union, and for this reason we have attracted and created collective karma with union and sexuality. This fear lies in the Akasha of our collective and sometimes the

Akasha of our soul. This Akasha holds a fear of vulnerability and loss within the feminine, and a fear of persecution and judgment within the masculine.

Your Akasha of union and sexuality begins to clear itself when you look at the truth that lies beneath your present feelings and thoughts regarding your own sexuality, your heart connection, and your union with another. Karmic absolution may be called upon, and through a journey toward forgiveness, all can transmute. This can only be explored if you are willing to accept the feelings and thoughts and recognize they are symptoms of your Akasha, and they show you a story of what your conditions and boundaries are and how you see your tantric vital force. All that does not emanate love will be sourced from the control mechanisms within your etheric body, influenced by your old Akasha or karma.

As you discover yourself in this way and embrace all you have discovered, the core truth arises in your consciousness. Once you connect to that core truth and make changes in your life in accordance with it, you release a part of your old Akasha, and the part of your consciousness that was bound by these conditions, boundaries, and beliefs shifts into oneness. Your ideas change, your consciousness feels freer, and you experience more of your divinity. As our personal power of creation is deeply entwined with our sexual energy, embracing your karma with union and sexuality not only changes the energy flow in your body but also brings you to a new level of empowerment within every other part of your life.

The most beautiful reward from a deep journey like this is that although it takes a longer time to heal, when it is healed it not only lifts the karma from you personally but also lifts the karma from your family's lineage and from the planetary body. Through this form of karmic clearing, we truly offer our service in the lifting of humanity's deepest burdens. Embracing loss in this way, although it is not exactly what any being wants to experience, is one of the highest forms of service to all beings.

These deep, painful, yet ultimately healing journeys arise when karma has created the chakras to be locked, resulting in profound loss in one area of your life. If this loss is your home or Earth connection, your Earth star chakra will be locked by the karma. If it is your family connection, it will be your link chakra that is locked by the karma. If this loss is within your physical body, then it will be the base chakra through many dimensions that is locked by the karma. If it is loss of your sexuality, the sacral will be locked by the karma. If it is loss of your will or freedom, the hara will be locked by the karma. If it loss of your mind, your solar plexus will be locked by the karma. If it is loss of love, then your heart will be locked by the karma. If it is loss of union, it will be your thymus. If it is loss of your expression of your truth, it will be your throat. If it is loss of guidance or direction, it will be your brow. If it is loss of your spirit, it will be your crown. If it is loss of your Presence, it will be your soul star chakra that will be locked by your karma. Know that all that you may feel you have lost can be reclaimed if you are willing to be patient and forgive each day and take responsibility for the karma that has created this loss.

The following prayer may be used for any deep journey that holds its grip on your life through many dimensions of your personal energy field as well as your spiritual bodies. By saying this prayer, you will begin to be assisted deeply on your healing journey.

Prayer to Release the Akasha of Your Soul or the Akasha of the Collective from Your Chakras

Mother, Father, God/Goddess, or Divine Presence of Love and Light,
I call for the highest form of love and assistance with clearing and balancing the collective karma, family karma, and personal karma I hold, locking my _____ chakra and consciousness, related to _____ (insert a positive description of your personal, family, and collective karma with which you hold karma of loss). As a representative of humanity, I ask for the healing of the loss of my _____ in divine order for my being. I call on the love to fill every part of me and for this to continue to flow until this karma is balanced or healed.

I embrace my personal, family, and collective karma now and accept that it creates a relationship between different parts of my consciousness that locks my consciousness into this karmic pattern. I ask for karmic absolution through all dimensions of my being and ask that the source of this karma be blessed and transmuted through all time, space, and dimension. I ask that the cause, core, and Akashic records that hold this karma within me be absolved as I forgive the hold it has had over me. I call on the laws of love, oneness, grace, divinity, forgiveness, karma, and liberty to flood through me and ask for the teams of enlightened healers and masters to assist all dimensions of my energy body and chakras to unlock so this karma may release with love and grace. I call for the frequency I need for this to occur and ask to receive the codes I need for this healing in divine order for my being.

I ask that I be guided to be in self-realization of all that I need to love and forgive to create this to take place, and to be aware of all unconscious beliefs in order to release the control mechanisms in my consciousness that may create me to experience this karma so deeply. I ask for karmic absolution for any acts, deeds, words, energy, or consciousness that have created this karma and for all I may have projected upon myself or the collective of humanity that has closed any of my consciousness down in any lifetimes I may have held in ancient civilizations on Earth such as Lemuria, Atlantis, and Ancient Egypt.

I ask that all seals I may have placed on my dimensional bodies and chakras from any ancient lifetimes that create this karma to be locked in any of my bodies be now broken and released into the light. I call on the laws of grace, love, forgiveness, wisdom, divinity, truth, karma, sacred resonance, liberty, oneness, faith, compassion, charity, service, communion, reflection, expansion, divine bliss, creation, and manifestation to flood through me, my collective consciousness, and my genetic line to create balance in all dimensions of my field. I ask for my chakras and energy field to be balanced as this takes place.

I call on the assistance of all my ancestors and ask that they forgive all with me that they may have experienced through loss. I call on my spirit from all other worlds to also forgive all we may have lost or given away. I call on my Divine Presence to merge with me at all times when this karma is present and to guide me on my path. I ask for the Enlightened Masters' assistance and for my ancestors and aspects of my spirit to simply accept what is taking place in life and to enter deep forgiveness.

I ask for the unlocking of all my chakras, and for the balance of my Earth bodies and my higher spiritual bodies within all dimensions. I ask for karmic absolution for all of humanity regarding this form of karma, and as a representative of humanity, I ask this for myself, my family, and my community and offer to forgive all souls connected to this experience so this karma can be lifted from our whole collective.

I call and pray for the healing of all other people on the Earth who may have their own personal, family, and collective karma with this. I acknowledge that I have attracted this situation to me to learn from and ask that all obstacles be removed so I may open my spiritual eyes and see the truth of what I need to forgive within myself, my family, and my community so I may learn my lessons in life. I ask that this clearing benefit not only me but also all of my family, all future generations, the collective of humanity, and Mother Earth and that it be lifted from the Earth grids, the Earth Crystal, and my lightbody and DNA. I ask for this karma to be lifted from any chakras that have been locked, from my DNA and my brain, my nervous system, and the cells of my body. I give thanks for this divine assistance. So be it.

Clearing Your Planetary Karma with Love and Acceptance

In the deepest aspects of your etheric body lies the seed that holds your planetary karma. Generations of souls have lived lives on Earth without being affected by this form of karma, as it does not affect a soul unless they activate their mission or highest contract of their life purpose. Planetary karma is very subtle, but it is the karma that will block your life work, your legacy or gifting to your society. This karma is based on what you have given to the world in your previous lives and what you have consciously chosen to withhold that you knew you needed to share with the world. Planetary karma can be debilitating and can cause great struggle for a soul in manifesting support for their mission, and it can even create a soul to choose not to continue their life work.

As a spiritual teacher, I was blessed to be shown by the Enlightened Masters that my planetary karma would block my life mission and that the only way to heal this was to leave my comfortable lifestyle and my partner, whose life purpose at the time was not fully aligned with mine. Even though this was the most difficult decision to make in this lifetime so far, I chose this for Mother Gaia, and in fact not long after this named my business Gaia, in honor of her. This was my baby for many years and was the doorway for my planetary work to begin its service to the world. I was deeply blessed by the choice I had made as I found little blockage to creating all I needed to create for my mission to flow powerfully.

The Enlightened Masters share that the planetary work or mission of a soul is their highest work, yet it is not the most important work. It is simply the work that has the greatest affect on the world. I had already chosen this path consciously when one day the Masters came and asked me which path I wished to take—a path as a community teacher, or a path as an international teacher where I would help more heal their hearts and be of greater service to the Earth Mother. They showed me a vision of the difference in numbers of people I could assist, and how many more people would be helped if I chose the latter path. I could see their hearts were lit up, whereas in the vision of me as a community teacher, I saw beautiful people but their hearts were not as lit up, as if the healing was not as deep.

At this stage, I had no idea what my life would look like if I took either of these paths. I simply did not think to ask. I sat in my heart and chose the international path where I could help more people. I made that choice about a year before I was shown what I would have to do to follow this path all the way through, that is, release my attachment to my lifestyle and my previous partner, Dreaming Heart.

Planetary karma does not usually make sense; it is not as easily understood as other forms of karma and therefore is the greatest challenge to our minds. The symptoms of planetary karma are threefold. The first and strongest symptom is a belief that you will not receive Mother Earth's support for your Earth mission. The second strongest symptom of planetary karma is an experience of encountering obstacle after obstacle in your life as you work toward your goals, which makes you feel so guilty and imagine you must be a fake in regard to your Earth mission. The third symptom of planetary karma is an attachment to something in life that is not serving you. This attachment creates comfort and security, but it does not resonate with your Earth mission and the development of this path.

If you have chosen this path, planetary karma can be dissolved easily through the following steps. Honor the attachment you have that creates your sense of security, and choose to release this attachment with unconditional love. Call on the divine assistance of your God Presence and begin the work of owning this karma, asking for it to be absolved and for the part of your consciousness that holds fear of your Earth mission to be held in love. Guide your consciousness to forgive all that may have taken place when you last connected to this mission. Work with universal law until this is healed or 51 percent clear, so you may continue on a clear path and allow your life work to flow here.

Know that as you do this, a great blessing is returning from your spirit to the spirit of Gaia, and this will allow your planetary service work to flow forward without your deepest unconscious fears creating obstacles on your path. This also supports a deeper grounding of your Presence. The following prayer is offered to support this process.

Prayer for Clearing Your Planetary Karma

Mother, Father, God/Goddess, or Divine Presence of Love and Light,
I call for the highest form of love and assistance with the clearing
and balancing of the planetary karma I hold between my antahkarana,
my chakras and energy body, and Mother Gaia's planetary field. I call

on Mother Gaia and ask for forgiveness for holding back my
_____ (insert a positive description of anything
you held back in your life work or Earth mission that you may not
have been able to complete on Earth in previous lifetimes) and choosing to close down my spiritual empowerment and planetary service in
any time, space, or dimension. I ask for the seeds of my planetary
karma to be absolved, and I choose to let go of my attachment to
_____ (insert the attachments you are needing
to release) so I may release this karma and open my heart fully to
Mother Gaia and her abundance, her love, and her support of my life
work and mission on Earth.

I accept and embrace my planetary karma now as the limitations
and conditions I placed on my relationship with Gaia in previous Earth
missions that I left unresolved. I call for my Akashic records to be brought
forth to me regarding my planetary karma, and I ask for the highest
form of support from my Divine Presence, Mother Gaia, and the
Enlightened Masters.

I ask for karmic absolution for any acts, deeds, words, energy, or consciousness that have created this karma and for all I may have
projected upon myself or the collective of humanity and Mother Gaia
that closed down any of my consciousness so I could not fulfill or complete
my Earth mission in any lifetimes I may have held in ancient civilizations on Earth such as Lemuria, Atlantis, and Ancient Egypt.

I ask for all karmic cords between me and any portals of Mother
Earth to be cleansed as I own this karma as a part of my planetary consciousness that needs love and forgiveness. I call for my Divine Presence
to clear any old spiritual cords of attachment bound within my
antahkarana, linking my spiritual body to parts of my spirit in the other
worlds and the Earth's lightbody and portal system. I ask that this take
place every day until this planetary karma has cleared from my energy
body and physical body.

I call on the laws of grace, love, forgiveness, wisdom, divinity, truth, *karma, sacred resonance, liberty, oneness, faith, compassion, charity, service, communion, reflection, expansion, divine bliss, creation, and manifestation to flood through me and all of my collective and planetary consciousness to create balance in my planetary connection and mission. I ask for all of my chakras and my energy field to be balanced as this takes place. I ask that all of my selves through all worlds be protected and given grace, and if there be a blockage in our collective heart and mind, may this now be gently released with grace and ease.*

I call on the assistance of all my ancestors and ask that they forgive all with me. I call on my spirit from all other worlds to also forgive as we receive the universal laws and ask for karmic absolution. I call on my Divine Presence to merge with me at all times when this karma is present and to guide me on my path. I ask for the Enlightened Masters' assistance and for my ancestors and aspects of my spirit to simply accept what is taking place in life and to enter deep forgiveness.

I ask for karmic absolution for all of humanity regarding this form of karma, and as a representative of humanity, I offer to forgive all souls connected to this experience so this karma can be lifted from our collective. I pray for the healing of all members of my soul family and all others who share this with me so they may also balance their karma with Mother Gaia. I acknowledge that I have attracted this situation to me to learn from and ask that all obstacles be removed so I may open my spiritual eyes and see the truth of what I need to forgive within myself, my family, my community, the collective, and the planet so I may learn my lessons in life. I ask that this clearing benefit not only me but also all of my family, all future generations, the collective of humanity, and Mother Earth and that it be lifted from the Earth grids, the Earth Crystal, and my lightbody and DNA. I give thanks for this divine assistance. So be it. Blessed be. Blessed be. Blessed be.

CHAPTER EIGHT

Our World's New Cities of Light: The Celestial Project 2009–2013

The Celestial Project is a gift from the enlightened realms that offers humanity the opportunity to work in group-consciousness with Mother Gaia, their Divine Presence, the Celestial Guardians of the Earth, and the Enlightened Masters for the clearing of humanity's collective karma that is held specifically within the etheric bodies of our world's cities, communities, and portals.

The project is coordinated worldwide by volunteers of the Divine University Project and overlighted by the Enlightened Masters. The project began in September 2009 via a series of worldwide linkups, focused on specific cities and communities. These specific celestial linkups will continue to occur worldwide until 2013, gathering many representatives of humanity together in planetary service as a support to the new alignment and consciousness shift within the Earth's field.

Twenty-five cities of North America and the United Kingdom, Europe, Russia, and the Middle East were the first cities in the project to receive the celestial activations and karmic clearings. This occurred between September 2009 and November 2010. As each representative of humanity joined the linkups from within their own community, they not only supported the karmic clearings of these cities, but also received personal, family, and collective karmic clearing and recalibration of their own etheric bodies and supported the celestial activation and karmic clearing of their communities.

As a portal project, CELESTIAL (Christ Energization, Love Expansion, Synergization, Transformation, Illumination, and Ascension of the Lightgrids) has been designed by the Enlightened Masters specifically to bring forth the greatest assistance to humanity for their shift into the fifth dimension via the clearing of the etheric field of Earth, the heart chakras of our cities and communities, and the etheric bodies of our collective. This takes place as giant celestial spheres that come from the same universal centers that feed our Earth are grounded into each city and community, opening a light portal between the worlds.

These celestial spheres carry the frequencies to absolve collective karma and ground the light frequency that is thousands of times more powerful than the frequencies presently held on Earth. As the celestial spheres anchor, the old grids of duality, control, and hierarchy and polarity are partially dissolved. As deeper focus is placed upon each city and community, the old grids are to be purified and absolved of our ancestors' karma, allowing our cities to begin to activate as new cities of light on the Earth. This in turn causes the grid structure of the Earth to shift significantly, as light is directly fed into the ley lines via the new Earth portals that have opened in this process. As these celestial light portals are activated, positive energies are fed to all inhabitants so they can be less affected by the collective karma. These activations are assisting members in our communities and cities to become responsible for their own karma as the fears left behind by the ancestors who originally lived in these areas are lifted.

The Celestial Project has been created by the Enlightened Masters in response to the many prayers for world peace and to Mother Earth's prayers for humanity's awakening. All ascended beings from other worlds of the Earth are supporting the celestial activations and karmic clearings of our cities and communities. The project is based on opening and clearing each city's or community's energy portal into the Earth by grounding the celestial spheres and opening a heavenly and Earth portal for the whole city or community. Each new celestial portal is reactivated by each new linkup, drawing in the frequencies that hold the power and purpose of dissolution of the fourth dimensional fear-based grids held in the etheric of the Earth.

The Enlightened Masters have shared that as the linkups of the Celestial Project complete, each celestial sphere will expand and extend for six hundred miles in each direction from the heart of the city through the etheric field of the Earth. This will ignite many other communities and cities and create a chain reaction, transforming the collective karma so a new etheric body may be received by Mother Earth.

As this chain reaction occurs, much of the old Akasha that is held in the old portals of the Earth is being absolved. The old fourth dimensional grids of duality, control, and hierarchy, which lock a soul's consciousness into a lower state, will begin to dissolve. The Celestial Project is supporting many souls under the influence of the duality, control, and hierarchy grids to gently awaken as these old etheric grids are dismantled.

As each city in the project is ignited by the celestial activations, the first manifestation will be a clearing of the collective heart chakra. As representatives of humanity link together, the collective heart chakra of the community receives its first level of clearing, and all souls within the community receive deeper levels of love into their lives. The Celestial Project's plan serves to ignite a new collective consciousness grid for humanity based on fifth dimensional frequencies, so as to invite love and peace to flow to all souls. As each city ignites a new etheric structure they will generate and share this via the Earth grids with all other cities and communities around the world.

The ancient creation portals linking all seven worlds of the Earth are raising their vibration and aligning for the shift to the fifth dimension. Yet, small number of these portals are still locked in fourth dimensional purposes that no longer serve the Earth and all beings. These portals have been holding our ancestors' deepest karma in regard to the use of resources and power and are influenced by the Atlantean karma of our ancestors and our own souls.

One aspect of the Celestial Project's plan is the dismantling of this old Atlantean portal system, so the portals and lightgrids of Earth can be free of the energies of duality, control, and hierarchy that affect us to self-sabotage or disempower ourselves. Thirty-eight sites on the Earth, at the time of writing, carry the Atlantean karma of our souls and our ancestors. Through each of these sites, there is an immense city of light in the Second World, the Middle Earth, which holds this karma and has been locked in the lower nature of the fourth dimension and in connection to the astral plane. These thirty-eight cities inside the Earth have been assisting to build a false form of power structure, via the energy field of the Earth that some have been negatively influenced by or given their power to, through the interconnection of their karma from Atlantis. The old grids of duality, control, and hierarchy are connected into the Middle Earth via these thirty-eight sites. The clearing of each of these thirty-eight cities of light within the Second World is taking place at the same time that the Celestial Project focuses on our physical world's cities.

The cities that have been chosen as primary focuses for the project all have large populations, or their etheric bodies carry a large percentage of a specific form of collective karma that needs to be released from the grids of the Earth. Some cities have also been chosen because the etheric field is directly influenced by one or more of the thirty-eight Atlantean cities of light that have been locked in the fourth dimension in Middle Earth and guided by unresolved memories or the karma of the fall of Atlantis.

The cities that are presently most influenced by the collective karma of Atlantis are of the highest priority within the project, as the clearing of this karma will support a deep level of clearing of our collective karma with power, responsibility, and war. The Enlightened Masters are focused upon supporting this shift first, as war often drives the economic fortunes or misfortunes of our world and is significantly responsible for many other forms of karma such as greed, poverty, and abuse.

The Celestial Guardians of the Earth are the original caretakers of the Earth who assisted in the original star-seeding of our planet and all seven worlds within. As representatives of our humanity, we are invited by the Celestial Guardians of the Earth to enter a deeper state of heart connection and receive divine energy and celestial frequencies for the karmic clearing of our world's cities and communities, and as we offer our service in this way, our personal, family, collective, and planetary karma is also supported to shift from our own etheric bodies.

The Celestial Project focuses on each specific city on a specific date at 11:11 a.m. in the time zone of the city. People from all around the world gather in groups for each worldwide linkup as it focuses on a specific city. Each group or any individual that participates acts as a representative for humanity while linked through a live internet or teleconference broadcast at the specified time, and is guided in how to work in group-consciousness with their Divine Presence, the Celestial Guardians, Mother Earth, the ancestors, and the Enlightened Masters in the clearing of humanity's collective karma.

During these worldwide linkups, celestial frequency is downloaded as each representative supports the celestial portal to be opened by Mother Earth, the Enlightened Masters, and the Celestial Guardians of the Earth and works directly with the souls and Divine Presences connected to each city to assist the overlighting archangel with the clearing of the collective heart chakra. This celestial frequency holds the power to absolve all forms of karma for the purpose of freeing souls and igniting their collective consciousness, as well as freeing their etheric bodies so their essence and unique soul gifts can be more freely accessed. All who participate work with the spiritual guides of all souls in the city, as well as the overlighting archangel of the city to support as many souls as possible receive karmic clearing. All who participate experience an energy shift from offering this service as well as work with their ancestors to support karmic clearing of their own family tree. During the linkup and for up to twenty-four to seventy-two hours after the linkup completes, the portals between the physical and celestial realms of the Earth in each city are held open by the Enlightened Masters so the transformation and clearing work can complete in accordance with the Divine Plan for Earth. Each time another linkup occurs, these portals are opened and the karmic clearing takes place again.

The project has been designed in this way to support a rapid shift in humanity's collective. It will not create the full shift as this can only occur as 51 percent of humanity awakens and each individual makes life choices that are directly sourced from their open hearts. Yet without the release and cleansing of a these cities' etheric bodies, the awakening process would be significantly slower. The collective karma held in a city has a locking effect upon the heart and soul star chakras of the individuals within these cities, and the fact is that until the karma carried by the etheric body is balanced, no one can be free, as we all share the collective field.

This project is taking place from 2009 to 2013, as this is a peak period on the Earth in regard to the transcension of the grids of Mother Earth's lightbody. The inner, nonphysical worlds are shifting dimensional frequencies and a new planetary portal system is activating through the recalibration of the Earth's etheric field.

Imagine each city's field becoming crystalline, all shadows transforming, and the collective's heart chakra freeing itself. In each of the cities that are to receive these clearings are hidden some of the darkest memories of our collective from experiences our ancestors were unable to forgive. These traumas have been held in the city's etheric body, affecting the frequency and flow of energy in the city. As each city's etheric body is activated and cleared of karma, specific aspects of collective karma begin to unlock from the entire etheric field of the Earth. The power of each linkup grows as each city is activated, and the cities that have already been activated are also reactivated through each new linkup. This profound chain reaction throughout the lightbody and grid system of the Earth will release the Earth's old etheric body once all cities in the project have been activated and cleansed. This is set to occur in 2012 and 2013.

This sacred work takes place in communion with Mother Earth, your ancestors, the Celestial Guardians, and the Enlightened Masters, with the support of your Divine Presence and the Divine Presences of all on Earth. This project is supported by 1,011 species of ascended light beings that form what is known as the Galactic Federation. Some of these 1,011 species are well known by some awakened and self-aware souls and include Sirians, Pleiadians, Andromedans, Arcturians, and Venusians. The transformational activations and downloads of vast frequency into these cities are also supported by the Elohim, the creation council for our universe.

Each linkup is an activation of the creation matrix of Mother Gaia. Codes are delivered in large packages of energy into our bodies and our fields for our evolution. This is the gift of the Celestial Project. You may deeply enjoy becoming a part of it or extending your heart into it. It will enhance all in your life, activate the Divine Plan for your soul, and accelerate you on your life path. You are invited to join the Celestial Project to work in worldwide community. Your contribution would be a blessing.

Our World's New Cities of Light

Sananda, Kuthumi, Maitreya, and Mary appeared to me with immense auras of light and shining hearts. Their eyes held the love of the universe, and I instantly melted inside. They spoke in group-consciousness to me as I was bathed in their love and light. They had come to share with me what was taking place as groups in the Celestial Project gathered in service to Mother Earth and all beings.

We come to you, our dear child, blessing you and your world and honoring all of the souls who have given their time and love to become representatives of humanity within the Celestial Project. This is a project of love that is created through the union of humanity's hearts and spirits and the communion with ascended beings from many dimensions. The light anchoring in each city as it is activated by the worldwide linkups is seeding much more than you presently know, our dear one.

The filaments of light that connect each soul to another are being freed, relationships are changing, abuse is releasing, ancestors are healing, children are activating their gifts more deeply, and the soul star chakra of all in these cities is beginning to open. They are all receiving energy to support them to discover their inner truth and follow it. The angels are able to enter the city once it has been activated as a celestial portal on Earth. The archangelic guardian of each city is then supported by the opening of this celestial portal and each linkup after this continues to weave a new etheric body for the city. These new etheric bodies are opening doorways for all souls to expand beyond the knowing within their minds, and this is leading toward their awakening.

As the city ignites and clears via its heart chakra, an angelic gateway opens so that when they are ready, all souls in the city can receive love and super-consciousness from their angelic guardian. This angelic spirit that is held in the Fourth World of the Earth is a soul's angelic guide until the soul has fully awakened their heart. Once this occurs, beloved, a soul in the Third World begins to share the consciousness and qualities of their angelic nature from the Fourth World. Each world carries a different light frequency, and as the angelic gateway in a city opens, more people are supported by the angelic frequency of their higher self, beloved.

These gateways between the worlds are opening now, as it is time on Earth for consciousness to free itself from the energies of duality, control, and hierarchy that have held humanity in a state of ignorance and created great suffering in your world. These gateways were closed in ancient times, and it is only now that they are ready to fully open as enough people on the Earth are prepared to take responsibility for the collective karma of the Earth.

As the cities are activated to higher levels, the archangelic and Christ gateways are opened, allowing souls to connect to their super-consciousness and love that is held in the Fourth and Fifth worlds above. We say *above* as these are heavenly worlds, or what many religions on Earth refer to as *heaven,* beloved. Yet the worlds of the Earth expand far into the universe, linking with other worlds beyond human understanding. Just as you witnessed your grandfather leave your world when he crossed the bridge of light into the next world, so will all souls on Earth travel this bridge. It is a portal into the next world where all humans become angels, archangels, or presences of immense love. These ones that watch over your world from above are truly with you and hold only love and light for each one of you.

The blessing of opening these doorways to allow the consciousness of humanity to awaken when each soul is ready is our greatest gift to you. We are unable to take away the cause of your suffering until each one has made the forgiveness in their heart and is willing to take responsibility for their karma. Karma is indeed a magnificent manifestation of the power humanity has, and the balancing of karma in your world will be the magnificent manifestation of your collective in the creation of peace on Earth.

Each linkup has been designed to initiate a chain reaction in the etheric body of your collective, and as each new city awakens, the codons of light are shared with smaller cities and communities all over the world. Thus, this project ignites the heart chakra of every city, whether or not the city is a focus of the project. We are working deeply with the portals within your oldest mountains, the mountains that carry the seeds of evolution for all of humanity. As the creation lines of the Earth are purified of the oldest karma, the original codons of light for humanity's super-consciousness to ground into their bodies are released into the land, so as each person walks upon these sites of the Earth, they receive these codons of light through their feet, beloved. Know each linkup is a special gift to Mother Earth and all of the future children of the Earth. These linkups are preparing humanity's collective for the greater shift that is its destiny.

As they completed, they lifted me into a cocoon of pearlescent and golden light. I felt like a child being held by the mother, cushioned and illuminated with love and all that is holy and sacred. I felt my heart release a cord of fear that I had not known about, a fear that humanity would not be held. I could see a beautiful mother holding me. Her eyes soft with tears of light, joyful tears she was shedding for me. As she held me, I knew it was Mary, mother of grace, who had a small part of her consciousness incarnate two thousand years ago, to birth Jesus. As I looked into her eyes, a transmission passed from her to me. I knew in that moment that humanity was further on their path of evolution than was recognized by me.

She lifted me up and we traveled into the enlightened realms of the Earth, the Seventh World. Everything was light. I had no body, no mind, no sense of my self, but I could see and feel the oneness of all life. This experience was not new to me; it had occurred regularly since I first met the Enlightened Masters. It always felt like I was returning home, into the heart of God. I call this experience my God Presence. It always gifts me a new view of life and a renewal of my source energy. Filled to the brim by the Holy Mother and Holy Father, overflowing with grace, I could see through the eyes of all children who were waiting for the Earth to change and carry this higher frequency, so they could be free.

Such patience I felt in their hearts, all souls on Earth, these children of light. I saw some had been waiting for millions of years, others for thousands, silently, knowing all is in its natural flow of evolution. I could see the source within every soul on Earth. I saw that the veils some carry are so small in comparison to what they truly carry as a soul. Before me these souls gently rose up and lifted their veils from their hearts. I saw some bring the veils back down, knowing they needed them until their selves in the other worlds were ready to forgive the collective karma. I saw every soul in their wisdom knew the timing for the release of the veils. I understood from this vision Mary and my God Presence gave me that all was in divine timing.

Mary gently placed me on a small table made of golden light, and I felt like a baby. She placed her hand upon my heart. She spoke, "This is a blessing I give to all of humanity through you. You will carry this for them and as they meet you, they will receive this blessing from me directly."

A great light filled me so powerfully, the cocoon dissolved, and I merged through hundreds of lightbodies flying into the core of the Earth. I transformed from one form to another as the light grew stronger. I felt like I was traveling into the center of the Earth. White light poured forth through me and surrounded me. I became a great white dove, then transformed into many kinds of birds—eagles, owls, hawks, and then many different forms of tiny birds, each one with its own song. My wings kept changing, and my form took on new colors and body sizes, each with a new view and song for the world. I felt the hearts of all birds over the Earth, and as a sea eagle, I swooped down into the ocean.

I grew large and entered the sea, then melted again and became the sea. I felt my waves and movement, feeding all of life within me. So many colored forms of life breathed through me, and my breath gave life and a depth held all beings. Out of the sea, I spouted my light and swam as a mermaid deep down through the water. I saw my body changing again; I became a white whale, with baby whales following me as I swam. I soared through the light as it intensified, and I became a pod of dolphins swimming through aquamarine light, a sea of love that expanded, rippling as we swam. I felt the hearts of all dolphins call to me as I was drawn into the light. I became a turtle, coiled inside my big shell, with ancient wisdom, sleeping and then awakening, one eye opening and seeing all within the water world. I was an ancestor of the water and land, bridging the worlds. The water melted away and I stood up and I was a beautiful young girl, stepping out the shallows of the water. I stepped onto a beach of white crystal sand and lay down and gently started to fall through the sand. As it melted under me, I became a large golden lizard in a cave; crystal veins of light fed me. I was ancient; I held scars on my body from thousands of years.

The light intensified, and I became a serpent snaking through long grass, and my body shimmered all colors of the rainbow. I was a caretaker of the land. I traveled down into the Earth through a hole and became very large. I traveled through the ley lines and into the crystal matrix, and I became even larger. I traveled all the way through the creation lines and matrix, deeper and deeper, and I became larger and larger. I entered the core of the Earth and was filled with molten liquid plasma fire, and I felt the power of creation and all it held. The many forms I had been and was were still held in the spiritual realms for me.

I rose out of the Earth as a giant winged rainbow serpent and flew into the heavens and then traveled over the land, leaving parts of myself on the land. I became an ancestral spirit in the mountains and a deva of the forest. I became one with every tree as I traveled to become an old grand-mother banyan tree. A part of me became a golden elk, another part became an otter, and another a golden mare. Another became a spider. I felt myself become many forms of animal and plant, deva and nature spirit. I returned down into the Earth and coiled myself around her heart. I felt myself in all bodies and all realms as I melted into Mother Earth's heart.

I heard a voice within speak gently and softly to me. "These are your dreaming bodies. This is your deepest connection, your oneness, and your spirit. You are vaster than you know."

I became aware of myself in the physical again with Mary, Sananda, Maitreya, and Kuthumi standing around me. I was in a state of deep bliss and could not move my body. I felt as if every molecule of my body and photon of my consciousness had just been rearranged and then united through the power of God's love. There were no words. There was only love.

They spoke gently to me and said, "You will gift this to all you meet, simply by sharing your love. This is the gift the Mother gives to all her children, the journey of returning to their dreaming. These codes will open the heart. Our message for humanity is that the mystery of spirit lives within them. They are vast and hold many forms, and when they accept this they will truly experience love."

In Loving Service to All of Humanity

The Enlightened Masters shared with me that every woman, man, and child on Earth is being supported through the Celestial Project, even if their city or community is not a focus of one of the project's linkups. I asked how this could be, and Sananda shared the following with me.

Deep within the heart of every soul incarnated into human form is their illumined energy. Sometimes this special spark is lost or hidden, but it can always be reignited, dear child. No matter what a soul may have lost or how hard life has seemed, they will be able to transform the circumstances in their life if they accept and release their karma. The project is serving every man, woman, and child by creating an opportunity for the souls who represent humanity to ignite their special spark as they receive the linkups that activate their energy and consciousness.

Each one of these souls will ignite another soul, and then another and another. Each soul ignited will then begin to clear their DNA, unlock their genetic code, and balance their personal and family karma. Each one will become a sphere that will affect others, we share. Codons of light will be exchanged through the eyes and heart, and the love will spread through hugs, we say. All will be touched, subtly at first, and then more powerfully as the awakening continues. This is the Celestial Project's service, and it is the service of many other wonderful endeavors that are being created in group-consciousness and are also inspired or directed by Holy Spirit.

The Celestial Project's Birth at the
Grand Canyon, Arizona

The Celestial Project was a surprise to me when it arrived into my life, via a document I received from the Enlightened Masters in the autumn of 2009. I had been sponsored to travel from my home in Australia to the United States by a small group of amazing women who had all been my students some years before. Vonnell had heard that I had been called by the Enlightened Masters to travel to the United States for a North American tour but that I was having second thoughts about the timing. My professional life felt too busy to organize the journey, and my finances needed to fulfill other commitments. She rallied others and encouraged me to come. They arranged everything to make it so easy that I could no longer consider it a difficulty to travel at that specific time.

I had received previously that my travel to the United States would be to assist in the karmic clearing of the grids and portals. I would be given a series of teaching events in different areas of North America that ran along the spine of a beautiful old creation snake deep within the Earth. This serpent line was moving, the Masters had shared, and a lot was being prepared for the creation matrix through North America to be opened, so I would be traveling back and forth to North America for the next few years. The serpent crossed through some centers along the east coast, so I was asked to spend time in New York and Montreal and then travel back down the coast and on to Mexico City.

I had been asked to create the Karmic Clearing Program with the Enlightened Masters, and they shared with me that as I traveled, unique pieces of the program would be offered to the different groups I worked with, and as groups received it, the blessings and activations given by the Masters would seed into the collective via the grids of the Earth. I had cocreated many educational healing programs over the previous ten years, so I knew it would be an amazing journey and like the previous programs it would advance my evolution and ground more of my Presence as well as all who received the program. A lot would be revealed as I delivered the teachings and transmissions, and I was excited about it. They gave me the names of the cities I would need to travel to and shared the program would need to be recorded for people from all over the world to receive at a later date.

I was also planning to visit Montana, where another friend, Katherine, who also worked with the Enlightened Masters, had been creating the base structure for the twelve universal pillars of the Elohim Temple to anchor on Earth, for the overlighting of a new etheric temple for North America. Over three years, the creation of thirteen powerful sacred sites, built from sacred light technologies, designed by the Elohim and charged with crystals, standing stones, and sacred geometries, were developed and activated in unique areas of her three-hundred-acre property, not far from Glacier National Park.

I planned to make it to the property for the lunar activation of the last of these sites and visit this wondrous manifestation that I had been hearing about. I knew it was an important puzzle piece for the Divine Plan and had shared with Katherine that when I arrived, we would need to build another gateway from the technologies, large stone discs, carved and encoded with sacred geometries. She got to work with the Elohim very quickly, and within six weeks had the new technologies made from large stone discs, some ready to bury in the earth with large crystals to connect into the Earth portal, and others to sit on the surface to be charged by the heavenly frequency through other crystals.

Once I arrived in United States, I headed to the Grand Canyon, for me one of the most treasured and endearing portals in the world. I had always gone to the Grand Canyon when traveling in the United States and usually received a new piece of my Earth mission while I was there. It felt like a source home for me, a power spot to connect to all of the seven worlds.

I had no idea about the Celestial Project at this stage. All I knew was there was some karmic clearing of the grids to focus on with the

Enlightened Masters. I knew I would receive the rest when I was at the Grand Canyon. Once I got there, the Enlightened Masters starting downloading the Divine Plan of the Celestial Project to me, in the form of a large document that described the overview of this worldwide service project. It began with a general outline of the North American clearing and a four-year process of clearing a number of cities on all continents.

In this moment I was so glad I had come to the United States when I did, and I now knew why Spirit had pulsed these beautiful women to make sure I got there in time. God had a much bigger plan than I had thought. This had been the first time in my work with the Enlightened Masters that I had thought about altering the timeline they had given as guidance to me, and I was having some big realizations about the subtleties of choice and one's alignment to timing. All I could think was, Thank God I didn't postpone this trip. When I received the document I could see why this needed to take place now, in preparation for the 2012–2013 planetary portal shift. It simply could not wait six months, as there were too many continents and cities within the project. It would take four years to complete if we started now.

The project seemed enormous as I already had about six very large projects going on with the Enlightened Masters and others in the world. I wondered how it would take place with my already busy schedule. Enormous as it was, it felt like the project I had been in training for over the last twelve years. With the potential for such a profound impact on our world, I knew that I would place all of my heart and energy into it, as it was truly a divine gift and a powerful opportunity for humanity to do some amazing planetary service work. Everything else in my life would have to take a small step back. Since that time, many have come to help this project manifest with all of its power and beauty, with God's grace.

CELESTIAL—Christ Energization, Love Expansion,
Synergization, Transformation, Illumination,
and Ascension of the Lightgrids

One of the primary aims of the Celestial Project is to clear and dissolve the old polarity grid of control within at least nine of our world's largest cities over these next four years. The nine cities are:

- Tokyo, Japan—via the Asian Karmic Clearing
- Mexico City, Mexico—via the North American Karmic Clearing
- Mumbai, India—via the Asian Karmic Clearing
- São Paulo, Brazil—via the South American Karmic Clearing
- New York City, United States—via the North American Karmic Clearing
- Shanghai, China—via the Asian Karmic Clearing
- Lagos, Nigeria—via the African Karmic Clearing
- Los Angeles, United States—via the North American Karmic Clearing
- Calcutta, India—via the Asian Karmic Clearing

The project's aim is also to open, clear, and activate the heart chakras of at least thirty-three cities worldwide. The following cities have been the first to receive these celestial activations and karmic clearing. The linkups for these cities took place in 2009 and 2010.

North America—New York, Chicago, Philadelphia, San Francisco, Los Angeles, and Washington DC in the United States; Vancouver, Ottawa, Toronto, and Montreal in Canada; Mexico City and Guadalajara in Mexico.

Europe and the Middle East—London, England; Paris, France; Berlin, Germany; Madrid, Spain; Saint Petersburg and Moscow, Russia; Budapest, Hungary; Istanbul, Turkey; Rome, Italy; Cairo, Egypt; Baghdad, Iraq; Tehran, Iran.

Some of the other cities that have been chosen to represent all cities of our world and receive the Celestial Project clearings:

South America—Bogotá, Colombia; Lima, Peru; Santiago, Chile; Buenos Aires, Argentina; São Paulo and Rio de Janeiro, Brazil; Caracas, Venezuela.

Africa—Lagos, Nigeria; Cape Town and Johannesburg, South Africa; Algiers, Algeria; Casablanca, Morocco; Khartoum, Sudan; Addis Ababa, Ethiopia; Abidjan, Côte d'Ivoire; Kinshasa, Democratic Republic of the Congo.

Asia—Dhaka, Bangladesh; Calcutta, Delhi, and Mumbai, India; Karachi, Pakistan; Shanghai, Beijing, Guangzhou, and Hong Kong, China; Tokyo and Osaka, Japan; Seoul, South Korea; Jakarta, Indonesia; Bangkok, Thailand; Manila, Philippines; Sydney, Australia.

The intention of the project is to activate the collective consciousness of humanity's grids over primary cities to allow as many souls as possible to open their soul star chakra. It focuses on clearing enough of the collective karma of humanity held within old grids of duality, control, and hierarchy to allow the divine manifestation of many more higher selves to ground through the cities. The project also aims to balance the portals of the Earth in alignment with the timing of portal shifts, to assist in the preparation of the Earth grids for their natural transitions in accordance with universal alignments and galactic influences. Other priorities of the project include opening the awareness of humanity to the presence of the collective influence and assisting as many light workers as possible to release from the old grids so they can receive clear guidance without the veils of collective karma affecting their awareness.

Through this project, representatives of humanity are invited to work in unity rather than as individuals and thus assist in a more powerful way to create transformation. Another long-term aim is the development of a Celestial Project library, which will be offered as a gift from the Divine University Project to all light workers of the world as a free source of information about sacred sites, Earth portals, grids of the Earth, and karma and the collective of humanity.

Other important aspects of the project involve the clearing of the collective consciousness grids held within the etheric body that lock the higher chakras of a soul's energy field from opening and from receiving their super-consciousness, and the regular infusion of the collective consciousness grids with celestial energy and frequency to dissolve collective fears held in these grids. The project also assists the illumination of the awakened souls within our collective to raise their consciousness and actively live in their divine connection, where their soul star chakra is no longer affected by the fears of the collective consciousness when they travel into any dense populations to do their sacred work.

A specific intention held through the project is the illumination of specific chakras of humanity's collective. The opening and ignition of the soul star chakra of the collective supports all of humanity to shift in vibration, and the clearing of the heart and soul star chakras of the collective supports humanity to receive their true spiritual direction as caretakers of the Earth.

During each linkup, lost souls who are trapped between the dimensional doorways of the Earth are assisted to be freed, the universal grids of divine love are activated through the portal system of the Earth, and the old Atlantean portals that feed the collective karma of power, responsibility, and war are cleared. All connected to this worldwide project act in service toward the manifestation of world peace.

The Celestial Earth Portals Energizing the Celestial Project

On September 21, 2009, the twelve primary celestial portals were activated in preparation for the Celestial Project. Over the duration of the project, thirty-two more portals will be activated for a total of forty-four. These portals are not cities but natural power sites on Earth, also known as creation sites. The portals are an amazing gift to us on Earth, for they are able to balance our biorhythms and activate our pineal and pituitary glands. These are the first two centers of the brain that need to activate in order to share the consciousness sourced from the light of one's spirit. As you connect to the portals that have been activated for the project, you may place your intention to receive the codes to ground the light through your pituitary and pineal glands for the integration of your super-consciousness and the activation of your higher spiritual gifts.

Each of the twelve primary portals works in a trinity with two others. These twelve original portals hold a specific celestial connection for the Earth and for all beings on Earth. A direct and potent infusion of the celestial frequencies from the stars, suns, and moons is received by the Earth through these twelve portals specifically for the purpose of the Celestial Project. Each of these portals is held in the higher dimensions as a magnificent light city or series of light cities. The light cities allow the higher dimensional currents of divine energy from the heavens to be anchored into the Earth and to feed the Earth and all her kingdoms via her ley lines and crystalline grid structure.

The twelve primary portals are as follows:
The first trinity of celestial portals:

- Mount Kilimanjaro, Tanzania
- Mount Kailash, Tibet
- The Grand Canyon, United States

The second trinity of celestial portals:

- The Great Pyramid, Egypt
- Uluru, Australia
- Machu Picchu, Peru

The third trinity of celestial portals:

- Mount Shasta, United States
- Mount Fuji, Japan
- Lake Taupo, New Zealand

The fourth trinity of celestial portals:

- The Alps—Switzerland, Liechtenstein, Austria, Slovenia, Germany, France, and Italy
- The Baltic Sea—Russia, Scandinavia, Latvia, Estonia, Lithuania, Poland, and Germany
- The Great Lakes—Canada and the United States

The Ceremony and Master Activation of the Twelve Primary Celestial Portals: The Enlightened Masters' Preparation for the Celestial Project

It was September 21, 2009, in the afternoon. I was sitting on the rim of the Grand Canyon with my dear friend Vonnell, who was traveling with me. I was in awe of the canyon; the stillness of the light, the spirit in the air always reminded me of the vastness of spirit we all share. I sat quietly in wonder, preparing for the sacred ceremony the Masters had shared was about to take place within the canyon.

This was a sacred ceremony with the Family of Light for the purpose of activating the first level of preparation of the Earth portals for the Celestial Project. It had been an absolute joy to receive the full download of the plan earlier that day, a twenty-page document regarding the project, so it was exciting to prepare to enter ceremony where we would meet with all of the portal keepers, the ancient ones who lived in the canyon, and begin the work of our Presences, the Enlightened Masters, the Galactic Federation, Mother Earth, and the guardians and ancestors.

I entered into group connection as many translated from the higher realms and began the ceremony as a representative of humanity and the Family of Light, giving thanks to Gaia and the portal keepers, elders, guardians, ancestors, and Inner Earth temple workers, and calling to Gaia and all councils of the Family of Light, God's Presence or Universal Spirit, the Elohim, the Eloha, the Enlightened Masters, the Divine Mothers, the Galactic Federation, Ashtar Command, the ancestors, guardians, and portal keepers, the archangels and angels, and the Divine Presences of humanity and all Earth kingdoms for the universal plan of the Celestial Project to activate.

The response was powerful as councils from all worlds and dimensions of the Earth began to gather in the portal, and from the heavens the Elohim sent a large solar sphere from the great, great central sun and a large lunar sphere from the great, great central moon through the solar and lunar gateways to the Earth.

As these huge celestial spheres traveled via the great central sun and great central moon and the central sun and central moon, thousands of lightships joined them. The lightships were created from angelic, archangelic, and Master consciousnesses merging in group merkabahs to form beautiful vehicles. These ships were not physical, but were made of the highest frequencies of light. As I witnessed them traveling through the central sun and moon into the stellar atmosphere of the Earth, the sky began to fill with concentrated orbs of light, as Presences began bilocating from the ships to work in the canyon portal.

As these giant spheres traveled through the universal, celestial, and galactic portals, igniting and opening each of the portals, the lightships began to travel into the Christ planes of our Earth system. I had never before seen so much focus on one project or world ceremony. They stopped in the outer atmosphere, and I became aware that the large, pyramid-shaped vehicle the Enlightened Masters traveled in was hovering over the Earth, transmitting directly into the Grand Canyon. The energy became very strong at this time. Light began to fill the canyon, my body, and my mind. I rose in vibration, and all my gifts started to open. My vision opened to all the worlds inside the portal of the canyon.

I then witnessed an astonishing event. Many hundreds of star beings, possibly even a few thousand, grounded around the rim of the canyon with me. We entered a state of group-consciousness through our hearts, brow chakras, and central pillars. I saw the grids between each of our chakras light up, expanding like a sacred matrix over the canyon as far as my inner vision could see. Our chakras began linking in with the central pillar of the ships and the central Mother Crystal of the Grand Canyon portal. We were all receiving and transmitting simultaneously, through group heart and group mind linkup. Pulsations of light from our collective matrix began to transmit as one large stream down into the core of the canyon, through the canyon floor and into Middle Earth and Inner Earth.

Through this stream of divine consciousness, we began making contact with the guardians of the portal within the Grand Canyon, as a bridge for the Universal and Galactic Federation's light fleet. Our communications streamed into the portal so the guardians would know why the fleet was here and why we needed to receive access to the portal.

All was explained about the Divine Plan of the Celestial Project, how the spheres contained the Celestial Mother Crystals for the Grand Canyon portal's upgrade, so the Celestial Project could activate and begin to do the collective karmic clearing for the Earth and humanity via the cities. It was shared how many other portals were also to be upgraded to drive larger volumes of Earth current into the cities for the duration of the project. All that was shared took place via an almost instant telepathic transferal.

The guardians and portal keepers were asked to give permission to fully open the portal into the cities of light that were deep beyond the canyon, through the canyon doorway within the Inner Earth. We entered a celestial temple with some of the Enlightened Masters and emissaries of the Galactic Federation. I became aware that within the lightships, there were celestial beings from 1,011 species of the Galactic Federation, and 80 percent of them were Celestial Angels for the Celestial Project's mission.

I was astounded to recognize that there were millions of Celestial Angels overlighted by the Enlightened Masters for this project, and they were all in group mind and group heart connection, receiving the transmissions I was receiving. I became aware that many more celestial beings will be traveling to Earth to serve with humanity during the next three to four years and that they will be preparing for the shift of the portals in alignment with the galactic portals, beginning in 2012–2013.

As we continued to receive the transmissions that the Enlightened Masters were sharing with the guardians, the portal began to open and a massive rainbow column opened up from deep within the Earth and expanded up through the canyon into the heavens. A giant blue Celestial Mother Sphere, a blue crystal as large as the canyon itself, began to ground into the Earth. It was so vast and I was so small, it filled me with blue celestial frequency in a split second, and I again rose in vibration.

Many of the celestial beings from the ships then traveled into the portal. I floated down with them into a city of light. We traveled on crystal platforms made of pure light via the huge rainbow column. There was a river of light with massive light cities on either side. We anchored and entered a large celestial temple where some of the Enlightened Masters were gathering with the guardians.

At this time, the guardians of several of the other twelve primary portals were also being contacted. The portals held through Mount Shasta, Mount Kailash, the Baltic Sea, Machu Picchu, the Great Lakes, Mount Kilimanjaro, and Mount Fuji opened and received giant blue celestial crystals, which began to ground through them and into the cities of light deep in the Inner Earth. The angelic oversouls, archangelic oversouls, and Christ oversouls of every city of the Earth were called to connect in the ceremony, and the plan of the Celestial Project was transmitted to all.

The Enlightened Masters in their pyramid ship then traveled to the Great Pyramid to activate this portal with a crystal three times larger than the others. Uluru, in Australia, also received a blue crystal sphere three times larger than the others. These are the two keystone portals of the planet—Uluru within the Divine Mother portal of creation and the Great Pyramid within the Divine Father portal of creation. The Grand Canyon is the third primary portal of creation, also known as the I Am or Divine Child portal.

As these first ten portals were activated by the gigantic celestial blue fire crystals, the Enlightened Masters sent the codes, geometries, and blueprints to every heart chakra of every city on Earth to create the synchronization of all crystals. The crystals began to interconnect and draw down the current from the blue celestial spheres, and the spheres then traveled back through all suns and moons, continuing to feed all of the crystals from the celestial realms.

As all ten portals synchronized, the celestial blue frequency from all of the large crystals fed the ley lines and song lines down into the crystal grid through the creation matrix into the Earth core, anchoring the activation of the celestial portals to ignite and open through all worlds of the Earth via these sacred sites.

Finally, guardians within the last two portals of Lake Taupo and the Alps were contacted. They were offered the Akashic records and were asked to let go of the fear that humanity would not shift into a higher state of awareness and love. These guardians chose to forgive and to open the portals to the Celestial Project. Then the blue celestial crystal spheres began grounding through Lake Taupo and the Alps, and the Enlightened Masters from the great pyramid ship began synchronizing all twelve primary portals in unity for the activation of the grid work via the Earth's ley lines and meridian streams. The ley lines began to fill with the sacred geometries. All twelve portals activated together and sent vast currents into the core of the Earth. The Mother Crystals were gently spinning, drawing in the celestial frequency from the unified field and emanating it from a central voidal vortex within their hearts. This opened a current that began to weave the crystalline celestial sound frequency of blue into the Earth Mother's heart.

Mother Earth received this and from her heart sent the celestial beams into the heart chakra of each city of the Earth. The heart chakra of each city began to connect to the portals and receive the sacred geometries from the ley lines, and also connect into the Celestial Mother Crystals held in each of the twelve portals.

Each heart chakra activated and expanded, merging with the hearts of the angelic, archangelic, and Christ oversouls, and transmitted the blue celestial frequency through the etheric fields of each city. Thousands of gigantic angels appeared, one over city each, with wings expanded and hearts filling the collective heart chakra of the city to open the lower dimensional pathways that store the collective karma of duality, control, and power dynamics. Gently these pathways were opened for the clearings that would be taking place city by city and country by country over the next three to four years.

As all of this was sealing, a great focus went to the heart of Montana, where Katherine and others had been building the Elohim Temple over the past years. I was shown that this site was a new Earth portal for celestial doorways and universal doorways to open for millions of light beings to come in service. Many enlightened presences would travel from beyond the great, great central sun and great, great central moon in support of the Earth's grid and portal system as it aligned into the new galactic cycle. I saw this temple structure made of pure light, expanding three hundred miles in every direction. Waves of blue celestial frequency were being directed from the twelve primary portals across the seas and lands toward this property and new portal site. The temple and new portal were being woven by the twelve portals as the Enlightened Masters anchored on the property to open the new portal completely.

Thousands of Celestial Angels were sent to this temple site in preparation for the Celestial Gateway opening, which was to occur on Saturday, October 3, 2009. I witnessed the thirteen primary sacred sites on the land and the seven pillars of the Divine University—love, wisdom, divinity, faith, service, communion, and charity—activate on the land, and each formed a golden bridge up through the heavens and to each of the twelve portals.

The cities of light deep within the Montana portal in the Earth beneath the temple structure also received a giant blue Celestial Mother Crystal over the next hour as it slowly anchored into the Earth. The crystal activated the grids in the region and sent blue celestial fire traveling down through the Rockies, into Mexico, and down into the Andes all the way into Argentina. The site in Montana was activated as a new celestial portal of the Earth. Thousands of Elohim disks spun through the Montana site, activating the new temple structure to be woven into twelve dimensions of Earth and preparing the site to be a Celestial Gateway, so celestial beings could enter the Third World more easily.

I became aware of myself on the rim of the canyon again. I was aware of so many Earth guardians and native ancestors, grandfathers and grandmothers that had been on this land and in the portal in spirit forms through all of their lineage, standing behind us on the rim. They blessed us as they laid gifts by our side, thanking us for the healing, deeply overwhelmed by the power of the sacred work brought to the Grand Canyon by white people and star people united. It was a great healing, they said, for them to have faith in all of humanity again. The Enlightened Masters in the giant pyramid ship sealed all with God's love. All of the emissaries and guardians would continue to work on this activation for the next seven days and nights, allowing it to complete on September 28–29, 2009. All in all it was an extraordinary experience, which was highly unexpected!

The Planetary Portals, Light Cities, and Grids of the Earth

Mother Gaia has many portals, and each one of these holds a divine connection to the heavens. Imagine a bridge of light that extends from the sun and moon directly into the Earth core. This light then streams out through specific sacred sites of the Earth. The sun and the moon are both exchanging frequencies with the Earth through the Earth core. Our sun feeds our Earth with many forms of light and plasma. Most of the light from the sun is unable to be seen and is stored as a source within the Earth core as a plasma frequency. This plasma core is like a giant sun inside our Earth that feeds all of the worlds of the Earth.

Our sun is more than one million times larger than our Earth. The plasma light bridge from the sun expands millions of miles to the Earth. The bridge from the moon is much smaller and works with the Earth field and the Inner Earth core. The bridges between the sun and the Earth and the moon and the Earth are the primary forces that support luminaries many times larger than our sun to direct their higher frequencies to the Earth.

The Inner Earth is driven by an internal current that is sourced from the void, a realm we are presently unable to investigate in its full nature. The plasma core of the Earth surrounds this void and attracts the frequency from even larger celestial bodies. In our heavens are celestial bodies, such as Arcturus and Antares, that are so large that the sun appears to be a small dot in comparison. The frequencies that come from these huge celestial bodies into our sun and moon are then transferred via the plasma and light bridges into the plasma and voidal core, where they are mirrored out through the diamond plates of the Earth Crystal through the Earth's planetary portals. This is how the balance of the Earth's creation matrix is held by these great celestial bodies and luminaries.

The depositing of all this sacred frequency supports the creation of all our Earth's resources such as crystals, diamonds, precious gems and ores, gold, silver, copper, metals, minerals, fossil fuels, and even our water. It also feeds all of the seven worlds of the Earth with the frequency needed for all of creation.

Excessive mining of these substances from the Earth disturbs the sacred frequency they hold for the balance of the Earth's grid and plate system and the balance between the seven worlds. Because these resources are being disturbed and removed from specific areas of the Earth without conscious awareness, the creation lines are being disturbed and are not always able to transfer and ignite the currents that normally source from the Inner Earth and extend through the portals into the greater field of the Earth. Thus, many of the diamond plates of the Earth Crystal are not always receiving the flow of liquid light from the plasma voidal core of the Inner Earth. Some of the Earth portals have closed because the creation currents in the Earth have been disturbed so deeply. The creation lines are the deepest currents in the Earth that carry the highest frequency, feeding all of creation with divine energy.

The portals are doorways into the seven worlds of the Earth as well as to specific stars or celestial bodies, so when a portal closes, beings from the First and Second worlds can become trapped inside it, and those from the Fourth to the Seventh worlds who are using the portal can become trapped in the First or Second world. The frequency from specific celestial bodies can then no longer travel freely through the worlds of the Earth.

When spirits become trapped in the portals, the lines and grids of the Earth through these sites become very sick. The creation lines or serpent lines are the first to become ill and stop flowing. Then the crystalline matrix and ley lines become affected. If the creation lines, the crystalline matrix, and the ley lines of an area are all closed, it is a sign that too much of the Earth's resources have been taken without respect and the devic energies are out of balance; Earth healing needs to take place to restore balance.

The Celestial Project focuses not only on opening portals in primary cities but also on clearing the grids, the crystalline matrix, and the creation lines so the diamond plates and portals of the Earth can flow with the liquid light energy. The release of guardians, elemental or nature spirits, Earth spirits, or devic energies that have become trapped within the ley lines, the crystalline matrix, or the creation lines allows a portal to open again so the Earth can receive the unique frequency from the luminaries and celestial bodies to regenerate its diamond plates and also energetically replenish the Earth resource.

If the ley lines, the crystalline matrix, or the creation lines are not flowing on a piece of land, this affects the health and energy of the people who live on the land. When people receive the pranic currents from the Earth they also receive any illness if it is held in the land. The energy of trapped spirits in the ley lines, the crystalline matrix, or the creation lines can also create the waterways to carry sickness within them and the land to be unhappy and carry a lack of peace.

The power of a portal opening on Earth takes place through the etheric field being unlocked, enabling it to receive the celestial frequency from the heavens that it needs to be able to shift into the fifth dimension. This also opens a doorway between the worlds, and the frequency of oneness or connection to the unified field is received. Just as the unlocking of the genetic code in our bodies via the clearing of our personal and family karma is the key for our personal shift in consciousness and experience of oneness, so too, is the unlocking of the etheric fields of our cities the key for our nations and communities to clearly shift into the fifth dimension and unite as one family on Earth.

Prayer for Earth Healing through the Clearing of the Earth Grids, the Crystalline Matrix, and the Creation Lines of the Earth

Mother, Father, God/Goddess, or Divine Presence of Love and Light,
We ask and pray for an Earth healing of this sacred site, _____
_____ (insert name of Earth site), and a cleansing of all of the Earth grids, waterways, and ley lines, the crystalline matrix, and the creation lines that feed or directly flow through this site. We call on Mother Gaia and the Ancestral Masters, and we ask for the holy flame of creation to flood through this site. We call on the power of our God Presences and the overlighting deva and angel of this land to open a healing portal and activate a pillar of light deep into the crystalline matrix and through the creation lines inside the Earth.

We ask for the highest healing dispensations for this land and ask that the guardian of this land forgive all that may have taken place to create the spirit of the land to be sick. We call to all of the nature spirits, devas, crystalline and elemental spirits, and angels to forgive all that may have taken place to bring stagnancy to the land or any Earth portals, doorways, or pathways that Spirit travels upon.

We ask for the opening of all portals, doorways, and pathways now and ask Mother Gaia and the Ancestral Masters to bring the flame of love, forgiveness, compassion, grace, oneness, divinity, karma, creation, and liberty. We ask that all trapped spirits, elementals, crystalline spirits, nature spirits, angelics, devas, and guardians be gently released from the land and supported to travel through the pillar of light. We call for for-giveness of any disrespect that may have taken place on this site. We call on all souls that are not incarnate to be lifted from this site if there are any attachments to it. We ask that this light pillar expand to fill the whole portal and that the blue, golden, and pink celestial fire flood through this site as the Ancestral Masters open the land and ignite a portal for the Earth healing to take place. We call on the holy flame of forgiveness. We give thanks for this. May this healing continue until it is complete. Blessed be!

Clearing the Karmic Grids for Los Angeles, California, 2009

A personal account written by William Asa Kniceley,
Palm Springs, California

Participating in the first level clearing of the collective karma for Los Angeles on November 9, 2009, in meditation I became distinctly aware of the larger geographic overview I was being drawn to. My view encompassed the entire West Coast, extending north toward San Francisco and south into Mexico.

As I watched, golden pyramids of higher dimensional light frequency were lowered over the Los Angeles metropolitan region, anchoring themselves deeply into the heart of the Earth beneath. A celestial blue light frequency preceded this arrival. Once anchored, this golden energy began to infiltrate the grid lines running through and around the entire coastal region, expanding out in all directions. I noticed that the density held in these grids was beginning to lighten through this transmutation process, and the collective consciousness of the region began to feel lighter and more open.

Before, Los Angeles had always felt to me as though there were an underlying competitive edge holding everything in deep separation because the density there was so intense that there were very few open creative fields through which to function. Thus there existed a lack of cooperation in Los Angeles, an attitude of "me against the world" and "every man for himself."

As the higher dimensional fields of golden Christ light opened the grids, creating more fluid space between the dense patterns of human thought forms, it began spreading outward and connecting to the grids of other cities—San Diego to the south; east toward Riverside, Palm Springs, and the Mojave desert; and north toward San Francisco.

I live in the small village of Palm Springs, which sits atop the San Andreas Fault, one of the most active fault lines in North America. As the light anchored through the San Andreas Fault it increased in velocity and intensity, suddenly shooting simultaneously north up the coastline through Oregon and Washington and into Canada, and south through Mexico. I was startled by the instantaneous intention carried by this energy as it moved throughout Southern California and then outward, anchoring these energetic gifts in direct connection to one another to form a new foundational structure of light, filling and transmuting the old structures and energetic patterns.

Southern California is known for its earthquakes, which are often large enough to shake objects off shelves and walls. Since the collective clearing of the Los Angeles grids, there has been a noticeable absence of earthquakes in the region. I have heard reports on the local news about small tremors and have spoken to locals who have felt them, including people in my own house, yet interestingly enough, I have not felt any since the clearing began.

My understanding is that as this energy has lifted and begun to clear the collective grids of the region, it has also had a profound effect upon my own individual field. As I participate, continuing to clear and bring my own energy through this alchemical process of transmutation, I have entered a higher, more expanded consciousness where I am not having the same experience as others who are still participating in some aspects of the collective energy that is manifesting as earth movement and tremors. There is an overall difference in the energetic characteristics of the region, and it is expanding to link with the grids of the rest of the North American continent in every moment as we continue to personally expand as One.

The Bridge between the Physical Realm and the Spiritual Realm

The Celestial Project linkups do take place in the higher dimensions of the Earth. The reason the linkups occur in this altered state is that consciousness work is always more powerful when a soul's energy is in a higher vibrational field than in a lower one. In fact, the higher the state of one's consciousness and energy, the stronger the effect will be of the planetary service you cocreate via the linkup. For this reason, during the linkups, each representative of humanity receives an upgrade in their own energy so they can sustain the vibration that is activating the city and ground it into the cells of their physical body.

Many light technologies are used within the project to support the sustainability of the high vibrational field. The Celestial Gateway was built from light technologies and crystals and was activated through the celestial portal technologies of the Enlightened Masters and Celestial Guardians specifically to support every linkup to be a safe process, ensuring that every soul who joins the linkups is protected.

This gateway is a physical site, part of the Elohim Temple in Montana. The gateway is called the Celestial Gateway but is also known as the Universal Angelic Gateway, as it acts as a bridge for all souls to the universal angelic planes where sound vibration, light, and love create beauty, oneness, and the activation of the higher qualities of celestial and universal love. It is a higher dimensional gateway that allows all souls to open their higher chakras and their super-conscious awareness more deeply than they usually can. This gateway opens the journey for every person that joins in the linkups, as all travel through it to do the higher dimensional work and also return through it as they are completing their journey. Gateways such as these were used as technologies in ancient civilizations and are returning to the Earth for purposes such as planetary portal work. The Celestial Gateway carries a twelfth dimensional frequency and has the power to lift souls into a higher vibration.

A bridge connects the spirit world and the physical world. Many don't experience this bridge until their physical body dies and their eternal soul leaves this world. But this bridge can be accessed for the purpose of embodying your higher dimensional self and grounding your spirit.

Wherever you are joining the linkup, as the linkup begins, the Enlightened Masters and the Celestial Guardians open an energy portal so as to pierce the veils between the physical and spiritual realms. The Enlightened Masters simply focus on you and open the bridge between the spiritual and the physical realm for you. This can be an unusual experience for someone the first few times it occurs. I remember my first experience of divine energy where my state of consciousness and perceptions altered.

I was sitting in meditation one day as a neophyte, not knowing what I was doing. My entire body had started to gently tingle, and as I had never felt this before, I was unsure of what was happening. I became hot and flushed, then cooled off, then became hot again. I remember feeling light as energy filled different areas of my body and my field. I simply witnessed as this happened. I was in my early thirties and had opened up all of my chakras, and I was having an unusual experience of energy. How did this occur? My spiritual current had opened inside my chakras as I opened them.

These are the sorts of experiences and sensations in the body many take for granted on the spiritual path. No, you are not going crazy. This is something we all experience on the spiritual path. If you are not experiencing energy and you are sincerely on the spiritual path, you have something you really need to surrender so you can receive the experiences of your energy.

Some years ago, I was facilitating a two-week retreat in Hawaii. The group of about seventy people were elated and happy, rising in vibration and shifting in consciousness easily, and many were having regular divine experiences. Some had never done this kind of work before, and as they opened deeply, they experienced powerful energies flowing through them. It made some of them wonder if they were being drugged, as the power of the frequency created them to experience altered states so easily.

Many had never met before the retreat, but they were soon forming deep bonds, as the field we were held in was blissful, filled with love, and genuine in its concentration of divine energy. Hearts were opening. Sometimes, as we finished our sessions together, everyone would bounce out of the hall we gathered in states of bliss and joy or wonder, but other times the energy left the body feeling so heavy it was not possible to walk without first grounding the energy. This took place when the frequency transmissions were so strong that we needed to integrate the frequency before our bodies could rise in vibration. Our collective field rose in vibration over the two weeks. I was told some years later that the experience of entering a state of unconditional love or bliss so quickly and unexpectedly had made some question what had created this. I explained that deep, concentrated transmissions of divine energy created with love have the power to completely dissolve old energy and shift consciousness.

The nature of your spiritual current is based on three factors. The first is the openness of your crown chakra. This is essential to receive the flow of your spiritual current. The second is the expansion of your heart chakra so the spiritual current can merge through the crown chakra and travel down and into the back of your heart chakra. This is important, for the heart must heal the unconscious beliefs and feelings that lie between your heart and spirit to allow the spiritual current through. The third factor is based on whether or not Spirit is real to you, and whether you fully hold faith in Spirit. Without faith in your own spirit and other forms of spirit, there will be no grounding of the current. It is important to release any beliefs that do not serve your divine experiences to take place.

Your spiritual current is your own personal bridge between the spiritual and the physical realms. It develops as you receive divine frequency and share it with others. Through the linkups, you receive an activation of your spiritual current to allow your higher chakras to expand and your lower chakras to clear. The journey of transformation occurs powerfully once your spiritual current becomes developed enough to be of support to you in your everyday life, so you may have the choice to raise your vibration and alter your state of consciousness when you are guided to.

My Experience of the First Level
Clearing of Montreal, Canada

A personal account written by Kishalah, Montreal, Canada

On Sunday, February 7, 2010, seventeen people gathered in Montreal with me for the Celestial Project. It was just wonderful that most of these people did not understand English and yet they came with an open heart, as pillars of love for this project. A beautiful pillar anchored in the center of our group, and a vortex was activated above it. As we connected with others around the world who were linking with us for the clearing, the pillar got wider and wider.

Mary came and was embracing the city, as it used to be called Ville Marie. Some people in our group saw the grey clouds above the city lifting, others felt the energies of the trauma experienced by the natives and the first Europeans that came to establish themselves in Montreal. Someone else saw the sacred geometries being activated and anchored in Montreal. Another saw the pillar of Montreal connecting to the heart of Gaia, and from there, the heart of Gaia started to pulse outwardly to each pillar and heart of the previous cities, and into the universe. It was a great experience and I felt blessed to share this moment with all who came and all of you around the world. Thank you, thank you, thank you and we love you all.

Prayer for Karmic Clearing of Our World's Cities and Your Community

Mother, Father, God/Goddess, or Divine Presence of Love and Light,

I pray for all people on the Earth to open their heart so the collective karma of humanity may be absolved and released into the light. I call forth my Divine Presence and all Enlightened Masters, archangels, angels, and the Divine Presences of humanity to be with me now. I ask to be held within the Universal Angelic Gateway with the angels and archangels so I may receive the highest frequency of healing for myself and others who are doing this service work via this worldwide linkup. I call on the Universal Spirit of Love, the Holy Spirit, and my God Presence to fill me with grace, love, and divine energy so I may be an anchor of peace and love for all beings on Earth and specifically for all within our world's cities.

I ask that my chakras be cleansed and aligned so I may be even more open in my heart to be a transmitter of divine love to all beings. God/Goddess, I ask for the grace, love, forgiveness, healing, and karmic absolution of all souls within humanity and specifically for the city of _____ (insert name of city) and for all in my community _____ (your community and the country you live in). I call on my ancestors to join me in this karmic clearing and ask that all within my family tree benefit from this. I ask that every soul within humanity and all of our ancestors be freed of the collective karma and any effect it may have over them in any way, through the highest dispensations and karmic clearing of our collective consciousness and the grids over our cities and communities.

I ask for all dispensations to come to humanity and to the heart chakra of all cities and communities so that all souls may awaken and open their hearts. I ask for the heart chakra of _____ (insert name of city, e.g., Mexico City) and my own community _____ (insert name of community) to be flooded with pure love and the blue celestial rays and frequency of the universal heart of God/Goddess for the next twenty-four hours as a cleansing of the collective karma held by all within this city and my community. I call on all universal laws to flood through these heart chakras and my heart chakra. I ask that all of the spiritual guides of every living being within this city and community be present.

I ask that the angels and archangels bless all of the souls in this city and community with the light and love, to be able to forgive all that may have taken place in this community and city. As a representative of humanity, I ask for a focus on _____ (insert the name of the city) as well as my own community, _____ (name of your community) and ask that the highest blessings come into the heart chakra of _____ (insert name of city) and into my community.

I call to all of the divine messengers of peace, love, light, and healing to assist me to be a divine transmitter of love and blessings to_____ _____ (insert city, e.g., Mexico City), and to my community. I ask for all of my chakras to be filled with love, light, and divine energy for me to transmit my love far across the world. I ask to be linked with all others doing this linkup and for the heart chakra of _____ (insert city) and my community to be ignited, opened, cleared, and illuminated.

I ask the angelic, archangelic, and Christ oversouls of this city and all cities of my community to open the heart chakra of these places so all of the collective energies held by the collective heart chakra of these places can be cleansed, purified, energized, and filled with love. I ask that all fear that may lie as veils over the collective heart chakra of all who live in these cities and in my community and that may form old grids of duality, control, or hierarchy be now lifted into the light by the Archangelic Light League, the archangels of the Earth and the heavens, and the Galactic Federation.

We call on all souls of _____ (insert name of city) and my community, _____, to receive together now, via the assistance of their guides, the tablets and codes of forgiveness, love, karma, grace, and divinity and ask that these tablets and codes be spun through the heart chakra of this city and my community now. We ask for karmic absolution for all souls if they carry any karma that presently blocks their soul star chakra or heart chakra. We call for a cleansing of the highest order of all old grids of duality, control, or hierarchy and ask all souls to break all agreements to accept the grids of duality, control, or the old hierarchy as an influence on any level of their being at this time.

We call forth the Divine Mother and Divine Father to bless every soul that chooses this, and we ask that all cords, ties, bonds, or energy blockages in or around these ones be freed through the laws of liberty, love, oneness, divinity, grace, forgiveness, karma, and creation. We ask that all levels of dissonant energies from this city or community that may lie in the unconscious or conscious realms of any soul be filled with love and forgiveness. We ask that these souls be bathed in love and choose now to receive deep love from the angels and archangels that assist them to be freed. We call forth to the Universal Spirit of Love, Peace, and Joy to flood into the hearts of humanity all over the world, and I ask to be a bridge to transmit love into the heart chakras of this city and my community now.

We call forth the Celestial Angels and the universal peacekeepers from all sacred realms and the Divine Mothers and Divine Fathers to bless the heart chakra of _____ (insert name of city) and lift any collective karma as we call for karmic absolution for any energy or form of consciousness that may be blocking the collective heart chakra of humanity within this city and my community.

I give thanks for this and ask the archangels and Enlightened Masters to ignite, open, and clear all fears held by our collective from this city and my community's heart chakra. I give thanks to the archangels, angels, and Enlightened Masters and to my Divine Presence and ask that they continue this work for me until the heart chakra emanates divine love from the heart of this city and my community.

We now ask that this work be sealed with the divine golden, blue, and white light and that a golden dome of love and light be placed over every city in the world to strengthen and protect its energy and all souls within it. We ask that as this occurs, the heart chakra be filled with universal love and light to begin the process of lifting the vibration of each city, my community, and the collective of humanity. Blessed be, blessed be. Blessed be all beings.

Prayer for Collective and Personal Karmic Clearing via the Celestial Linkups

I call forth to Mother, Father, God/Goddess, or Divine Presence of Love and Light, the Universal Spirit of Love, the Holy Spirit of Light, the Enlightened Masters, the celestial presences, archangels, and angels, the Divine Presences of all of humanity, the Holy Spirit of the Earth, all guardians and caretakers of the Earth from all kingdoms and realms, and Mother Earth to open a divine celestial portal for the clearing of collective karma within my heart, my family, my community and the city of _____ (insert city of focus) for the establishment of peace on Earth.

I ask for my celestial presence to merge with me and for a chamber of divine protection, healing, and love to be placed over, through, and around me. I ask for the Divine Mother to bless the focus of this linkup now and for the Enlightened Masters and emissaries of the Archangelic Light League to link me through the Celestial Universal Angelic Gateway of Love in group connection with all others linking in from around the world for the karmic clearing of this city.

I give thanks for the love I am about to receive and offer myself in service as a light pillar in this linkup and as a representative of humanity and our collective. I ask that my ancestors do this work with me. I call on the archangels of love and light to merge with me for this linkup and open my group heart and group mind connection to the Family of Light. I invite the Enlightened Masters to activate my merkabah for soul travel into the celestial crystal that is anchoring in the city so I may receive the healing, karmic absolution, and clearing in my energy and consciousness so I am less affected by the old grids of duality, control, or polarity. I ask for the wings of my angelic and archangelic bodies to sweep through my heart as I choose now to let go_____ (insert anything that is a burden in your life), and I ask for the clearing of my personal and collective karma related to this.

I invoke the holy power of love and the power of my eternal soul to open my heart and forgive _____ (insert any people, events, situations, or circumstances connected to your burdens) so I may be a clear vessel for the celestial blue frequency.

I call on the vast waves of universal love, all of the universal laws, and the dispensations of forgiveness and absolution for myself, for all souls, and for the ancestors of the city of_____ (insert city of focus) and of my community. As a winged one, in my protected and ascended body of light, I choose now to travel into the heart chakra of this city and clear the grids of duality, control, and polarity so it may become a city of light. I call on the Angelic and Archangelic Presences of this city to ignite the love and light within the etheric field of the city as many begin to clear the heart chakra of the old grids.

As a representative of humanity, I choose now to call forth the ancestors of this city and my community and ask them to step into the light by forgiving any deeds, words, feelings, actions, and projected thoughts that were not sourced from light and love. I choose to forgive all of you as the ancestors of this city and my community, _____

_____ (insert name of your community), if you at any time closed your heart and gave your energy to the creation of the grids of duality, control, or false hierarchy.

I ask you all to forgive this, open your hearts, and choose to receive your Akashic records as the Enlightened Masters step forth to you now in the temple of love and karmic absolution, which is anchoring through this city now and my community. I ask you to sit in the violet flame of forgiveness with me and receive love and healing now.

I call forth the Divine Presence of Archangel Michael to be with you and to bring the legions of light so you may receive the love and healing you need to forgive any karma you hold within this city or my community and any collective karma you may be responsible for.

I call on all of your family who are still on the Earth to receive the love from your Divine Presence and Angelic Presence, so they may give permission for the genetic healing of any memories of these deeds and receive a clearing of their ancestral line via your forgiveness. I call to the Enlightened Masters to offer you and all your family members karmic absolution now. I also ask for this for my family and ancestors now. I give thanks for this. I give thanks for this. I give thanks for this. So be it. It is now done.

My Experience of the First Level Clearing of Washington DC

A personal account written by Lelama Sjamar, Australia

Wow, Washington DC is a very happy place now. On the night of December 12–13, 2009, we traveled with many souls to this precious city to support the clearing of any residue and present unresolved energies that are held in the energy field of the city, in the consciousness of the people that live, create, share, and pray there. We were offering to clear the control patterns for this city as well as for all that it is connected to. As I arrived I was taken straight down into the Inner Earth portal below the city. My Presence together with many Inner Earth temple workers, ancestors, angels, and master beings commenced immediately the loosening, clearing, and dissolving of dark, old cords that were held from the heart of the city and the hearts of many people into the Earth and the portal below.

Simultaneously, I was taken straight above the city into the pillar that connects the city with the celestial realms. From there my Presence, united with many master beings, healers, and karmic board members, was infusing light and karmic absolution and the waves of the creation current to support the cords that were dissolving to be filled with new truth and the power of creation. A great celestial energy of cosmic blue fire was brought into and around the energy field of the city and all people to create the release of the karmic energies held. I was told that this would continue to operate for the next three weeks in order to fully reconnect the antahkarana and divine connection of this powerful city. I am so grateful to be present for this, as I feel the power of the clearing move through a part of our beloved Earth and humanity, and also through my own being and all that I am connected to. Thank you so much!

A Celestial Project Transcript: Worldwide Linkup for First Level Clearing of Guadalajara, Mexico—February 9, 2010

We're about to begin the Guadalajara clearing, and I wish to thank you all for being on the linkup and bringing all your beautiful energy to our world in planetary service. It's an important one because it's our last of the first level clearings of North America. It's the twelfth city, and it's bringing everything together in a way; all of the grid work and everything's that already taken place will be enhanced fully through this linkup, the twelfth of the first level of clearings of North America.

So to begin, allow yourself to deeply go inside now. Close your eyes and enter your chakra pillar by simply calling on the light to be with you. As each one of you begins to receive a blessing directly from Archangel

Michael now, he begins to focus on all who are joining in this linkup worldwide ... beginning to activate the crown chakras first, as Michael invites you to go into your heart to the pure light inside and breathe into it, expanding that light, concentrating it simply by focusing on the light inside of your being in the center of your heart chakra. As you take all of your consciousness and awareness into your heart in this way, send that light from your heart down into Mother Gaia, into the Earth core by creating a bridge of light, linking her heart and your heart now. As you do that, ask Mother Gaia to open an Earth portal underneath you so all of your sacred work can ground 100 percent and you can receive the energization as the divine frequency flows through you.

The celestial presences who are joining us in this sacred linkup begin to activate each one of us now, align our chakras, our energy fields, our merkabahs, preparing us, filling our auric bodies with pure color rays. Gold and silver, peach, aquamarine, white, emerald, blue sapphire, ruby, pearl, diamond, platinum, and yellow rays of light begin to flood into our auras now. Beautiful rainbow colors begin to fill us now. Breathe that light in and send it down through the bridge of light between your heart and Mother Gaia's heart, the Earth core, visualizing a rainbow bridge of light as three Archangels step forth to you.

Archangel Michael continues to ignite each one of your chakras now, as the three Archangels begin to support you, asking you to ground into your bridge of light more deeply. They ask you to become aware of your eternal flame of love inside of your heart chakra and to expand it out with your breath in every direction around you now. Transmit love to all beings to open your heart deeply now as they begin to fill each of your chakras with diamond, platinum, golden, silver white light, beginning to raise your vibration a little now. They invite you to call on your Divine Presence to merge with you ... all of your higher selves and your extended body of light to ground through your auric field now, as these blue celestial fire archangels, these three that surround you in a circle, begin to fill your heart chakra with celestial fire. They ask you to receive this blue light and send it down into Mother Gaia's heart, into the Earth core now, to ground your bridge of light. As you do this, they place platinum spheres in each of your chakras, and these begin to spin gently, multidimensionally, to open your bridge of light wider.

They ask you to expand the light bridge up from your heart through all of your chakras, through your crown and soul star chakra above your head, and to send this rainbow bridge of light directly up through the sun and the moon in the heavens above you. Send it through the sun and moon and into the central sun and central moon that lie beyond our sun and moon in the heavens, and intend for it to travel through the central sun and central moon and through to the great central sun and great central moon and larger suns and moons beyond that ignite the universal field of light and love, opening your energy body to the universal currents of love and light so you can be a transmitter and receiver of divine energy.

As you send the bridge, intending this in your heart connection, or visualizing, imagining, simply knowing it is connecting now through the great central sun and great central moon, ask that your divine connection activate through your source connection now. Breathe in the frequency from the heavens and from deep within the Inner Earth and draw in the divine energy from the universe through this rainbow bridge down through your higher chakras into the Earth core and then back up into your heart energy. As you do this, beloved heart, the three archangels with you begin to merge their pillars with your pillar, inviting you to enter group merkabah with them to rise into a higher dimension.

Draw in the love that they send you now, directly into your heart. One is to the left, one is to the right, one in front of you, beloved heart. Open your heart to these three archangels now, inviting them to merge with you to empower your energy . . . the gift you hold as a representative of humanity. They hold beautiful rainbow bridges of light, and they offer to deeply merge with your rainbow bridge now. Open your chakras to them. These are ascended celestial presences from the project that will raise your vibration and assist you to travel into the higher dimensions where it is safe for you to do your sacred work, beloved, of the karmic clearing of your community, your family, and Guadalajara.

They merge their pillars deeply with yours to activate a group merkabah now. Your merkabah is beginning to merge with their merkabahs to form a greater group-consciousness, and they begin to lift you through the Celestial Gateway into a blue field of light, where you are beginning to be filled with the blue celestial frequency and your lightbody is turning to a solid blue light. As this potentized energy concentrates through your field, you begin to become saturated with this blue frequency through every chakra, every energy body. As you begin to travel through a blue pillar of light with these celestial archangels, grounding in the Celestial Universal Angelic Gateway, there you begin to receive dispensations, tablets, codes, ki's, and special frequencies into your energy body that you will be able to share with the rest of humanity.

As you meditate, allow yourself to see yourself as pure blue light in a blue body with blue wings, beloved, in an angelic body, as your celestial body begins to activate . . . and this blue lightbody is that which you begin to travel in now through the sacred gate and into the spiritual realms of the Earth. You travel to other portals or into Guadalajara now. Each of you travels to different places, and a large team travels with you. Twelve celestial presences now begin to join you, merging their energies with yours, working in a council with you, and linking their heart with your heart now. Some of you are beginning to travel to some of the other cities, some to other portals on the Earth, and some into the stars. Each one of you travels through a gateway and lands in a temple where many other beings gather who also support this work to take place—the clearing of the Earth karma. Your soul star is activated now. It lies six inches above your head, and you are asked to say a prayer for all of humanity for their soul star chakras to be opened now, freed of all that may lie in their etheric bodies connecting them to any grids of duality, control, polarity, and hierarchy.

In a blue body of light, you continue to be filled and flooded with blue celestial frequency. Twelve blue celestial presences surround you, merging with your heart chakra. As you say your prayers for humanity, again they ask you to say prayers for all of humanity's heart chakras to be opened freely without any interference that may come through the old grids of duality, control, or old hierarchy and authority.

Dispensations from the Enlightened Masters begin to flood through Guadalajara as they begin to focus through their great mother ship upon this sacred city now, and these dispensations also flood through your community as a great golden dome begins to anchor around the community you are in. The Ashtar begin to focus in, and a golden dome around Guadalajara begins to weave grids of light through the etheric body of Guadalajara and over your community, weaving with golden, platinum, white, diamond light these domes of protection as gold and silver disks of light are spun into the portals now and the twelve master celestial portals of the Earth, through the Grand Canyon, Mount Kailash, Mount Kilimanjaro, Mount Fuji, Uluru, Machu Picchu, the Great Pyramid, Lake Taupo, Mount Shasta, the Baltic Sea, the Great Lakes, the Alps, now begin to activate celestial pillars of light through all twelve dimensions.

Great pillars begin to activate through twelve dimensions of these portals now, creating great rivers of blue celestial frequency to flood through the Earth body in all directions through the North American grids. This whole continent is focused upon, and each of the grid points through Canada, Mexico, and North America are beginning to be ignited now with golden, diamond, platinum, and white light from many ships in the heavens above, and in the Inner Earth, beings opening the grid points. They begin to work with the old grid structure of the old etheric body of the Earth through North America, the creation lines that lie deep underneath these grids, and through the crystalline matrix of the Earth. All of the Holy Spirit energy within the Earth body begins to awaken, and the portal keepers within the Earth begin to open pillars of light through the grids of the Earth now like acupuncture points, and beautiful golden pillars begin to open up through the grids of light that have been seeded with the ascension of the Earth.

Take a deep breath now, and visualize Mother Gaia opening her current fully through North America and beginning to receive the blue celestial frequency. She begins to direct it into the heart chakra of

Guadalajara in Mexico for all souls in this city now, as all spiritual guides travel to their souls within this city and within your community now. Call now for the karmic clearing of this city and your community and of North America [prayers in ancient language are spoken] as the ancient prayers are spoken now as the universal laws of karma, forgiveness, oneness, reflection, grace, creation, expansion, liberty, love, divine bliss, truth manifestation, sacred resonance, and divinity begin to activate through the grids of North America now.

The universal laws begin to flood through you now [prayers in ancient language are spoken] as we gently ask for the alignment of the grids of North America and that any points along the North American continent or through the ocean body surrounding this continent that hold the karma of the collective of humanity be purified, enlightened, activated, and illuminated with the blue celestial frequency. Each of the original cities that have been activated through the Celestial Project begin to be activated once again, and each of the celestial spheres within the Earth begin to multidimensionally spin, opening up the heavenly Earth portal through each of these cities now. This activates through the heart chakras as Mother Earth begins to activate a pure white light bridge up from her heart through all twelve cities, through New York, Chicago, Philadelphia, Mexico City, San Francisco, Los Angeles, Washington, Vancouver, Ottawa, Toronto, Montreal, and now up through Guadalajara ... and as these white light pillars activate, the codes from Mother Gaia are released for the rewriting of her etheric body and the release of the old grids.

The activation of the new grids that are seeding her ascension into the fifth dimension and seeding humanity's ascension as a collective into the fifth dimension takes place now while the disks of light are offered to you. They are placed in each of your chakras and they are beginning to spin through your energy body now, opening you to a higher dimensional connection, and each one of you is becoming a bridge of light. You are asked to contact all of the souls in your community and Guadalajara now, telepathically speaking to them as representatives of humanity, calling them to forgive anything that may have occurred for them as a soul regarding this life or any of their last three lives on Earth that may create them to be karmically bound, limited in their connection here, or holding any fear here. The heart chakras of Guadalajara and your community are worked with now and the ships of the Galactic Federation and Ashtar Command begin to focus on the heart chakras, laser beaming them with pure platinum diamond white light. They begin to illuminate the grids, the Archangelic, Christ, and Angelic Grids of Light through the etheric body of Guadalajara and of your community [prayers in ancient language are spoken] as the angelic, archangelic, and Christ oversouls of Guadalajara are contacted now.

As this takes place, the angelic, archangelic, and Christ oversouls of all previous cities begin to connect in group-consciousness and begin to transmit to the heart chakras in every other city of North America now. Through their own heart chakras, they begin to activate other cities within North America now as the tablets of karmic absolution are offered to all souls [prayers in ancient language are spoken] and karmic records are brought to all souls by their spiritual guides. All implants, programs, soul fragments are offered to be removed now from the heart chakra of Guadalajara and your community and the heart chakras of all souls that are willing to receive assistance [prayers in ancient language are spoken]. As your soul star chakra begins to activate with blue celestial fire, you are asked to transmit it directly now into the heart chakra of Guadalajara and your community and all dispensations, codes, and tablets you have received will begin to spin and activate through the heart chakra as you do this, beloved [prayers in ancient language are spoken].

Gently now, a blue celestial sphere in the heavens beyond the great central sun begins to travel with many celestial presences through the central sun and our sun into the Earth, focusing now toward Guadalajara, to begin the celestial activation of Guadalajara for the karmic clearing of the etheric body of this city and all beings within the city [prayers in ancient language are spoken]. Divine Mother begins to offer blessings now as waves of love begin to flood through all the pillars that have opened up in the grid structure of North America, and into the cities through the heart chakras of all cities of North America. A beautiful matrix between the heart chakras of all cities of North America begins to activate. Dispensations begin to flood through the blue celestial frequency through the heart chakras of all twelve cities and into all other cities of North America through this matrix [prayers in ancient language are spoken] as the bridge to Iraq, which was originally opened through a previous linkup, is ignited again and the pillars within the power grid structure of the old Atlantean portals are ignited by the Enlightened Masters with blue celestial frequency and beginning to be flooded now as veils are being lifted through the etheric body, through all of these old Atlantean portals all over the Earth now.

You are asked to say prayers for all of the original souls that lived on Atlantis on the Earth and all those that stayed on the Earth from this time that believed themselves to be caretakers of the Earth now ... to say prayers for their healing, enlightenment, purification, their karmic absolution at this time [prayers in ancient language are spoken]. As representatives of humanity, you have the power to call as a group now for the clearing of all these beings that hold power back from the rest of society and do not share the power, or take power from others. Say the prayers for the balance of power between all humans now and call for the old Atlantean power grid structure to be dismantled from the collective consciousness of humanity [prayers in ancient language are spoken].

Call to all of humanity, asking those that are in a state of disempowerment to step up into the light and open their hearts, and asking those that hold empowerment that do not share it, that do not benefit others with it, to let go of all need to control and hold onto the power or the need to overpower others [prayers in ancient language are spoken].

The blue Celestial Mother Sphere is beginning to merge through the heart chakra of Guadalajara now, and smaller spheres through the heart chakra of the community you are in [prayers in ancient language are spoken] as the pure white light bridge expands up through Guadalajara, opening the portal through the Earth's grid structure now, and the crystalline matrix of the Earth is beginning to be activated with the blue celestial fire.

As this is flooded through, the whole of the crystalline matrix of the Earth releases rainbow light out of all crystals where the Akashic records are held [prayers in ancient language are spoken].

You are asked to thank all of the crystalline kingdoms of the Earth now for housing the old energy and choosing to be purifiers of the old energy that has been unable to resolve through the field of the Earth through all of history [prayers in ancient language are spoken]. As you call on the purification of all of the crystals of the Earth now, as representatives of humanity, ask for the old Akashic records of Atlantis that create control, old hierarchy, authority, and duality to be purified and lifted from the crystalline matrix of the Earth now [prayers in ancient language are spoken], as many tablets are given to you by the Enlightened Masters. An Enlightened Master steps forth directly in front of you now, this one supporting your sacred work with humanity, sharing you have a great power as a representative of the collective to take these tablets, to use them in your sacred work now.

You will be guided in your own way of how to work with these, where to place them on the Earth and through the grid structures of the Earth. You are asked to call on your own families and to work with your community also at this time, to activate the karmic clearing with these tablets of karmic absolution that are offered to you at this time. Allow yourself to go into your sacred work now and utilize the puzzle pieces that you carry, whether it is through sacred sound or traveling more deeply, beloved. Allow yourself this time to go deep with your sacred work to support the peace to take place through the karmic clearing of our collective, through the grids of the Earth.

The golden light matrix deep inside of the Earth, the Christ matrix, begins to activate now, and the diamond light rays, the platinum golden white light penetrating into the etheric body of your community and Guadalajara activates a thousandfold in strength and quantity. The Galactic Federation begins to raise the vibration of the transmissions now. The blue Celestial Mother Sphere begins to ground fully through the city into the Earth, having activated the heart and the etheric body fully.

Hundreds of thousands of celestial presences have been working with us through the city's etheric structure and throughout the other cities previously activated to create the strongest etheric body, the greatest clearing of the etheric structures of the cities. As the golden matrix of Christ consciousness activates through the Earth body now, the Enlightened Masters begin to ground dispensations into Mother Earth directly, and to humanity as a collective, beginning to place seals on the old portals of Atlantis ... blue celestial fire seals.

They begin to weave them over all grid structures, grid points that cross through any of the old Atlantean portals that hold any sources of energy for control, old authority, or duality. They place out the clarion call to all beings on the Earth that may be in any way utilizing the control energy or duality energy or placing themselves in positions of old hierarchy over others ... to release their false beliefs of power and invite all of the souls or spirits to enter into the light and reconnect to their own source connection where they may have infinite energy. As these ones are contacted, all souls and spirits on the Earth that are not presently resting in the light but are lying in the shadows or working through the uncnscious in the darkness are focused on now, whether they be incarnated in human form or living within old cities of light in alternate dimensional energy forms. All are contacted by the Enlightened Masters and offered their karmic records now, and their overlighting guides travel to them to offer them the potential for karmic clearing with the flames of holy forgiveness, which burns brightly now in the pockets of the Earth where dissonance lies.

The places of the deepest suffering are beginning to be flooded with the violet flame now, and a special blessing is beginning to activate in these areas over the Earth, in the grid structures, for underneath the areas of greatest suffering lie pockets of darkness in the Earth. You are asked to say a prayer now for all the sacred sites that hold the old karma of war, the old karma of greed, the old karma of abuse, and to ask that every portal that presently holds many souls in suffering be focused on now with the blue celestial fire and the power of all these twelve cities and the power of the original twelve celestial portals, and the power of your prayer, joining in group heart with many others as representatives of humanity. Call on the Divine Presences of all humanity now to activate the karmic clearing of the Earth in these areas of the deepest suffering where there is the most poverty, violence, abuse, war, anger, closure of the heart, and fear, and ask now for karmic absolution for all souls within this portal and for all the grids of control, duality, old hierarchy, and authority to be lifted from these portals.

The blue Celestial Mother Sphere grounds fully to Guadalajara now and activates, and a great portal of light begins to open all the way from the Earth core through this city, up through the sun into the great central sun, as a great bridge of light through the universe. The blue celestial fire begins to flood in high concentrations now through this city, and this begins to take place through all other eleven cities now, a bridge begins to open from deep within the Inner Earth, the Earth core, up through each city, through the sun, the central sun, and into the great central sun, opening a universal bridge of light. Each of these bridges of light interconnects through the heart chakras of each city, and these heart chakras begin to activate through all heart chakras of all cities, not only through North America, but through the whole of the Earth now. The power of the celestial frequency begins to flood through the heart matrix of the collective of humanity, through the heart chakras of all cities. Ask for the heart chakras of all cities and communities to be opened now as a dispensation so all may receive the vibrational frequency that clears the old karma from the collective of humanity and from the etheric body of Mother Earth, Mother Gaia.

Golden white spheres begin to travel from the central sun, flooding to the Earth now ... hundreds and thousands of spheres activating through the communities of the Earth and through the city's heart chakras as the Christ Presences of many beings, humanity's Christ Presences, begin to travel to meet with their souls on the Earth, offering dispensations of deep love and healing. These Christ Presences will stay on the Earth for the next twelve weeks, moving through the etheric body, as the Enlightened

Masters share that through these twelve linkups, we have opened the celestial matrix of North America and much great work can take place now. The beginning of the dismantling of a city that lies underneath the city of Washington DC will begin to take place now through that which has been created through these twelve linkups, the first level clearings.

Send all of your love now into the heart chakra of Washington DC and say the prayers for all governments to open to the light, for all in government to move through their ascension process, to release all from their etheric bodies connected to any control grids, any old hierarchy, any influence from the old Atlantean power structures that no longer serve humanity, releasing them from the grids of duality. Calling for this now, as the angels and the archangels focus deeply on Washington and the Enlightened Masters anchor a bridge of karmic absolution deep down into the Inner Earth through Washington DC, where underneath the city lies an old city of light that they will begin to purify now. For all of the interdimensional beings of light that live within the city that do not presently step into the light, that have in the past been working through the control matrix, offer forgiveness now, send love . . . to any energy, spirit, or soul connected to the city underneath Washington DC, the city of light originally seeded in Atlantis, which through the fall became a place of control where those that were unwilling to forgive made their home, beloved, interdimensionally.

Call on these old beings that consider themselves caretakers of the Earth to forgive now and to release their belief that they are superior and they need to consume all of the resource, hold onto all of the resource, control all of the resource, and not share the resource. As the Enlightened Masters begin to ground thirty-three dimensions of dispensations through this pillar now, they place a seal on the pillar.

They seal this city of light now in accordance with the Divine Plan and call to all within this city to move into the light, sharing that otherwise they will be blocking Mother Earth's ascension and that through karmic law and the law of protection they are now being called to heal their wounds that create them to need to control, beloved. As the prayers are spoken now for all to be freed from any connection to this old Atlantean portal, you are each asked to take your power back as a sovereign being now, to go deeply into your heart and to call to all of humanity to take their power back, to own their sovereignty as divine beings on the Earth [prayers in ancient language are spoken].

Call to humanity to receive karmic absolution for any connection through Atlantis or any influence they may have received etherically, through their dreaming state via the astral planes, of connecting to these old portals that were seeded in Atlantis and became portals of control over humanity as the violet flame blazes through you in protection now [prayers in ancient language are spoken] as the tablets of karmic absolution are offered to beings connected within this old city of light and a great light begins to flood up through Washington DC now as much begins to release. The first level of this clearing of this old city of light begins to release, and a portal between Washington and Sirius begins to open now as the old Sirian energy begins to release into the light to open a clear light connection between Washington and this portal and Sirius, the star that guides humanity's ascension into mental clarity, into alignment to truth [prayers in ancient language are spoken].

An alignment of divine truth is beginning to activate through Washington DC now as celestial presences in many ships over this city begin to connect a bridge of light between Washington, Guadalajara, Mexico City, and the cities of Ottawa, Vancouver, Montreal, and Toronto, and a bridge between the United States, Canada, and Mexico is beginning to form now, and much is beginning to release that has been held karmically between Canada, the United States, and Mexico. Each of you receives the violet flame flooding through. You are asked to ground the blue celestial fire now deep into Mother Earth's core. Call on the guardians, the ancestors of the Inner Earth, the caretakers to receive and ground all of this healing now, and invite them to bring their power into this clearing, to activate the Earth portals so the old karma may be lifted into the light now. Gently the Enlightened Masters ground over Guadalajara through their master mother ship, this great pyramid of golden light. They begin to activate the grid structures there. They hold other ships and they also anchor over all eleven other cities, and three lightships anchor over Washington.

They will stay for the next three weeks, working through the grid structures of North America with the specific focus of serving Mother Gaia and her etheric body restructuring the release of the karma that has been blocking this from flowing. They thank each one of you for being a representative of humanity and share that there are many other star races working with you, also representing their races, working in a similar way, sharing that not only humanity lives upon the Earth, but many other races also live within cities of light within the Earth and in the higher dimensions. A rebalancing is taking place now through the grids of North America, and this will directly affect the Asian grids, and balancing these will also prepare the way for the South American grids to be worked with. They begin to offer you a blessing personally now, asking you to invite all of your family, your blood and soul family, to receive this with you. It is for your personal life on Earth, for the clearing of your power of creation. They offer a special frequency through you now that empowers your creation of your reality, and as you receive this, they gently remind you, let your heart, your pure heart with the light inside, be your guide in life and release all desire from your life, beloved, for it is a false guide and your pure heart is your true guide.

They ask you to meditate upon this now. Receive the light of this frequency for your pure heart connection as it fills your etheric, spiritual, mental, emotional, physical, genetic, and soul bodies. They seal this work through your energy body and share that if you have received all twelve linkups, you have opened a connection to your celestial presence, which is the nature of all you have received through these twelve linkups.

They recommend that if you have not received all of the linkups, you receive each one so that you may open this connection and open into the second level clearings of North America, and then into the first level clearings of Europe, Russia, and the Middle East, where a whole new level of connection will open for you, beloved. They bless you and thank you deeply and share they are sealing the sacred work for this first step in the Celestial Project over the next few weeks. They invite you to join them for the second and third level clearings of the three primary cities within the North American grid structure. They say Namaste to you now. Blessings . . . Let yourself sit in the frequency for as long as you wish.

Healing the Avenger

A personal account written by Colleen Faye Maguire, Kila, Montana

I've been participating in the celestial cities project and would love to share one of my experiences. This account comes from the Guadalajara clearing on February 9, 2010.

The avenger is one of my strongest archetypes. I believe it comes from a strong Templar lifetime and many other significant lifetimes where I took up the sword to defend right and honor. These lifetimes sometimes roll before my eyes like a movie on fast-forward.

During the final activation of the fourth trinity of cities on February 9, I had a vision of this archetype, in the form of a Knight Templar standing in what I'll call a crystal cave of creation. He was dressed in a white tunic with a red cross on the breast. He wore a helmet and carried a shield and a sword. As I watched, he lay down on the floor of the cave, semi-curled, at the base of a ten- or twelve-foot crystal. After he lay there for a while, the energy of him was slowly absorbed into the crystal. It was as if he was vapor and there was a suction coming from the crystal to pull him in. I had the sense that I/he would emerge from the crystal transmuted into another form.

I was anxious to discover what form I would emerge in. I remember having a few ideas—maybe a magician or a wizard or a powerful angel. Instead, I was slightly surprised to see a huge eagle emerge from the crystal. I came out standing, wings opening as I walked forward.

Then came the strangest part. I was hovering over North America, not far above, but covering the whole of the continent. My wings were spread in what felt like a very protective posture. I landed gently with wings still spread, covering the entire United States, like a bird opening her wings for the chicks to gather in the warmth of her body. At this point the vision ended. It took me some time to process what had happened.

I can see for myself, in a karmic sense, that it's time for me to let go of the avenger and the karma that goes with it. The sword has had its place, but it's now time for a peace-filled world. To me, the eagle carries a similar energy of strength and honor, but without the avenging attribute. The eagle has long been one of my totems, but I'm just beginning to understand the significance of my personal journey.

It also has occurred to me that the United States can be seen as the avenger archetype and, as a country, we certainly carry the eagle totem. Maybe my vision is about both me personally and the nation as a whole clearing our avenger karma so we can become the eagle.

As I was writing about my vision, two bald eagles flew past my window and perched themselves on a tree thirty yards away. I couldn't quite believe the synchronicity, but I saw it with my own eyes. I am in gratitude for my growth and this insight. I would like to thank the Celestial Project for the opportunity to participate in this amazing karmic clearing experience.

Your Journey

The journey is inviting you to illuminate yourself, your life, your family, and your world in a way that you have not known before today. What must you take into your hands and heart to do more than consider this, beloved heart? How will you sculpt your reality to be that which you know is your path ahead? What will your priority be, we ask? Do you wish to see beyond your mind and how you now believe yourself to be?

Your super-consciousness awaits. It is excited and illuminated. The distance between your head and chest is the distance you must travel inside yourself to experience your divine consciousness, which is held within the depths of your heart, awaiting.

Beings of light will come, they will go, but you will stay in the space you choose to be. You may experience your divinity. You may experience your pain. You may experience both if you wish. You have the choice to will what you would like to experience here.

Yes, your karma will show what you need to see, that otherwise you may have placed a blindfold over thy eyes, silently. To look beyond is to know the truth, to guide thy way between the worlds, for you are no longer only a physical form. You are multidimensional and spiritual, and within your soul is the wisdom of all you have created, learned from, invested in, manifested, healed, illuminated, and done your best with.

Your soul holds the path ahead, and although at times your mind may wish for another path, your karma turns the wheel of life for you. Some things are destined, as your karma must be received so it may be brought into a new light, so you may be eternally free of what you have carried, sometimes unknowingly.

Fibers of your very source nature are being ignited as you absorb your true reality and what you must acknowledge and allow to receive the highest attunement for you. Happiness is based not upon what you have, who you are, or what you do. It is based upon your ability to live in resonance with what is true inside of you—this resonance that goes far beyond the methods of the mind, the small feelings of your inner child, the knowledge of your past, the wishes of your personality. Your soul is larger than all of this, older and wiser, and already knows the path ahead.

Your listening for the truth within is the only map your soul requires of you. Enjoy the platters of spiritual food laid before you. The innocence may still be held in sacred balance with the wisdom. It may still be sweet, and you may still hold a vulnerable aspect of yourself within. The karma of your soul, your family, your collective, and your relationship with Mother Gaia seeks only one thing from you and will give everything back you have ever asked for. Your karma seeks only to receive, and it will serve you and give you something you deeply need. To be touched, to be held, to be gathered in the arms of the Holy Mother and Holy Father . . . to be given what you truly need is the blessing and gift Spirit holds for you.

Let no fear rush into your mind to take this gift away. Let no doubt destroy what you know is helpful to you. Let not another come between your mind and heart and your truth, no matter how much you love. Let your soul expand your wings through your back, and break all attachments that hold you from the one thing Spirit wishes to give to you—your evolution, your experience of your Presence and your divinity. As you acknowledge this and accept this as a priority in your life, your spirit arranges for you to receive all you need to open your spiritual eyes to what is before you and what lies already within.

Your spiritual eyes, soft, kind, sensitive, deep pools of love within, melting upon your angel's wings, helping, giving, playing, and laughing. So wise they are, to be all these things, multidimensional, with many feelings. Your spirit, so vast, so expansive, invites you to go beyond the beyond that you know could be for you . . . beyond your fear and into your heart, more deeply than before. This is the call of your Divine Presence to you. Your Presence awaits you in the wings, collaborating with Love.

SPIRITUAL EYES

Spiritual eyes
seek not what they can see . . .
Unveil what is
allow the way to unfold . . .
Accept the wisdom of the old
with the truth of the new
growing within you . . .
Your gift of love
to another
knows no boundary
condition or wish . . .
Only that which God grants thee
To be soothed
held and whispered to
called inside
blessed to be unveiled
to be no more hidden

to meet the breath ...
Wind of song
that hallows thou name
to kingdom come
to journey, no longer in vain ...
He taketh the path of truth
it leadeth him to his heart
where a small dove lies
wounded in love ...
With his breath of life
he giveth the dove a kiss
eternally awakened, through this ...
With spiritual eyes
he seeks not, wants not ...
He sees only himself through this
as the dove ...
Heavens expand and great light symphonies ...
The moon rises and orbs the sky ...
Our journey, to be held in between the preciousness of life
and the eternal awakened state of truth ...
Our faith in one hand
sacred keys in another
unlock all doors
all paths, all possibilities ...
To illuminate
our sacred chalices
overflowing with grace
from the Holy Mother ...
He tempteth not his fate ...
His arms rested on the archways
of golden light
that leadeth into the heavens ...
He is called once again

to know the eternal chalice of light
the breath of infinite love
the gift of possibility of Presence . . .

ABOUT THE AUTHOR

During the past fourteen years, Sri'ama Qala Phoenix has received over four thousand visitations from the Enlightened Masters. These divine interventions have led her to become an international teacher and founding mother of the Divine University Project in Byron Bay, Australia. Qala came to spontaneous spirituality in 1997 after an extraordinary journey that inspired her to discontinue her full-time university studies in natural medicine and train personally with the archangels and Enlightened Masters within the Divine University of Light on the spiritual planes to become one of their representatives on Earth. As a spiritual teacher, she feels she was granted divine access that is rarely received. Since that time, Qala has cocreated many advanced programs in the field of new education, in which she works with students to accelerate their frequency and energy connection for access to higher levels of consciousness. She travels the world as a loving bridge for the illumination of the Divine Presence, facilitating retreats, self-mastery schools, and sacred journeys. You may connect with her teachings and programs through www.qalasriama.com.